THE FUTURE OF
THE INTERNATIONAL LEGAL ORDER
VOLUME II

Wealth and Resources

THE FUTURE OF THE INTERNATIONAL LEGAL ORDER

EDITED BY CYRIL E. BLACK
AND RICHARD A. FALK

Volume I. *Trends and Patterns.* 1969.
Volume II. *Wealth and Resources.* 1970.
Volume III. *Conflict Management.* Forthcoming.
Volume IV. *The Structure of the International Environment.* Forthcoming.
Volume V. *Toward an International Consensus.* Forthcoming.

Written under the auspices of the
Center of International Studies,
Princeton University

A list of other Center publications
appears at the back of the book.

THE FUTURE
OF THE INTERNATIONAL
LEGAL ORDER

VOLUME II

Wealth and Resources

EDITED BY RICHARD A. FALK

AND CYRIL E. BLACK

PRINCETON UNIVERSITY PRESS

PRINCETON, NEW JERSEY, 1970

Foreword

THIS SERIES has been organized and edited under the auspices of the Center of International Studies, Princeton University, with the assistance of a grant from the Ford Foundation. The views presented in these volumes are those of the authors of the individual chapters, and do not necessarily represent those of the contributors as a group, of the Center of International Studies, or of the Ford Foundation.

The publication of this second volume of *The Future of the International Legal Order* has been considerably delayed beyond the intentions of the editors. The complexities associated with publishing a multi-volume work of this sort are greater than even we imagined. Our present schedule calls for the publication of Volume III (*Conflict Management*) and Volume IV (*The Structure of the International Environment*) before the end of 1971.

The editors wish to thank Marjorie Putney of the Princeton University Press and Elsbeth B. Lewin, Jane G. McDowall, June Traube, and Mary Merrick of the staff of the Center of International Studies at Princeton University for the careful attention that they have given to the preparation of this manuscript.

CYRIL E. BLACK
RICHARD A. FALK

Introduction

THIS VOLUME focuses upon the capacity of the international legal order to cope with the course of international economic development in a setting that will be heavily influenced by rapid and dramatic technological progress. Emerging problems will certainly include the search for nonviolent means by which to reconcile the interests of rich and poor countries during the decades ahead, and the rising demands of secondary countries to participate in and benefit from the scientific wave of the future.

Vivid incidents such as the Torrey Canyon disaster and the Santa Barbara oil slick illustrate the dangers and costs that are likely to be increasingly associated with technological progress. The pollution of the oceans and of the atmosphere is beginning to arouse widespread concern around the world. Peaceful uses of nuclear energy appear to contain serious, not yet fully grasped, dangers of radioactive fallout. The mass use of modern agricultural techniques involves vast increases in the use of insecticides and fertilizers which simultaneously tend to prevent, or at least defer, the occurrence of serious famine and to aggravate the density of pollution.

Above all else, the problems being posed by the new technologies appear to depend for solution on multinational, if not global, regimes of control. National governments, so long able to control events within their own territory and to exercise "freedom" on the oceans and in the skies, seem likely to become more and more dependent on cooperative regimes both to serve the common good and to prevent the common disaster. By the end of the century the idea of the nation-state as the principal independent actor in the world may be significantly eroded and qualified by the existence of a variety of functional actors carrying out specific mandates on the basis of some sort of transnational orientation. The sovereign state is likely to lose some of its dominance in international society as a result of the emergence of other political forms that will be needed to deal with the kind of problems created by the new technologies of social and economic progress. Unlike the sort of direct transfers of power from national to international institutions that are associated with most disarmament schemes the buildup of international functional institutions is likely to take place more indirectly, less frontally, and may, for this very reason, proceed more rapidly.

The main impetus for this forced growth of international institutions comes from the expanding spatial locus of operations for many areas of human endeavor. The radioactive fallout spread by nuclear reactors or tests enters the entire atmosphere of the world; if this fall-out endangers world health, then it becomes intolerable to vest exclusive control in national governments by deference to such traditional doctrines of international law as "territorial jurisdiction," "jurisdiction over national airspace," or "freedom of the high seas." The regime of law must come to correspond roughly with the locus of primary concern. The adaptive capacity of the international legal order will be tested by the degree to which it can establish these correspondences under conditions of rapid change. This capacity will be especially tested by whether more rational forms of control can be brought into being prior to the occurrence of high-level catastrophe and before trends toward the expropriation of scarce resources or toward the contamination of the oceans or skies reach disastrous or irreversible thresholds. We have witnessed how ineffectual have been the cooperative efforts to protect endangered species of marine life, such as the blue whale, from extinction; too little power has been vested on the foundation of a consensus that crystallized too late.

In some areas the problem of international control illustrates the paradox of aggregation. The individual fisherman (or the fishing nation, for that matter) receives a greater marginal reward as a result of catching as many fish as he can, although the cumulative effect of what he and others do tends to diminish or even eliminate the reward for the community of fishermen. The paradox of aggregation does not exist so long as the renewable fish population exceeds the total demand of all fishermen. Such a condition of abundance, with some limited exceptions for certain regions and species, has existed for several centuries with respect to the ratio between the supply and demand of fish. As soon as scarcity becomes a general attribute of an endeavor the paradox of aggregation applies and what is rational for the individual is damaging to the community. Under such circumstances the rational pursuit of self-interest takes precedence over any claims asserted on behalf of the general welfare, the ethics of self-restraint are ineffectual, and the source of wealth and benefit tends to become a vanishing asset unless a system of community controls backed by coercive machinery to enforce public policy on an equitable basis can be negotiated into being. The international legal order as one organized around the dynamics of national self-interest is being subjected to increasing challenge by the growing relevance of the paradox of aggregation to the conditions of human life.

The shift of power within a federal state from the level of internal units of sovereign control to the central unit of sovereign control usually occurs as a result of changes in the dimensions of problems before the overall society; it is less a matter of conscious design than an expression of shifting functional imperatives. The scale of the requirements pertaining to the buildup of modern industry in the area of electronics and nucleonics has demonstrated that only the very largest states in the world command a sufficient base of resources and skill to sustain a competitive position. The effort of smaller states to compete on the basis of national capabilities is likely to place a severe strain on their economies and to produce, in any event, a position of inferiority and dependence in relation to the most powerful national societies. It is this situation that has been mainly responsible for European fears about becoming subject to American economic dominance. Such a situation has stimulated proposals and caused certain limited progress toward economic integration in Europe; it also prompts an increasing effort to develop nuclear facilities through the joint action of two or more countries.

The fantastic technologies of the future may require resources that exceed the capabilities of even such generally autonomous states as the United States and the Soviet Union. There have been, for instance, a series of recent proposals emanating from both Soviet and American scientific circles that rest on the cooperative international pooling of resources for the development of climate control. The computer requirements alone suggest that it would be much slower, as well as most wasteful, to rely on national competition as the principal engine of joint progress. Businesses, so often more adaptive to changes in their environment than are governments, have tended to carry on an increasing amount of their activity through the medium of world companies, managerial units of enterprise that pool resources and operate free from the constraints of any given national environments. These world companies are a new form that may facilitate the process of adapting to the future, provided that these companies are themselves brought within some framework of control that is expressive of general community interests. Proposals for the creation of a "world company law" reflect an effort to subordinate the profit-seeking pursuits of these new types of corporations to norms of welfare and progress for the world as a whole.

In the decades ahead there will be a continuing series of demands to reform the international legal order in such a way as to raise the standards of the poorer countries, to close the gap between the rich and poor countries, and to enable the poorer and less-developed countries to participate in the achievements of the new technologies. It is, as yet, unclear whether the international legal order will make significant adjustments in response to these demands, and what will be the consequence in the future of their partial or total rejection. At the present time, national centers of political control seem unwilling to give up privileged positions with respect to matters of wealth and military power. Whether the functional pressures toward some form of community management of many key activities will also tend to undermine the present stratification of international society is one of the great questions that will become increasingly more prominent toward the close of the century. In any event, it seems clear that the search for new modes of international control will be accompanied by a struggle of the weaker and poorer peoples of the world to obtain more significant participation in global processes of decision bearing on trade, wealth, and technological development and to secure for themselves a larger and larger share of the fruits of human endeavor. This global struggle seems likely to overshadow in importance the competition between the more capitalist and the more socialist systems of economic organization, although this prediction presupposes that the level of political and ideological conflict is kept below that of large-scale sustained violence and certainly that nuclear war is avoided during this time period.

The chapters in this volume attempt to call attention to some of the more critical new and anticipated developments and to provide frameworks for relating these developments to the requirements of international legal order. Their especial contribution is to provide instruments for coherent and comprehensive analysis, rather than to offer specific substantive solutions. The authors represented in this volume have been asked to articulate a point of view that will enable a future-oriented appraisal of any given problem. These points of view have been organized around certain critical and illustrative subject-matter areas: social and economic development, the control of foreign wealth, and ocean and space activities. In this way we hope to introduce the reader to creative and responsive ways to think about the future, especially as new technologies unfold and have a major bearing on the wealth-producing and wealth-distributing processes of international society. Detailed substantive studies are necessary to bring the orientation of this volume down to the level of practical legal and political policy; this is not the task of this volume which is more in the nature of a mapping operation, but it is our hope that this urgent complementary task will be facilitated by the studies that we present here.

RICHARD A. FALK
CYRIL E. BLACK

Contents

THE FUTURE OF
THE INTERNATIONAL LEGAL ORDER
VOLUME II

Wealth and Resources

CHAPTER 1

The Relevance of International Law
to the Processes of Economic
and Social Development

WOLFGANG FRIEDMANN

INTRODUCTORY OBSERVATIONS

A GENERATION ago, an article on this theme could hardly have been written. Notwithstanding the establishment of the League of Nations and several notable efforts centered around the League concerning matters of human welfare, the concern of international law and organization with matters of economic and social development[1] was, at best, sporadic.

The organized international pursuit of objectives of economic and social development is essentially a post World War II phenomenon, although objectives of both economic and social development were included in the Constitution of the International Labour Organisation which was established in 1919. The Preamble to the Constitution states, in part, as follows:

> Whereas conditions of labour exist involving such injustice, hardship and privation to large numbers of people as to produce unrest so great that the peace and harmony of the world are imperilled; and an improvement of those conditions is urgently required: as, for example, by the regulation of the hours of work, the regulation

---

[1] The terms "economic" and "social" are often used jointly and without any sharp distinction. The definition of "social" that is most pertinent to social development is, "implying action directed in some sense toward the welfare of others —and usually toward the welfare either of a whole society or its less privileged members." Julius Gould and William L. Kolk, eds., *A Dictionary of the Social Sciences* (New York 1964), 643. Taken in that sense, social development comprises economic development. More specifically, social development will usually be understood as concerned with the general improvement of the conditions of living in a community, whereas economic development is concerned with the improvement of the means of satisfying material needs. Thus, the provision of religious services, debating clubs, or playgrounds may be described as predominantly social objectives and the fixing of minimum wages for seamen or agricultural laborers as an economic objective. Both objectives may be simultaneously pursued, for example, in an international convention for the preservation and protection of forests. Its economic objective is the conservation of soil fertility. Its social objective is the preservation of open spaces and plant life. For the remainder of this article no specific distinction between the two objectives will be regarded as necessary.

of the labour supply, the prevention of unemployment, the provision of an adequate living wage, the protection of the worker against sickness, disease and injury arising out of his employment, the protection of children, young persons and women, provision for old age and injury, protection of the interests of workers when employed in countries other than their own, recognition of the principle of equal remuneration for work of equal value, recognition of the principle of freedom of association, the organisation of vocational and technical education and other measures;

Whereas also the failure of any nation to adopt humane conditions of labour is an obstacle in the way of other nations which desire to improve the conditions in their own countries;

The High Contracting Parties, moved by sentiments of justice and humanity as well as by the desire to secure the permanent peace of the world . . . agree to the following Constitution of the International Labour Organisation.[2]

The great enlargement of the fields of international economic and social welfare organization after World War II was mainly due to two factors. First, the horizontal widening of the areas of cooperation through the specialized agencies of the United Nations concerned with such matters as cultural relations and education (UNESCO), health (WHO), food and agriculture (FAO), air transport (ICAO), the international utilization of atomic energy (IAEA), currency stabilization and monetary supply (IMF), economic reconstruction and development (IBRD). Second, the postwar structure of international law has been deeply affected by the advent to statehood of a large number of countries which were not only hitherto politically unfree[3] but were also economically underdeveloped.

The concept of economic and social development as a public international responsibility is far and away the most important new departure in contemporary international law and organization. It has added to the enlargement of international activities concerned with matters of human welfare, and to the vertical reach into the manifold processes of economic activity and organization. The prices of agricultural commodities, the methods and terms of the exploitation of mineral resources, the instrumentalities of international trade, and the structure and mechanisms of economic development within the underdeveloped nations have become integral parts of contemporary inter-

[2] See text in Amos J. Peaslee, ed., *International Governmental Organizations*, 2nd edn. rev. (The Hague 1961), II, 1233.

[3] This was also true of the states constituted after World War I from the ruins of the Austro-Hungarian Empire.

national law and organization. Hence, the Constitution of the International Bank for Reconstruction and Development, and—though less specifically related to the needs of less-developed countries—the Articles of Agreement of the International Monetary Fund, both in the Bretton Woods Agreement of 1944, must be regarded as the most significant documents developed within the purview of international law over economic and social matters since the original Constitution of the International Labour Organisation. But exclusive preoccupation with the objectives, the structure, and the techniques of the World Bank and other international financial agencies would be inadequate to describe the concern of contemporary international law with economic and social development. The concept of development assistance as a transnational concern has also given rise to a multitude of new organizations and techniques on the national and binational level.[4] Development aid on a nation-to-nation level dates back to the Marshall Plan of 1947, from which has sprung a network of public national aid agencies in a growing number of countries and corresponding institutions in recipient countries. These agencies conclude, year by year, a multitude of binational agreements for grants, loans, commodity exchanges, and technical assistance, usually on a government-to-government or public agency-to-public agency level. No less significant for the structure of international law, and especially for international contractual relations, has been the transformation in the character and terms of concession and economic development agreements between the governments of underdeveloped countries on the one side and private foreign investors on the other side. As will be shown later, the growing importance of these bilateral relationships has brought a whole new sphere of "transnational"[5] situations within the purview

[4] For a discussion of the aid agencies in the major donor countries (e.g., United States—AID, France—Caisse Centrale, United Kingdom—Ministry for Overseas Development) see Columbia University School of Law Research Project on Public International Development Financing, Report No. 2, *Methods and Policies of Principal Donor Countries* (New York 1962); and Report No. 12, *Seminar on Politics and Experiences in International Development Financing* (New York 1965). For the institutional structure in developing countries see, *inter alia*, Report No. 3, *Turkey* (New York 1962); Report No. 9, *India* (New York 1964), of the aforementioned project.

[5] The compass of these relationships has been described by Judge Philip C. Jessup as follows:

Transnational situations . . . may involve individual corporations, states, organizations of states, or other groups. A private American citizen, or a stateless person for that matter, whose passport or other travel document is challenged at a European frontier confronts a transnational situation. So does an American oil company doing business in Venezuela; or the New York lawyer who retains French counsel to advise on the settlement of his client's estate in France; or the United States Government when negotiating with the Soviet Union regarding the unification of Germany. So does the United Nations when shipping milk

of modern international law, i.e., relationships formerly regarded as purely private have been transformed into matters of public concern. This new development has also been accompanied by, and in turn stimulated, new international concepts on the rights of a state over its natural resources[6] and the mutual rights and obligations pertaining between private foreign investors and the host governments in under-developed countries.[7]

These new concerns and objectives have given rise to an interrelated network of institutions, treaties, and international transactions. Included are: international conventions (such as the convention sponsored by the World Bank for the settlement of investment disputes between states and the nationals of other states);[8] many United Nations declaratory resolutions (such as the Resolution on the Permanent Control over Natural Resources); bilateral treaties (such as the Friendship, Commerce, and Navigation treaties concluded between the United States and many other countries); and a multitude of agreements between foreign investors and host states for the development of resources. Most recently, this new and complex type of relationship between developed and developing countries has produced a new United Nations agency, the United Conference on Trade and Development (UNCTAD), specifically designed to develop and systematize relations between developed and developing countries. In short, there has been a basic change in values and policies resulting in many new

---

for UNICEF or sending a mediator to Palestine. Equally one could mention the International Chamber of Commerce exercising its privilege of taking part in a conference called by the Economic and the Social Council of the United Nations. One is sufficiently aware of the transnational activities of individuals, corporations, and states. When one considers that there are also in existence more than 140 intergovernmental organizations, and over 1,100 nongovernmental organizations commonly described as international, one realizes the almost infinite variety of the transnational situations which may arise. Philip C. Jessup, *Transnational Law* (New Haven 1956), 3.

See also Myres S. McDougal's emphasis on the need for a contemporary study of international law that would include not only the nation state, but also international government organizations, transnational political parties, pressure groups, private associations, and the individual human being. McDougal, "International Law, Power and Policy: A Contemporary Conception," *Académie de Droit International, Recueil des Cours*, LXXXII (1953), 137 [hereafter cited as *Recueil des Cours*].

[6] Tentatively formulated in the U.N. General Assembly Resolution on Permanent Sovereignty over Natural Resources of December 20, 1962. G.A. Res. 1803, U.N. *Official Records*, 17th Sess., Supp. No. 17 (A/5217), 1962, 15.

[7] Embodied in numerous recent investment laws and codes, e.g., the Kenya Foreign Investments Protection Act of 1964. For an interesting survey of such legislation in one region see *Investment Laws and Regulations in Africa*, U.N. Doc. E/CN. 14/Inr/28 (Rev. 2), 1965.

[8] See International Bank for Reconstruction and Development, Convention on the Settlement of Investment Disputes between States and Nationals of other States and Accompanying Report of the Executive Directors (March 18, 1965).

patterns in international organizations and transactions, as well as in other multilateral and bilateral relationships. They cover a wider range of international organizations, a wider range of participants, and a much greater variety of international legal relationships. The most basic significance of this new phase in international relations is that the human being—singly, in groups, or through his nation or state— has become the direct concern of international law.[9]

ECONOMIC AND SOCIAL WELFARE AND THE EXPANDING SCOPE OF INTERNATIONAL LAW

A generation ago Georges Scelle—applying the sociological concepts of Durkheim and Duguit—spoke of a *droit intersocial* derived from the phenomenon of social solidarity which "déborde les sociétés étatiques pour former les sociétés internationales."[10] We need today a wider conception of the scope of international law with regard to matters of human welfare, a conception that reflects the realities and aspirations of the postwar world. The trend of things was brilliantly forecast by Maurice Bourquin.[11] Although at that time most of the new international economic and social activities had hardly begun, and the impact of the since emancipated developing countries was not yet felt, Bourquin saw that the subject matter of international law was not enclosed in "immovable boundaries," that it was "a mounting flood which is far from having exhausted its momentum." From the rapidly expanding number of fields affected by international legal regulation such as labor, human rights, education, science, refugee assistance, civil aviation, agriculture, international money and banking matters, Bourquin deduced that international law was in for both "quantitative and qualitative renovation."

Another characterization of the impact of the concern with human welfare on the scope of international law is that of Wilfred Jenks:

[T]he emphasis of the law is increasingly shifting from the formal structure of the relationship between States and the delimitation of their jurisdiction to the development of substantive rules on matters of common concern vital to the growth of an international community and to the individual well-being of the citizens of its

[9] "We may find that some of the problems that we have considered essentially international, inevitably productive of stress and conflict between governments and peoples of two different countries, are after all merely human problems which might arise at any level of human society—individual, corporate, interregional, or international." Jessup (fn. 5), 15.

[10] Georges Scelle, *Précis de Droit des Gens, I* (Paris 1932), 29.

[11] Maurice Bourquin, "Pouvoir Scientifique et Droit International," *Hague Recueil*, LXX (1947), 331.

member States. We shall also find that as the result of this change of emphasis the subject-matter of the law increasingly includes cross-frontier relationships of individuals, organisations and corporate bodies which call for appropriate legal regulation on an international basis. . . .[12]

The Dutch jurist Röling, in a perceptive monograph on "International Law in the Expanded World" (1960), emphasized particularly the importance of the shift in the subject matter of international law, from the more or less formal regulation of diplomatic relations between states to an international law of welfare. At the same time, Frederick van Asbeck singled out six factors as the most important new forces accounting for the growth of international law.[13] First, the extension of intergovernmental consultation and cooperation from the foreign relations field to technical, economic, and social affairs; second, the increasing substitution of a collective framework for bilateral dealings; third, the extension of the activities of international unions and other organizations to the non-European world; fourth, the entry of the technical expert on the international scene; fifth, the growth of regular political conferences and assemblies, fixed in composition and procedure, and based on a permanent secretariat of officials; and sixth, the quasi-parliamentary conference representing social groups as well as governments, as in the ILO.

COEXISTENCE AND COOPERATION IN INTERNATIONAL LEGAL RELATIONS

The present writer has sought to rationalize these manifold developments in a basic distinction between the "international law of coexistence," and the "international law of cooperation."[14] The former

---

[12] C. Wilfred Jenks, *The Common Law of Mankind* (New York 1958), 17.

[13] Frederick M. van Asbeck, "Growth and Movement of International Law," *International and Comparative Law Quarterly,* xi (October 1962), 1054.

[14] Wolfgang Friedmann, *The Changing Structure of International Law* (New York 1964), Chap. 6. The distinction has been accepted, e.g., by Richard A. Falk, Review, *Columbia Journal of Transnational Law,* iii, No. 2 (1965), 256; D. M. Johnson, Review, *International and Comparative Law Quarterly,* xiv (January 1965), 313; R. J. Barnet, "Coexistence and Cooperation in International Law," *World Politics,* xviii (December 1965), 82. However, it has been sharply criticized by McDougal and Reisman in the following terms:

The artificiality of the distinction between the laws of "coexistence" and of "cooperation" should by now be clearly apparent. All the actions of participants in the international social process are taken, it is assumed, for what is perceived to be self-interest in an attempt to maximize overall value positions. In certain value processes, it is widely perceived that self-interest can be achieved through cooperation; self-interest is supplanted by a perceived common interest. In these

comprises the bulk of traditional international law, that is, the regulation of diplomatic relations between states which are the exclusive subjects of international law. Essentially these relations embody rules of abstention. They are concerned with the delimitation of national sovereignty. As such, they are international rules on the bounds of, and the mutual respect for, the attributes of national sovereignty. They regulate such matters as: the dimensions of rights pertaining to territorial waters and continental shelves; national jurisdiction on the seas; national sovereignty over air space and tentatively the uses of outer space, for which national sovereignty has not so far been claimed; the attendant prerogatives of national jurisdiction over nonnationals; governmental immunities from jurisdiction; and principles of state responsibility for injuries caused within the state's jurisdiction to the personal and property interests of foreigners. Another part of traditional international law has been concerned with the respective

---

value processes, recurring patterns of decision give rise to institutions which can have positive effects as a conditioning factor in other value processes where self-interest clashes. Such other value processes, in which effective elites think (possibly correctly) that their objectives are better served by protracted conflict than by cooperation, are the primary problems for contemporary international law. Assuming that the interest in cooperation is strong enough, it may be possible to manipulate this interest so as to modify or regulate the areas of conflict. If the distinction between coexistence and cooperation is employed in this sense—that is, as a strategy for community decision-makers—then it is justified. If, on the other hand, it is used to circumvent the pressing problems of the so-called law of coexistence, it hinders rather than helps the cause of world order. Myres S. McDougal and W. Michael Reisman, " 'The Changing Structure of International Law,' Unchanging Theory for Inquiry," Columbia Law Review, LXV (May 1965), 810, 834.

It is difficult to understand the precise purport and meaning of this critique. That the laws of "cooperation" as well as those of "coexistence" are directed by "self-interest" is stressed throughout the book, where indeed the development of an international law of cooperation is regarded as a matter of survival. McDougal and Reisman are prepared to accept the distinction between coexistence and cooperation "as a strategy for community decision-makers," but object to the distinction being used "to circumvent the pressing problems of the so-called law of coexistence." Nowhere in the book is there any suggestion that the law of cooperation would make the law of coexistence less relevant, or diminish the need for arrangements of coexistence responding to contemporary conditions and needs. What is stressed is that the techniques of the international law of cooperation may offer ways of response to urgent international concerns, and corresponding developments of international law, not attainable by institutional blueprints such as a wholesale revision of the U.N. Charter. The difference between the two types of international law is particularly important with respect to sanctions.

Certain rules of coexistence, e.g., agreement to abstain from claims of national sovereignty in the Antarctic or in outer space, are the bases for possible cooperative efforts such as joint weather stations or communications systems. This in no way derogates from the importance of distinguishing both objectives and techniques in the two areas.

rights and duties of belligerents and neutrals in time of war. Until the advent of the League of Nations Covenant and the United Nations Charter, the waging of war was the ultimate and unchallenged expression of national sovereignty. The legal instrumentalities of the international law of coexistence have been almost exclusively custom and treaties.

By contrast, the newer and incipient international law of cooperation is concerned with the organization and implementation of joint endeavors on a binational, regional, or multinational level directed to human welfare. In any field, rules of abstention may give way to rules of cooperation, as common purposes and endeavors supersede a "hands-off" posture.

The exclusivity of national fishing rights in territorial waters, or competitive fishing in the open seas, may be replaced by joint arrangements for the conservation of breeding grounds or—as has been attempted in a widely violated convention—the regulation of whaling. The competitive launching of outer-space satellites or moon rockets may give way to joint weather stations or moon expeditions. The competing national claims for jurisdiction over crimes committed on the high seas may be replaced by joint judicial institutions. Most important of all (though not relevant to the present enquiry), the absolute right to make war for the pursuit of national objectives may be limited— as imperfectly attempted by the League Covenant and the U.N. Charter—by common organizations for international security. The pursuit of these objectives widens the range of participants in the international legal process from states to public international organizations, nongovernmental international organizations, and private corporations insofar as they enter into relations with states or public international organizations in the pursuit of international economic and social objectives.

The growing scope of international law has also widened and diversified the *sources* of international legal rules of conduct. Because so many of the new concerns of international law deal with matters formerly entirely within the ambit of private law, the categories and norms of private law must increasingly be used to develop public international relationships. The addition of "the general principles of law recognized by civilized nations" to the Statutes of the Permanent Court of International Justice and its contemporary successor, the International Court of Justice, as a third source of law has now become much more important; it goes beyond the still very limited field of jurisdiction of the International Court itself. As will be shown later, the "general principles" are being increasingly used in international economic agreements to characterize the law applicable between the parties—largely states on the one part and private corporations on the other. Declaratory Resolutions of the United Nations General Assembly, draft conventions for the protection of foreign investments (even if not formally adopted by the requisite majority), drafts prepared for Reports of the International Law Commission, bilateral treaties, and national investment laws (insofar as they come to represent a general pattern of international relationships) must now be used as supplementary sources of the new international law of economic and social development.

The most universally accepted and continuing efforts in connection with the international law of welfare tend to be embodied in permanent international organizations. The World Bank and its two affiliates (the International Development Association and the International Finance Corporation), the new United Nations Conference on Trade and Development, the majority of the specialized agencies of the United Nations, the General Agreement for Tariffs and Trade (GATT), and various regional organizations (most notably the European Economic Community) represent institutionally organized endeavors in economic and social development. They are supplemented by a multitude of international conventions, treaties, and agreements, some of which may eventually be consolidated into international organizations. The distinction between the international law of cooperation and the international law of coexistence corresponds to the distinction recently articulated by H.L.A. Hart between the prohibitive and punitive aspects of law as a coercive order, and the concept of law as "the power . . . conferred on individuals to mold their legal relations with others by contracts, wills, marriage, etc. . . . Or as a means of social control. . . ." Or, as "used to control, to guide and to plan life out of court."[15] The importance of this distinction between the different functions of law is, in the international sphere, considerably greater than in municipal law. In the latter, the legal order normally provides full civil or criminal sanctions—whether in the form of punishment, damages, or nullity of transactions—for all types of legal relationships, prohibitive as well as permissive ones. This is in fact one reason why analytical jurists, such as Austin or Kelsen, have denied the validity of the distinction. But in international law, the coercive sanction is still lamentably weak. Recourse to international legal processes and the force of sanctions to reprove the illegal conduct of states is still very restricted. To some extent a substitute can be found in the reciprocity of interest.

15 Herbert L. A. Hart, *The Concept of Law* (Oxford 1961), 28, 39.

SANCTIONS IN THE INTERNATIONAL LAW OF ECONOMIC AND SOCIAL COOPERATION

Reciprocity is the most important sanction of an international law of coexistence based on a decentralized structure of nation states. Except for the very limited authority of the United Nations with regard to control over the use of force, and leaving aside the recently qualified theory of Kelsen that war and reprisals used by states are sanctions of international law used in behalf of the international community,[16] reciprocity is the principal guarantor of respect for the territorial and jurisdictional aspects of national sovereignty.[17] In the analysis of Georg Schwarzenberger, the international law of reciprocity which expresses a state of equilibrium of power stands between the "law of power" and the "law of coordination."[18] The development of rules governing diplomatic immunity—which are a characteristic feature of the international law of coexistence—owe their development and effectiveness largely to the principles of reciprocity.

In this writer's slightly different approach, the law of reciprocity characteristically represents a "society" as distinct from a "community."[19] Such endeavors as the organized efforts in international development aid, or the objectives of the ILO, the Special Development Program of the United Nations, the European Development Fund, and the proposed Southeast Asian Development Fund cannot be adequately understood in terms of reciprocity. The borderlines between the two concepts are, of course, fluid. A strong degree of mutual reciprocal interest may lead to a closer degree of structural integration and hence to a "community." The relativity of the distinction between society and community may be compared to that between interest and values. One of the leading books on the subject of values describes "value" as the unifying idea of the "interests of life," and it defines "value" as the "principle which determines the subordination of one end to another."[20] The "balance of interests," which has been

[16] Hans Kelsen, *General Theory of Law and State* (New York 1961), 330.

[17] It is much more effective in the relations between states of roughly comparable power than in the relations between states of very unequal power. One may contrast, for example, the importance of reciprocity in the relations between the Western powers and the U.S.S.R. in Germany (especially Berlin) or the resolution of the Cuban missile crisis of October 1962, with the occupation of Tibet by Communist China in 1959, the annexation of Goa by India in 1961, or the United States intervention in the Dominican Republic in 1965.

[18] Georg Schwarzenberger, *The Frontiers of International Law* (London 1962), Chaps. 1-15, 29.

[19] The distinction has been classically formulated by the German sociologist Ferdinand Tönnies, *Gemeinschaft und Gesellschaft* (Leipzig 1887).

[20] W. G. Everett, *Moral Values* (1918), 6.

categorized in particular by Roscoe Pound in many of his works,[21] could equally well be described as a balance or conflict of "values." It remains true, nevertheless, that in the formulation of Tönnies, members of a society remain isolated in spite of their association while the members of a community are united in spite of their separate existence.

In this respect both the structure and the purpose of international development aid are quite different from that of the law governing diplomatic immunity. The latter is strictly conditioned upon reciprocal interest and reciprocal enforcement. The former incorporates a community goal of mankind in the pursuit of which the interests of the various participants are quite uneven. In a wider sense it may be said that the quotas contributed, for example, by the United States to the World Bank, or its substantial bilateral aid for economic development is essentially inspired by a long-term interest in national survival. In any meaningful sense, however, there is no reciprocity between the interest of the United States or Britain or France in assisting, bilaterally and through multilateral institutions, the development of Tanzania or India or Colombia and the interest of these countries in receiving such assistance. Granted, much of the bilateral development aid given by the major developed countries is "tied" to the utilization of the loans for purchases in the aid-giving countries. Nevertheless, a very large portion of this aid in the form of grants, surplus food, untied loans, technical assistance, and contributions to multilateral agencies means a net burden on the donor country and a—not always strictly corresponding—net benefit for the recipient country. Their respective parts in the bilateral aid schemes, e.g., for the financing of roads, harbors, or industrial projects, or the fact that developed and underdeveloped nations are classified as two distinct categories by the International Development Association, with one supplying the major share of the capital and the other being exclusively entitled to "soft" loans granted by the IDA,[22] cannot be explained by the law of reciprocity. It is predicated upon a community interested in international economic development in which the roles and functions of the different participants are deliberately unequal and different in kind.

These differences are reflected in the differential effects of the "sanction of nonparticipation," i.e., exclusion from participation in development activities, on the various parties. Reduction or termination of aid on the part of the United States or Britain may in the long

---

21 See among others Roscoe Pound, *Jurisprudence*, III, Pt. 4 (St. Paul 1959); *Social Control through Law* (New Haven 1959); "A Survey of Social Interests," *Harvard Law Review*, LVII (October 1943), 1.

22 See Articles of Agreement of the International Development Association (IDA), Schedule A-Initial Subscriptions, with Part I and Part II differentiation.

perspective be politically unwise, but the only direct effect will be a lightening of the national tax burden. By contrast, a developing country excluded from institutionalized development aid may find itself vitally hampered in its national existence or development. The threat of nonparticipation is therefore very different for one side than it is for the other. A willful default on a loan granted by the IBRD or the IDA may not incur any stronger direct punitive sanction than the violation of any other international obligation.[23] But such a default would almost certainly have the consequence of ineligibility for further loans. This sanction of "nonparticipation," comparable in national affairs to the exclusion of a member from his union or professional association, could be more serious than many a "punitive" sanction.[24]

The importance of the sanctions of exclusion or nonparticipation is proportionate to the importance of the activity to the excluded party. In this respect, the various institutionalized or noninstitutionalized international economic and social activities differ considerably. In the international development aid field, the status of the World Bank as lender, manager, or technical adviser has become so universally accepted that refusal of the Bank to cooperate any further with a particular state has a very bad effect on its general international creditworthiness. Willful default on a loan, or grossly negligent handling of resources in such a manner that the payment of interest or capital becomes impossible, will normally induce the Bank to refuse further loans or other assistance. The effect of such defaults would be so detrimental that they have not occurred in the history of the Bank. Here the sanction of nonparticipation is effective with regard to the fulfillment of international financial obligations—although it does, of course, affect borrower states much more than lender states.

On the other hand, international labor and social security standards have not as yet achieved sufficient universal respect and acceptance to make nonparticipation an effective sanction against a defaulter. Whereas, with the exception of the Soviet bloc, membership in the World Bank and its affiliate agencies is almost universal, ILO conventions are normally signed only by a minority of the members. Not to be bound by ILO conventions that prescribe certain minimum standards of wages or working conditions is often still a distinct advantage

---

[23] I.e., it is dependent either on the availability of external assets that may, in theory, be seized—but which are usually immune from seizure under the international principles governing the immunity of governments, or on the acceptance of a judgment by the defaulting state.

[24] See for a perceptive analysis of the "Emerging Field of Sanction Law" in the municipal sphere, Richard Arens and Harold D. Lasswell, *In Defense of Public Order* (New York 1961).

in an international society which, in this field, has very weak community features. Nonparticipation of the states concerned in the various conventions that constitute the so-called Seafarers Code makes it possible and profitable for large numbers of commercial ships to be registered under the flags of Panama, Liberia, Honduras, and others. This compares with the situation of trade unionism in the Western countries one or two generations ago. Minimum standards and collective bargaining had not yet reached the legal and social status which makes compliance with the terms of collective agreements a practical if not a legal necessity for the employer in modern industrial societies. In the international community, the divergencies of national interests and standards still prevail by far over the community interest in joint minimum standards of social welfare. But this may not be a permanent state of affairs. The rise of welfare state ideologies in a growing number of countries, or the chaos of international trading conditions caused by stark discrepancies in living standards and working conditions may, in due course, lead to a far more general acceptance of international labor and welfare law, and, to the same extent, may make nonparticipation in the relevant international organizations and conventions as unenviable a status as it is today for most industrialized countries in the major occupational fields. Exclusion from participation in an organization may then result in the unavailability of labor or preclusion from commerce with complying countries.

Much of this is music of the future. What matters is the shift of emphasis in cooperative economic and social activities from the punitive sanction to the sanction of nonparticipation. It is impossible to predict how soon and with what intensity mankind will realize the overwhelming importance of cooperation in such matters as the conservation of fisheries or whales, the international fight against erosion of the soil and deforestation and, above all, population control in a world whose population is likely to more than double between now and the end of the century. It is, however, at least possible that insight into the overwhelming urgency of these matters and the corresponding importance of participation will develop more quickly than the constitutional organization of mankind into a world community whose governing organs will dispose of effective coercive and punitive sanctions.

THE WIDENING OF PARTICIPANTS IN THE PROCESS OF ECONOMIC AND SOCIAL DEVELOPMENT

The vertical extension of the scope of international legal relations to economic and social matters has been the principal, though not the only, stimulating agent in the progressive widening of the participants in the international legal order beyond the nation states. Public international organizations and, to a more limited extent, also private corporations are today major participants in the development of new fields and techniques of international law. Before proceeding to analyze some of these new principles and techniques, we must dispose of the main objection to such an extension derived from the traditional definitions of international law. Until recently, international law was unanimously defined by authoritative writers as "the law which is effectively applied in the relations of states by reason of the obligatory character that they recognize in it."[25]

But some recent writers have a different approach. Reference has already been made to the "transnational law" concept tentatively developed by Philip Jessup and Myres McDougal.[26] The insufficiency of an international law defined solely in terms of interstate relations has been put clearly by Wilfred Jenks: "International law can no longer be adequately or reasonably defined or described as a law governing the mutual relations of states . . . it represents the common law of mankind in an early state of development, of which the law governing the relations between states is one, but only one, major division."[27]

THE ABSORPTION OF PRIVATE INTO PUBLIC INTERNATIONAL LAW

Such a widening of the sphere of public international law can be accepted only on the assumption—clearly brought out by Jenks—that the scope of international law is at no time authoritatively determined by the statutory definition imposed by a lawmaker. Rather, it is a developing body of rules reflecting the changing pattern of transna-

[25] Charles de Visscher, *Theory and Reality in Public International Law* (Princeton 1957), 133. A similar statement is found in the third French edition at p. 169, though this may be regarded as a description rather than a definition of international law. Among well-known definitions confining international law to relations between states are those of Holland, Hall, Pollack, and Hackworth. See Jean Gabriel Castel, *International Law Chiefly as Applied in Canada* (Toronto 1965), 3.
[26] See footnote 5.
[27] Jenks (fn. 12), 58. For recent definitions, which include entities other than states among the subjects of international law see also Marjorie M. Whiteman, *Digest of International Law*, 1 (Washington 1963), 1: "International law is the standard of conduct, at a given time, for states and other entities subject thereto." Or Joseph G. Starke, *An Introduction to International Law*, 5th edn. (London 1963), 1, 2, where international law is stated to include not only "the principles and rules of conduct which states feel themselves bound to observe," but also "the rules of laws relating to the functioning of international institutions or organizations, their relations with each other, and their relations with states and individuals; and certain rules of law relating to individuals and non-state entities are the concern of the international community."

tional relationships. The reasoning of those who continue to exclude entities other than states from the field of international law[28] must, therefore, be predicated upon the immutability of custom in international relations. But, whereas, within a municipal system, the scope of law can be constantly readjusted and redetermined through the interplay of legislative, administrative, and judicial organs, there is no equivalent in international legal relations. The redefinition of the scope of international law must proceed through periodical reappraisals of the character and scope of international legal relationships that can properly be ascribed to public international law. The only proper criterion for distinguishing the scope of *public* as distinct from that of *private* international law is the characterization of the relation or activity in question as predominately public rather than private in purpose. There is, surprisingly enough, very little discussion of the differentiation of these two spheres in terms of international legal relations. The distinction between public and private concerns, in municipal as in international legal relations, however elusive, has to be attempted. For a great number of purposes—such as the determination of the law properly applicable to the relations between the parties, or for deciding the question whether public authorities should properly concern themselves with the relationship in question, or for determining whether the analogy of private contract law or that of revocable public concessions is more applicable to an arrangement between a government and private investor—the allocation of a relationship to public or private law is important.

Writers on international law have generally avoided or bypassed the question. Thus Jessup, in describing the sphere of transnational law, suggests that "it would be unnecessary to worry whether public or private law applies in certain cases."[29] Students of jurisprudence have not found it easy to agree on the relevant criteria either, although the great majority of them accept the necessity of the distinction between public and private law.[30]

Generally, we may say that public law pertains to public purposes and private law to private purposes. But the definition of what is public or private at a given time clearly varies greatly depending upon the political, social, and economic structure of a society. A century ago when states generally confined themselves to minimal protective func-

---

[28] See, for example, Lord McNair, "The General Principles of Law Recognized by Civilized Nations," *British Yearbook of International Law*, XXXIII (1957).

[29] Jessup (fn. 5), 15.

[30] Significant exceptions are Hans Kelsen and Leon Duguit, on whose rejection of the relevance of any distinction between public and private law see, inter alia, George W. Paton, *A Textbook of Jurisprudence*, 2nd edn. (Oxford 1951), Chap. 14; W. Friedmann, *Legal Theory*, 4th edn. (London 1960), 179, 233.

tions such as the administration of defense, justice, and police, it was fairly simple to exclude economic and commercial activities from the sphere of public law. This clearly is no longer true in view of the manifold and far-reaching activities of governments nationally and internationally in commercial matters. In the legal systems which have a jurisdictional division between "ordinary" and administrative courts, such as the French legal system, the allocation of legal transactions to one or the other jurisdiction has caused considerable difficulty.[31] But even if we can give only a loose and flexible characterization of the respective spheres of public and private law,[32] the distinction remains necessary and valid.

Returning to our original subject of inquiry, international economic relations which can be characterized as predominantly pertaining to the public purposes and policies of the community, rather than to the commercial considerations of *quid pro quo* that dominate contracts as a characteristic instrument of exchange in private economic life, may be ascribed to the sphere of public international law. The problem has confronted the administrative tribunals constituted by the League of Nations and the United Nations, with regard to the characterization of the relations between the international organization—of which there are now a vastly increased number—and employed individuals. In the first study of the problem of the relative shares of public and private law in the characterization of these relations, Suzanne Basdevant concluded that it was necessary to resort to the rules of internal public, especially of administrative, law as most closely analogous to this type of contractual relationship.[33] This theory, first applied in the Monod case[34] to the principles governing the termination of the contract of an employee, has since been developed in many subsequent judgments, especially those of the United Nations Administrative Tribunal.[35]

Once we concede the basic and surely elementary assumption that

[31] See notably the distinction between *gestion publique* and *gestion privée* as analyzed in Marcel Waline, *Droit Administratif*, 7th edn. (Paris 1957), Par. 132; John D. B. Mitchell, *The Contracts of Public Authorities* (London 1954), 167; W. Friedmann, *Law in a Changing Society* (London 1959), 371.

[32] See, for example, Paton (fn. 30), 261: "Private law is thus the residue of the law after we subtract public law. This approach seems to involve fewer assumptions as to the nature and quality of state activities than any other."

[33] Suzanne Basdevant, *Les Fonctionnaires Internationaux* (Paris 1931).

[34] See League of Nations, *Official Journal* (Geneva 1925), 144.

[35] For a comprehensive survey of the jurisprudence see C. Wilfred Jenks, *The Proper Law of International Organizations* (Dobbs Ferry 1962), 59; also W. Friedmann and A. A. Fatouros, "The United Nations Administrative Tribunal," *International Organization*, XI (Winter 1957), 13, 22. See also Alan H. Schechter, *Interpretation of Ambiguous Documents by International Administrative Tribunals* (London 1964).

the scope and structure of international law is conditioned by the changing patterns of international relations and the expanding scope of relevant international activities, we will have no difficulty in regarding public international organizations as full public subjects of international law within the functional limitations of their task.[36] The navigational regulations issued by the International Civil Aviation Organization, the Sanitary Code of the World Health Organization, the technical assistance arrangements negotiated by the Food and Agriculture Organization, the joint transactions of the World Bank or of the European Development Fund, the arrangements for the use and inspection of nuclear energy installations entered into by the International Atomic Energy Authority, all these clearly pertain, on both sides, to public purposes. Even insofar as sales, leases, service contracts, and other commercial contracts are involved, these are used as instrumentalities derived from private law but used for the benefit of the community as a whole—national, regional, or international as the case may be—and not of specific individuals.

CONSTITUTIONAL ASPECTS OF INTERNATIONAL ECONOMIC AND SOCIAL ORGANIZATIONS

The growing importance of economic and social objectives in international organizations has led to significant structural and constitutional developments. The following five features may be mentioned. First, the increasing need to insure certain universal or near-universal minimum standards in fields of essential international communication has led, for two of the specialized agencies of the United Nations, to an advance toward quasi-legislative powers—as distinct from the usual purely advisory functions. The World Health Assembly, the "legislative" organ of WHO, has been entrusted with powers to adopt regulations concerning sanitary requirements and the prevention of disease. It also has the power to establish certain nomenclatures and standards with regard to the safety, purity, etc. of biological, pharmaceutical, and similar products. These regulations—of which the WHO Sanitary Code is the outstanding example—come into force for all members after due notice has been given of their adoption, except for such members as may notify the Director-General of rejection or reservations within a certain stated period. Similarly, the International Civil Aviation Organization's Council has the power to enact certain international standards, practices, and procedures of air navigation

---

36 In other words, their status is not equivalent to that of states which still have a monopoly of international legal status in the spheres affecting the bulk of the international law of coexistence, i.e., the delimitation of national sovereignty and jurisdiction.

by a two-thirds majority, subject to disapproval within a certain period by a majority of the contracting states. In the absence of disapproval by such a majority, decisions taken by the qualified majority are binding on all of the members. While health and air transport are essentially nonpolitical in character, they signify the growing importance of universal international standards in the pursuit of mankind's welfare. In their approach to near-legislative powers, the procedures of the ICAO and WHO may foreshadow a pattern of future international organizations in other fields.

Second, the Constitution of the International Labour Organisation is characterized by the so-called tripartite pattern. Only one-half of the delegates, both to the General Conference and in the governing body, are chosen from government nominees. The other half are nominated, in equal proportions, by the national organizations representing employers and workers. This tripartite composition reflects the horizontal extension of international law into the social patterns and processes of collective bargaining on labor conditions, as developed in the industrial countries. It also reflects a pluralistic philosophy insofar as it is predicated upon the autonomy of employers and labor organizations within the state. The adoption of this pattern has caused considerable difficulty with regard to the admission of Communist or Fascist states, since in these political systems both employers and labor organizations are state-controlled organs without autonomy of decision.

Third, the international financial agencies, i.e., the World Bank and its affiliates and the International Monetary Fund, differ in structure and powers from the typical international agency because of their financial autonomy. The capital is supplied by quota subscriptions from the participating states. This enables them to make loans and enter into other financial transactions without recourse to the participating states (except insofar as the Executive Directors represent one or several states). Experience has shown that the Executive Directors have come to function more as permanent representatives of these institutions than as national delegates. On the basis of the original quota subscriptions, the World Bank has been able to multiply its financial resources by recourse to the international bond market. It has also increased its reserves through the income from its loans. The relative independence of the international financial organizations has become an increasingly important factor of international life and greatly serves to enhance their *international* as distinct from a *multinational* status.

Fourth, the European Communities, and most particularly the European Coal and Steel Community, represent an advance toward *supranational* as distinct from *multinational* decision-making. The High Authority of the ECSC—now administratively merged with the EEC Commission—is empowered to act by a simple majority vote. This is, however, restricted by the need for consent in many important matters by the multinational Council of Ministers. In the European Economic Community the executive body, the Commission, has in theory only advisory powers. It is in effect the growing predominance of these permanent bodies of high-level officials that has been the main motive behind French moves to delay the advent of the next phase provided for in the EEC treaty, under which certain decisions can be made by a qualified majority of the members.

Fifth, the international organizations created for the administration of certain international commodity agreements reflect, in their composition and function, the distinction between capital-exporting and capital-importing countries, between producers and consumers, or, as in the new Trade and Development Board of the United Nations Conference for Trade and Development,[37] between developed and developing countries.[38]

ECONOMIC DEVELOPMENT AGREEMENTS BETWEEN GOVERNMENTS AND FOREIGN INVESTORS

A more complex problem is that of the status of international transactions between governments on the one part and private investors on the other. Here, the motivations and purposes on the part of the private investor, usually a large "multinational" corporation, are essentially commercial, i.e., dominated by the commercial profitability of an operation within the context of the corporation's total business. But, on the government's part, the main purpose is that of using the best available means for the development of the national economy. Usually, these agreements form part of a long-term national economic development plan and many of them are in part financed by loans from a public, national, or international aid agency.

In the Aid India and Aid Pakistan consortia, for example, in which aid commitments on the part of the major international and Western public development aid agencies are worked out in regular consultations with the recipient governments, the government will frequently list projects of this kind, i.e., development agreements concluded with private foreign investors as part of its national development plan. The

[37] See G.A. Res. 1995 (XIX), 1965.

[38] This distinction is also reflected in the Annex to the International Development Association, which distinguishes, for the purposes of qualification for "soft loans" between a stated number of "developed" countries, which are not eligible, and the rest which are. See footnote 22.

principles governing foreign investors with regard to taxation, labor permits, repatriation of earnings, etc., are often laid down in investment laws. Thus, the provisions governing these transactions form part of the public law system of the country.

In deciding whether agreements of this kind pertain essentially to public or to private international law, the decisive criterion must be their *predominant* purpose and function. Surely the public purposes in this instance clearly prevail over the private purposes. As Adolph Berle observed some years ago, the Iranian Oil Agreement of 1954, which terminated a severe international political crisis caused by the Mossadegh government's confiscation of the Anglo-Iranian oil properties in Iran and under which a consortium of private oil companies concluded a new and complex agreement with the government of Iran, fulfilled quasi-diplomatic as well as commercial functions.[39] The entire agreement had, in Berle's view, certain "quasi-treaty aspects."

It is not only through the participation of private corporations in complex international transactions of a strongly political character that the public purposes of such transactions are apparent. It is in the *content* and purpose of the mutual rights and obligations that the modern economic development agreement differs decisively from the traditional concession agreement. The traditional agreement was typically between a foreign investor and the host government (or, as in the case of the vast concessions obtained by Cecil Rhodes in what subsequently became Rhodesia, from a native chief) under which the investor obtained certain exclusive rights and privileges from the exploitation of certain resources in consideration of a lump sum payment or a concession fee. It is not only the terms of such concessions that have drastically changed, for example, in the modern oil concession agreement. Whether in the form of an equity joint venture or of a contractual arrangement, the host government now is a partner in the exploitation, and its share is measured by the dramatically changed evaluation of the host state's sovereignty over natural resources. In the international oil agreements which have multiplied since the last World War, the typical arrangement became that of a fifty-fifty share in profits based on the so-called posted price of the crude oil at the port of shipment. More recently, these terms have shifted further in favor of the host government in two respects. First, the host government has obtained what is in effect a seventy-five percent share of the profits by using as its agent a government corporation which shares with the foreign investor at the rate of fifty-fifty while the for-

[39] A. A. Berle, *The Twentieth Century Capitalist Revolution* (New York 1954), Chap. 4.

eign investor has to split his own profits at the same rate with the host government.[40]

Second, due to the collective organization of the Middle Eastern oil producers in the Organization of Petroleum Exporting Countries (OPEC), a foreign investor can no longer deduct the royalties due per ton or barrel of produced oil from the profits payable to the government. He can only deduct them as expense before net profits are ascertained. The difference is significant.[41]

But it is not only the greatly increased participation of the host government in the economic benefits of international commercial arrangements that distinguishes the contemporary economic development agreement from the old concession agreement. These agreements are now typically marked by a series of obligations on the part of the investor—and corresponding promises and permissions on the part of the host government—designed to foster the national development of the whole country. Any important agreements of this type (such as the Iranian Oil Agreement of 1954, or the LAMCO joint venture in which the government of Liberia is one party and a consortium of foreign commercial steel producers and industrial consumers form the other party) contain the following obligations: the development of "infrastructure" utilities and services in conjunction with the exploitation of the commodity involved, such as iron ore or crude oil; the training of local labor and experts, designed to reduce progressively the dependence upon foreign experts; the development of social facilities, such as housing schemes, schools, and hospitals; the maximization of the use of domestically produced raw materials and other commodities; the restriction of imports and the consequent use of foreign exchange for stipulated essentials; the corresponding obligation to maximize exports; and, to an increasing extent, the participation of local public or private capital through the device of the "joint venture." The more important of these economic development agreements are built into five year or other national development plans which in turn form the basis for international loan requests made to the World Bank, AID, or other public aid agencies.

It is this transformed character of the contemporary concession agreement which makes its public purpose prevalent over the purely

[40] See, for examples, the agreements concluded by the state-owned Italian ENI with Iran and the United Arab Republic (1963), and the 1957 AGIP-NIOC Agreement.

[41] See in detail Muhamad A. Mughraby, *Permanent Sovereignty over Oil Resources: A Study of Middle East Oil Concessions and Legal Change* (Beirut 1968), Chap. 6.

commercial purpose and, therefore, justifies its inclusion in a widened public rather than a private system of international law.

The frank acknowledgment of the *vertical* widening of the ambit of international law through the inclusion of transnational economic development transactions and the *horizontal* widening through the participation of private parties in the public purposes of economic development is the only approach that can satisfactorily respond to the challenge put to the science of international law by economic development itself—now a vital part of contemporary international relations. This approach recognizes the gap between the immensely widened scope of contemporary public international law and the inadequate substantive principles of public international law as developed in past centuries to regulate interstate diplomacy not economic and social development processes. The gap must be filled by the gradual absorption of the principles of contract or property, and of other fields developed in private, national, and international commercial transactions. This may be done by specific reference to the "general principles of law recognized by civilized nations" which has been an acknowledged source of public international law since 1919 for the Permanent Court of International Justice and the International Court of Justice. It may be done through reference to principles of equity, good faith, etc., as guideposts to the interpretation of the economic development agreement. Or it may be read into the construction of such an agreement where there is no specific reference to the law to be applied. Contemporary writers and judgments still tend to shy away from the frank recognition that, because of the essentially public purposes of international economic development transactions, contemporary public international law includes many types of institutions and transactions formerly either unknown or considered to be a matter of private international commercial relations, in an entirely different economic and social climate. Reference has already been made to Lord McNair's difficulty in considering economic development agreements as governed by public international law *stricto sensu* because international law, in his view, can only apply between states. His solution is to have recourse to "general principles of law" as a kind of separate system of law hovering between public and private international law.[42]

Professor Verdross draws what is perhaps the logical conclusion from such an approach by maintaining that commercial transactions between a state and a foreign corporation are "quasi-public international contracts . . . governed by the *lex contractus* agreed between the

[42] McNair (fn. 28), 10.

parties."[43] This means that the law agreed upon between the parties —which often means the invocation of general principles of law—is a kind of legal order of its own, allocable to neither public nor private international law. This solution has been strongly criticized by Dr. Mann.[44] The construction of an ad hoc legal order between two parties is neither theoretically nor politically desirable. It would tend to confer upon the parties a degree of autonomy in the formation of law which would have ominous parallels to the international cartel law developed in a number of internationally important industries in the inter-war period.[45]

Dr. Jenks, despite his clear insight into the new challenges and the widened scope of modern public international law, appears to adopt a view similar to that of Lord McNair, although he hesitates to follow the view of Verdross that general principles of law are a separate legal system.[46] For this approach, which leaves the application of general principles of law somewhat in the air, Dr. Jenks also invokes the authority of Judge Jessup whose concept of transnational law "includes both civil and criminal aspects, it includes what we know as public and private international law, and it includes national law, both public and private."[47] Judicial tribunals, national and international, are in Jessup's view to be "authorized to choose from all these bodies of law the rule considered to be most in conformity with reason and justice for the solution of any particular controversy."[48] This surely does not mean that transnational law has to be regarded as a third and separate system of law, rather than a widened and modernized version of public international law which has absorbed and continues to absorb many principles of private law. Modern international arbi-

---

[43] Alfred Verdross, "Die Sicherung von ausländischen Privatrechten aus Abkommen zur wirtschaftlichen Entwicklung mit Schiedsklauseln," *Zeitschrift für ausländisches öffentliches Recht und Völkerrecht*, XVIII (June 1958), 635. The same view is related in a more recent contribution, *Year Book of World Affairs*, XVIII (New York 1964), 230.

[44] F. A. Mann, "The Proper Law of Contracts Concluded by International Persons," *British Yearbook of International Law*, XXXV (1959), 34. See Friedmann (fn. 14), 175.

[45] This technique was developed particularly in the incandescent lamp industry and other highly cartelized international consortia which found means to evade the application of national laws and jurisdictions through arbitration clauses backed by economic sanctions such as boycott, exclusion from licenses, dumping, and financial guarantees. The powerful international cartels were often able to establish a kind of independent "federation," exercising their power over members, or even outsiders, without worrying too much about the complications which might arise from the application of private international law, let alone public international law. See for a more detailed analysis of these techniques and their consequences W. Friedmann and V. van Themat, "International Cartels and Combines" in W. Friedmann, ed., *Anti-Trust Laws* (London 1956), 477.

[46] Jenks (fn. 35), 152.   [47] Jessup (fn. 5), 106.   [48] Same.

tration awards appear to incline in this direction. Thus Lord Justice Asquith, as he then was, in the much quoted "Abu Dhabi" award[49] used a reference in an agreement between a private petroleum company and the ruler of Abu Dhabi to "good-will and sincerity of belief and . . . interpretation of this agreement in a fashion consistent with reason" as implying the application of a "Modern Law of Nature."[50]

More recently a Swiss federal judge as arbitrator in the Sapphire arbitration used a reference in the agreement—which had no specific choice of law clause—to "the principles of good faith and good-will" as leading to the application of general principles of law based on a comparative analysis of leading civil and common law systems with regard to breach of contract.[51] The learned judge came at least near to acknowledging the direct application of public international law when he said that "the present contract . . . was concluded between a state organ and a foreign company, and depends upon public law in certain of its aspects; it has therefore a quasi-international character which releases it from the sovereignty of a particular legal system and it differs fundamentally from an ordinary commercial contract."[52]

The ARAMCO award,[53] in the dispute between Saudi Arabia and the Arabian American Oil Company, came to a somewhat similar result by a tortuous road. Having first stated that "as the agreement of 1933 has not been concluded between two states, but between a state and a private American corporation, it is not governed by public international law," it proceeded to apply public international law to the *effects* of the concession on the grounds that "objective reasons lead [the tribunal] to conclude that certain matters cannot be governed by any rule of the municipal law of any state, as is the case in all matters relating to transport by sea, to the sovereignty of the state on its territorial waters and to the responsibility of states for the violation of its international obligations."

The importance of the "internationalization" of contracts of this kind has been noted by Dr. Mann who stresses the importance of public international law in such contracts but limits it to cases in

[49] Reported in *International and Comparative Law Quarterly*, I (April 1952), 247.

[50] Same, 251.

[51] See analysis by David Suratgar, "The Sapphire Arbitration Award, the Procedural Aspects: A Report and a Critique," *Columbia Journal of International Law*, III, No. 2 (1965), 152, and by Jean-Flavien Lalive, "Contracts Between a State or a State Agency and a Foreign Company," *International and Comparative Law Quarterly*, XIII (July 1964), 987, 1002-21.

[52] Same, 1018.

[53] Award rendered in 1958 (unpublished), reproduced in full: *Revue critique de droit international privé*, LII (April-June 1963), 272ff.

which the contracting parties—one of whom is an international person—expressly or by implication choose public international law as the proper law of their contract.[54]

The difference between this approach and the present writer's view that in case of doubt public international law must be held to govern the relations between the parties, is perhaps one of emphasis and relevant only where the parties fail to give any indication as to the applicable law. There are, however, strong reasons why the presumption should be thus reversed, why public international law through the incorporation of general principles of law recognized by civilized nations should, in case of doubt, be held to be the proper law in transactions of this kind. Since some states will need assistance for many years, economic development agreements are concluded between economically underdeveloped states that are legitimately proud of their political and legal sovereignty and foreign private corporations from highly sophisticated industrial and legal systems. In many cases, neither party wishes to subject itself to the law of the other party. The host state does not wish to give even the appearance of subjugation to foreign private capitalist entrepreneurs through the application of their law. The private investor does not wish to subject himself to the substantive and procedural uncertainties of the host state. The result is quite often vagueness or even complete failure to refer to any choice of law. Silence may be wisdom in such situations but it does not preclude the need to apply some legal order if the necessity arises. The application of public international law, enriched by the absorption of private commercial law principles, offers a satisfactory way out of the dilemma. Perhaps the strongest confirmation for this approach is found in the consistent practice of the World Bank which, contrary to its earlier practice of referring to the law of New York for the interpretation of legal terms in its agreements, no longer incorporates any choice-of-law clause in its loan agreements with governments or private borrowers (backed by government guarantees). In view of those most qualified to interpret the silence, this is taken to mean the applicability of public international law.[55]

---

[54] Mann (fn. 44), 34, 43.

[55] See in particular Aron Broches, "International Legal Aspects of the Operations of the World Bank," *Recueil des Cours*, xcviii (1959), 301. For an excellent brief survey of the various reasons which make the traditional choice of law techniques awkward and ineffective in this kind of international transaction, see Lester Nurick, "Choice-of-Law Clauses and International Contracts," *Proceedings of the American Society of International Law*, LIV (1960), 56. In this survey Mr. Nurick refers to two opposite ways of solving this problem, neither of which is satisfactory. One is the subdivision of a complicated transaction into many component parts and thus immensely complicates unity of interpretation. A partial list of the laws ap-

JOINT INTERNATIONAL BUSINESS VENTURES

The joint international business venture between developed and developing countries has, in the last decade, become an increasingly important aspect of international economic relations and in particular of economic development agreements. The chief reason for the growth of the joint venture as a substitute for wholly foreign owned operations in developing countries is the desire of the developing countries to retain a controlling or at least a substantial interest in the enterprises developed within their territories, while making the maximum possible use of the capital and know-how resources of investors from the developed countries. This is not the place to discuss the many different modalities as well as the advantages and disadvantages of such joint ventures.[56] Suffice it to say that the great majority of developing countries have increasingly resorted to the joint venture device as the best possible compromise between national sovereignty and foreign participation in development, and that the majority of foreign investors, however reluctantly, have come to accept the sharing of controls, whether as majority or minority shareholder, as offering the only prospect of continuing operations.[57]

---

plicable to the various parts of the Upper Volta Agreements reveals the following fragmentation:

1) Master Agreement and related agreements—Ghana law with qualifications.
2) Two trust agreements—New York law.
3) IBRD loan agreement—no provision.
4) Ex-Im Bank loan agreement—New York law.
5) AID loan agreement—District of Columbia law.
6) U.K. loan agreement—no provision.
7) Currency agreement; arbitration pursuant to the rules of the ICC; agreement itself governed by Swiss law.

However cumbrous, this is the technique preferred by most lawyers who like to lean on the legal system most familiar to them. The second solution is that of silence in the absence of any stipulation as to the applicable law. This Mr. Nurick describes as "essentially a nihilist position, a confession of defeat." See also, for a persuasive argument against the truncation of complex international transactions and in favor of the application of public international law, D. Sommers, A. Broches and G. R. Delaume, "Conflict Avoidance in International Loans and Monetary Agreements," *Law and Contemporary Problems*, XXI (Summer 1956), 463.

[56] For a comprehensive analysis, with many case studies, see W. Friedmann and George Kalmanoff, eds., *Joint International Business Ventures* (New York 1961), and W. Friedmann and J. P. Béguin, *Recent Developments in Joint International Business Ventures* (to be published in 1970). See also *Columbia Journal of World Business* (Spring 1966), 19.

[57] Among the countries that in recent years have increasingly emphasized the encouragement of joint international business ventures, as part of their foreign investment policy, are Brazil, Chile, India, the Philippines, and Zambia. Both Chile and Zambia have, by recent legislation, converted foreign copper holdings into minority interests. The governments have, directly or through state corpora-

The joint venture is often a particular aspect of an economic development or concession agreement. It couples with the basic agreement on the exploitation of natural resources and the development of basic utilities or industries, an equity partnership which is usually constituted under the company law of the host country. To this extent, i.e., with regard to the statutory requirements and other "status" aspects of the joint enterprise, it is the law of the host country that must control. The joint venture rests, however, on contractual agreements between the parties. Where the local partner is either the government itself or a government-owned development corporation—as is often the case—the problem of the proper law is the same as in the type of economic development agreement discussed earlier. Although the fact that a joint enterprise has been constituted between the parties in the host country would indicate some gravitation toward that law, this is not always the controlling factor. With regard to the basic contractual relations, the same difficulties pertain regarding the choice between the one or the other legal system as the locus of reference. So do the considerations which point toward public international law as the legal order most acceptable to both sides.

New Legal Techniques in Interstate Economic Relations

While the cooperation of private foreign investors with the governments of developing countries has gained outstanding significance in postwar international law, economic transactions have also acquired increasing importance in the relations between states—the traditional subjects of international law. This is due in part to the increasing involvement of many governments in economic activities, not only as controllers but also as owners and managers. The increasing range and importance of interstate economic agreements also result from the fact that most developing countries have state-directed economies and need to earn the greatest possible amount of foreign exchange through the export of their produce (usually agricultural staple products or mineral raw materials) in return for needed capital, consumer goods, and technical services. Some of these needed commodities and services are supplied by national or international public agencies on a grant or loan basis. But this method is neither permanent nor adequate. Nor is

---

tions, acquired 51 percent of the shares. Brazil has, after many years of negotiations, nationalized the telephone and telegraph operations of the (Canadian) Brazilian Traction Company and insisted on investment of a major part of the price paid to Brazil in various minority ventures with Brazilian enterprises. For details see the case studies in Friedmann and Béguin (fn. 56).

the receipt of aid a permanently acceptable way of life for nations which aim at real, as distinct from nominal, independence.

The ideal of free international trade—through the widest possible use of the "most favored nation" clause, through the abolition or at least a general reduction of protective tariffs, and through the abolition of import quotas—is the long-term objective of the General Agreement on Tariffs and Trade. Even in the relations among the industrially advanced countries, who are the main parties to GATT, this ideal is far from realization. Almost every one of the contracting parties has entered into the Agreement with a considerable range of qualifications.

The European Economic Community, while aiming at free trade and the gradual elimination of tariffs between its six members, has, by the same process, erected a protective wall against the outside world. The reduction of this barrier through mutual concessions between the EEC and other countries (especially the U.S.) was the objective of the so-called Kennedy Round which, after prolonged negotiations, resulted in an agreement on mutual tariff reductions in 1968. Even if the industrially developed nations should increase free trade with each other, the great majority of developing countries are scarcely in a position to join. The advantages which the developed countries enjoy with regard to scientific development, technical know-how, and labor productivity have greatly increased the gap between their economic competitiveness and that of the developing countries which are still struggling to get away from their traditional position of suppliers of agricultural staple commodities and raw materials. Moreover, the supplies of the latter available for export have, for more than a decade, been in surplus. This has a further depressing effect on prices and competitive position in international trade. The chronic inferiority of the developing countries—dependent upon the export of such commodities as coffee, cocoa, cattle, cotton, palm nuts, copper, or tin—led to the formation of a common front of the underprivileged at the Geneva Conference on Trade and Development in 1964. Seeking to formulate common policies vis-à-vis the developed world at a level reaching at least one percent of GNP, the international trade policies of this bloc have found expression in two major demands: first, the attainment of a special status with regard to tariffs and import quotas for their products to be granted by the developed countries;[58] and second, the con-

[58] A new chapter on Trade and Development, adopted as an amendment to Article XXXVI of the GATT, in February 1965, recognizes this special status, by committing the developed contracting parties "to the fullest extent possible," to

(a) accord high priority to the reduction and elimination of barriers to products currently or potentially of particular export interest to less-developed

clusion of commodity agreements that would assure to exporting members a minimum share for commodities such as coffee (threatened by a surplus of competing supplies), with a corresponding commitment on the part of the importing members, and, in some cases, the conclusion of price agreements that would protect them from fluctuations within certain limits.

The question of possible arrangements for supplementary financing for countries suffering from disruption of their export earnings was the subject of a staff study published by the World Bank in December 1965; it was undertaken as implementation of the Resolution passed at the Geneva Conference on Trade and Development.[59] This study suggests arrangements aimed at insuring that assistance will be given only to countries whose development policies give assurance that the assistance will be used for the intended purposes. It proposes an "administering agency" (presumably the World Bank) which would receive commitments for a five-year period and enter into arrangements with each of the assisted countries. Such arrangements would incorporate a projection of a "reasonable expectation" for export earnings over a period of, say, five years, and a "policy package" which the recipient country would agree to carry out in order to be eligible for assistance if its export earnings should fall below the projected amount. The agency would maintain continuous contact both with the recipient countries and with other aid-giving institutions. This mechanism combines certain administrative with quasi-judicial functions and would constitute a further step in the institutionalization of development aid.

Trade agreements between developing and developed countries and commodity stabilization agreements imply the adaptation of old techniques to new objectives. Any bilateral or multilateral trade agreement is, of course, a departure from the model of a free flow of trade across national boundaries carried out by private traders and deter-

---

contracting parties, including customs duties and other restrictions which differentiate unreasonably between such products in their primary and in their processed forms;
(b) refrain from introducing, or increasing the incidence of, customs duties or non-tariff import barriers on products currently or potentially of particular export interest to less-developed contracting parties; and
(c) (i) refrain from imposing new fiscal measures, and
    (ii) in any adjustments of fiscal policy accord high priority to the reduction and elimination of fiscal measures
    which would hamper, or which hamper significantly the growth of consumption of primary products, in raw or processed form, wholly or mainly produced in the territories of less-developed contracting parties, and which are applied specifically to those products.
[59] See IMF *International Financial News Survey*, XVII, No. 50 (December 1965).

mined, in the quality, quantity, and pricing of goods, by the laws of supply and demand. It is hardly necessary in this day and age to point out that reality has always been far removed from this theoretical model. For many decades, virtually all states have, to a greater or lesser extent, protected their national economy by tariffs imposed on imported goods (which threaten nationally produced agricultural commodities or industrial products), by import quotas limiting the volume of importations from abroad, by export subsidies designed to improve the competitive position of national industries or services with foreign competitors, or by outright prohibitions of imports. The range and intensity of these essentially economically motivated interferences and restrictions have been greatly widened by two factors which have removed the actual patterns of international trade even further from the theoretical model of free trade. First, the deep political and ideological tensions which have made the regulation of trade through restrictions on both imports and exports a major *political* weapon in the cold war. Second, the growing extent of state control and direct state management over the economic system, including foreign trade, which has made the model of an international free trade operated by private enterprise increasingly inapplicable. The distortion has been made more severe by the fact that state interferences have been very uneven in range and direction. In the Communist system—now comprising one-third of mankind—basic state control of all economic activities has been a fundamental faith and the directing factor in national as in international economic movement, from which even relatively free trade arrangements have been special exceptions, made for specific purposes. Since the second World War, a great majority of the newly independent countries have also developed essentially state-directed economies and systems of international trade under a national economic development plan. The impetus comes not so much from Communist or Socialist ideology, as from the paramount need to develop a national economy starting from a very low level and almost universally characterized by a shortage of foreign exchange and low competitive capacity. The international aspects, i.e., the import of vital raw materials, products, and services and the payment for such commodities and services either through export or through foreign public and private credit naturally are essential parts of such economic development planning. The fact that so many states have, for a variety of reasons, regarded international trade as an aspect of state-directed planning, has in turn influenced the methods and techniques of the relatively more liberal and economically developed states.

The most far-flung and ambitious effort to restore relatively free conditions of international trade, the General Agreement on Tariffs and Trade of 1947, was essentially directed to the removal or reduction of the many economic barriers that had developed between the older and economically more developed states, i.e., quotas, tariffs, and discriminatory arrangements. Its effectiveness has, therefore, been inevitably limited almost entirely to the economically more developed countries. The key provisions of this effort are the Articles describing the general elimination of quantitative restrictions, the nondiscriminatory administration of such quantitative restrictions as remain, and above all, the general most-favored-nation treatment.[60] The parallel effort made between the six member states of the European Economic Community also aims at the gradual removal of all the impediments to a free flow of trade although it also incorporates more positive efforts at economic integration of the national economies.

What distinguishes the more recent techniques of bilateral trade agreements or multilateral commodity agreements in which state-directed systems participate, is that the negative pattern—the removal of restrictions—cannot meaningfully apply. It has been pointed out by many commentators[61] that the most-favored-nation clause, which aims at the indirect growth of international trade through the extension of any benefits reciprocally arranged between the two states to any third state, has no meaningful application to the trading objectives of a mutually planned economy—Communist or non-Communist—in which international trade is part of a general plan and which often couples its international trade objectives with political objectives. Hence, the predominant pattern of bilateral trade agreements in which at least one of the parties is a state-directed economy tends toward global quantitative exchange or direct barter agreements. Where Communist states make trade agreements with developing countries this can often be effected by the purchase on the part of the more industrially developed Communist state of a specific staple commodity, such as cotton, coffee, or wool, in bulk, in exchange for machinery and services needed for development. But even where one of the parties is a more or less free-trading country, such as Japan, trade agreement with developing countries may tend to fix overall targets of mutual trade so that imports and exports are roughly held in balance.[62]

The intergovernmental commodity agreement openly aims at the "establishment of a degree of managed trade economy for such com-

---

[60] Article XI, No. 1; Article XIII, No. 1; Article I, No. 1.

[61] See inter alia, J.E.S. Fawcett, "State Trading and International Organizations," *Law and Contemporary Problems*, xxiv (Spring 1959), 341; J. N. Hazard, "Commercial Discrimination and International Law," *American Journal of International Law*, lii (July 1958), 495; Friedmann (fn. 14), Chap. 21.

[62] See, for a comprehensive analysis, Gilbert P. Verbit, *Trade Agreements for Developing Countries* (New York 1969).

modities."[63] While each of the relatively few intergovernmental commodity agreements hitherto concluded differs from the other, three key elements have been singled out by an authoritative commentator:[64] (1) The buffer stock device, designed, through the buying up and selling of stock, to hold price fluctuations within a minimum-maximum range; (2) quantitative limits on imports and/or exports; (3) quantitative allocations as among suppliers and takers.

While any more detailed analysis of international trade and commodity agreements goes beyond the task of the present article, it is clear that these new types of international economic agreements add significantly to the modern range of transnational arrangements, and that they are characterized by *positive* state action far beyond the range of Communist or Socialist systems. The whole wide range of international economic transactions is thus brought within the purview of public international law and organization. The conclusion of, or accession to, an international trade or commodity agreement becomes a public and political act which, in the case of the United States, often means submission to the political and constitutional processes of Congressional approval and legislation.[65] It also means the development of an important new type of international organization such as the International Wheat and Coffee Councils. With regard to the structure of international organization, an important result of this new type of arrangement is that it makes relevant certain economic group distinctions, such as those between exporters and importers of certain commodities, of producers and consumers, or, more widely, between developed and developing countries.[66]

A New Type of International Lawyer

It is an important corollary of the increasing extension of international law into economic and social matters that the training and outlook of the traditional expert in international law is no longer adequate.[67] Until recently, international law used to be taught widely

---

[63] Herman Walker, "The International Law of Commodity Agreements," *Law and Contemporary Problems*, XXXVIII (Spring 1963), 393.

[64] Same, 394.

[65] U.S. participation in GATT was, however, effected by executive agreement.

[66] See, for example, Annex A. V, I to the Final Act of UNCTAD (United Conference on Trade and Development), "Institutional Arrangements, Methods and Machinery to Implement Measures Relating to the Expansion of International Trade," U.N. Doc. E/Conf. 46/141, Vol. I, 1964, 58. See A. Etra, "Time for a Change: The U.N. Conference on Trade and Development," *Revue Belge de Droit International*, No. 1 (1966), 50.

[67] See American Society of International Law, Report of the meeting of the Board of Review and Development, "Law and Developing Countries," July 16-17, 1965, LX (April 1966).

as a part of political science. This reflected the basically diplomatic character of the traditional international law of coexistence. But modern international legal arrangements need both international lawyers with a much wider and differently oriented training and outlook, and the cooperation of legal experts in different fields of common objectives. Arrangements of an economic and social character also need the cooperation of economists, sociologists, and scientists. In an international labor convention, the international lawyer must collaborate with experts in law, labor relations, and social welfare. In international trade and commodity agreements, he must have the advice of economic and social experts. Loan transactions of national and international public aid agencies are, as already mentioned, linked with, and often based on, an appraisal of the objectives and techniques of economic development plans. International agreements on the conservation of fisheries or other resources must be based on the studies of agricultural or forestry experts and ecologists. Agreements on joint meteorological stations must be predicated on the advice of the meteorological experts. The scientist, from the geologist to the nuclear scientist, now plays an ubiquitous role in international arrangements. Most important of all, all of these international treaty agreements and transactions are now part and parcel of an overall political strategy. Even if the U.S. investor in some country in Latin America, Africa, or Asia, continues to be dominated by business motivations, the other party, i.e., a government or a governmental development corporation is not and cannot be so directed. The essential need, in our generation, therefore, is for greatly widened training in international law, and an equally great extension of interdisciplinary collaboration on the governmental, academic, and private levels.

CHAPTER 2

International Law and the Deprivation
of Foreign Wealth:
A Framework for Future Inquiry*

BURNS H. WESTON

"Get off this estate."
"What for?"
"Because it's mine."
"Where did you get it?"
"From my father."
"Where did he get it?"
"From his father."
"And where did he get it?"
"He fought for it."
"Well, I'll fight you for it."

—Carl Sandburg

AMONG THE several reasons why the United States Supreme Court declined to adjudicate "the merits" of the now famous case of *Banco Nacional de Cuba v. Sabbatino*[1] was its majority observation that "[t]here are few if any issues in international law today on which opinion seems to be so divided as the limitations on a state's power to expropriate the property of aliens."[2] While acknowledging "the view that a taking is improper under international law if it is not for a public purpose, is discriminatory, or is without provision for prompt, adequate, and effective compensation," the Court pointed out that Communist and newly independent and underdeveloped countries have come to question the admissibility of this perspective.[3] Accordingly, although stopping short of saying that "there is no international standard in this area," the Court found it "difficult to imagine the courts of this country embarking on adjudication in an area which

* This essay was published substantially as follows in the *Virginia Law Review*, LIV (October and November 1968), 1069, 1265. I take pleasure in thanking the Rockefeller Foundation and the Yale Law School for their generous support which has enabled me to begin inquiry into the many problems that form the basis of this essay.

[1] 376 U.S. 398 (1963).   [2] Same, 428.   [3] Same, 429-30.

touches more sensitively the practical and ideological goals of the various members of the community of nations," and so held that it would "not examine the validity of a taking of property within its own territory by a foreign sovereign government, extant and recognized by this country at the time of suit, in the absence of a treaty or other unambiguous agreement regarding controlling legal principles, even if the complaint alleges that the taking violates customary international law."[4]

There are several grounds upon which this particular judgment can be criticized.[5] Perhaps most important is that the Court, in taking no more than "a cursory look at relevant authorities,"[6] gave the clear impression that the "basic divergence between the national interests of capital importing and capital exporting nations and between the social ideologies of those countries that favor state control of a considerable portion of the means of production and those that adhere to a free enterprise system"[7] cannot be reconciled by international law (at least not in the near future) save in the case of that rarest of phenomena, the "unambiguous agreement." Detailed investigation of past practice in this area, as well as an abiding conviction that international law can and should be an effective shaping force in the economic and other affairs of man, compels us to reject this suggestion outright.

For the suggestion, however, we students of international law have largely ourselves to blame. Had the Court scrutinized the "relevant authorities" yet farther than it did, it might justifiably have concluded that the law in this area is, to recast Sir Winston Churchill's famous phrase, but "a riddle wrapped in a mystery inside an enigma." That is, it would have found a bouillabaisse of "anecdotal historicism"[8] from which has been spooned a string of allegedly precise (but demonstrably ambiguous and contradictory) doctrines, principles, and rules which, serving more as magic talismans than as sharply honed tools for legal analysis, have tended to divert attention away from the adjustment of the very real value conflicts of the kind to which the Supreme Court displayed commendable sensitivity.[9]

---

4 Same, 428; 430 n.26.

5 See, e.g., Richard B. Lillich, *The Protection of Foreign Investment* (Syracuse 1965), 81-85; Eugene F. Mooney, *Foreign Seizures—Sabbatino and the Act of State Doctrine* (Lexington 1967), 73-124; see also Burns H. Weston, "L'Affaire Sabbatino: A Wistful Review," *Kentucky Law Journal*, LV (Summer 1967), 844.

6 Lillich (fn. 5), 83.   7 376 U.S., 430.

8 The expression belongs to Myres S. McDougal and may be found in his more extensive treatment of some of the grievances mentioned here. See McDougal, "Some Basic Theoretical Concepts About International Law: A Policy-Oriented Framework of Inquiry," *Journal of Conflict Resolution*, IV (1960), 337, 344.

9 For a brief foray into the ambiguity and complementarity of some of these

For anyone concerned about "the future of the international legal order" as regards foreign-wealth deprivations,[10] specifically, or foreign trade and investment, generally, this is an unacceptable state of affairs. Needed, as one concerned observer has urged, is "a radical change of approach, a reassessment of the objectives sought by the international law rules in this field."[11] It is the purpose of this essay to make a modest beginning in this direction.[12]

Two preliminary caveats are in order, however. First, to persons familiar with what Professor Falk has recently dubbed "the New Haven Approach"[13]—the "configurative" and "policy-oriented" jurisprudence

---

doctrines, principles, and rules, see Burns H. Weston, "Community Regulation of Foreign-Wealth Deprivations: A Tentative Framework for Inquiry," in Richard S. Miller and Roland J. Stanger, eds., *Essays on Expropriations* (Columbus 1967), 117.

[10] The term "wealth deprivation" and such derivatives as "deprivation measure" and "deprivation claim" are used principally to avoid the simultaneous and, hence, ambiguous reference to both facts and legal consequences which so often characterizes the more popular "expropriation," "confiscation," "condemnation," "taking," "forfeiture," etc. It is therefore conceived as a neutral expression which describes the public or publicly sanctioned *compulsory* imposition of a wealth loss (or blocking of a wealth gain), by whatever means, with whatever intensity and for whatever claimed purpose, which, in the absence of some further act on the part of the depriving party, would involve the denial of a *quid pro quo* to the party who sustains the deprivation (the component "wealth" being preferred to the more popular "property" because it refers to all the relevant values of goods, services, and income without sharing the latter's common emphasis upon physical attributes or the Civil Law's stress on "ownership"). Depending on a multitude of factual variables, a wealth deprivation may be found lawful *or* unlawful. As implied and as thus defined, however, the term is superior in ways other than its descriptive neutrality. By stressing more the final results than the implementing procedures of the institutional practice, it underscores the ultimate gravamen to which all claims arising out of any interaction are addressed: value change. At the same time, but without straint of legal-technical language, it affords a broad mantle under which a variety of institutional procedures may take shelter, whether the archetypal "direct taking" or its many "indirect" functional equivalents (the latter, because of obvious evidentiary difficulties, serving less often than the former as the basis of illustration and discussion herein). Finally, it more readily admits that there can be a loss by one party without there being a one-for-one gain by another.

Throughout this essay, the shorter expressions "wealth deprivation" or "deprivation" will be used instead of the longer "foreign-wealth deprivation" unless clarity or emphasis otherwise require.

[11] A. A. Fatouros, "International Law and the Third World," *Virginia Law Review*, L (June 1964), 783, 809.

[12] For an earlier and more tentative beginning by the author, not now wholly subscribed to, see Weston (fn. 9).

[13] See Richard A. Falk, "On Treaty Interpretation and the New Haven Approach: Achievements and Prospects," *Virginia Journal of International Law*, VII (April 1968), 323, 330 n.11. See also John N. Moore, "Prolegomenon to the Jurisprudence of Myres McDougal and Harold Lasswell," *Virginia Law Review*, LIV

of Harold D. Lasswell, Myres S. McDougal, and their associates—the approach here recommended can hardly be called "radical" if that term is to mean complete originality on the part of the author.[14] Nor should it be considered "radical" since, like all the Lasswell-McDougal studies, it seeks mainly to inject a minimum of common-sense clarity into a welter of technical confusion. But to the extent that no systematic, multifactoral, and policy-oriented analysis has ever before been ventured in this area, it is, regrettably, quite "radical" indeed.[15] Second, what this author understands to mean by the term "international law rules" is not simply a set of logically rigorous constructions that may be found to refer indiscriminately to what has been, to what will be, and to what should be among nation-states and other transnational participants. More precisely, the term represents the separate total flows of a number of different kinds of decisions (intelligence-serving, recommending, invoking, prescribing, applying, appraising, and terminating), internal as well as external to nation-states, which, as expressions of community policy, both authorize and control the

---

(October 1968), 662; Burns H. Weston, "Book Review," *University of Pennsylvania Law Review,* cxvii (February 1969), 647.

[14] For the central initiatives of the New Haven Approach from which the author draws inspiration, see Richard Arens and Harold D. Lasswell, *In Defense of Public Order* (New York 1961); Lung-chu Chen and Harold D. Lasswell, *Formosa, China and the United Nations* (New York 1967); Rosalyn Higgins, *The Development of International Law Through the Political Organs of the United Nations* (London, New York 1963); Douglas M. Johnston, *The International Law of Fisheries: A Framework for Policy-Oriented Inquiries* (New Haven 1965); Harold D. Lasswell and Abraham Kaplan, *Power and Society* (New Haven 1950); Myres S. McDougal and Associates, *Studies in World Public Order* (New Haven 1960); Myres S. McDougal and William T. Burke, *The Public Order of the Oceans: A Contemporary International Law of the Sea* (New Haven 1962); Myres S. McDougal and Florentino P. Feliciano, *Law and Minimum World Public Order: The Legal Regulation of International Coercion* (New Haven 1961); Myres S. McDougal, Harold D. Lasswell, and James C. Miller, *The Interpretation of Agreements and World Public Order* (New Haven 1967); Myres S. McDougal, Harold D. Lasswell, and Ivan A. Vlasic, *Law and Public Order in Space* (New Haven 1963); B. S. Murty, *Propaganda and World Public Order: The Legal Regulation of the Ideological Instrument of Coercion* (New Haven 1968).

For introductions to other major works now in progress, see Myres S. McDougal, Harold D. Lasswell, and Lung-chu Chen, "Human Rights and World Public Order: A Framework for Policy-Oriented Inquiry," *American Journal of International Law,* LXIII (1969), 237; Myres S. McDougal, Harold D. Lasswell, and W. Michael Reisman, "The World Constitutive Process of Authoritative Decision," *Journal of Legal Education,* XIX (1967), 253, 403. This article appears as Chap. 3, Richard A. Falk and Cyril E. Black, eds., *The Future of the International Legal Order,* Vol. I, *Trends and Patterns* (Princeton 1969).

[15] The only known, but neither sufficiently systematic nor comprehensive, attempt in this regard is Kenneth S. Carlston, *Law and Organization in World Society* (Urbana 1962). Professor Carlston's study is restricted primarily to the role of "international economic development contracts" in the international economy.

variegated patterns of international intercourse.[16] It is a *process of international decision* we are exploring, not merely a confused and confusing body of international rules.[17]

A reassessment of the objectives, or policy goals, sought by the process of international decision that regulates the deprivation of foreign wealth and responses thereto is neither easily nor quickly done. If neither blindly conventional nor arbitrary reassessment is to be had, then the full (and concededly sometimes vexing) performance of all the tasks of rational inquiry must be undertaken: the clarification of goals, the description of past trends in decision, the analysis of conditions affecting decision, the projection of future trends in decision, and the invention and evaluation of policy alternatives—in respect of all points of past and probable disagreement. This cannot be done, however, without a practical means for organizing and reflecting upon the many variables that may have policy relevance for the particular case. In other words, a framework for rational inquiry is needed, a framework which, as contextual, problem-oriented, and multimethod (and so attuned to the needs of all who would affect and understand the interrelation of law and community process), would include the most significant features of a *process of deprivation* (within which participants act and react in pursuit of certain objectives), a *process of claim* (within which participants invoke authority in defense of claims and counterclaims arising out of the process of deprivation) and the above-mentioned *process of international decision* (within which established decision-makers respond authoritatively to the claims and counterclaims asserted).[18]

[16] For extensive discussion of these seven "decision functions," see Harold D. Lasswell, *The Decision Process: Seven Categories of Functional Analysis* (College Park, Md. 1956); see also McDougal, Lasswell, and Reisman (fn. 14), 415-37.

[17] This clarification is indispensable for any conception about law which purports to account for the demands of justice in the particular case. Unhappily, our inherited theories about international law, upon which the bulk of contemporary international legal decision remains premised, have largely failed to acknowledge this central thesis. In this connection, see the penetrating analysis by Myres S. McDougal, Harold D. Lasswell, and W. Michael Reisman, "Theories about International Law: Prologue to a Configurative Jurisprudence," *Virginia Journal of International Law*, VIII (April 1968), 188, the most exhaustive comparative jurisprudential statement by the New Haven policy-oriented theorists to date.

[18] It is not this author's intention to suggest that the analytical model thus fleetingly proposed and hereinafter partially expanded upon is the *only* right scheme for rational factual and policy clarification. It has proved remarkably well suited, however, to the delineation of the myriad variables which can and do affect decision in this area. For a particularly informative presentation of the character and function of models and model theory in the legal-policy decisional context (replete with helpful references), see Louis H. Mayo and Ernest M. Jones, "Legal-Policy Decision Process: Alternative Thinking and the Predictive Function,"

The remainder of this essay is devoted to an extensive description of the important features of the Process of Deprivation only;[19] it does not purport to "state the law" relative thereto. It is tendered in the belief that even so limited a contextual orientation, far from propounding analytical categorization for its own sake and thereby, in Kingsley Amis' wonderful phrase, "casting pseudo-light on nonproblems," can point the way to the most critical legal policies at stake in this troublesome area and thus bring us closer to the reconciliation of basic divergencies.

THE PROCESS OF DEPRIVATION

Each hour of each day men are seeking the production, conservation, distribution, and consumption of wealth across national boundaries. The Process of Deprivation may be seen as one of many interaction patterns which affect, and are in turn affected by, this global wealth process. It is most efficiently described in terms of two reasonably distinct (but nevertheless highly interdependent) subprocesses of *action* and *reaction* whose sequential treatment herein, if not always true-to-life, is justified by the exigencies of clarity. In the first, principal emphasis is given to the participants who impose foreign-wealth deprivations (i.e., *deprivors*). In the second, the stress is upon those who sustain and react to them (i.e., *deprivees*). The point of demarcation between these two subprocesses may be found in the initial post-Outcome (or Special Effects) phase of the Process of Deprivation. The following brief outline should prove helpful:

George Washington Law Review, xxxiii (October 1964), 318. Nor is it this author's intention to suggest that analytical models, whatever form they take, are without their own deficiencies. For a discussion of some of these, see Abraham Kaplan, "Some Limitations on Rationality," in Carl J. Friedrich, ed., *Nomos VII: Rational Decision* (New York 1964, 55; Max Black, *Models and Metaphors* (Ithaca 1962), 153-69. But as one analyst has observed, "no model, of whatever sort, even purports to reproduce the *real world* in all its detail. Rather, it is a means of spotlighting and examining selected properties of real situations by postulating what would happen if the model *did* accurately portray behavior. In accounting for discrepancies between models and empirical events, models are improved and actual behavior is more satisfactorily explained." Martin Shubik, ed., *Readings in Game Theory and Political Behavior* (Garden City 1954), Foreword, x. To similar effect, see Harold D. Lasswell (fn. 16), 2: "[T]he requirements of research and policy change as the context of knowledge and controversy changes in response to the unceasing flow of human experience. Classifications are serviceable when they are tentative and undogmatic, and when they guide scholarly activity in directions that are presently accepted as valuable."

19 For a tentative, but less descriptive and thus more abstract, account beyond the Process of Deprivation, see Weston (fn. 9).

Participants (Deprivors)
Objectives
Situations
Strategies
Outcomes
Effects
  Special
    Participants (Deprivees)
    Objectives
    Situations
    Strategies
    Outcomes
  General
Conditions

Each of these phases may now be separately considered.

PARTICIPANTS

Since the end of the Napoleonic Wars especially, all who have en-gaged in transnational economic activity have also participated in the Process of Deprivation.[20] While some parties have been more directly involved than others and while participation has varied among differ-ent actors at different points in time (these variables being among the many that must be considered if the background of authoritative de-cision is to be properly understood), for purposes of clear analysis it is

[20] This is not to suggest that wealth deprivation devices were unknown before 1815. That it was firmly established in ancient Egypt, for example, is well known. See M. Rostovtzeff, "The Foundations of Social and Economic Life in Egypt in Hellenistic Times," *Journal of Egyptian Archeology*, VI (London 1920), 161; see also Coleman Phillipson, *The International Law and Custom of Ancient Greece and Rome* (London 1911), 166, where the author notes that the "confiscation" of the property of aliens ("meteocs") specifically, at least for penal purposes, can be traced back to ancient Greece. Louis Frederick Vinding Kruse, *The Right of Property*, P. T. Federspiel, trans. (London 1939), 170, reports that "[t]he legal form corresponding to the expropriation of modern times . . . was . . . established in German and Scandinavian law in the Middle Ages, particularly in the towns." But it was not until after about 1815—thus making that date a convenient starting point—that the deprivation of foreign wealth took on either economic importance or substantial legal interest. The reasons are mainly two. First, it was not until the years following that the world economy, with the final dismantling of the old mercantilist structure, first assumed truly international proportions. Second, it was not until that time, as Morton A. Kaplan and Nicholas deB. Katzenbach have remarked, that " 'positivism' tended to replace natural law and [that] the con-ceptually universalistic 'law of nations' became international law" as we know it today. Morton A. Kaplan and Nicholas deB. Katzenbach, *The Political Foun-dations of International Law* (New York 1961), 56.

helpful to identify all the concerned parties in terms of the roles with which they are directly or indirectly associated in this process: *deprivors* (those who impose deprivations) and *deprivees* (those who sustain and react to deprivations).[21] Such characterization permits us, without sacrifice to relevant diversities (indeed, in spite of them), to identify common perspectives and, hence, to cut through to distinctions which are meaningful for both policy and decision.

As indicated, we may in this initial subprocess of action limit our focus to the deprivors; or to put it in policy-relevant terms, to the identification of the participants who may be legally competent to deprive and legally responsible for the infliction of foreign-wealth losses. Identification and description of the deprivees is reserved for subsequent discussion.[22] It is now necessary only to point out that the latter may include any of those who participate in the global wealth process—nation-states, international governmental institutions, private associations, and individual human beings—and that they have thus far come principally from the West.

Among the deprivors it is obvious that the nation-state has long played the most decisive role. Recalling only some of the better known deprivations over the years—whether the taking of the lands of Mr. Finlay, a British subject, for the royal gardens of King Otho of Greece in 1836[23] or the nationalization of American-owned properties in Cuba in 1959-60[24]—we are struck at once by the primacy of the nation-state in this role. This is so notwithstanding that we are today witnessing, as Wolfgang Friedmann has aptly observed, "both the climax and the

[21] It should be understood that these terms are in no way intended to impute fault or liability. They are meant to be descriptive only.

[22] See pp. 99-107.

[23] See Correspondence between Great Britain and Greece, 1842-1849, respecting the claim of Mr. Finlay to receive compensation for his land, which was enclosed in the Garden of the Royal Palace at Athens, *British and Foreign State Papers* [1849-1850], xxxix (London 1863), 410.

[24] Among the laws of the national Cuban Government effecting the deprivation of American-owned interests were the following: Agrarian Reform Law of May 17, 1959, Official Gazette of June 3, 1959 (Special Issue No. 7 of the Annual Series); Labor Law No. 647 of November 24, 1959, Official Gazette No. 224 of November 25, 1959; Law No. 351 of July 6, 1960, Official Gazette No. 130 of July 7, 1960 (affecting oil, banking, and other interests); Law No. 890 of October 13, 1960, News Digest of October 20, 1960 (affecting Cuban as well as American sugar interests). For brief summaries, see Richard C. Allison, "Cuba's Seizures of American Business," *American Bar Association Journal*, xlvii (January-February 1961), 48, 187; International Law Commission Report, "The Cuban Situation," New York State Bar Association, lxxxiv (1961), Rep. 151; Leland L. Johnson, "U.S. Business Interests in Cuba and the Rise of Castro," *World Politics*, xvii (April 1965), 440. See also Frank G. Dawson and Burns H. Weston, "Banco Nacional de Cuba v. Sabbatino: New Wine in Old Bottles," *University of Chicago Law Review*, xxxi (Autumn 1963), 63.

profound crisis of the era of the national state and of national sovereignty."[25]

Obvious though this may be, however, it is also apparent that the nation-state is not alone as deprivor. Other territorially organized communities, such as internal and external subnational entities, can be included as well. One is reminded of deprivations undertaken, for example, by provincial and municipal communities (especially in federally constituted and other "composite" bodies-politic), as when in 1893 a public market concession negotiated between the National Government of Venezuela and one Henry Rudloff, an American citizen, was unilaterally and prematurely terminated by the authorities of the Federal District within which Rudloff was operating.[26] Similarly, in 1962, the Brazilian State of Rio Grande do Sul nationalized a claimed six to eight million dollars worth of holdings of the Companhia Telefonica Naçional, a subsidiary of International Telephone and Telegraph.[27] External subnational entities, too—"colonies," "protectorates," "suzerainties," "territories," etc.—each with varying degrees of dependency, have assumed deprivor functions. Among other examples, the wealth losses imposed upon certain British subjects and "protected persons" in the protectorate of the Spanish Zone of Morocco during the rebellions of 1913-21[28] and upon certain Italian phosphate prospecting interests in the French Zone of Morocco in 1920[29] are perhaps the best known.

Furthermore, deprivors have been restricted neither to territorial communities nor to bodies-politic. They have included mixed governmental-nongovernmental agencies,[30] private associations,[31] private

---

[25] Wolfgang Friedmann, *The Changing Structure of International Law* (New York 1964), 31.

[26] See Rudloff (United States v. Venezuela), J. Ralston and W. Doyle, Venezuelan Arbitrations of 1903 (1904), 182, United Nations Reports of International Arbitration Awards [hereafter cited as U.N.R.I.A.A.], ix (1903), 244.

[27] See Decree No. 13,186 of February 16, 1962, of the Government of the State of Rio Grande do Sul, described in *New York Times*, February 18, 1962, p. 1, col. 6.

[28] See Affaire des Biens Britanniques au Maroc Espagnol (Great Britain v. Spain), U.N.R.I.A.A., ii (1925), 615.

[29] See Phosphates in Morocco [1938], Permanent Court of International Justice [hereafter cited as P.C.I.J.], Ser. A/B, No. 74.

[30] See, e.g., Dickson Car Wheel Company (United States v. Mexico), Opinions of Commissioners under the Convention Concluded September 8, 1923, as extended by Subsequent Conventions, between the United States and Mexico (1930-31), 175, U.N.R.I.A.A., iv (1931), 669. The case involved an American-owned debt incurred and allegedly repudiated by the National Railways Company of Mexico which, though temporarily "taken over" by the Mexican Government at the time, was partially owned by the Mexican Government both before and after the temporary seizure and which, even during the temporary dispossession (which served as the basis for repudiation), was held never to have lost its "property rights" nor "its own juridical identity." See also Hofmann and Steinhardt (United States v. Turkey) [c. 1925-34], Frederick K. Nielsen, American-Turkish Claims Settlement (under

individuals[32] and, in at least one case, an international governmental institution.[33]

Still, despite this profusion, the nation-state continues as in the past to figure most prominently. The principal reason is not hard to see: the nation-state remains unsurpassed among sociopolitical institutions

---

the Agreement of December 24, 1923, and Supplemental Agreements between the United States and Turkey) (1937), 286. This case concerned the "destruction" of certain bearer bonds issued by the "Anatolian Railways" which, according to the American Application, "was operated by a semi-public corporation directly under the supervision and control of the Turkish Government." The claimants sought unsuccessfully to attribute responsibility to the Turkish Government by virtue of its participation in and actions affecting the "semi-public corporation." Consider also the deprivative role played by government-controlled trade associations in the Soviet Union in 1929 against the British-owned Lena Goldfields Company, Ltd., as elaborated in the award of the Lena Goldfields Arbitration [1930], set forth in the Appendix to Arthur Nussbaum, "The Arbitration between the Lena Goldfields, Ltd., and the Soviet Government," *Cornell Law Quarterly*, XXXVI (Fall 1950), 31, 42 of Appendix.

31 Private railway and utility companies in the United States, for example, have long enjoyed a "delegated power" of eminent domain. See Philip Nichols, *The Law of Eminent Domain*, 3d edn. (Albany 1964), I, §§ 3.23, 3.231, 3.232. Less explicit examples may be seen in the deprivative role played by the German Nazi Party and its individual members against Jewish nationals and aliens during and before World War II. See, e.g., Vladimir Pozner, "Pogroms for Profit," *The Nation* (January 7, 1939), 33; Jewish Black Book Committee, *The Black Book* (New York 1946), 57, 82-83, 89-95; William L. Shirer, *The Rise and Fall of the Third Reich* (New York 1960), 338-40, 580-99; G. Warburg, *Six Years of Hitler* (London 1939), Chap. 6. See also Board of Editors, "The Measures Taken by the Indonesian Government Against Netherlands Enterprises," *Nederlands Tijdschrift Voor International Recht*, V (July 1958), 227 (reporting deprivative measures taken by Indonesian labor unions and industrial worker organizations against Dutch-owned properties in 1957-59). For an account of deprivative measures taken by Indonesian labor unions and industrial worker organizations against American and British holdings in 1965, see *New York Times*, April 4, 1965, p. 7, col. 1.

32 Of key concern in The Mavrommatis Jerusalem Concessions [1925], P.C.I.J., Ser. A, No. 5, for example, was a concessionary option granted to one Rutenberg by the Crown Agents for the Colonies on behalf of the High Commissioner for Palestine authorizing Rutenberg to "annul," on payment of compensation, any preexisting concessions which might be found to conflict with his own. Similarly, at least two cases affecting foreign landowners in Panama involved a Panamanian law that permitted private persons to sue to recover lands for the Panamanian Government in exchange for "cultivation permits" on the lands so recovered. See Marguerite de Joly de Sabla (United States v. Panama), *United States and Panamanian General Claims Arbitration*, 432 [hereafter cited as *Hunt's Rep.*], U.N.R.I.A.A., VI (1933), 358; Mariposa Development Company and Others (United States v. Panama), *Hunt's Rep.* 573, U.N.R.I.A.A., VI (1933), 338. For authority in support of the right of an individual to acquire deprivative power in the United States, see Nichols (fn. 31), at § 3.24. Not to be forgotten are cases in which private persons (singly and in groups) have performed deprivative functions without cover of explicit authority but under circumstances suggesting "public" inspiration or collusion. See, e.g., The Ashmore Fishery (United States v. China) [1884], John B. Moore, *International Arbitrations to Which the United States Has Been a Party*, II (Washington 1898) [hereafter cited as Moore, *Arbitrations*]. See also footnote 138 and accompanying text.

33 See the abridged report of Public Prosecutor v. Aerts [1938-40] in *Annual*

in achieving a wide freedom of effective decision and control. It is still, to use Rupert Emerson's expression, the ultimate "terminal community"; that is, "the *effective* end of the road for man as a social animal, the end point of working solidarity between men."[34]

Of course, when distinguishing the "nation-state" from other deprivor participants we must not allow its label (any more than other corporate or group names) to obscure the fundamental role that is played singly and collectively by individual human beings.[35] Any realistic identification of the nation-state or other composite form, whether for determining competency to deprive or for attributing responsibility for particular burdens, must first account for the individual persons and elites who presume to speak or act on "its" behalf, both before and, by subsequent involvement or succession, after deprivation. Doctrinal strictures about the "subjects" and "objects" of international law or about "state continuity" and "corporate personality" aside, the individual human being is, after all, the ultimate actor always. Whatever surrogate role he plays, his particular class, interest, personality, and past exposure to crisis—that is all of his particular identifications, demands, and expectations—will determine or reflect the acts and communications of his mandator. Second, realistic identification must account for the important peripheral role that is oftentimes played by individuals within particular sociopolitical systems. Political parties, interest groups, private associations, and influential persons, though not necessarily the surrogates of official act and communication, all bring to bear a wide range of pressures through a wide

---

Digest and Reports of Public International Law Cases, Case No. 23 (London 1942), 52, which came before the Appeal Section of the Mixed Tribunal of Tangier in 1939 when the Zone of Tangier was administered by an international body under powers delegated by the Sultan of the French protectorate of Morocco. The case involved a law passed by the Legislative Assembly of the Zone in 1938 which, in prohibiting the installation or exploitation of broadcasting stations, provided that owners, possessors, or users of broadcasting stations should, without indemnity, dismantle the same. A Belgian-owned station which continued operations after the deadline promulgated in the law was "seized" by the Tangier authorities.

[34] Rupert Emerson, *From Empire to Nation* (Cambridge, Mass. 1960), 96 (emphasis added). As Reinhold Niebuhr had described it: "The modern nation is the human group of strongest social cohesion, of most undisputed central authority and of most clearly defined membership. The church may have challenged its preeminence in the Middle Ages, and the economic class may compete with it for the loyalty of men in our own day; yet it remains, as it has been since the seventeenth century, the most absolute of all human associations." *Moral Man and Immoral Society* (New York, London 1932), 83.

[35] The label "nation-state" is not the happiest of terms. But it is adopted here because of its common usage and because it is reasonably distinguishable from the other participants mentioned herein. For an indication of some of the difficulties inherent in the term, see Myres S. McDougal, "International Law, Power, and Policy: A Contemporary Conception," *Hague Academie de Droit International Recueil des Cours*, LXXXII (1953), 137, 192-94 [hereafter cited as *Recueil des Cours*].

variety of techniques upon the objectives and strategies of official deprivor policy. These pressures are clearly strong in times of intense crisis. But the significance of peripheral participation as a constant shaping force upon deprivor policy should never be overlooked. In sum, accurate analysis compels recognition that deprivations do not take place in legalistic vacuums; they occur, rather, within a wide and flexible human context—wider and more flexible than the syntactical consistency of the label "nation-state" (or, indeed, the label "deprivor") would lead us to believe.

The mere identification and classification of particular *types* of deprivors, however, is not all that is required for policy clarification. A richer indication in terms of who in particular they have been (or where they have come from) and how in detail they may be characterized is indispensable both to a proper understanding of the precedential value of past trends in decision and to a fuller appreciation of the significant factors that have shaped deprivor perspectives toward all other phases of the Process of Deprivation. In the discussion that immediately follows, the emphasis (by way of illustration) is upon the principal deprivor identified: the nation-state.

While not rare during the approximately one hundred year period preceding World War I, neither were foreign-wealth deprivations then common. As any examination of the various adjudicated and negotiated disputes reveals, the deprivations that did take place (which, except for recurring revolutionary depredations, entailed primarily the seizure of vessels, their cargo, and other chattels in the claimed enforcement of trade and revenue laws and, from time to time, the unilateral suspension of agreements and public debts) were imposed almost exclusively within the comparatively weak and usually fragmented communities of Latin America, especially "Middle America" (i.e., Central America, Mexico, and the Caribbean).[36] Few were undertaken in what remained of the politically independent world as repre-

---

[36] A survey of most of the international arbitrations pertaining to the "peace time" (as between the immediate parties) deprivation of foreign wealth before World War I clearly suggests that this was largely the result of the coincidence of newly won Latin American political independence on the one hand, and of geographically proximate and increasingly expansive United States commerical interests on the other. See the many and varied deprivative disputes digested and reported in Moore, *Arbitrations*, Vols. I-V; John B. Moore, ed., *International Adjudications*, Vols. I-VI (Modern Series, New York 1929-1933); Henri La Fontaine, *Pasicrisie Internationale* (Berne 1902); Albert G. Lapradelle and Nicolas Politis, eds., *Recueil Des Arbitrages Internationaux*, Vols. I-III (Paris 1905, 1923, 1954); Jackson H. Ralston and W. J. Sherman Doyle, *Report of French-Venezuelan Mixed Claims Commission of 1902* (1906); U.N.R.I.A.A., Vols. VI, IX-XI. For general guidance, see Alexander M. Stuyt, *Survey of International Arbitrations 1794-1938* (The Hague 1939).

sented by Europe and North America.[37] The reason is clear. This was a century of relative harmony in which the principal powers enjoyed a virtual universal adherence to *laissez-faire* notions of common justice and fair dealing, to a credo of individualistic capitalism that was transmuted into broad patterns of acceptable behavior beyond the confines of their own economies to far-flung empires and commonwealths. To free the factors of production was a major objective of the rising bourgeoisie and this required the elimination of complex trade and other restrictions, the limitation of governmental supervision, the free flow of technical ideas and skills, and an international specialization based on comparative advantage.[38] Indeed, these notions of individual liberty, of the inviolability of private wealth, and of the sanctity of contract served generally as common ground upon which economic relations could be established and maintained even in the new nations of Latin America, embodied as these notions were in their own fundamental, Western European derived laws.[39] Far from representing

[37] The principal and obvious explanation is that what remained of the then politically independent world—that is, what was not, with varying character and degree of political dependency, but an extension of Western hegemony—was mainly a world of primitive societies that had little or no awareness of outside life and which, for one reason or another, had yet to prove important to external economic interests. China and Japan, of course, were clear exceptions, especially toward the end of the nineteenth century. And in the former particularly, with a Dowager Empress agitating the fanatical expulsion of Westerners and Western influence, foreign-wealth owners were subjected to deprivations of the severest kind. On the origin and development of the Boxer Movement, see George N. Steiger, *China and the Occident* (New Haven 1927). On the more general theme of the methods, ideas, and aims of Western economic interests in China before World War I, see Westel W. Willoughby, *Foreign Rights and Interests in China*, 2 vols. (Baltimore, rev. edn. 1927).

[38] This is not to say, of course, that the *laissez-faire* system was complete. As Douglass C. North has pointed out: "Tariffs declined but did not disappear. Minor wars occasionally interfered with the system, and cyclical instability, transmitted from one country to another, sometimes resulted in longer periods of readjustment than the classical economist or his contemporary counterpart would find 'natural' to a self-regulating mechanism. Indeed, even at the zenith of relative economic freedom, some individual economies were moving in the direction of further protection." "International Capital Movements in Historical Perspective," in Raymond F. Mikesell, ed., *U.S. Private and Government Investment Abroad* (Eugene, Ore. 1962), 10, 11-12. But as North himself concedes, "notwithstanding these aberrations it was a remarkable era, set off from the preceding century and in marked contrast to the post-World War I era of the present century." Same, 12.

[39] It is not mere artfulness that has prompted Phanor J. Eder to write that "[w]hen Columbus sailed westward, he carried with him a cargo seldom referred to by historians—the law." "Law and Justice in Latin America," in Alison Reppy, ed., *Law, A Century of Progress 1835-1935* (New York 1937), I, 39. For as the late Professor Yntema has written, "the hereditary umbilical relation of legal science in the United States to European influences has its counterpart beyond the Rio Grande. Substitute *Las Partidas* for the *Yearbooks*, Pothier for Blackstone, the Code Napoléon for the English Reform Acts, France for England, and the parallel is in essential aspects complete. To borrow from the expressive folklore, all Latin

a primal assault upon fundamental beliefs, the wealth deprivations imposed in Latin America and elsewhere during these years were the result largely of unpremeditated, though chronic, internal disorder and instability.

World War I tolled the death-knell of the *laissez-faire* era. Radically dislocating European and other ascendent economies, the war heralded the renascence of the restrictionist policies that had marked international economic relations a century and a half earlier.[40] Economic nationalism, with all its discriminatory trappings, became the major order of the day. Despite overwhelming proof of global economic interdependence (made distressingly obvious by the Great Depression), nations turned inward to their own domestic problems. This interwar perspective had a profound effect upon the Process of Deprivation. No longer were deprivations restricted mainly to the Latin American republics. Nor did they remain simply the product of chronic internal disorder and instability. Though these patterns continued, especially in Mexico during its turbulent revolution of 1910-20,[41] foreign-wealth deprivations became both more widespread and more

---

Americans originally came from Paris." Hessel E. Yntema, "Research in Inter-American Law at the University of Michigan," *Michigan Law Review,* XLIII (December 1944), 549, 550.

[40] See U.N. Department of Economic and Social Affairs, *International Capital Movements During the Inter-War Period* [hereafter cited as *International Capital Movements*] (New York, U.N. Pub. Sales No. 1949.II.D.2). As one observer has put it, "the twentieth century gave evidence of becoming an era in which politics ruled economics—when governments moved into close control over business enterprise." Jeannette P. Nichols, "Hazards of American Private Investment in Underdeveloped Countries," *Orbis,* IV (Summer 1960), 174, 182.

[41] See the many and varied deprivative disputes reported in: Opinions of Commissioners under the Convention Concluded September 8, 1923, between the United States and Mexico (February 4, 1926 to July 23, 1927), U.N.R.I.A.A., IV, 15-320; Opinions of Commissioners under the Convention Concluded September 8, 1923, as extended by the Convention of August 16, 1927, between the United States and Mexico (September 26, 1928 to May 17, 1929), U.N.R.I.A.A., IV, 327-545; Opinions of Commissioners under the Convention Concluded September 8, 1923, as extended by Subsequent Conventions, between the United States and Mexico (October 1930 to July 1931), U.N.R.I.A.A., IV, 551-746; Opinions of Commissioners under the Convention Concluded September 10, 1923, as extended by the Convention Concluded August 17, 1929, between the United States and Mexico (April 26, 1926 to April 24, 1931), U.N.R.I.A.A., IV, 783-913; Decisions and Opinions of the Commissioners in accordance with the Convention of November 19, 1926, between Great Britain and the United Mexican States (October 5, 1929 to February 15, 1930), U.N.R.I.A.A., V, 17-129; Further Decisions and Opinions of the Commissioners in accordance with the Conventions of November 19, 1926 and December 5, 1930, between Great Britain and the United Mexican States (subsequent to February 15, 1930), U.N.R.I.A.A., V, 133-306; La Réparation des Dommages Causés aux Etrangers par des Mouvements Révolutionnaires—Jurisprudence de la Commission Franco-Méxicaine des Réclamations (1924-32), U.N.R.I.A.A., V, 325-560. See also the relevant bibliography listed in Vols. IV and V of U.N.R.I.A.A.

deliberate, a development which Dupuis was once led to call "une régression lamentable."[42] But however lamentable, it was probably inevitable. Born mainly of the experiences and necessities of war, the wealth deprivation device became an important strategy of conscious social engineering, complementing other techniques for reallocating wealth and other values. Recall, for example, the major deprivations undertaken by the so-called Succession States of Eastern Europe following the peace treaties of World War I, perhaps most notably immortalized in the celebrated litigation between Germany and Poland concerning the "expropriation" of certain German interests in Polish Upper Silesia.[43] Recall, too, the revolutionary assaults upon domestic and foreign wealth by the Soviet Union in 1917 and the years immediately following.[44] Elsewhere in Europe, particularly during the nadir of the Great Depression, Fascist Italy and Nazi Germany inflicted deprivations upon foreign as well as domestic proprietors and entrepreneurs.[45] And across the Atlantic, though less the offspring of World War I than the consequence of long-standing inequities,

[42] Charles Dupuis, "Régles Générales du Droit de la Paix," *Recueil des Cours*, XXXII (1930-II), 1, 163. For similar but more recent misgivings, see Gottfried Dietze, "The Disregard for Property in International Law," *Northwestern University Law Review*, LVI (March-April 1961), 87.

[43] Case Concerning Certain German Interests in Polish Upper Silesia, P.C.I.J., Ser. A, No. 6 [1925] (Jurisdiction), No. 7 [1926] (Merits), No. 9 [1927] (Jurisdiction), No. 13 [1927] (Interpretation); Case Concerning the Factory at Chorzow, P.C.I.J., Ser. A., No. 17 [1928] (Indemnity). See also German Settlers in Poland, P.C.I.J., Ser. B, No. 6 [1923] (Advisory Opinion); Treatment of Polish Nationals and Other Persons of Polish Origin or Speech in the Danzig Territory, P.C.I.J., Ser. A/B, No. 44 [1932] (Advisory Opinion); Appeal from a Judgment of the Hungaro-Czechoslovak Arbitral Tribunal, P.C.I.J., Ser. A/B, No. 61 [1933]; Minority Schools in Albania, P.C.I.J., Ser. A/B, No. 64 [1935]; Emeric Kulin Père c. Etat roumain, *Recueil des Décisions des Tribunaux Arbitraux Mixtes*, VII (April-August 1927), 138 [hereafter cited as M.A.T.]. This last case served as the decisional model for a number of claims arising out of certain agrarian reforms proposed to be carried out by Rumania against, among others, landowners who had opted for Hungarian nationality, with the result that the case is sometimes referred to as "The Hungarian Optants' Case." The other claims are listed in M.A.T., VII, 150-51.

[44] See Ivan A. Gladkov, *Nationalization of Industry in the U.S.S.R.* (Moscow 1954) (in Russian), where the texts of Soviet nationalization enactments, federal and local, between 1917 and 1921 are set forth. For discussion, see Donald D. Bishop, *The Roosevelt-Litvinov Agreements* (Syracuse 1965); Samy Friedman, *Expropriation in International Law* (London 1953), 17-23; Konstantin Katzarov, *The Theory of Nationalisation* (Neuchâtel 1964), 34-36; Ben A. Wortley, *Expropriation in Public International Law* (Cambridge, Eng. 1959), 61-62.

[45] See Wortley (fn. 44), 64. As to Italy during the interwar period, see Mario Einaudi, Maurice Byé, and Ernesto Rossi, *Nationalization in France and Italy* (Ithaca 1955), 189, 194-200; William A. Robson, *Nationalized Industry and Public Ownership* (London 1960), 495-98. As to Germany, see Katzarov (fn. 44), 36-37; authorities cited in footnote 31. See also Paul Weiden, "German Confiscation of American Securities," *New York University Law Review Quarterly*, XVII (January 1940), 200.

Mexican history records the widely transformative nationalizations of foreign oil and agrarian interests beginning with the Constitution of 1917 and following into the next two decades.[46]

"What is past is prologue." Especially is this Shakespearean truth apparent in the relationship between the interwar and post-World War II deprivation eras. No mere disinheritors of conditions past, the Mexican, Soviet and, "Succession State" experiments of the interwar years were previews—indeed, progenitors—of events future. For all its validity, however, the axiom cannot be permitted to gloss over the distinctly divergent character of post-World War II deprivations. If any single conclusion must be drawn from events since 1945, it is that wealth deprivations in general, and foreign-wealth deprivations in particular, lost whatever incidental and parochial quality they may previously have had. Little by little over the years, but now overwhelmingly by comparison, direct and indirect interference with private (and public) wealth, through regulation, transfer, redistribution, and outright abolition, on a major and minor scale, became a fundamental strategy—a "determined system"[47]—of national policy, not only in Latin America and Europe, but the world over. Recalling some of the more notable deprivations since the onset of World War II (all of which affected foreign wealth to some degree) confirms the point.[48] Significantly, the vast majority of deprivations during these years have taken place within two geopolitical spheres: the so-called Communist World and, as Vera Micheles Dean has dubbed it, "the Land of Bandungia,"[49] with nearly all of the most recent in the latter—a pattern

[46] See Josef L. Kunz, "The Mexican Expropriations," *New York University Law Review Quarterly*, XVII (March 1940), 327, 342-84; Friedman (fn. 44), 23-29; Katzarov (fn. 44), 31-34; Wortley (fn. 44), 64-65. It may be recalled, as Friedman has done, that the Mexican reforms preceded those of the Soviet Union "by almost a year" (fn. 44), 23.

[47] Katzarov (fn. 44), 75.

[48] *Eastern Europe*: Estonia (1940), Latvia (1940), Lithuania (1940), Bulgaria (1942, 1946-49), Czechoslovakia (1945-48), Poland (1945-48), East Germany (1945-49), Hungary (1945-49), Yugoslavia (1946-47, 1956), Rumania (1946-50). *Western Europe*: France (1944-46), Holland (1945), Austria (1946-47), Great Britain (1946-47). *Latin America*: Argentina (1946, 1963), Bolivia (1952), Guatemala (1953), Brazil (1959-60, 1962), Cuba (1959-61), Mexico (1960), Colombia (1962), Chile (1964, 1969), Peru (1968). *Asia*: Burma (1948, 1962), Communist China (1950, 1955-57), India (1953), Philippines (1954), Indonesia (1957-59, 1963-65), Ceylon (1958, 1962). *Middle East*: Iran (1951), Syria (1951, 1965), Iraq (1957, 1961-62). *Africa*: Egypt (1956-57, 1960-61), Tunisia (1960, 1964), Guinea (1960-61), Kenya (1962-64), Algeria (1964-65), Congo (1964, 1966-67), Tanzania (1966-67). For a brief summary of many of the deprivations undertaken since the beginning of World War II, not all of which involved foreign wealth, see Katzarov (fn. 44), 42-73.

[49] Vera M. Dean, *The Nature of the Non-Western World* (New York 1957), 12-16.

that is likely to continue in the future. Plagued by poverty, antiquated institutions, and political instability, and lacking in progressive technologies, rapid rates of capital accumulation, and strong entrepreneurial classes, the backward countries are understandably turning to the broad integrative influence of direct public participation in the economic process.[50]

In the particular case, of course, all the significant characteristics that have shaped perspectives toward the deprivation of wealth, generally, and toward the deprivation of foreign wealth, specifically, must be deliberately surveyed if rational policy clarification is to be achieved. Concentrating on the nation-state as deprivor, for example, such questions as the following will invariably prove relevant: Is it old or new? What is its aggregate strength and what is the nature of that strength? What degree of industrialization has it achieved? How and to what degree are its internal social processes institutionalized? Is its power structure narrowly based or widely shared? Does it seek to exclude all private wealth or does it look to a more or less mixed economic regime? Does it actively solicit foreign capital and skills or does it abjure them in whole or in part? With what nation-states does it maintain (or has it maintained) alliances and affiliations, and what is (or has been) the nature of those alliances and affiliations? Is it a member of an important power bloc? What type of world public order does it demand? And so on.

Clearly, this kind of detailed inquiry is more than can be entertained in so general a statement as the present one. In the absence of a detailed, case-by-case analysis of specific controversies, the emphasis must here remain essentially suggestive and commendatory.[51]

OBJECTIVES

The immediate objective of the deprivor, nation-state and otherwise, is obviously to deprive. But further reflection indicates that far more is involved. Stated in most general terms, deprivor objectives embrace all the demands that are commonly projected into the more comprehensive world scene for the protection and enhancement of wealth, power, respect, and other values. Of course, these particular value demands vary from case to case and from one historical context to another. They vary, too, depending on the situations within which

[50] See generally Albert H. Hanson, *Public Enterprise and Economic Development* (London 1959).

[51] See Irving L. Horowitz, *Three Worlds of Development* (New York 1966), 44-46, for a "digest" of economic, political, social, and military factors characterizing the underdeveloped "Third World" wherein, as indicated, most deprivors are to be found today. To the extent that deprivors may be found elsewhere, however, see the equivalent "digests" for the "First" and "Second" worlds, 39-44.

they arise and on the strategies actually employed to achieve them. Naturally, all this variation greatly complicates the task of comparative analysis over time and between controversies. Moreover, given the unreliability of self-serving statements (official and unofficial) and the confusion in most cases of a mixture of value goals, there is considerable difficulty in isolating the objectives that are actually being pursued in the given case. But difficulties such as these do not excuse systematic analysis. Not only are deprivor objectives likely to challenge authoritative norms, but they are likely also to condition fundamentally the actions and reactions which ultimately are undertaken.

Deprivor demands can be typed by reference to any one or a number of possible criteria. Provided that the typology employed relates them to the variables which do and should effect the prescription and application of policy, the methodology employed seems unimportant. Here we may suitably and conveniently refer to certain general value categories.[52] It must be borne in mind throughout, however, that all analytical constructs—including the one here recommended—always cast rather synthetic shadows. Objectives rarely travel except in combination, sometimes at cross-purposes. Still less frequently are they clearly articulated, if at all. And, more commonly than is to be wished, they are sometimes unrecognized or uncomprehended even by those who pursue them, often working as they do below the level of conscious awareness and rationality. Nevertheless, it is believed that even a somewhat artificial typology can bring clarity to what has too long been a much neglected question. As one keen observer has put it, "[i]f action is viewed in terms of the realization of values of the members of a group, the amount of group energy it will use, the direction it will take, and the control it will accept can be anticipated."[53] For clarity and economy, it is helpful to distinguish between "welfare values" (wealth, well-being, skills, and enlightenment) and "deference values" (power, respect, rectitude, and affection), the former being those "whose possession to a certain degree is a necessary condition for the maintenance of the physical activity of the person," and the latter those "that consist in being taken into consideration (in the acts of others and of the self)."[54]

Welfare Values

It is difficult—often impossible—to separate one welfare value demand from another (or in some cases, indeed, from all other value demands).

---

[52] Detailed discussion of value objectives sought in other processes of interaction can be found in McDougal and Burke (fn. 14), 17-20; McDougal, Lasswell, and Vlasic (fn. 14), 17-31.

[53] Carlston (fn. 15), 72-73. [54] Lasswell and Kaplan (fn. 14), 55-56.

Yet it would seem implicit in the very nature of the process under consideration that of all the welfare values being demanded by deprivors, *wealth* should be the most apparent, if not the most important. Over the years, communities at every level have demanded protection for, and improvement of, their bases of wealth through limitations severe and mild upon foreign access to, use of, and benefit from wealth processes and values.

But when we look, first, to the century preceding World War I we find that wealth deprivations rarely were motivated by demands for wealth as such; that is, for wealth as the dominant or end goal of public policy. The pre-World War I era was, as noted, the heyday of *laissez-faire*. Wealth was considered most socially productive when left to private initiative, free from public interference. It was conceived (if not wholly respected) as a natural right conditioned only by the most utilitarian needs.[55] Its outright acquisition, whether in the enforcement of health and penal statutes (which, in the name of social *well-being*, stands as one of the few instances where welfare value demand distinctions are possible) or in the administration of customs regulations or utility "condemnation" laws (in the name of improving all welfare values generally), was therefore seen less as a final reward than as a highly circumscribed means for safeguarding and enhancing other (usually welfare) values.[56] This is, indeed, the essence of what B. A. Wortley has called "the 'classical' type of expropriation"; that is, "an exceptional procedure for special needs"[57]—in fact, the very pith of the so-called rule of public utility.

Of course, wealth has continued to serve as an auxiliary deprivor objective in the years since World War I (a point too often forgotten by international law scholars). It is, after all, one of those fundamental human values upon which the full realization of most others so often depends, not only in the minor sense characteristic of the nineteenth century, but also as a means for achieving true societal transforma-

[55] The nineteenth century "coalescence" of "natural right" and "utilitarian" notions about private wealth ownership has been noted in Richard B. Schlatter, *Private Property* (London 1951), 249:

. . . it was not strange that the classical economists of the early nineteenth century were both utilitarians, and exponents of the rights of property as those were defined in the Lockean tradition. The idea that each man ought to own what his industry created was, according to one's philosophical preferences, either a rule of natural justice or a correct counsel of expediency. Ricardo and his interpreters could defend private ownership on either ground. Their only problem was to demonstrate that a liberal economic society did in fact distribute property on this principle.

[56] For demonstration, see the authorities cited in footnote 36.

[57] Footnote 44, 24-25. Wortley's use of the term "expropriation" includes "adequate compensation before taking."

tions. As Kunz once observed of the revolutionary Mexican reforms of the interwar period, *"La Revolución Mexicana* is the all embracing name for a vast social transformation, an attempt to give the masses land, hygiene, education, to reshape the country completely, to create a true Mexican nation, to emancipate the Indian . . . and to liberate the *peón* through an economic and spiritual higher standard of living."[58] In sum, all welfare values, today principally in the underdeveloped lands and usually in the name of "nationalization," may be simultaneously demanded when deprivations are broached. "Nationalization is in many sectors of underdeveloped nations . . . thought to be an essential step in reaching the stage of development of an industrially organized state with an ability to provide for the *welfare* of its citizens."[59] But the point is not limited to emergent economies alone. In the sense that wealth deprivations may contribute significantly to more efficient economic administration and planning, higher rates of saving, effective control of currency and credit, increased investment expenditure, reduction of competitive waste, and so forth, the general welfare of the peoples of industrially advanced societies may be believed to be benefited as well.[60] Indeed, in at least one case, betterment of the national welfare generally, through the deprivative device specifically, was seen as a matter of life and death. Thus is former French Minister of Finance René Pleven reputed to have declared in 1945: "Nous moderniser en nationalisant ou mourir."[61]

[58] Kunz (fn. 46), 328.

[59] Carlston (fn. 15), 6 (emphasis added).

[60] For discussion of these considerations in post-World War II Britain, for example, see Symposium, "The Nationalization of British Industries," *Law and Contemporary Problems*, xvi (Autumn 1951), 620; Albert H. Hanson, ed., *Nationalisation* (Toronto 1963), 22-63; Ben W. Lewis, *British Planning and Nationalization* (New York 1952), 43-45; Robson (fn. 45), Chap. 2. For contrasts in expectations and programs elsewhere in Western Europe, see *Les Nationalisations en France et à L'Etranger: Les Nationalisations en France*, Leon F. Julliot de la Morandière and Maurice Byé, eds. (Paris 1948); Einaudi, Byé, and Rossi (fn. 45); Douglas V. Verney, *Public Enterprise in Sweden* (Liverpool 1959). A number of these demands are found also in some of the preambles to post-World War II Eastern European deprivative legislation. See Gillian M. White, *Nationalization of Foreign Property* (New York 1962), 18-24. As to post-World War II Eastern Europe, see generally *Les Nationalisations en France et à L'Etranger: Les Nationalisations à L'Etranger*, Henry Puget, ed. (Paris 1958), 125-299; Samuel Herman, "War Damage and Nationalization in Eastern Europe," *Law and Contemporary Problems*, xvi (Summer 1951), 498; Samual L. Sharp, *Nationalization of Key Industries in Eastern Europe* (Washington 1946). As to Europe as a whole, see Nicholas R. Doman, "Postwar Nationalization of Foreign Property in Europe," *Columbia Law Review*, xlviii (December 1948), 1125. For a general but somewhat dated bibliography, consult U.N. Technical Assistance Administration, *Some Problems in the Organization and Administration of Public Enterprises in the Industrial Field* (U.N. Doc. ST/TAA/M/7), July 28, 1954, 67-87.

[61] See Albert G. Lapradelle, "Les Effets Internationaux des Nationalisations," Rapport et Projet de Résolutions Définitifs (Troisième Commission), *Annuaire*

All that has been said, however, should not obscure the fact that in this era of worldwide economic development, wealth (upon which other welfare values depend) has become an end goal of distinctive significance, especially in "the Land of Bandungia." It is in this light that one may at least partially interpret, for example, the preamble to the Bolivian decree of May 14, 1952 establishing a commission to prepare for the nationalization of the massive and largely foreign-owned Patino, Hochschild, and Aramayo tin mining combines.[62] Accusing the mining companies of having "for half a century exploited Bolivia's mining riches, exporting nearly all their profits and reserves and incorporating them to foreign economies," the preamble recalled that one of the primary objectives of the "national revolution" (which installed Paz Estenssoro as President of the country) was "to correct this state of affairs by adopting the necessary measures for the benefit of the collectivity" and so declared that "the most important of such measures is the nationalization of the great mining enterprises so that the future yield of the industry may be incorporated to the country's economy."[63] Illustrations of this kind abound.

Regrettably, students of this field have too often disregarded (or perhaps too glibly assumed) the status of wealth, specifically, and of all welfare values, generally, as end goals of contemporary deprivor policy. Such recognition as has been shown is usually found, and then only incidentally, in connection with the definition of such terms as "expropriation" and "nationalization." When twentieth century deprivor objectives are considered at all, emphasis is given to those demands (often frowned upon by Western eyes) that are implicit in so-called political, nationalistic, or ideological "motives."[64] Whether this emphasis (or lack of recognition) reflects a too rigid preference for "classical" nineteenth century patterns, thereby making suspect "legal" conclusions about more recent deprivations, we can only conjecture. More important is that we recognize that wealth and other welfare values today loom large among the congeries of value demands that are sincerely believed to be advanced by the deprivation of foreign wealth.[65]

---

de L'Institut de Droit International, XLIII (I) (Bath 1950), 42, 45. For discussion bearing upon French attitudes about State ownership and supervision of key industries, especially during France's post-1945 era of intensive economic planning, see John Ardagh, The New French Revolution (New York 1968), 12-66.

[62] Quoted in New York Times, May 15, 1952, p. 16, col. 1.

[63] Same.

[64] See, e.g., Isi Foighel, Nationalization and Compensation (London and Copenhagen 1964), 37-47.

[65] The conviction is manifest not only in the underdeveloped world. American and "reform Marxist" economist Martin Bronfenbrenner, for one, has sought to

Deference Values

It should not be assumed that welfare values are always the sole or even the dominant values demanded by deprivors. Deference values, too, play a significant role. Like the former, however, they are not easily separated. More often than not they are projected in multiple combination. But distinctions among them are nonetheless more noticeable and for this reason they may be separately treated.

Power. The deprivation of foreign wealth may spell a net improvement not only in the development and reallocation of important resources, goods, and services, but also—and perhaps more consequentially—in overall economic and political power. For example, demands for power appear to have been an important factor when in 1899 Portugal unilaterally annulled and seized the American- and British-owned Delagoa Bay Railway concession interests in what was then Portuguese East Africa.[66] This was at a time when, as Herbert Feis has recalled, "the territorial division of Africa was proceeding rapidly" and when "Great Britain and Germany suspected each other of designs upon these colonies, and Portugal entertained fear and suspicion of both." Noting the concession controversy, Feis concluded: "Portugal defended its action on technical grounds in the contract but its real motive was unquestionably fear of British dictation."[67]

Other pre-World War I examples could be cited. More significant to contemporary and future policy, however, are the situations in which demands for power have played a dominant (often decisive)

---

demonstrate through arithmetic models that the "confiscation" of private foreign wealth (i.e., without compensation) in "reasonably representative" underdeveloped economies can significantly accelerate economic development "by shifting income to developmental investment from capitalists' consumption, from transfer abroad, and from unproductive 'investment' like luxury housing." "The Appeal of Confiscation in Economic Development," *Economic Development and Cultural Change*, III (April 1955), 201. Cf. Daniel H. Garnick, " 'The Appeal of Confiscation' Reconsidered: A Gaming Approach to Foreign Economic Policy," *Economic Development and Cultural Change*, XI (July 1963), 353; Bronfenbrenner, "Second Thoughts on Confiscation," same, 367. In more general terms, without explicit reference to the deprivation of foreign wealth as such, Hanson (fn. 50), 23, notes:

> Whatever the ultimate perspective may be, the country anxious to develop economically has no alternative but to use public enterprise on a considerable scale, at the very least in order to "get things going." How much is left to private initiative will depend, partly on ideology, but to a much greater extent on social and economic circumstances. If these are such that private entrepreneurship can be effectively stimulated, then the policy of concentrating governmental effort on certain basic but unremunerative essentials and leaving everything else to the private entrepreneur has much to recommend it.

[66] See Delagoa Bay Railway (United States and Great Britain v. Portugal) [1900], *Foreign Relations, U.S.* (Washington 1902), 903; La Fontaine (fn. 36), 398.
[67] Herbert Feis, *Europe the World's Banker 1870-1914* (New Haven 1930), 248.

role since that time—more significant because they illustrate not only that the exigencies of power have from time to time been the *primum mobile* of deprivative activity, but also and more importantly that deprivor demands since World War I and especially since World War II largely reflect, if they do not epitomize, the rise and reaction of non-Western nationalism to the imperial expansion (economic as well as political) of Western civilization over the face of the earth.[68] This historic development has manifested itself in the Process of Deprivation in two principal ways.

On the one hand, it has involved specific demands for total or primary control over particular—usually politically sensitive—bases of wealth, generally in the name of economic "self-determination."[69] As Dunn once stated, the "obvious purpose" of Article 27 of the Mexican Constitution of 1917 (pursuant to which Mexico appropriated foreign-owned petroleum deposits) "was to break the control of foreign interests over the extremely prosperous oil industry of Mexico and to vest that control in Mexicans. This was part of the general program [of the Mexican Revolution] of making the Mexican people economically independent."[70] To similar effect was Iranian Premier Mossadegh's *Déclaration* of June 9, 1952, before the International Court of Justice (following Iran's nationalization of the British-owned Anglo-Iranian Oil Company) in which he spoke of Iranian demands for control of its national oil resources, emphasizing that the British company "devenue un État dans l'État, détermina les destinées du pays."[71] In

---

[68] Precision compels our acknowledging, however, that this motivating nationalism cannot be characterized simply as non-Western and/or anti-Western. As we are taught by recent developments in Burma and Tanzania (where Chinese and Indian capitalists have become the targets of deprivative action) and by earlier events in Eastern *and* Western Europe (where Westerners deprived each other), it has been more generally xenophobic and to a substantial extent ideological.

[69] On the "principle of self-determination" within the emergent world, see Emerson (fn. 34), 293-359. Myrdal has referred to these demands as part of the "process of economic liberation." Gunnar Myrdal, *Beyond the Welfare State* (New Haven 1960), 214.

[70] Frederick S. Dunn, *The Diplomatic Protection of Americans in Mexico* (New York 1933), 332. Dunn notes the not surprising result that "the nationalization of petroleum deposits received the first attention and generated the greatest amount of heat in the diplomatic relations between the United States and Mexico."

[71] The Anglo-Iran Oil Company Case, International Court of Justice Pleadings (1952), 437, 439. That Premier Mossadegh's concern was not wholly imagined is clearly evident from a public account that at the time of nationalization "there were only three Iranians in the whole company who had ever been in the control room of the power plant that supplied not only the refinery but the towns of Abadan, Khurramshahr and vicinity." *New York Times*, January 31, 1953, p. 6, col. 3, quoted in Jerrold L. Walden, "The International Petroleum Cartel in Iran —Private Power and the Public Interest," *Journal of Public Law*, XI (Spring 1962), 64, 72. Similar concern was later expressed in Canada by the Royal Commission on Canada's Economic Prospects:

this context, the words of Senator John Sherman, father of United States antitrust legislation, seem strikingly relevant: "If we will not endure a king as a political power, we should not endure a king over the production, transportation and sale of any of the necessities of life."[72]

On the other hand, some deprivations have been born less of a desire for economic self-determination than of a wish to press compliance with, or to retaliate for failure to gain acceptance of, a preferred policy otherwise wholly or largely unrelated to the bases of wealth actually at stake. Several recent examples are well known. In 1958, in apparent retaliation for refusal of the Netherlands to transfer sovereignty ("liberate") Irian Barat (West New Guinea), Indonesia took over most of the privately owned Dutch possessions then within its territory.[73] In

---

The benefits of foreign investment that we have mentioned are real and tangible. It is more difficult to state in similarly precise terms what the dangers are in the present situation and what conflicts might occur between the interests of Canadians and the interests of the foreign owners of wholly-owned subsidiaries of foreign companies operating in Canada. In the course of the Commission's hearings, concern was expressed over the extent to which our productive resources are controlled by non-residents, mostly Americans. Many Canadians are worried about such a large degree of economic decision-making being in the hands of non-residents or in the hands of Canadian companies controlled by non-residents. This concern has arisen because of the concentration of foreign ownership in certain industries, because of the fact that most of it is centered in one country, the United States, and because most of it is in the form of equities which, in the ordinary course of events, are never likely to be repatriated. Some people think it is foolish to worry too much about the possible dangers of foreign investment in this country. However, the contrary opinions on this subject which we have mentioned do in fact exist and if a period of political or economic instability should occur, they might develop into demands for restrictive or discriminatory action of an extreme kind, the consequences of which would be unfortunate for all concerned. *Final Report* (Ottawa 1958), 389-90.

For recent consideration of the role of American enterprise in Canadian life, see Daniel Jay Baum, "The Global Corporation: An American Challenge to the Nation-State?" *Iowa Law Review*, LV (December 1969), 410.

[72] Quoted in Alan D. Neale, *The Antitrust Laws of the United States of America* (Cambridge, Eng. 1960), 25. On the general theme of alleged "economic exploitation" by foreign oil interests in the Middle East, see Edith Tilton Penrose, "Profit Sharing Between Producing Countries and Oil Companies in the Middle East," *Economic Journal*, LXIX (June 1959), 238.

[73] See generally the article by the Board of Editors of the *Nederlands Tijdschrift Voor Internationaal Recht* (fn. 31); Martin Domke, "Indonesian Nationalization Measures Before Foreign Courts," *American Journal of International Law*, LIV (April 1960), 305; H. W. Baade, "Indonesian Nationalization Measures Before Foreign Courts—A Reply," *American Journal of International Law*, LIV (October 1960), 801; Lord McNair, "The Seizure of Property and Enterprises in Indonesia," *Nederlands Tijdschrift Voor Internationaal Recht*, VI (July 1959), 218. Similar factors appear to have been at work in 1964 when Indonesia, as part of its policy of "confrontation" with Malaysia and in apparent retaliation for Britain's support of Malaysia, undertook deprivative measures against British-owned properties. See *Keesing's Contemporary Archives* (January 9-16, 1965), 20518, Pt. A, col. 1.

1960, Cuba nationalized extensive American holdings in admitted reprisal against United States suspension of a preferential Cuban-sugar import quota,[74] in turn a response to prior Cuban seizures. And later in 1960, the United Arab Republic appropriated private Belgian interests in Egypt on the grounds that Belgium was responsible for the severance of diplomatic ties between the Republic of the Congo (her former colony) and the U.A.R.[75]

In sum, demands for power—whether in terms of increased internal control or of tactical advantage in international dealings—have recently assumed a highly critical posture among deprivor objectives. In almost all cases they have been directed against nationals closely identified with, if not always originating from, the *anciens régimes* of a bygone colonial era. That this may—indeed should—bear heavily upon policy recommendation in general, and upon such formulations as the "rule of nondiscrimination" in particular, is axiomatic.

Respect. It is only recently that demands for respect have taken their place among the major objectives sought by deprivors, again because of that tumultuous nationalism which resounds in the emergent world. In a sense this seems paradoxical. After all, foreign-wealth deprivations are hardly calculated to enamour the aliens against whom they are directed. But the inconsistency is not quite so rigorous as first it might seem. "*Respect*," write Lasswell and Kaplan," is the value of status, of honor, recognition, prestige, the 'glory' or 'reputation' which Hobbes classes with gain and safety as one of the three fundamental human motivations."[76] In other words, it may or may not summon affection, approbation, or esteem. In this sense, the paradox all but vanishes and

[74] Thus the first paragraph of the preamble to Cuban Law No. 851 of July 6, 1960, Official Gazette No. 130 of July 7, 1960 (affecting oil, banking, and other interests) reads:

> WHEREAS, the attitude assumed by the government and the Legislative Power of the United States of North America, which constitutes an aggression, for political purposes, against the basic interests of the Cuban economy, as recently evidenced by the Amendment to the Sugar Act just enacted by the United States Congress at the request of the Chief Executive of that country, whereby exceptional powers are conferred upon the President of the United States to reduce the participation of Cuban sugars in the American sugar market as a threat of political action against Cuba, forces the Revolutionary Government to adopt, without hesitation, all and whatever measures it may deem appropriate or desirable for the due defense of the national sovereignty and protection of our economic development process.

[75] See *The Times* (London), December 3, 1960, p. 6, col. 3. More recently, Cairo threatened to nationalize West German property and to sequester West German funds within the U.A.R. in the event that West Germany were to establish formal diplomatic relations with Israel. *New York Times*, March 11, 1965, p. 1, col. 5.

[76] Lasswell and Kaplan (fn. 14), 56.

the manner in which deprivations occasion respect thus becomes more readily discernible.

As already noted, the deprivors of the last few decades are to be found mainly in the underdeveloped Third World; the deprivees, generally, in the formerly politically imperial West. In this context, deprivor demands for respect can be seen largely as claims to "status" and "recognition," to an equal and independent place among nations, to the dignity of self-determination. For emerging peoples, then, foreign-wealth deprivations have served as convenient expressions of their desire to eradicate what are to them humiliating remnants of past political and economic subservience, to achieve a sense of independent worth. Thus was Premier Castro's announcement in August 1960 of the nationalization of about two-thirds of the total value of all American private investment in Cuba declared to mark the beginning of the "Week of Jubilation," or what the Cuban press and radio called the beginning of the "final independence of Cuba."[77] Especially illustrative are excerpts from President Nasser's speech of July 26, 1956, announcing the nationalization of the Universal Company of the Suez Maritime Canal (hereafter referred to as "the Suez Canal Company"):

Citizens,

We shall not let imperialists or exploiters dominate us. We shall not let history repeat itself once more. We have gone forward to build a strong Egypt. We go forward towards political and economic independence. We go forward towards national economy for the sake of the whole people. We go forward to work. But, whenever we look behind, we do so to destroy the traces of the past, the traces of slavery, exploitation and domination.

Today, citizens, rights have been restored to their owners. Our rights in the Suez Canal have been restored to us after 100 years.

Today, we actually achieved true sovereignty, true dignity and true pride. The Suez Canal Company was a state within a state. It was an Egyptian Joint Stock Company, relying on imperialism and its stooges.

. . .

Today, when we build the edifice of our dignity, freedom and pride, we feel that it will not be completely found until we eradicate domination, humiliation and submission. The Suez Canal constituted an edifice of humiliation.[78]

[77] *New York Times*, August 9, 1960, p. 3, col. 1.

[78] Quoted in U.S. Department of State, *The Suez Canal Problem* (1956), 28-30. For a brilliant "contemporary history" of Suez, see Hugh Thomas, *Suez* (New York and Evanston 1967).

Whether such nationalistic self-assertions are justified by the objective record and whether they are wholly genuine is, if answerable, almost irrelevant. For the fact is that they reflect an attitude generally shared by those who have been more on the receiving than the giving end of political and economic hegemony. There is no gainsaying that the emerging peoples of the world do win for themselves, through deprivative activity, a sense of respect from others—"honor" and "prestige" from the peoples and elites with whom they are historically, ideologically, or strategically associated, and "recognition" from the great financial and political interests in faraway London or New York or Paris[79]—and out of this a sense of self-respect. These are "plain, plump facts" that must be understood if a rational approach both to the dynamics of deprivation and to the enlightened formulation of community policy is to be expected.

Rectitude. Common to all legal systems is the assumed competence to prescribe certain conduct as *contra bonos mores* and, hence, punishable. Sometimes the punishment may be directed against the individual person (as in cases of incarceration, banishment, or the taking of life), sometimes against his wealth (as when fines are imposed or possessions "confiscated"), and sometimes against both. Our concern is of course with the deprivation of wealth[80] and, more specifically, with the manner in which wealth deprivations have been employed to help institutionalize prevailing or ascending notions about right and wrong behavior.

Examples are legion. Traditionally, they appear to fall into three basic categories. First are the deprivations imposed following the commission of particular—usually "criminal"—acts; e.g., the forfeiture of burglary instruments or disinheritance upon life sentence.[81] Second,

[79] Thus, for example, was Egypt's nationalization of the Suez Canal Company warmly endorsed in the press and in the official circles of the Arab and Communist worlds as a "daring and important step" in the "struggle for independence." See *Keesing's Contemporary Archives* (July 28-August 4, 1956), 15004, col. 2. The presence of demands for respect in connection with this nationalization were regretfully recognized by then U.S. Secretary of State Dulles in his joint radio-television report with President Eisenhower to the American people of August 3, 1956. See *Department of State Bulletin*, XXXV (August 13, 1956), 259-60. As to demands for respect in the Third World generally, see Harry G. Johnson, "A Theoretical Model of Economic Nationalism in New and Developing States," *Political Science Quarterly*, LXXX (June 1965), 169.

[80] This is not to say that the taking of human life, incarceration, and banishment may not themselves result in severe wealth losses, both to the immediate party and to his lawful heirs and assigns. Such measures, however, are not within the principal focus of this essay.

[81] It perhaps deserves mention that insofar as United States practice is concerned, the state of "civil death" does not ordinarily prohibit the descent and distribution of wealth. See "Descent and Distribution," *American Jurisprudence* 2d, XXIII (1965), 743; Annotation, *American Law Reports*, CXXIX (1942), 1308. The author has not yet investigated the practice elsewhere in the world.

and clearly more important to the global wealth process, are those resulting from the pursuit of "noxious or immoral trades,"[82] such as gambling, counterfeiting, smuggling, narcotics peddling, trading in alcoholic beverages, piracy, or slave trading.[83] Finally, there are deprivations that are imposed because persons maintain or propound political or religious loyalties antithetical to the particular internal order. In the early claim of *The Reverend Dr. Jonas King*,[84] for example, the American Reverend's "alleged offenses against the established religion of the state"[85] probably contributed (it is not wholly clear) as much to the Greek Government's "taking" of his land as they did to his sentence of banishment. Similar factors appear to have been at work in the events which led to the *Affaire des Propriétés Religieuses*,[86] wherein certain foreign-owned Jesuit properties were seized, damaged, or destroyed during the Portuguese Republican Revolution of 1910. More recently, we can point to anti-Semitic spoliations undertaken by the former Axis powers[87] and to the post-World War II Eastern European deprivations against German nationals and other "enemies of the state."[88]

Conspicuous among deprivor objectives since the Bolshevik Revolution, however, is still another type of rectitude demand which has contributed to a number of wealth deprivations (domestic and foreign) in this century: the demand for the fulfillment of the essentially ethical notion that the net product of labor should belong, collectively, to those who labor.[89] This is not to say that the idea of collective ownership was the work only of the Bolshevik Revolution or of its mentors, Marx and Engels. Even in antiquity its contours had been traced;[90] it

[82] The term belongs to Ben A. Wortley. See his discussion on this point in *Expropriation in Public International Law* (fn. 44), 42-44.

[83] For a classic and oft-cited example, see J. Parsons (Great Britain v. United States), Nielsen, American and British Claims Arbitration 587, U.N.R.I.A.A., VI (1925), 165, which involved the destruction by American authorities in the Philippines of a stock of British-owned "bootleg" liquor on the grounds that its manufacture and sale was in violation of United States prohibition laws. For a number of other examples falling within this category see Friedman (fn. 44), 1-2, 50-51.

[84] The claim arose in 1835 and was ultimately settled through "diplomatic intervention" on the part of the United States. For a synoptic account, see John B. Moore, *A Digest of International Law*, VI (Washington 1906), 262.

[85] Same.

[86] (France, Great Britain, and Spain v. Portugal), U.N.R.I.A.A., I (1920), 7.

[87] See, e.g., the authorities cited in footnote 31. See also Siegfried Goldschmidt, *Legal Claims Against Germany* (New York 1945).

[88] See Doman (fn. 60), 1125, 1143-58.

[89] See generally, Gérard Fouilloux, *La Nationalisation et le Droit International Public* (Paris 1962), 93-104. Schlatter has argued that socialist theories about wealth ownership are in a substantial sense but "natural right" theories of property "restated to fit a complex system of cooperative production." Schlatter (fn. 55), 262-77, 281.

[90] See Katzarov (fn. 44), 17-18.

did not spring suddenly like Minerva from Jupiter's head. But it was for the Bolshevik Revolution, buttressed by the famous litany "to each according to his needs" and the fervent commandment "expropriate the expropriators," first to give it worldwide significance. Of course, it is common knowledge that Marxist theories have not had upon all societies the extreme impact that history has recorded in the Soviet Union and its allies. Whatever the inevitabilities of Marxist dialectics, fundamental economic transformations have been taking place in a variety of different ways in a variety of different political and social orientations. Yet there is no denying that socialist notions of economic rectitude have had a profound influence, particularly in the under-developed world where, rightly or wrongly—and to some extent bor-rowing from Lenin—capitalism has been equated with imperialism and colonialism.[91] Planning, social welfare, collective controls, out-right public ownership—each is testimony to the widespread conviction that government has a necessary role to play in the economic process. Whether we are talking about the foreign-wealth deprivations that have taken place in Great Britain or Ceylon, France or Algeria, this is a fact whose fundamental importance for policy clarification needs neither sponsor nor justification.

Affection (Solidarity). The struggle for the loyalties of peoples at home is a phenomenon unique to no age. Emotive appeals to na-tionalistic sentiments have mobilized the energies of even the oldest of nations. But nowhere have demands for group solidarity been so universally conspicuous as in today's emerging countries where "ele-ments of social resistance to economic change" have been strongly marked by the centrifugal forces of "factionalism," by "the tendency of the society to be divided by caste and class cleavages, ethnic or re-ligious distinctions, differences in cultural tradition and social patterns, kinship loyalties, and regional identifications."[92] "The primary task facing the political leaders of the underdeveloped countries," Gunnar Myrdal has observed, "is to attempt to lift the masses out of apathy and frustration; to give them a vision of economic development; to inspire them to enterprise and cooperation; and to instil among them

[91] Former Burmese Premier U Nu voiced concise expression of this equation before the Chamber of Commerce in Burma over a decade ago: "Burma has been for over a century under Imperialist domination, and Capitalists have during the entire period been regarded as the handmaids of Imperialism. During the entire course of our struggle for freedom, therefore, Capital and Imperialist domination have been closely associated in the minds of all of us who have taken part in the struggle, and it has been impossible to view the two in isolation." *From Peace to Stability* (Rangoon, Ministry of Information, 1951), 75.

[92] U.N. Department of Economic and Social Affairs, *Processes and Problems of Industrialization in Underdeveloped Countries* (New York 1955), 19-20.

the discipline needed to strive effectively, to work diligently, and to make sacrifices to improve their conditions"[93]—only to be done, he concludes, "by inspiring them to unity of nationhood":[94]

Nationalism in the underdeveloped countries as it is now rising is . . . not—as it mostly is in the developed countries—associated with reactionary political attitudes, but with the movement towards modernization and reform. It is increasingly a force for equalization of opportunities and for democratization of social and economic conditions. That this is so constitutes an immensely important political difference, the significance of which is only slowly dawning in the Western world. The instigation of nationalistic feelings among backward peoples is a precondition for social and economic progress. If progress is the goal, to foster these emotions becomes a rational means for accomplishing it.[95]

In many quarters, foreign-wealth deprivations are deemed especially well-suited to the achievement of these ends, carried out as they often are "in a spirit of demagoguery which expresses rather the desire to identify the ruling party with the spirit of the nation than any true economic necessity or desirability."[96] (Indeed, it is not unknown for political leaders to seize foreign wealth and at the same time to appeal for foreign investment within their country.) What more expeditious ways are there, it is asked, to summon *us* to "the common purpose" than by striking at *them* where it hurts most, especially when *they* are (as *they* usually are) from the white and Judeo-Christian and economically powerful West? The psychology is as old as history itself. So it is that we daily read of the "Mexicanization" or the "Egyptianization" or the "Cubanization" of economies. Thus did the Iranian Single Article Law of 1951 (resolving "that the oil industry throughout all parts of the country . . . be nationalized") begin by invoking "the Happiness and Prosperity of *the Iranian Nation*."[97] And hence did Premier Castro's anti-American campaign of 1959-60 permit him, as one writer has recently noted, "to keep his hold over the masses through 1960, consolidate his power, and move firmly into the Soviet Bloc."[98] The examples are many. Singularly vivid, however, was Mex-

[93] G. Myrdal (fn. 69), 207.

[94] Same.

[95] Same, 208.

[96] International Commission of Jurists, *The Dynamic Aspects of the Rule of Law in the Modern Age* (Report on the Proceedings of the South-East Asian and Pacific Conference of Jurists) (Geneva 1965), 60.

[97] For the texts of the laws pertaining to the nationalization of the oil industry in Iran in 1951, see Alan W. Ford, *The Anglo-Iranian Oil Dispute of 1951-52* (Berkeley 1954), 268 (emphasis added).

[98] Johnson (fn. 24), 440, 448.

ico's nationalization of certain foreign electric companies in 1960. Shortly after Fidel Castro's accession to power in Cuba, the Mexican National Congress resolved that the Administration of President Lopez Mateos should favor and follow Cuban policies, a resolution that created a critical situation by dividing the nation over a sensitive issue of foreign relations. The seizure of the electric companies, we are told, was the Administration's answer to demands for national unity, demonstrating anew its dedication to the principles of the Revolution of 1910.[99]

It can be wisely argued, of course, that the price of such xenophobic appeals and actions may be high indeed, particularly when they are made to distract public attention from divisive economic and political failures. As Reinhold Niebuhr has reminded us, national patriotism may be an exalted form of altruism when compared to lesser loyalties, but it is also a form of selfishness on a grand scale[100]—a selfishness, it should be added, that may do more harm to those in whose name it is projected than may be done to those who are its immediate targets. But it is nevertheless important to understand that foreign-wealth deprivations can and do link "the people" more closely to the national framework which increasingly determines so much of their daily life.[101] This, too, is a fact which must be weighed into "the balance of relevant considerations" if rational policy is to be achieved.

SUCH, THEN, are the variety of objectives sought by deprivors. It perhaps deserves reemphasis, however, that objectives vary widely from case to case, that they rarely stand alone and that they are never so

[99] Miguel S. Wionczek, "Electric Power: The Uneasy Partnership," in Raymond Vernon, ed., *Public Policy and Private Enterprise in Mexico* (Cambridge, Mass. 1964), 97-98.

[100] Niebuhr (fn. 34), 48, 49.

[101] Thus, Horowitz (fn. 51), 223, has written:

> Confiscation . . . unites a sizable portion of the population in a common historic endeavor; mobilizes the masses behind the political system over against the entrenched economic system; makes it possible to introduce changes such as urbanization and rapid mobility which have been thwarted by conditions of economic and monetary polarization. It is easy to see why confiscation has become a principal feature of the national revolutions of our age. That such policy directly affects foreign credit arrangements and threatens existing securities is a small matter when put together with the country's need to "close the gap" and enter the modern world. The *ideological* advantage of take-over is based on the mobilization and integration of anti-imperialist forces; the economic substance of such take-over is basically anti-traditional. This strategy produces political independence from the old ruling classes and creates a nationalism which serves to unify the popular classes.

See also Johnson (fn. 79); Edward Shils, "The Concentration and Dispersion of Charisma: Their Bearing on Economic Policy in Underdeveloped Countries," *World Politics*, XI (October 1958), 1.

rationally conceived or pursued as our categorization or description might suggest. Confused or confusing though they may be, these value demands do bear heavily upon policy recommendation, prescription, and application, and so summon us all—decision-makers, practitioners, scholars, and interested observers alike—to strive earnestly to isolate and assess them in each case. This must be done not only in terms of the intensities with which they are pursued and the priorities which are attached to them in time and conflict dimension. It must be done also with an eye to the degree to which the demands may be found inclusive or exclusive and to the extent to which they may be found to involve the expansion, conservation, or destruction of other values —not merely from the propagandist's word, but from deliberate empirical investigation. Comprehensive rational appraisal requires no less.

SITUATIONS

The situations (or particular contexts of confrontation) within which foreign-wealth deprivations take place are manifold. An exhaustive itemization at this most general juncture, therefore, approaches the impossible. Nevertheless, the most important situations—from the standpoint of a world of acts and events which most commonly confront decision-makers and, hence, most frequently influence decision —can be examined by referring to four basic and often interdependent dimensions: space, time, institutionalization, and crisis. Such organization, by calling attention to the most relevant variables, permits us to achieve a more rational delimitation through time and from case to case of the many situational factors that have affected decision.

Space. In the vast majority of cases, deprivors have proceeded against foreign wealth—"tangible" and "intangible," "movable" and "immovable"—which has been located, if not physically, at least conceptually within the terrestrial confines of their immediate or extended communities. At times, however, the target has been situated in the "territorial sea,"[102] sometimes in outlying zones "contiguous" there-

[102] E.g., Compañía de Navegación Nacional (Panama v. United States), *Hunt's Rep.* 765, U.N.R.I.A.A., VI (1933), 382, which involved a seizure by Canal Zone authorities of a Panamanian ship in the territorial waters of the Canal Zone pursuant to a libel against the ship for collision with an American vessel outside those waters. McDougal and Burke (fn. 14) have stated that this appears to be the only instance "in which a coastal state saw fit to seize a vessel passing in the territorial sea." But cf. the table prepared by the U.S. Department of the Interior in 1963 on "seizures and harassments of tuna vessels" for the period September 15, 1951 to June 28, 1963, reprinted in *International Legal Materials*, III (Washington 1964), 61. As to claims to authority to apply policy generally in the territorial sea, see McDougal and Burke (fn. 14), 269-89. For an example of the application of deprivative authority in the territorial sea against other than vessels, see footnote 111.

to,[103] and sometimes on the "high seas."[104] At other times it has been within territory belonging to the deprivee's community.[105] And on still other occasions it has been located in communities with which neither of the immediate parties has been politically affiliated.[106] Potentially it may even be located in outer space.[107] Wherever found, however, its precise location is of no mere academic interest.[108]

In the first place, any realistic expectation that deprivations can be successfully imposed will invariably hinge upon the extent to which deprivors and deprivees can assert or maintain at the "situs" the formal authority or effective control (or both) that is indispensable to the achievement of their objectives. It is easily observed that assertions of competence against foreign wealth which is located outside the "territorial jurisdiction" of the deprivor community stand on a lesser legal footing than those which are directed within territorial limits. As Kaplan and Katzenbach have pointed out, "[t]his relationship of law to physical power rests, in part, upon the truism that the effectiveness of any prescription ultimately depends upon power to coerce compliance. . . ."[109] The observation is less an acknowledgement of the "principle of territoriality" than an acceptance of fact.

In the second place, the location of the foreign wealth will generally bear some correspondence, albeit rough, to the intensity with which deprivor and deprivee objectives will be pursued and to the degree to which these objectives may be found inclusive or exclusive. Mere casual reflection points up that the more closely the target of deprivation is identified with the distribution of values within the deprivor or deprivee communities, the more manifestly pronounced will be the respective concentrations of interest in the foreign wealth involved. It

[103] See McDougal and Burke (fn. 14).

[104] Same, 876-85.

[105] Among the critical issues arising out of the nationalization of the Suez Canal Company in 1956, for example, was whether or not Egypt intended to affect British- and French-owned assets within Great Britain and France. White (fn. 60) has concluded that such was the case. But cf. Robert Delson, "Nationalization of the Suez Canal Company: Issues of Public and Private International Law," *Columbia Law Review*, LVII (June 1957), 755, 781.

[106] A number of the nationalization measures enacted in post-World War II Eastern Europe, for example, appear to have been directed against the foreign-owned assets of local enterprises wherever externally situated. See White (fn. 60), 102-04.

[107] See McDougal, Lasswell, and Vlasic (fn. 14), Chaps. 6, 8.

[108] It deserves emphasis that the reference here is to the location of the wealth target before or at the time of deprivation. Considerations pertaining to its location after deprivation (actual or purported) will be noted later. See pp. 111-12.

[109] Kaplan and Katzenbach (fn. 20), 175. Of course, this is not to say, as Kaplan and Katzenbach have themselves further remarked, that the possession of physical power should *ipso facto* "determine appropriate policy, the wisdom of its exercise, or the substantive rules to be applied (domestic or foreign) as the guide to decision."

is, of course, the varying intensity and exclusivity of interest in the foreign wealth that is important for policy. "As the impact upon values of [the] national community becomes more remote, the public interest is less and the area of tolerance for divergent rules correspondingly increases."[110] But it must not be forgotten that geographic proximity, even in this age of advanced technology, looms large among the factors which vitally affect this question.

Time. Temporal dimensions can also prove critical, and in many respects. The more important may be noted here.

Consider, first, the so-called *punctum temporis*, or moment, of deprivation: the "date of first projection," the "date of decree," the "time of notice," the "date of filing of declaration," the "date of initial physical interference," the "date specified by legislation," the "date of confirmation and judgment," and so forth. In contrast to other situational factors, this has perhaps the most pervasive relevance, for upon its determination (the criteria for which require the most careful deliberation) depends a whole complex of critical judgments. In some cases it may affect the spatial position or location of the target of deprivation (whether "tangible" or "intangible," "movable" or "immovable") and, hence, the very competence to deprive.[111] In others, regardless of the type of wealth involved, the time of deprivation may determine the "national character" of the particular target; that is, whether or not there is to be a *foreign*-wealth deprivation at all.[112] And on still other occasions, location in time may help to characterize the deprivation itself. The United States Court of Appeals for the Second Circuit in *Banco Nacional de Cuba v. Sabbatino*,[113] for example, quite properly indicated that a verdict of "discriminatory" or "retaliatory" deprivation may rise or fall depending on whether the particular measure is or is not one of a series of previous, concurrent, or future deprivations.[114]

[110] Same, 179.

[111] The point has been recently and vividly demonstrated in the American courts in Banco Nacional de Cuba v. Sabbatino, wherein it was held that Cuba was competent to affect the nationalization of a shipload of foreign-owned sugar because at the time of the "effective date" of the relevant decree the sugar shipment was located within four to six miles of the Cuban port of Santa Maria or, in other words, within Cuba's claimed "territorial jurisdiction." 193 F. Supp. 375, 379 (S.D.N.Y. 1961), affirmed, 307 F.2d 845 (2d Cir. 1962), reviewed on other grounds, 376 U.S. 398 (1964).

[112] In other words, a particular deprivation may affect an owner who, at the determinative time, may be said to be a national of the deprivor community. This has bearing, obviously, on the whole question of "international responsibility." See p. 114.

[113] 307 F.2d 845 (2d Cir. 1962).

[114] Same, 866-67. The court was able to conclude from a "quite significant" lapse of ten weeks time between the nationalization of an American-owned sugar enterprise and similar Cuban-owned enterprises that Cuba had pursued "discrimi-

Another important variable may be the duration of deprivation. Anyone concerned with the deprivations in Eastern Europe after World War II and more recently in Indonesia, for example, has had to consider whether so-called temporary (as opposed to permanent) deprivations—that is, measures passing under such rubrics as "detention," "intervention," "protective custody," "supervision," or "conservation" —engage or mitigate "international responsibility."[115]

Finally, understandings about the duration of special relationships may affect expectations about commitment and, hence, about the feasibility, if not the legality, of particular deprivations. Strong expectations of continuity may make disregard of certain relationships (formal and informal) wholly impolitic. On the other hand, short-range commitments may command less respect and thereby make renunciation an attractive choice. A key issue in the dispute over Egypt's nationalization of the Suez Canal Company in 1956, for example, was whether the Company's concession and related agreements required that the Company be allowed freely to operate the Canal until 1968.[116]

Institutionalization. To consider the institutional framework within which deprivations take place, it is unnecessary to mount a detailed description of formal governmental structures, the traditional subject matter of the political scientist. The activities which bear upon the deprivation function cut across so many branches, departments, and agencies of government that it is difficult, if not impossible, to relate them to these formalisms with any meaningful precision. For analytical purposes, therefore, it is better to look upon "institutions" not as formal structures, but as specialized patterns of practice (integrated and recurring perspectives about, and ways of doing, certain things) which, traversing formal structures, demonstrate both positive and negative impact upon the production and distribution of values within and without territorial communities. Given our present

---

natory" or "retaliatory" objectives, notwithstanding the court's admission that "[a] short lapse of time between similar provisions in the same program, standing alone, would not create discrimination." For a discussion of some of the inadequacies of the court's holding in this regard, see Dawson and Weston (fn. 24), 63, 88-91.

115 As to Eastern Europe, see, e.g., "In the Matter of the Claim of Sabine G. Helbig," Claim No. Hung-20,590, Decree No. Hung-941, Foreign Claims Settlement Commission of the United States [hereafter cited as FCSC], *Tenth Semiannual Report to the Congress for the Period Ending June 30, 1959* (Washington 1959), 51 (Final Decision). For a discussion of some of the problems pertaining to this temporal issue, particularly with reference to Eastern Europe, see George C. Christie, "What Constitutes a Taking of Property Under International Law?" *British Yearbook of International Law*, XXXVIII (London 1962), 307. As to Indonesia, see Board of Editors, *Nederlands Tijdschrift Voor Internationaal Recht* (fn. 31).

116 See generally, *The Suez Canal Problem* (fn. 78).

reference, analysis must of course seek to isolate and describe those practices that actually environ and, hence, condition the deprivation of foreign wealth.

Particularly conspicuous is the practice of hosting foreign invest-ment. Most often the target of deprivation will have been originally received on an informal basis within a setting involving relatively wide but tacit understandings about accepted modes of operation and about the necessity for mutual tolerance and self-restraint. Sometimes, however, special promises (explicit and implicit, exclusive and non-exclusive, etc.), perhaps inappropriate for wider participation, have been tendered by way of express invitation, as in the case of loan agree-ments, concessionary joint-venture and "know-how" contracts, or "instruments of approval."[117] At other times, a middle course has been struck through more inclusive promises in commercial and other treaties or in investment codes and other municipal laws[118]—perhaps even in mere official utterances.[119] Consider also the practice of depriva-tion itself. Sometimes it is major in scope, affecting vast economic sectors and requiring the mobilization of extraordinary collaborative effort. At other times it is less comprehensive (in absolute and relative terms) and but part of routine procedure. Sometimes, too, it has been highly circumscribed by constitutional and statutory designations both general and detailed in character. In other cases few if any stip-ulations have been articulated, thus leaving wide disparities from one deprivation to another in the procedures of prescription and applica-tion. Finally, no consideration of the institutional environment would

---

[117] See, e.g., A. A. Fatouros, *Government Guarantees to Foreign Investors* (New York 1962), Chaps. 5, 6 [hereafter cited as *Government Guarantees*]; Fatouros, "The Quest for Legal Security of Foreign Investments—Latest Developments," *Rutgers Law Review*, XVII (Winter 1963), 257, 268-75. See pp. 118-21.

[118] See pp. 121-24.

[119] See, e.g., *Ceylon Ministry of Planning and Economic Affairs, Government Policy on Private Foreign Investment* (Ceylon, March 1966), reprinted in *Inter-national Legal Materials*, V (Washington, July 1966), 591. In light of subsequent events, consideration might also be given to the numerous speeches and press con-ferences of Dr. Fidel Castro on the occasion of his "unofficial" visit to the United States after his swearing-in as Prime Minister of Cuba in early 1959. In the com-pany of his Ministers of Finance and National Economy and the President of the Central Bank of Cuba, Dr. Castro repeatedly stressed that his Government would not only *not* "confiscate" foreign property but would actively promote foreign in-vestment in Cuba in order to provide for the greater employment of his people. See *Keesing's Contemporary Archives* (July 11-18, 1959), 16901, Pt. A., col. 1. Similar assurances are often published as advertisements in leading commercial and financial publications abroad; for example, in the Sunday financial pages of the *New York Times*. Still another illustration is seen in a 1955 "statement of policy" of the Burmese Council of Ministers in which the Council expressly as-sured that it would "guarantee new enterprises against nationalization for an agreed period which will normally be not less than ten years." *Burma, Statement of Policy of June 8, 1955,* 4 (a).

be complete without accounting for the underlying socioeconomic and political system prevailing within the deprivor community—whether it is more or less monocultural or multicultural, monopolistic or pluralistic, collectivist or capitalist, authoritarian or democratic, monolithic or polycentric, and so forth.[120]

The point is that, notwithstanding historical and cultural diversities, the institutional environment within which deprivations are imposed can be found to exhibit characteristic differences in the degree to which controlling practices are patterned or unpatterned, stable or unstable, centralized or uncentralized, organized or unorganized—or, in a word, institutionalized.[121] The point is of crucial importance, for out of respect for the differences that distinguish the institutional levels of pertinent practices (and, consequently, for the similarities that bind them together) comes both a policy-relevant delimitation of the aptness of past "precedents" and a richer appreciation of the extent to which particular practices have reached a plateau of "normalcy" (or stability) from the standpoint of community expectation, departure from which *may* be lawful or, in any event, explicative of deviant behavior.

Crisis. In many cases, to be sure, little or no crisis surrounds the deprivation of foreign wealth. But to the extent that crises or expectations of crisis do influence such deprivations, they must be considered. These crisis situations can be conveniently divided into two working categories: those involving conflict and those involving no conflict.

The nub of the first category is that conflict (short- and long-term) between the host community and any one of three broadly typed adversaries is the parent of deprivation. These may be briefly noted.

First are deprivations which are the intended or unintended outcome of conflict between the host community (as deprivor) and the home community of the deprivee. The illustrations that come most immediately to mind are the wealth losses sustained by "enemy subjects" in the conduct of declared and undeclared hostilities.[122] But

120 It should be recalled that these institutional factors are among the many environmental conditions which should be considered, *ex hypothesi*, when approaching the identification and description of deprivor participants. See pp. 47-52.

121 This is not to say that a high degree of organization is necessarily the *summum bonum* of an institutional environment. Some decisions are better made and executed at low organizational levels. The point is stressed because of the popular tendency to equate effective and efficient, if not lawful, operation with highly structured order.

122 See McDougal and Feliciano (fn. 14), 587-610; Julius Stone, *Legal Controls of International Conflict*, rev. edn. (New York 1959), 434-41, 451-54. Consideration should also be given to deprivations inflicted in the course of foreign "belligerent occupation." See Stone, same, 706-19; McDougal and Feliciano (fn. 14), 809-32.

deprivations caused by crises "short of war" can also be included in this conflictual context. The struggles between the Netherlands and Indonesia in 1957-58 and between the United States and Cuba in 1959-61 are exemplary.[123]

Second, foreign-wealth deprivations have resulted from conflict between the host community and third party communities (communities of which the deprivee is not a member). Thus have nonparticipating ("neutral") aliens suffered wealth losses during periods of violent belligerency.[124] So too have they been deprived during less intense conflicts, as were British and Dutch nationals during the United States-Cuban encounter of 1959-60.[125] Two points relevant to this general conflict situation should not be overlooked, however. On the one hand, the host community may or may not be the manifest (i.e., actual) deprivor. Either of the protagonists or their agencies may perform this function, and the identification of the "responsible" party becomes then an essential task for decision. On the other hand, foreign-wealth owners are not always (or do not always remain) "neutral," with the result that they may themselves become primary antagonists in the conflict and for this reason alone the targets of deprivation. Following her rise to power in South Africa in 1902, for example, Great Britain (via its Transvaal Commission) "cancelled" a Dutch company's railway concession in the Transvaal and refused indemnity therefor because of that firm's admitted "organized hostilities" against the British during the Boer War.[126]

Finally, foreign-wealth deprivations have resulted from conflicts between the host community and internal factions. This is most evident during "revolutions," "civil wars," "rebellions," and other variants of intense internal disorder.[127] Again, however, the host community (in terms of the preconflict elite) may or may not be the actual de-

[123] While military authorities were sometimes the executors of deprivatory policy in both Indonesia and Cuba, while guerilla warfare against the Sukarno and Castro regimes was carried out by native dissident elements with more or less covert assistance from the Dutch and American governments, and while expectations of violence between these countries were ever-present, in neither case during these years did the Dutch-Indonesian or American-Cuban conflicts reach the level of open armed hostilities.

[124] McDougal and Feliciano (fn. 14), 435-519. Stone (fn. 122), 434-41.

[125] See *The Times* (London), July 2, 1960, p. 8, col. 3; same, July 4, 1960, p. 10, col. 1.

[126] "Netherlands S. A. Railway Company Ltd.," *Report of the Transvaal Concessions Commission*, Command No. 623 (1901), 33.

[127] See, e.g., the many deprivative disputes arising in this context in the references listed in footnote 41. Of these, see particularly Opinions of Commissioners under the Convention Concluded September 10, 1923, between the United States and Mexico, as extended by the Convention Concluded August 17, 1929 (April 26, 1926 to April 24, 1931), U.N.R.I.A.A., IV, 783-914.

privor, thus creating further problems of identification. Again, too, foreign deprivees have not always been nonparticipating, as the famous *Affaire Cerruti* makes clear.[128]

Of course, when approaching any of these conflict situations, one is struck immediately by the unhappy but traditional dichotomy between the so-called state of war and state of peace, upon which ostensibly hang distinct and mutually exclusive sets of rules about the deprivation of foreign wealth. However, the difficulty with this supposed state of affairs, as many have observed, is that it does not faithfully mirror the world in which we live. "War" and "peace" are but polar opposites in a continuum of policy-relevant stages, and the task of responsible decision is to ascertain the many nuances within that continuum which may determine the policies that are and should be prescribed and applied.[129]

As indicated, however, the crises which sire foreign-wealth deprivations need not be conflictual. History abounds with situations that are without conflict but which are nevertheless critical because they evince a marked and sometimes unexpected disruption of social processes capable of provoking deprivations in major and minor degree. This is not to say that nonconflict crises are never the product of conflict, for indeed they most often are. It is, simply, that they are not in themselves characterized by conflict in the adversative sense that this term has been used above. Some illustrations should make this distinction clear. In the celebrated *Oscar Chinn Case*,[130] for example, the cataclysmic depression of 1929 and the years following prompted Belgium to grant protective rate reductions and rebates to economically threatened fluvial transport enterprises in the Belgian Congo—measures which, though held not to be the cause of the economic loss sustained by the British claimant, Mr. Chinn, were at least arguably responsible therefor.[131] Consider also the spate of nationalization and other deprivative measures unleashed in Eastern and Western Europe (against aliens and nationals alike) by the ravaging effects of World War II, once dubbed "the greatest social shock yet felt by mankind."

[128] Italy v. Colombia, Moore, *Arbitrations* (fn. 32), 2117, U.N.R.I.A.A., XI (1897), 377. Colombian officials "occupied," "pillaged," and "sequestered" the property of Cerruti, an Italian national, because of his participation in internal revolutionary activities.

[129] Notwithstanding this observation, deprivations undertaken in the more intense conflictual contexts are mentioned here more for purposes of comprehensiveness than of analysis. Inasmuch as they involve policies substantially distinct from those applicable in "peacetime" situations, they have been treated as falling outside the ambit of this essay.

[130] P.C.I.J., Ser. A/B, No. 63 [1934].

[131] See J.L.F. Van Essen, "A Reappraisal of Oscar Chinn," in *Symbolae Verzijl* (The Hague 1958), 145.

Prominent, too, have been the major deprivations pressed in Mexico, the Soviet Union, Bolivia, Cuba, Algeria, and elsewhere over the last half-century in the generally crisis-ridden atmosphere of postrevolutionary upheaval. These illustrations are obviously not exhaustive. But other examples are not necessary to support the point that non-conflict crises, like the previously noted conflict crises, exhibit varying degrees of character and intensity, and that these variations do and should affect the prescription and application of authority. This, regrettably, is a matter that has thus far received only haphazard attention.

STRATEGIES

As the ancient debate about ends versus means makes abundantly clear, how participants pursue their objectives in any process of interaction must necessarily be of fundamental importance—often primary importance—for policy recommendation and decision. At any rate, the strategies that deprivors employ can of themselves be decisive in characterizing particular schemes as "lawful" or "unlawful." A call for discrete analysis is therefore axiomatic.

In the wider global wealth process within which the Process of Deprivation takes place, foreign-wealth deprivations are themselves economic strategies *par excellence*, of course. This is much emphasized by the leading commentaries. Indeed, this has been the principal if not sole emphasis of "strategy inquiry" in this field, with little or no attention given to the strategies *of* deprivation as such. Looking upon the deprivation phenomenon as a means rather than as an end in itself (that is, other than as the immediate objective of deprivor policy), few have sought systematically to account for the multiplicity of subservient or instrumental techniques by which, through action or refusal or failure to act, deprivations are themselves imposed. But as observers dedicated to the rational delineation of variables which do and should affect the prescription and application of authority about the permissibility or impermissibility of deprivative action or nonaction, it behooves us to do so.

The particular shape that strategies *of* deprivation may take depends, to be sure, upon a wide variety of conditioning factors, not the least being the perspectives or objectives of the deprivors themselves. Nevertheless, they can be conveniently typed and appraised in terms of the various instruments of policy that are commonly employed in most global interactions: diplomatic, ideological, economic, and military.[132] By this typology we can account both for the "direct

[132] For use of these categories in analyzing other processes of interaction, see McDougal and Feliciano (fn. 14), 309-30; McDougal, Lasswell, and Vlasic (fn. 14), 416-36.

taking" and for the increasingly but still insufficiently considered "indirect," "de facto," "surreptitious," or "creeping expropriation" whose distinguishing characteristic usually involves, at once or over time, the denial of access to, use of, or benefit from wealth processes and institutions (rather than the deprivation of wealth itself) and/or the spoliation of values other than wealth but upon which the production, conservation, distribution, and consumption of wealth vitally depend.[133] Whether or not the latter may be so classified in fact, however— whether particular exercises of public power may properly be held to be the functional equivalent of a "direct" deprivation—depends largely on the purpose of the measure involved. And this, as suggested above, requires (among other things) the careful evaluation of the perspectives or objectives of the alleged deprivor. As will be seen, most of these measures concern use of the economic instrument.

The *diplomatic* instrument groups together a number of deprivation strategies whose common distinguishing feature involves the use or nonuse of signs and acts which, short of actual force, are communicated directly to the potential deprivee or his surrogate. Here, for example, may be included all of those essentially persuasive and combined rituals of legislation and adjudication which generally obtain in one form or another, with varying "due process" and unilateralism, wherever organized legal systems are found (e.g. "eminent domain" condemnations or "forced" loans and sales). They are, indeed, by far the more common of all deprivor strategies, daily headlines notwithstanding. But strategies of direct negotiation between the concerned parties, as when forfeitures are explicitly or implicitly preordained in concessionary and other technical agreements[134] or when more or less

---

[133] Compare Fatouros (fn. 117), 167 n.202, who, citing Stanley Metzger, "Multilateral Convention for the Protection of Private Foreign Investment," *Journal of Public Law*, ix (Spring 1960), 133, 157, accepts "the virtual impossibility . . . of defining with precision the meaning of 'indirect' expropriation." For the only known extensive study of the complex issues of "creeping expropriation," see Luis J. Creel, Jr., " 'Mexicanization': A Case of Creeping Expropriation," *Southwestern Law Journal*, xxii (Spring 1968), 281. For an indication of some of the author's findings, in connection with postwar French international claims practice, see Weston, *International Claims: Postwar French Practice—Adjudication by National Commissions* (Syracuse 1970).

[134] See, e.g., Article 18 of the Contract between Yacimientos Petroliferos Fiscales (the Argentine Government petroleum agency) and Pan American International Oil Company of July 21, 1958, which provides that "[o]n expiration of this contract for the periods mentioned all the equipment, constructions and installations of the COMPANY used in compliance with the agreement shall become the property of Y.P.F. free of charge." *International Legal Materials*, iii (Washington 1964), 359, 362. It deserves mention that, together with several other oil production contracts granted to foreign firms by the Argentine Government during the presidency of Arturo Frondizi, this agreement was declared null by President Illía in 1963 pursuant to Argentine Decree No. 744/63. *International Legal Materials*, iii (Washington 1964), 1.

compulsory sales agreements are drawn,[135] are also employed. Not to be forgotten, either, is the possibility that mere threats of deprivation may serve as effectively as any other technique to bring about liquidation or deprivation in fact.[136]

Use of the *ideological* instrument concerns the creation and dissemination of symbols, slogans, and doctrines for the purpose of altering the identification, demand, and expectation patterns of local audiences vis-à-vis foreign-wealth ownership. Compared to other instruments, it has seldom been consciously employed in this context. Usually it has been limited to situations involving high intensities of crisis, with its frequency, as well as the shape and effectiveness of particular component strategies, depending on such factors as the availability and permeability of communication media. But some examples are well known: for one, the deliberate fomenting (concealed and unconcealed) of boycotts of foreign enterprises in a manner calculated to destroy or severely impair the continuity or well-being of foreign-wealth operations;[137] for another, as exemplified in the Indonesian-British "confrontation" over the formation of the Federation

---

[135] See, e.g., the Contract for the Sale of American and Foreign Power Company Properties in Brazil to Centrais Electricas Brasileiras S.A. (a duly authorized agency of the Brazilian Government) of November 12, 1964. *International Legal Materials*, IV (Washington 1965), 72, or the agreement for the sale of assets of P. T. Shell Indonesia to the Indonesian Government of Djakarta December 30, 1965, *International Legal Materials*, V (Washington 1966), 1136. The latest most publicized example of the more or less compulsory sales agreement is the recent contract between the Government of Chile and the Anaconda Mining Company, of June 26, 1969. See *New York Times*, June 27, 1969, p. 1, col. 1. See also "Chilean President's Statement on Negotiations for Government Acquisition of Anaconda Company Properties (June 26, 1969)," *International Legal Materials*, VIII (Washington 1969), 1073.

[136] See, e.g., The Mavrommatis Jerusalem Concessions (fn. 32). As noted earlier, the case concerned an option expressly granted by the British Palestine authorities to one Rutenberg to "annul" any preexisting concessions that might be found to conflict with his own. While the Court decided that claimant Mavrommatis (who held such a preexisting concession) was not entitled to compensation based on this threat because he had failed to prove any loss resulting therefrom, it nevertheless noted, 39, that "a right on the part of M. Rutenberg to require at any time the expropriation of pre-existing concessions . . . interfered with the right of holders of pre-existing concessions to utilize their concessions as such without being threatened with annulment," thereby leaving the clear impression that under appropriate circumstances threats as such may prove effectively deprivative. Support for this view is found in Mariposa Development Company and Others (United States v. Panama), *Hunt's Rep.* 573 (fn. 32), 338, wherein the U.S.-Panama Claims Commission stated, by way of dictum, that, though it would not ordinarily so find, it would "not assert that legislation might not be passed of such a character that its mere enactment would destroy the marketability of private property, render it valueless and give rise forthwith to an international claim. . . ." Same, 342.

[137] Consult Clement L. Bouvé, "The National Boycott as an International Delinquency," *American Journal of International Law*, XXVIII (January 1934), 19.

of Malaysia, the apparent official incitation of citizens to demand the deprivation of, or to riot against, the holdings of resident aliens.[138] By definition the emphasis is in this regard "indirect" rather than "direct."

As indicated, however, it is in connection with the *economic* strategies of deprivation that we find most of the claimed "indirect takings"; that is, the denial of access to, use of, or benefit from wealth processes and values for the alleged purpose of depriving aliens of the "use and enjoyment" of their wealth as effectively as if they had been subjected to outright seizure. Notable, for example, have been cases in which communities have established public and private monopolies to the manifest detriment of existing foreign concerns.[139] At other times, as in *Czechoslovakia v. Radio Corporation of America*[140] and in the case of *Marguerite de Joly de Sabla*,[141] they have granted special privileges to their own or other favored nationals in claimed derogation of existing foreign contractual and other "rights." Conspicuous, too, are measures that have placed foreign wealth under "national administration" or public "supervision," "management," or "control," as in Eastern Europe after World War II and, most recently, in Indonesia,

[138] See *The Times* (London), September 17, 1963, p. 12, col. 1; same, September 18, 1963, p. 12, col. 1. See also footnote 32. Such tactics would today seem especially possible when government-owned operations are involved. See the table prepared by the U.S. Department of State entitled "Damages to U.S. Government Buildings Overseas through Mob Violence, Riots, or Other Causes Since July 1962, Indicating Date, Place, and Damage," and reproduced in the *Congressional Record*, CXI, 1965, 468-69.

[139] See, e.g., Correspondence between Great Britain and Sicily, relative to the Sulphur Monopoly in Sicily [1893-40], *British and Foreign State Papers*, XXVIII (London 1857), 1163; [1840-41], same, XXIX (London 1857), 175; and Correspondence between Great Britain and Sicily, relative to the claims of British subjects for losses consequent upon the Sulphur Monopoly in Sicily [1841-42], same, XXX (London 1859), 111; The Savage Claim (United States v. Salvador) [1865], Moore, *Arbitrations* (fn. 32), 1855. On the establishment of a state-owned life insurance monopoly in Italy in 1911, see Edouard Clunet, *Consultation Pour Les Sociétés D'Assurances sur La Vie Etablies en Italie* (Paris 1912); E. Audinet, "Le Monopole des assurances sur la vie en Italie et le droit des étrangers," *Revue Générale Droit International Public*, XX (Paris 1913), 5; Gaston Jèze, "De la responsabilité pécuniaire de l'état italien envers les nationaux et les étrangers à raison de l'établissement d'un monopole public des assurances sur la vie," *Revue du Droit Public et de la Science Politique*, XXIX (Paris 1912), 433. Cf. Hans Wehberg, *Das Völkerrecht und das italienische Staatsversicherungsmonopol* (Vienna 1912). On the proposed establishment of a state-owned life insurance monopoly in Uruguay in 1912, see Jèze, "Le Monopole public des assurances en Uruguay," *Revue Scientifique et de Législation Financière*, XI (1913), 12; Georges Scelle, "A propos de l'établissement du monopole des assurances en Uruguay," *Revue du Droit Public et de la Science Politique*, XXX (Paris 1913), 637. See also Edwin M. Borchard, *The Diplomatic Protection of Citizens Abroad* (New York 1915), 125-26, and references cited therein.

[140] [1932], *American Journal of International Law*, XXX (July 1936), 523.

[141] United States v. Panama, *Hunt's Rep.* 573, U.N.R.I.A.A., VI (1933), 338.

Cuba, and Syria.[142] Of course, these by no means exhaust the economic techniques that may be employed for deprivative purposes. Any number of others *may* serve the same goal: compelling reorganization or liquidation of business enterprise; insisting upon domestic participation in the management and labor of foreign enterprise; disallowing sales without official consent; refusing to grant or renew necessary licenses; "blocking" or "freezing" vital assets; limiting the remission of capital and capital yield; prohibiting the importation of capital, materiel, or personnel; levying extraordinary taxes, tariffs, or other exactions; repudiating public issues and other debts; boycotting businesses; imposing prohibitive rate and price restrictions; diverting rental or other income; delimiting permissible zones of operation; and so forth. Whether such measures *do* serve the same deprivative goal is, surely, the primary question. But it is important at least to recognize that they *can* serve such goals.

The *military* instrument embraces all strategies which involve the use of direct force, ranging from the most mild to the most severe application (e.g., mere physical occupation or gun-point eviction). The amount of force applied, however, will generally depend on the nature and scope of the objectives being pursued, as well as, *inter alia*, the institutionalization and crisis situations within which values are being demanded. Essential for rational inquiry, therefore, is a determination of the degree of coercion that may be mete and proper in given contexts. It may be that the "wanton, riotous, and oppressive" official invasion and destruction of an alien's property, as per *Walter Fletcher Smith v. Compañía Urbanizadora del Parque y Playa de Maranao*[143]

---

[142] As to Eastern Europe, see, e.g., In the Matter of the Claim of Renata Estes, Claim No. CZ-4115, Decree No. CZ-3192, FCSC, *Seventeenth Semiannual Report to the Congress for the Period Ending December 31, 1962* (Washington 1962), 245 (Final Decision), following, Public Law 85-604 Panel Opinion No. 6; FCSC, *Eleventh Semiannual Report to the Congress for the Period Ending December 31, 1959* (Washington 1959), 28. As to Indonesia, see the article by the Board of Editors of the *Nederlands Tijdschrift Voor Internationaal Recht* (fn. 31). Mr. A. Sastroamidjojo of Indonesia protested the introduction of this article among the working papers of the Committee on Nationalization and Foreign Property of the 48th Conference of the International Law Association on the grounds *inter alia*, that "[i]n no instance has the Government of Indonesia proclaimed the nationalization of Dutch enterprises or any forced transfer of title over Dutch properties in Indonesia. The Indonesian Government has merely assumed supervisory control over Dutch-owned enterprises to assure their continued operation, especially in time of emergency." *International Law Association, Report of the Forty-eighth Conference* (New York 1958), 154. As to Cuba, see among others, Christie (fn. 115), 307. As to Syria, see the *Wall Street Journal*, December 9, 1966, p. 4, col. 1, reporting the Syrian "seizure" of property of the Western-owned Iraq Petroleum Company on a "nominal" basis that "didn't rule out the possibility of total nationalization in the future."

[143] United States v. Cuba, *American Journal of International Law*, XXIV (April 1930), 384, U.N.R.I.A.A., II (1929), 913.

is unlawful generally; or as Aneurin Bevan put it about a year after Suez, "if the sending of one's police and soldiers into the darkness of the night to seize somebody else's property is nationalisation, Ali Baba used the wrong terminology."[144] On the other hand, this is not to say that the use of force is or should be impermissible under international law in all cases.

A DISTINCT categorization of deprivative strategies, as above, can easily be deceiving. It would be wrong to assume that the various techniques employed are, and always remain, independent of each other. To the contrary, though they sometimes operate in isolation (particularly when diplomatic strategies are involved) they are most frequently employed in varying combination and sequence, especially when the so-called indirect approach is followed. The measures applied by the Soviet Union against the British-owned Lena Goldfields Ltd. in 1929 afford a classic example in this regard. In 1925, at the time of its relatively "conciliatory" New Economic Policy, the Soviet Government granted Goldfields a long-term concession to conduct vast mining and transportation operations within Soviet territory. In 1929, however, the Five Year Plan was introduced, and this "meant the development of the U.S.S.R. and of all its industries, commerce, banking, agriculture, transport, and indeed its whole economic life on purely Communistic principles, and brought with it a bitter class war against capitalistic enterprise and everyone connected with such enterprise."[145] But the Soviet Government chose not to confront Goldfields directly. It looked to indirect means instead. First, the ideological instrument was used. The firm was attacked in the press as an enemy of Communism, with the Russian people being asked to treat it as an economic outcast. Next, the economic instrument was applied. Sole purchaser of the company's yield and principal supplier of the company's needs, the Soviet Government refused to buy or supply anything. Further, it persuaded and pressured Russian employees to quit their employment. Finally, resorting to the military instrument, the Soviet Federal Political Police (O.G.P.U.) raided Goldfields' offices, seized Goldfields' documents, and terrorized what remained of Goldfields' employees. The end was inevitable. Goldfields withdrew. The Soviet Government acquired all.

OUTCOMES

The outcomes of this intial subprocess of the Process of Deprivation may be seen to refer most generally to the *immediate* results that

---

[144] Great Britain, *Parliamentary Debates* (Commons), 5th Ser., 570 (1957), 680.
[145] Lena Goldfields Arbitration [1930], set forth in the Appendix to Nussbaum (fn. 30), 31, 46.

actually obtain in particular cases. They are penultimate to the special and general "effects" (or structural consequences) that affect not only the immediate parties but all participants in the wider global wealth process.

One way of tabulating these outcomes might be to assess the extent to which deprivors succeed, if at all, in realizing the value demands that trigger their deprivative actions in the first place. But, while clearly relevant to total appraisal, an assessment of net value gains (or losses) immediately accruing to deprivors does not seem the most useful means for clarifying the fundamental legal policies that are here at stake. Moreover, in many cases—especially when deprivations are components of radical economic reorganizations—assessment may not even be possible. Whether or not State A, having undertaken deprivations against the nationals of State B for purposes of, say, overall economic betterment, increased economic control and/or wider international prestige, succeeds or fails in achieving increased welfare, greater power and/or heightened respect (more or less) is a question that can seldom be answered until a considerable period of time has elapsed— time enough at least to account for what are usually protracted responses and counterresponses. Better suited to policy clarification at this juncture, therefore, is an identification and appraisal of the wealth and possibly other value deprivations actually sustained by deprivees and their associates in the particular case. While this is not to suggest that there is always a one-to-one correlation between deprivor gains and deprivee losses, there does remain truth in the adage that what is one man's gain is another man's loss. The point is that by focusing upon deprivee losses rather than deprivor gains we can more easily anticipate the post-Outcome process of deprivee response which invariably follows. Knowing what specific deprivations have been imposed, if any, we are in a better position both to explain the intensity of deprivee response and to appraise its permissibility.

Preliminary, of course, is the need to determine whether a deprivation has been imposed at all, in fact or effect. Indeed, this is the primary issue which decision-makers must face when approaching any of the preceding phases of the Process of Deprivation heretofore discussed. Whether the alleged deprivee has already been satisfactorily repaid, whether a deprivation took place when first projected, or whether a particular tax was in fact excessive and so deprivative, are all exemplary of questions which bear upon this basic issue. Also essential is the further question of causal relation; whether the deprivee's loss is, in whole or in part, the outcome of the particular encounter upon which attention is focused or whether it can be attributed to other causes.[146] Hovering over and undoubtedly influencing the judgment of the Permanent Court of International Justice in the *Oscar Chinn Case*,[147] for example, was the question of whether "the loss and damage complained of by Mr. Oscar Chinn [were] the outcome of the measures for which the Belgian Government is blamed" or whether they were due to "the [1929] economic crisis and the decision taken of his own account by Mr. Chinn to close down certain branches of his business...."[148]

Assuming, however, that a deprivation is sustained and that it is the result of the particular measures complained of, there still remains for consideration the specific type or types of loss actually suffered. Naturally, the nature and degree of injury will vary between cases, ranging from the most mild to the most extreme. But the key questions which bear upon these critical considerations will remain the same: What, in fact, are the wealth losses which have been sustained? Are they important or unimportant? Are they partial or complete? Are they temporary or permanent? Has more than one foreign owner been deprived? If so, how many and who are they? Have the deprivees mitigated their damages in any way, either before or after the fact? What other values, if any, have been adversely affected and with what effect? And so forth. Important, in sum, is the necessity of facing squarely all the variable consequences of deprivation that are relevant to the overriding question to which decision-makers are commonly asked to respond, to wit: what is the nature and degree of relief, if any, that is warranted by authoritative community decision? Certainly no satisfactory solution to this question can be found without comprehensive assessment of the entire factual background of the particular case (both retrospective and prospective within the framework here recommended). But it is at least facilitated by describing as precisely as possible what it is that is really at stake and demanding of protection insofar as foreign deprivees and their associates are concerned. Description in terms of the value categories employed above, it is believed, provides a meaningful instrument for clarifying not only the specific prejudice which the manifest deprivee (private or public) has been made to suffer, but also the wider interests which may be at stake—more meaningful, in any case, than description in terms of the normative ambiguities of legal technicality.

146 For as Edwin M. Borchard is reputed to have said, "[e]very man whose property rights are diminished thinks that there has been a 'confiscation.'" Quoted in J. C. Witenberg, "La protection de la propriété immobilière des Etrangers," *Journal du Droit International Privé*, LV (Paris 1928), 566, 579.

147 P.C.I.J., Ser. A/B, No. 63 [1934].

148 Same, 68. See also the discussion concerning the decision in The Mavrommatis Jerusalem Concessions in footnote 136.

It is, of course, endemic to the process here being considered that *wealth* (in the sense of base resources and the yield therefrom) should be at the vortex of all values capable of being damaged or destroyed by deprivative devices. On the one hand, foreign nationals have been denied possession, if not "ownership," of a great variety of resources at their disposal: "tangible" and "intangible," "contractual" and "noncontractual," "movable" and "immovable," "real" and "personal," etc. Land, mineral resources, raw materials, emblements, livestock, buildings, vessels, machines, equipment, goods, so-called industrial, artistic, and literary property, commercial licenses, concessions, bank deposits and other credits, securities and cash itself are among the many which come to mind. On the other hand (or in addition), they have been denied the yield or income ordinarily derived from these factors of production. Indeed, this is usually although not inevitably the case whenever base resources are damaged or divested. Sometimes, however, it is the yield alone that has been the target of deprivation. Proscriptions on the use of base resources, limitations on profits, rentals, and royalties, moratoriums on interest (temporary and permanent)—all are familiar examples.

Were we to follow traditional inquiry, this description (with minor exception) would end the matter. To judge from the leading commentaries, wealth—i.e., "property as the subject matter of loss"—is virtually all that is at stake. Yet nothing could be more erroneous. True, the loss of wealth as such is the central concern. But in many cases wealth is neither the sole nor even the most critical value at stake. We cannot afford to ignore the spoliation of other values (well-being, skills, enlightenment, power, respect, rectitude, and affection) upon which the ultimate focus of our concern—the production, conservation, distribution, and consumption of wealth—so vitally depends. It is of course impossible wholly to separate the loss of these other values from the loss of wealth itself. Whenever there is a deprivation of wealth as such, whether by direct or indirect means, there is likely to be at least a partial loss of some or all other values, and probably a total loss in the case of a foreign national having no other wealth operations within the deprivor community (the effective scope of which must be realistically identified if precise appraisal of the extent of injury is to be had). In sum, it is not simply wealth which forms the "subject matter" of deprivation, just as it is not wealth alone which forms the "subject matter" of investment. All the values which form the basis of deprivation and, hence, of protective demand, must be considered. Otherwise, a decision-maker whose obligation it is to respond to a world of real acts and events will be unable to make a sufficiently rational policy choice.

Again it is convenient to distinguish between the now familiar welfare and deference values. We may do so to highlight the general point that additional or wider—and, hence, perhaps more consequential—interests may be affected by deprivations of the latter than the former. Whereas concern for the forfeiture of wealth and other welfare values has been limited largely to the foreign owners themselves (private and public), concern for the sacrifice of deference values has often extended beyond the owners to their own and sometimes other national communities (the former communities being sometimes hereinafter referred to as "deprivee communities"). Admittedly, this tends to contradict the venerable notion that injury to an alien represents a diminution of the total welfare of all the members of that alien's home community. Yet as Dunn once remarked,

> this concern which we feel whenever one of our fellow-citizens sustains injury at the hands of a foreign government is seldom in fact based on any conscious judgment that the material interests of the nation have thereby been damaged. It is more often a manifestation of the group consciousness that is represented in the concept of nationality, and is in some degree connected with the idea of relative prestige and importance of the group as compared with other competitive groups.[149]

Of course, the extent to which this observation has validity depends upon the importance that affiliated national communities attach to the values appropriated by the foreign government. In the case of the Anglo-Iranian Oil Company nationalization, for example, the British Government was itself the principal owner of the properties appropriated by the Iranian Government in 1951 and, hence, quite naturally possessed a direct and strong concern.[150] And in the case of the nationalization of the formally private Suez Canal Company, substantially owned by the British and French governments, exceedingly critical public interests were at stake, both for the deprivee communities themselves and for other national communities. The strong British

149 Frederick S. Dunn, *The Protection of Nationals* (Baltimore 1932), 39.

150 Ford, writing in 1954, stated that in 1914 "the British government acquired a 53 per cent interest in the company which it has continued to hold." (Fn. 97), 16. This interest represented great value in monetary terms. "In 1950 alone, the [Anglo-Iranian Oil] Company derived a profit of between $500 million and $550 million, or between £ 180 million and £ 200 million, from its oil enterprises in Iran, at international market prices," or in other words, "after deducting the share paid to Iran [i.e., 'only $45 million, or about £ 16 million as royalties, share of profits, and taxes'] . . . more than the entire sum of £ 114 million cited by the representative of the United Kingdom as the total sum paid to Iran in royalties in the course of the past half-century." Allahyar Saleh, U.N. Security Council, *Official Records*, 6th year, 563d meeting, October 17, 1951, 15.

protest to the Egyptian Government on July 27, 1956 made this abundantly clear: "The Egyptian Government have promulgated a law purporting to nationalise the Suez Canal Company. . . . H.M. Government protest against this arbitrary action, which constitutes a serious threat to the freedom of navigation on a waterway of vital *international* importance."[151] In such cases, obviously the old argument prevails that the welfare of the total community has been diminished. In general, however, the distinction here drawn does bear considerable validity.

Welfare Values

Of the remaining welfare values which have been exposed to deprivation and for which protection has been demanded, *well-being* (in the sense of enterprisory continuity and security) is perhaps the most apparent and, from the standpoint of foreign entrepreneurs, perhaps the most critical. As has frequently been pointed out, assurance of enterprisory well-being is often the single most important determinant of foreign investment, profit incentives notwithstanding.[152] But the loss of *skills* (in the sense of developed proficiencies in, or the liberty to acquire, particular techniques and practices designed to cope with general and specific problems) and *enlightenment* (in the sense of the freedom to procure or disseminate insight, knowledge, or information pertinent to local economic, political, cultural, or technological conditions) is also of high importance and should not be over-

[151] Quoted in *The Times* (London), July 28, 1956, p. 6, col. 1 (emphasis added). See also text at footnote 161. Significantly, it has been reported that the British Government owned 44 percent of the shares of the Suez Canal Co., *New York Times*, October 9, 1966, p. 17, col. 4. For extensive details, see Thomas (fn. 78).

[152] Basing their conclusions on a 1952 U.S. Department of Commerce survey of over 400 American firms having operations abroad, their own investigation of some 40 such American companies, and a number of individual case studies, Barlow and Wender have listed "the most important reasons" for investing abroad in the following descending order:

(1) Maintenance of markets for companies in the manufacturing field; (2) Availability of raw materials for companies in the extractive field; (3) Expansion of existing operations within a particular country to meet greater needs; (4) Development of foreign markets for present product lines; (5) Instigation of others desiring the company to operate within a particular country; (6) Possibilities of unusually large profits. Edward R. Barlow and Ira T. Wender, *Foreign Investment and Taxation* (Englewood Cliffs, N.J. 1955), 146.

See also the Department of Commerce Survey, *U.S. Department of Commerce, Factors Limiting United States Investment Abroad*, Pt. 2 (Washington 1954). For more recent indications of the importance of factors contributing to enterprisory well-being, see Jack N. Behrman, "Foreign Associates and Their Financing," in Raymond F. Mikesell, ed., *U.S. Private and Government Investment Abroad* (Eugene, Ore. 1962), 77, 88-91; National Industrial Conference Board, *Obstacles and Incentives to Private Foreign Investment 1962-1964* (New York 1965).

looked. Especially is this true of enterprises for which specialized skills and knowledge are decisive for successful operation. The deprivation of any of these values, like the deprivation of wealth itself, is bound to be strongly resisted. Not only are they (like other values) supportive of wealth values, but none are easily obtained by even the most affluent investors.[153]

Deference Values

As noted, the deprivation of deference values (power, respect, rectitude, and affection) implicates not only the interests of the deprivees themselves, but often, as well, the interests of their own and sometimes other national communities. In part, as the above quotation from Professor Dunn implies, this situation can be traced to that hazy nexus which exists between these values and the concept of nationality—a concept of group consciousness or "tribal solidarity" that inherently makes for wider identification. In earlier times, this may have been a sufficient explanation. But recent experience suggests that it is both this and something more—briefly, that deprivations today, particularly those of large scale, have become closely allied with the whole politico-ideological range of postcolonial and cold-war conflict about the proper ordering of these and all other values in international relations generally. Obviously, this is a conflict which threatens interests far wider than those of the immediate deprivees. Given the frequent

[153] Alfred P. Sloan, Jr., former President of General Motors, has given us a glimpse of some of the basic hurdles involved:

> Looking back on the rapid growth [of the Overseas Operations Division of General Motors] during the past four decades, one might regard our progress overseas as a kind of natural and inevitable extension of our progress in this country. In reality, there was nothing at all inevitable about it. . . . In building up our Overseas Operations Division, we were obliged, almost at the outset, to confront some large, basic questions: We had to decide whether, and to what extent, there was a market abroad for the American car—and if so, which American car offered the best growth prospects. We had to determine whether we wanted to be exporters or overseas producers. When it became clear that we had to engage in some production abroad, the next question was whether to build up our own companies or to buy and develop existing ones. We had to devise some means of living with restrictive regulations and duties. We had to work out a special form of organization that would be suitable overseas. All of these problems were considered fully within the corporation for a period of several years in the 1920's when basic policies were established. *My Years with General Motors* (Garden City, N.Y. 1963), 313-14.

See also the *Wall Street Journal*, August 20, 1968, p. 1, col. 1, for a current brief survey of the variety of routine difficulties encountered by American companies establishing ventures abroad. For a detailed study of the process of investment decision in the underdeveloped world, see Henry G. Aubrey, "Investment Decisions in Underdeveloped Countries," in Moses Abromovits, ed., *Capital Formation and Economic Growth* (National Bureau of Economic Research, Princeton 1955), 397.

link between severity of outcome and the intensity of response, consideration of these wider interests is also imperative.

Power. Consider, first, how and to what extent foreign-wealth owners may themselves be made to suffer a loss of power when deprivations are imposed. While naturally the nature and degree of such loss will depend on the strategies of deprivation employed, among other things, there are nonetheless at least two broad and interrelated patterns that can be drawn.

First, deprivation *may* mean a total loss of power or control over enterprisory activity as such. Indeed, this is the usual consequence of any wholesale enterprisory deprivation, whether effected by direct or indirect means. But the word "may" is used advisedly for two reasons. On the one hand, deprivations need not involve the wholesale appropriation of all enterprisory activity. A deprivation of but one or even a number of specific factors of production, for example, or of but one or more of a number of operational components, for another, while probably causing a loss of control over these factors and components, does not mean that there must be a complete loss in overall enterprisory control.[154] In such cases, of course, the single or combined importance of the factors or components commandeered must be carefully weighed since it is possible that their loss will prejudice, perhaps irreparably, the enterprisory control which can in fact be wielded overall, even though the indicia of such control have not been divested in any formal sense. On the other hand, it is at least possible to conceive of situations of total or partial enterprisory deprivation in which deprivors, by payment of certain remunerations, would wish to retain prior management to insure continuous effective operation. Several nationalizations in post-World War II Britain, for example, involved little actual change in this and other respects and, in the process, provided for a great deal of uninterrupted managerial decentralization.[155] As Katzarov has observed, "[i]t is important to determine whether [the] com-

[154] The 1963 Ceylonese nationalization of American and British-owned petroleum installations, for example, appears to have been limited to the appropriation of 108 Caltex, Esso, and Shell filling stations near Colombo, some storage facilities, and a pipeline. It did not involve the wholesale take-over of the foreign operations as such. For the texts of the pertinent Ceylonese legislation, see *International Legal Materials*, I (Washington 1962), 126; same II (Washington 1963), 951. See also *Keesing's Contemporary Archives* (December 1-8, 1962), 19115, Pt. A, col. 2; same (October 5-12, 1963), 19667, Pt. A, col. 1. According to one report, this meant that only about 20 percent of the entire Caltex and Esso installations in Ceylon were affected. *New York Times*, January 12, 1963, p. 9, col. 2. Caltex and Esso officials claimed, however, that this represented about 50 percent of the total worth of the American-owned facilities, due principally to the proximity of their filling stations to downtown Colombo traffic.

[155] See Lewis (fn. 60), 48-52; Robson (fn. 45), 78-118.

panies continue to exist after nationalization in a modified form or whether they cease to exist, and also whether there is any link between the companies and the new legal subjects responsible for the national-ised activities."[156] In many cases, to be sure, neither of these reserva-tions, nor the potential significance that they bear for the nature and degree of community protection warranted, holds true. Where the deprivation of an enterprise and the cognate value of enterprisory control is complete, the loss of power in this sense is rarely if ever singled out for special concern. But, somewhat paradoxically, when a deprivation affects only certain features of enterprisory activity, the loss of power in this sense appears (at least from the standpoint of the deprivee) to assume added significance. This is so if for no other rea-son than that most investors appear to insist upon complete or near-complete control over their foreign operations as the *sine qua non* of profitable enterprise.[157]

Second, foreign-wealth owners may lose power in the sense that they may suffer a total or partial loss of effective economic and/or political influence either within the deprivor community as a whole or within the local or world markets to which they are specialized, perhaps with-in both spheres. While the conditioning variables are many, much will depend upon the relative size and importance of the holdings appro-priated. As regards loss of influence within the deprivor community, for example, such injury will most likely be felt by the behemoth for-eign enterprise that commands a dominant, if not monopolistic, con-trol over the economic and political life of the host community.[158] Indeed, if any one-to-one correlation between deprivor value de-mands and deprivee value losses is anywhere to be found, it is here. And as regards loss of influence within local or world markets to which deprivees are specialized, likely as not it will be the small or individual entrepreneur who will suffer the most harm. Possessed prob-ably of little economic and political power, even a minor or temporary deprivation could prove ruinous of his ability to cope profitably with local or world market competition. Of course, these illustrations are but polar extremes of a many-leveled continuum of investor size and importance. Whether or to what extent power will be sacri-

---

[156] Katzarov (fn. 44), 172. See generally same, 172-79.

[157] See Behrman (fn. 152), 91-95.

[158] For an indication of the extent to which foreign enterprise sometimes domi-nates the life of a host community, see Robert Engler, *The Politics of Oil* (New York 1961), 183-84, wherein the author quotes extensively from a sales letter of Time, Inc., for the purpose of demonstrating the broad influence of the Arabian-American Oil Company in Saudi Arabia. See also Detlev F. Vagts, "The Multi-national Enterprise: A New Challenge for Transnational Law," *Harvard Law Review*, LXXXIII (February 1970), 738.

ficed in one or both of these spheres is bound to vary from case to case. What matters for policy is that the scope of inquiry include both a recognition and an assessment of the possibility and effect of these kinds of value losses.

The importance of this second inquiry is not limited to the manifest deprivees alone. It is in the sense of a loss of politico-economic influence that deprivee communities, too, may suffer injury to their power position when deprivations are imposed. Again, while the nature and degree of this loss will vary, two separate and interrelated patterns are apparent.

First, as above, it may mean a loss of effective influence within the deprivor community. On the one hand, this could be the natural consequence of the very manner in which deprivations are effected. The "Yanquiphobic" zeal which charted Cuba's seizures of American-owned holdings in 1959-60, for example, was surely contributory to (though by no means wholly explanatory of) the virtual elimination of effective United States influence within Cuba in the years since. But the loss can also be born of the special relationship which may exist between the foreign-wealth owner and his home government. As any student of international affairs well knows, foreign investors (particularly large corporate investors), whether in the heyday of the British East India Company or in the present era of the Arabian American Oil Company (Aramco), have often served as informal emissaries for, if not alter egos to, their own governments.[159] Referring to American enterprise abroad, Sigmund Timberg observed over two decades ago: "Particularly in the international sphere, corporations, whether they rely on American capital alone or involve cooperative international commitments, should be regarded as not only the carriers of their own private interests, but instrumentalities for effectuating social and economic [and political] interests which the national and international community regards as paramount."[160] Obviously, the deprivation of operations

[159] On the essentially public politico-economic functions performed by Aramco in Saudi Arabia particularly, and in the Middle East generally, see George Lenzowski, *Oil and State in the Middle East* (Ithaca 1960), 113-17; Benjamin Shwadran, *The Middle East, Oil and the Great Powers* (New York 1955). On the role of the modern corporation as a "private government," with special reference to overseas operations, see Arthur S. Miller, "The Corporation as a Private Government in the World Community," *Virginia Law Review*, XLVI (December 1960), 1539. Professor Miller provides abundant and rich references.

[160] Sigmund Timberg, "Corporate Fictions: Logical, Social, and International Implications," *Columbia Law Review*, XLVI (July 1946), 533, 580. To like effect, Timberg has more recently written:

England, Holland, and the other great trading powers of the seventeenth and eighteenth centuries were delegating *political* power to their foreign merchants, when they permitted those merchants to engage—collectively and under the

performing such functions may well have the effect of damaging, perhaps critically, the overall influence that their home governments can wield within the deprivor community.

In addition, one or more deprivations may seriously threaten the power posture of a deprivee community not only in relation to the deprivor community, but in relation to the world at large as well. Especially is this likely when economic interests vital to the nation's everyday welfare are at stake, even more so when those interests play an important role in the never-ending drama of international power politics. As former British Prime Minister Sir Anthony Eden declaimed to the House of Commons shortly after the Suez crisis of July 26, 1956:

> [T]he cause for the anger and alarm felt, not only here but among the Governments and peoples of the democratic world, at the action

---

corporate aegis—in foreign trade. In Maitland's classic phrase, there were "the companies that became colonies, the companies that make war." The same proposition holds for the modern large corporation. The modern state undeniably delegates *political* power to large private corporations, as it does to the large labor unions with which the corporate behemoths deal. The authorization of collective activity has, at least since the time of the early Christian and Jewish communities had their difficulties with the Roman Emperors, always been a state prerogative. Furthermore, the activities authorized for a large corporation involve such functions as price-fixing, the division of markets, the setting of wages, and the general development of local communities, functions which in a pre-Industrial Revolution era had been the primary responsibility of the State. It has been said of international cartels that some of the more powerful of them "are little empires in themselves, and their decisions are often more important than those of 'sovereign, political' entities like Holland, Denmark, or Portugal." "The Corporation as a Technique of International Administration," *University of Chicago Law Review*, xix (Summer 1952), 739, 742.

See also Baum (fn. 71); Vagts (fn. 158).

A glimpse of some of these "political" functions, as performed by large foreign enterprises, has been given us by an erstwhile official of the Standard Oil Company of New Jersey:

Regular contacts are maintained with economic representatives in the important United States embassies throughout Europe and with national bodies in the different nations responsible for energy matters. Valuable contacts and communications have been developed with government quarters in Washington and with the U.S. Regional Office and special embassies in Europe charged with representing United States interests in the main supranational groups. These are based on confidence and friendly relations between managements and local government departments which provide constructive backing for activities at the international level. U.S., Congress, Senate, *Joint Hearings on Emergency Oil Lift Program before the Subcommittee of the Senate Committee on the Judiciary and Committee on Interior and Insular Affairs*, 85th Cong. 1st Sess., Pt. 2, February 5-March 22, 1957, 1039.

For a general treatment of "the blending of public and private abroad" insofar as the worldwide petroleum industry is concerned, see Engler (fn. 158), Chap. 8.

of the Egyptian Government is due to the special character of the Canal. . . .

As the world is today, and as it is likely to be for some time to come, the industrial life of Western Europe literally depends upon the continuing free navigation of the Canal as one of the great international waterways of the world. . . . Last year, nearly 70 million tons of oil passed through the Canal representing about half the oil supplies of Western Europe. Traffic through the Canal moved at the rate of 40 ships a day and amounted to 154 million tons of shipping—prodigious figures. Nor does this traffic affect the West alone. Australia, India, Ceylon and a large part of South-East Asia transport the major proportion of their trade, or a large proportion of their trade through the Canal.

Therefore, it is with these reflections in mind that I must repeat the carefully considered sentence which I used in the House on Monday last, if I may quote it again:

> "No arrangements for the future of this great international waterway could be acceptable to Her Majesty's Government which would leave it in the unfettered control of a single Power which could, as recent events have shown, exploit it purely for the purposes of national policy."

This is still our position, and it must remain so.[161]

Here appropriated, then, were values of primordial importance to the overall economic and political strength, not merely of the manifest deprivees themselves, but of the entire national communities with which they were affiliated and even, indeed, of nations having no phyletic involvement whatsoever. What is more, as the subsequent twenty-two-power London Conference alone made clear, these interests weighed heavily in the wider cold-war contest for world power, generally, and for greater politico-economic influence in the "unaligned" Third World, specifically.[162] Under such or similar circumstances, one is led rhetorically to ask, as elsewhere, whether and to what extent traditional learned commentaries about "property as the subject matter of loss" are sufficient for policy clarification and decision.

---

[161] Great Britain, *Parliamentary Debates* (Commons), 5th Ser., 557 (1956), 1602, reprinted in *1956 Documents on International Affairs* (London 1959), 126. For further details, see Donald C. Watt, ed., *Documents on the Suez Crisis* (Royal Institute of International Affairs, London, 1956).

[162] See, *The Suez Canal Problem* (fn. 78). See also John G. Stoessinger, *The United Nations and the Superpowers* (New York 1965), 62-74; Thomas (fn. 78); Yves Van der Mensbrugghe, *Les Garanties de la Liberté de Navigation dans le Canal de Suez* (Paris, 1964), 87-99.

Respect. Just as demands for respect figure prominently among deprivor objectives, so is respect a value much cherished among foreign-wealth owners and their nation-states. Indeed, it is the threatened or actual loss of respect in its most comprehensive sense that lies at the heart of all deprivee concern—hence the oft-mentioned plea of "respect for acquired (or vested) rights."

In an overarching sense, then, all deprivations involve a withdrawal of respect from foreign-wealth owners. By definition they are disrespectful of the continuous possession of wealth. But a denial of respect in this rudimentary sense is not the concern here. Presumably, considerations relevant to this point—e.g., the "public" or "private" character of the foreign-wealth owner or the presence or absence of contractual or other promises not to deprive—shall have already been entertained. Our present focus, at least insofar as the manifest deprivees themselves are concerned, is upon those deprivations that withdraw respect from foreign-wealth owners in a secondary sense: principally, those which are said to be "discriminatory" because they are premised on such "human rights" considerations as race, creed, color, caste, status, or nationality and/or because they deny "equality of treatment" as between different groups of wealth owners, whether in terms of the implementation of the deprivative measure or in terms of the rendering of compensation due (if any), or both. Of course, what constitutes a "discriminatory" deprivation is a thorny question, one that has troubled international law scholars and practitioners for years. Still more difficult is whether a "demonstrably discriminatory" deprivation is of a kind against which community protection is warranted. Few are so easily judged as those that were imposed by National-Socialist regimes upon Jewish nationals and aliens several decades ago. In a complex international society where countless special environments create countless specialized experiences and perspectives about the substance of "simple human respect," manifestly there are no easy answers. In any event, few will be found without reference to the entire factual and authoritative background of the particular case. What matters is that we understand that the possibility of such deprivations, especially in this era of xenophobic nationalism, quite plainly exists.

As indicated, however, it is not the foreign-wealth owner alone who may suffer a loss of respect. The respect which a deprivee's nation-state can command from others may also be threatened when deprivations occur. This can be illustrated in at least two distinct but related dimensions.

On the one hand, the challenge may be to the respect position of the deprivee government (in contrast to the national community as a whole). Faced with deprivations to which it knows it is expected to respond, it may and often will feel constrained to prevent the impression from getting about that its interests and the interests of those it claims to represent may be mistreated with impunity. Potentially at stake are all those ephemeral but nonetheless fundamental notions and emotions (if not basic assets) of honor, status, prestige, and esteem, and perhaps, therefore, even self-preservation itself.[163] These are values which are seldom lightly relinquished, and the confirmative pattern has been traditionally to respond with promptness, firmness, and sometimes forcefulness—a pattern that may be, and often is, quite disassociated from any conscious perception of the economic loss itself.[164] Of course, the extent to which the elites of deprivee communities will feel their respect position threatened in this way and what manner of response they will choose will depend, as usual, upon a great number of variables. In relation to their own citizenry, much will depend on whether their control is democratic or authoritarian and whether the society for which they speak is pluralistic or totalitarian. And in relation to the inhabitants and elites of other nations, the success or failure of a government's past international encounters (deprivative and otherwise) and the degree of hostility with which the deprivations are themselves imposed will have considerable bearing.

It is in this last connection, indeed, that we find the second threat dimension alluded to above. On occasion the very dignity and worth of an entire national community for which a deprivee's government acts as surrogate—all the composite identifications, demands, and expectations—may be called into fundamental question. This is especially noticeable when, because of a host of different grievances, the deprivations are directed against a particular nationality group, as has increasingly happened in recent years. At a public gathering in Cuba in 1960, for example, at the time when American holdings were being nationalized in avowed retaliation for alleged United States "economic aggression," Premier Castro (among others) attacked "North American imperialism" as "the enemy of humanity," declaiming that "[w]e no longer believe in your lies . . . your false democracy, murderer

[163] On the importance of these factors as basic "policy aims" in international relations, see Ernst B. Haas and Allen S. Whiting, *Dynamics of International Relations* (New York 1956), 59-64.

[164] For an indication of French sensitivities in this regard following the nationalization of the Suez Canal Company in 1956—e.g., "Enough! This is enough! We will take no more defeats. It is time for a victory."— see Herbert Luethy and David Rodnick, in Lloyd A. Free, ed., *French Motivations in the Suez Crisis* (Princeton, December 1956), 59-101. For British reactions, see generally, Leon D. Epstein, *British Politics in the Suez Crisis* (Urbana 1964); Thomas (fn. 78).

of Negroes . . . your false liberty, sower of tyrants on our continent . . .
your hypocritical philosophy, which protects a Franco as well as a
Trujillo . . . your films from Hollywood. . . ."[165] The crisis for United
States reputation lay not alone in the reservoir of disenchantment that
was being built up against the United States within Cuba, but also in
the contagion of disrespect for American institutions, public and private, which such charges (given a certain credibility by the nationalizations themselves) tended to spawn beyond the geographic confines
of the immediate context, particularly as to institutions affiliated or
otherwise identified with the proclaimed symbols of "North American
imperialism."[166] Subsequent United States policy, whether in terms
of the abortive Bay of Pigs invasion or the more helpful *Alianza
para el Progreso* (the main purpose of which was to improve living
standards in order to avoid Fidelista-type upheavals elsewhere in Latin
America), may be seen as having been guided substantially by a desire
to redress the loss in respectability which the United States had been
made to suffer.[167]

Rectitude. Generalizations are always hazardous. But it is not unduly misleading to say that, with only very recent exception, deprivees

[165] Quoted in *Keesing's Contemporary Archives* (December 3-10, 1960), 17788,
col. 1.

[166] The point has been succinctly recognized by one commentator in a leading
American public utility journal:

> For many years now the handwriting has been on the wall for foreign opera-
> tors of electric power and other utilities in Latin America. It is believed in
> many quarters that in due time about all electric power will be government-
> owned and -operated south of the Rio Grande and as far as Puntas Arenas.
> Foreign investors, who earlier in this century were virtually the sole suppliers of
> electric power in this area, have long been locked in—hostages to local national-
> ism and resentment against "rich foreigners." These investors have been victims
> of domestic Latin American politics; of national economic and monetary mis-
> management causing dollar erosion, exchange control, and inflation; of com-
> munist propaganda and always latent anti-Americanism, although the victims
> have not been only American investors. The largest aggregate U.S. investments in
> Latin American public utilities have been those of the American & Foreign
> Power Company ("Foreign Power"), now operating in 11 of those countries.
> What Cuba's Castro has done to Foreign Power's Cuban subsidiary, Cia. Cubana
> de Electricidad, and to the mother company's earnings thus far is a sad lesson
> to international investors; and what more still lies ahead we do not venture to
> predict. Herbert M. Bratter, "Latin American Utilities' Nationalization Proceeds
> Inexorably," *Public Utilities Fortnightly,* LXVI (July 7, 1960), 1, 1-2.

[167] On the "Alianza para el Progreso," see the address by President Kennedy on
March 13, 1961, at a White House reception for Latin American diplomats and
members of Congress and their wives, *Department of State Bulletin,* XLIV (April 3,
1961), 471. As Professor Karst has written, "[t]he Alliance, as Fidel Castro boasts
and despite regular official denials, was a reaction to the Cuban revolution."
Kenneth L. Karst, "Latin-American Land Reform: The Uses of Confiscation,"
Michigan Law Review, LXIII (December 1964), 327, 328. See generally Tad Szulc,
The Winds of Revolution (Praeger 1963), 173-233.

and their communities have generally favored politico-economic creeds which, if not logically incompatible with governmental participation in the wealth process, at least vigorously endorse "private" or "free" market mechanisms in the ordering of economic and other values. As indicated earlier (and as will be elaborated later),[168] most of those who have sustained wealth deprivations in the past have come from the so-called liberal economies of the West where, in varying degree, "classical" theories about the "sacrosanctity of private property"—currently couched in terms of "free enterprise," "individual initiative," "the profit motive," "open competition," and so forth—have long been deeply embedded in popular and official thought. Particularly have they adhered in the comparatively conservative United States, probably the most important deprivee community today. But not exclusively. As Mario Einaudi has observed of post-World War II Western Europe generally:

> The tides of human affairs move slowly, and in a century that has seen the idea of private property modified and qualified and private property rights subjected to frequent restrictions and interpretations the ancient belief was kept alive in many political quarters that government was still confronted by an unchanging and rigid concept of property rights, and that the only way to go forward was to deal with title deeds as if they had the fearsome strength given them by the Napoleonic codes.[169]

Of course, it has been amply demonstrated (even in the United States) that these doctrines represent more the myth or "folklore of capitalism" than its reality.[170] But this is almost irrelevant to the fact that they can and do fundamentally condition how best to achieve the optimum satisfaction of human wants. Wealth deprivations, especially those born of socialist objectives, are seen to pose a serious threat to these capitalist-oriented notions of socioeconomic rectitude.

In any significant sense, however, this threat is of but relatively recent origin. Before World War I (or, more precisely, before the October Revolution), these notions were scarcely challenged in any practical sense. From the Code of Hammurabi (c. 1950 B.C.), belief

---

[168] See below, pp. 103-07.

[169] In Einaudi and others (fn. 45), 4.

[170] See Thurman W. Arnold, *The Folklore of Capitalism* (New Haven 1937); Daniel J. Baum and Ned B. Stiles, *The Silent Partners* (Syracuse 1965); David T. Bazelon, *The Paper Economy* (New York 1963); Adolf A. Berle, *The 20th Century Capitalist Revolution* (New York 1954); Berle, *Power without Property* (New York 1959); Berle and Gardiner C. Means, *The Modern Corporation and Private Property* (New York 1932); Earl Latham, *Political Theories of Monopoly Power* (College Park, Md. 1957); David Lynch, *The Concentration of Economic Power* (New York 1946); Andrew Shonfield, *Modern Capitalism* (London 1965).

in the absolute and exclusive control and disposal of private "vested rights" enjoyed an astonishing universality, and the importance of private wealth as the *sine qua non* of the social fabric scarcely wavered.[171] Whatever threats deprivations may have posed in this earlier era, they did not challenge fundamentally the ideological order of the day. But such has not been the case since 1917. Beginning in Mexico and the Soviet Union, wealth deprivations have come to represent a new and now constant challenge to these ancient faiths.[172]

It would appear, however, that the threat is not so theoretically restricted as it seems to have been in 1926 when, during an International Law Association discussion concerning the "inviolability of private property in international relations," it was asserted that the Soviet Union, because of its "attack upon this international agreement as to the sacredness of private property" and its failure to "agree with the common conscience of all other civilised nations upon this most fundamental question of morals and ethics," had "exclude[d] and excommunicate[d] itself from the society of civilised nations."[173] Even modern conservatives and spokesmen for "big business" would agree that the contemporary threat is not, as this assertion suggests, to some outmoded theory of "natural right."[174] The Lockean idea that "the right of private property" is "natural," and hence "inviolable," gave way long ago to Utilitarian, Saint-Simonian, and other "social function" arguments for a more equal distribution of wealth.[175] Today,

171 But see footnote 20.   172 See pp. 49-52.

173 *International Law Association, Report of the Thirty-fourth Conference* (Vienna 1926), 259. See also Sliosberg v. New York Life Ins. Co., 244 N.Y. 482, 499, 155 N.E. 749, 755, cert. denied, 275 U.S. 526 (1927): "[W]e do not think that the public weal requires that honest creditors should be made to abide the time when a law, inherently unjust and confiscatory, enacted by a governmental power then regarded as barbarous [i.e., the Soviet Union], might become an effective weapon of defense through the recognition of that power as a worthy member of the society of civilized nations."

As George Kennan has written, "In the twenties the Moscow communists had appeared to polite Anglo-Saxon society chiefly as a group of extremely bad-mannered people—anarchists and extremists, bristling with beards and bombs, misguided, motivated by all the wrong principles, unlikely to remain in power for any length of time, sure to be punished in the end for their insolent recalcitrance." *Realities of American Foreign Policy* (Princeton 1954), 24.

174 "The theorists employed by the National Association of Manufacturers to write *The American Individual Enterprise System* assert again and again that each man has a right to that which his own labour creates. But each time they qualify the classical theory: each man owns by right what he 'creates or *acquires*,' 'by his labour' or by his 'efforts' and 'activities,' 'either alone or in *co-operation with others*.' The qualifications are doubtless intended to adapt the theory in the light of modern facts. But they destroy whatever logical rigour the theory has and prove its uselessness as a defence of the modern capitalist system." Schlatter (fn. 55), 280-81.

175 "[T]he unconditional, inviolable nature of the right of property remains but one of those magnificent phrases which it is so easy to shout from the housetops

rather, the threat is conceived largely in terms of an assault upon liberty, upon freedom, upon democracy. Private ownership, it is argued, is essential for the defense of these values; collectivism breeds regimentation and the suppression of civil liberty.[176] "From the political and social point of view," writes *American* economist Eugene Staley,

> a vigorous growth of private business enterprise [in the underdeveloped countries]—provided it is widespread and not concentrated in a few hands—broadens the bases of political power, helps to create an independent middle class, promotes decentralization of authority and leadership, and helps to separate economic power from political and other forms of power. These are among the fundamental requirements . . . for development of democratic, free societies.[177]

A threat to private ownership, in sum, is a threat to political democracy. When seen in this light, the deprivation and particularly the socialization of foreign wealth assumes for many the color of that epochal conflict between collectivism and individualism which, with subtle variation, so divides our contemporary world.[178] It is this, indeed, which perhaps best explains why whole communities, as well as individual persons, may feel especially sensitive to the potential or actual deprivation of foreign wealth. It also helps to explain, subject to the intensity with which protection for individualistic values is demanded, the severity of response that sometimes ensues.

Affection (Friendship). After all that has been said, it seems almost superfluous to point out that the bonds of friendship that may exist between foreign-wealth owners or their nation-states, on the one hand,

---

in the enthusiasm of a revolution and in the dawn of constitutions, but which in the more sober aftermath it is impossible to live up to. It is well enough known that after 1789 laws and regulations of every country have imposed numerous and considerable restrictions on the right of property." Kruse (fn. 20), 7. To the same effect see Myrdal (fn. 69), 77-78.

[176] See, e.g., Friedrich A. von Hayek, *The Road to Serfdom* (Chicago 1944). Roger M. Blough, Chairman of the United States Steel Corporation, has stressed the nexus between liberty and economic progress in the following terms: "In a free society there is no other way than the voluntary corporate way. It is the key to a greater society. Any other way will constitute an abandonment of the voluntary way. . . . The voluntary cohesiveness and integrity of the productive group is vital. Without this we diminish for our society the values only competition can supply." *Free Man and the Corporation* (New York 1959), 122-24.

[177] Eugene Staley, *The Future of Underdeveloped Countries* (New York 1954), 239. Use of this quotation is not intended to suggest a doctrinaire attitude on Mr. Staley's part, for as he himself next states, "[t]o be *for* private enterprise is not the same thing as to be *against* enterprising government."

[178] See, e.g., Peter Adriaanse, *Confiscation in Private International Law* (The Hague 1956), 3-4; Dietze (fn. 42), 87.

and the inhabitants or elites of host communities, on the other, may be gradually or abruptly severed when deprivations are imposed. Nevertheless, a few remarks are in order. From the standpoint of the foreign-wealth owner, particularly those having a number of wealth operations within the deprivor community, deprivations may and often do mean not only the loss of goodwill among the general populace but also the erosion, if not the outright termination, of friendly cooperation with local governing elites (in the form, say, of tax relief, exchange concessions, and other special advantage). From the standpoint of the deprivee community, it may mean the severance of diplomatic relations or even the total disruption of peaceful intercourse. These are obvious points which require little elaboration. And it scarcely needs saying that the factors which qualify them are many. Among the more important, for example, is that it is sometimes less the deprivations themselves than other hard conditions (both immediate and long-standing) that are actually responsible for the losses incurred; deprivations may be more the consequence than the cause of ill will. This is the kind of question with which any decision-maker must be concerned, to be sure. But it is beyond dispute that deprivations can and do at least exacerbate enmities for months, years, and even decades to come—and at all levels.[179] Especially is this likely when they are unaccompanied by a payment or promise of indemnity or when they are pressed in seeming disregard of economic and social programs previously undertaken by the foreign parties out of demonstrable genuine concern for the needs of the host community. Whether and to what extent the values of friendly relations have been sacrificed, therefore, are questions which will necessarily have important bearing on policy clarification and decision.

EFFECTS

As mentioned above, the Effects phase of the Process of Deprivation may be said to refer to those post-Outcome structural consequences of deprivor activity that affect not only the immediate parties and their

---

[179] As Dunn, writing in 1933, has noted of U.S.-Mexican relations:

In the frequently troubled course of diplomatic relations between the United States and Mexico, no subject has been a more persistent source of controversy than that of the protection of American lives and property in Mexican territory. For a hundred years this subject has been almost continuously in the foreground of diplomatic discussions and has occupied more space in the official correspondence between Washington and Mexico City than any other. It has been intimately associated with all the major crises in the relations of the two nations and has led to sharp demands and threats of forceful action on a number of occasions. . . . It remains today perhaps the most serious threat to the continuance of harmonious relations between them. Dunn (fn. 70), 1.

associates, but in addition, all who participate in the wider global wealth process. As noted also, these consequences can be conveniently described and appraised in both special and general terms. It is to their separate consideration, then, that we may now turn.

Special Effects

Once a foreign-wealth deprivation is deemed possible or probable, or once it is actually imposed, there begins a process of response on the part of the deprivees, their communities, and others (the second subprocess mentioned earlier) that can have profound effect not only on the ultimate economic success or failure of the projected or imposed deprivation, but also on the aggregate flow of wealth activities within the deprivor and deprivee communities, specifically, and among all communities, generally. It might be argued that, so defined, this second subprocess is not altogether a "post-Outcome" phenomenon in that the reaction or response may not always be to a wealth deprivation actually sustained. But the argument would be unjustified. First, deprivor activity manifests a broad continuum of act and communication, ranging from the earliest contemplation to the later threat to the final confrontation, and any one or more of these stages may provoke a response. Second, this activity may or may not go so far as to involve injury to wealth as such, but possibly may harm other supportive values for which protection would be demanded. Finally, as indicated, the effect of this activity extends beyond the principal actors to parties who may respond simply because of real or imagined threats to themselves because of deprivations already imposed on others.

Description and appraisal of this second subprocess may be approached within the same framework used to describe and appraise the first subprocess heretofore noted. Separate and successive consideration may thus be given to the principal participants involved, their objectives, the situations which confront them, the strategies they employ, and the outcomes which flow therefrom.

Participants

As noted, the Special Effects phase of analysis is concerned mainly with the deprivees, actual and potential. Their precise identification, like that of the deprivors, is indispensable to the rational clarification of policy. Who they are may condition deprivor perspectives about the wisdom or importance of deprivation. Who they are may condition the feasibility or permissibility of deprivation. Who they are may condition the community protection warranted, if any. Who they are may condition both the character and intensity of their own response. And so forth. In sum, the identity of the deprivees is likely to condition practices (and so decisions) that are relevant to all phases of the Process of Deprivation (both retrospective and prospective as herein formulated).

In contrast to the deprivors, however, the deprivees appear somewhat less widely arrayed; as yet they appear not to have included international governmental institutions. Still, it is not amiss to suggest that such institutions, given the increased and proliferating activity of organizations like the International Bank for Reconstruction and Development (World Bank), the International Development Association (IDA), the International Monetary Fund (IMF), and the Inter-American Development Bank, may some day be subjected to deprivation.[180] The possibility seems particularly plausible in the case of international lending institutions whose financial credits could be unilaterally repudiated.

Actual past deprivees, however, are quickly identified. Most important and conspicuous are individual persons and private business associations. Even a cursory glance at the deprivations of the last century or more makes this abundantly clear: whether the Greek taking of the lands of the American Reverend Dr. Jonas King in 1835[181] or the myriad individual foreign losses in Eastern Europe following World War II,[182] whether the annulment and seizure of the British- and American-owned Delagoa Bay Railway interests by Portugal in 1889[183] or the "protective custody" seizures of the United States Rubber and the Goodyear Tire and Rubber plantations in Indonesia in 1965.[184] The individual human being is, of course, the ultimate deprivee. This is as true today as it was a century ago. But when we account for the recent burgeoning of corporate enterprise and institu-

---

[180] Wortley appears to be alone among the leading commentators to have noted this possibility, adding that, when they are so subjected, "the problem of protection will have to be faced; it would seem that, since the Advisory Opinion on Reparation for Injuries Suffered in the Service of the United Nations [(1949) I.C.J. 174], it would be less difficult to accord them the necessary international personality for the purpose of claiming reparation or restitution." Wortley (fn. 44), 151.

[181] For a synoptic account, see Moore (fn. 84), 262.

[182] For evidence of the many wealth losses sustained by individual United States citizens in Eastern Europe at this time, see the decisions reported in *Settlement of Claims by the Foreign Claims Settlement Commission of the United States and Its Predecessors 1949-1955* (Washington 1955) and in the semiannual reports of the United States Foreign Claims Settlement Commission published since 1954. For similar evidence in respect to British subjects, see Richard B. Lillich, *International Claims: Postwar British Practice* (Syracuse (1967). For similar evidence in respect to French nationals, see Weston (fn. 133).

[183] See Delagoa Bay Ry. (fn. 66), 903; La Fontaine (fn. 36), 398.

[184] See *New York Times*, February 27, 1965, p. 1, col. 5.

tional investment[185] (now on an extraordinary global scale[186]) we are forced to concede that the nexus between individual risk and individual loss is today much less clear than it was in the past. Today's individual deprivee must therefore be seen (more often than not) in terms of his membership—direct and indirect—as stockholder, partner, joint-venturer, and otherwise in a wide variety of different types of private business associations.[187] Private business associations, accordingly, are now the most important (and, if past trends are any indication, certainly the most likely) targets of public power.

Perhaps less conspicuous in this context, but no less noteworthy, are nation-states and their agencies. As is well known, they have many times suffered injuries, both severe and mild, to installations and materiel customarily reserved for the performance of official diplomatic and consular functions.[188] But sometimes they have been deprived of demonstrably commercial interests, as, for example, in the 1951 Iranian nationalization of the Anglo-Iranian Oil Company (better than 50 percent of the capital stock of which, as earlier noted, was then owned by His Britannic Majesty's Government).[189] Potentially significant in

[185] On the growth of institutional investment and its economic and political implications see Baum and Stiles (fn. 170).

[186] See Richard J. Barber, "Big, Bigger, Biggest—American Business Goes Global," *The New Republic* (April 30, 1966), 14. See also Howe Martyn, *International Business* (New York 1964).

[187] As A. A. Berle has confirmed,

[t]here is substantial evidence . . . that this is representative of the real pattern of the twentieth-century capitalism. The capital is there; and so is capitalism. The waning factor is the capitalist. He has somehow vanished in great measure from the picture, and with him has vanished much of the controlling force of his market-place judgment. He is not extinct: roughly a billion dollars a year (say 5 percent of total savings) is invested by him; but he is no longer a defensive force. In his place stand the boards of directors of corporations, chiefly large ones, who retain profits and risk them in expansion of the business along lines indicated by the circumstances of their particular operation. Not the public opinion of the market place with all the economic world from which to choose, but the directoral opinion of corporate managers as to the line of greatest opportunity within their own concern, now chiefly determines the application of risk capital. Major corporations in most instances do not seek capital. They form it themselves. (Fn. 170), 39-40.

See also Grant McConnell, *Private Power and American Democracy* (New York 1966), 127-34.

[188] See, e.g., the table prepared by the U.S. Department of State entitled "Damages to U.S. Government Buildings Overseas through Mob Violence, Riots, or Other Causes Since July 1962, Indicating Date, Place, and Damage," and reproduced in *Congressional Record*, CXI, 1965, 468-69.

[189] See footnote 150. As Fatouros has observed, however, "[i]t is interesting to note . . . that nowhere in its pleading before the International Court of Justice did the British Government refer to its control of the Company." Fatouros, *Government Guarantees* (fn. 117), 192, n.6. For another instance involving the deprivation of a state-owned enterprise, see The Panevezys-Saldutiskis Railway Case, P.C.I.J., Ser. A/B, No. 76 [1939]. In 1919, the then independent Lithuanian Gov-

this regard is the widening role that is being played by "state trading" agencies in the Soviet Union, the Eastern European countries, the People's Republic of China, and other countries involved in international economic exchange.[190] And obviously it bears recollection that, depending on the degree to which it perceives its vital interests to be at stake when its nationals are subjected to deprivation, the nation-state should also be considered within the deprivee category in an associative sense.

Of course, whether or not any of these particular participants—individual human beings, private business associations or nation-states—may be properly characterized as a "deprivee" in a given case is a question that has of itself often been of critical importance. Specifically, the appearance of additional participants by way of subsequent involvement, either as surrogates for, or as successors to, the manifest or actual deprivee (heirs and legatees, successor entities, surviving partners, assignees and grantees, subrogees, administrators and executors, guardians, etc.), is a common feature of daily life with which all decision-makers are obliged to contend. Accordingly, just as it is essential to identify precisely the persons or elites who presume to speak or act on behalf of the "deprivor," likewise must there be precise identification of the "deprivee." The importance this bears for policy may be seen in the fact that subsequent identifications can and do substantially influence not only the question of community protection warranted (if any), but, as well, the objectives that may be pursued in this second subprocess and the strategies that may be employed to achieve them. One need but reflect upon the role traditionally played by the nation-state as "subrogee" in the practice of "diplomatic protection" to see the relevance of this point.

As with the deprivors, however, mere identification of deprivee *types* is not all that is required for policy clarification. Again, richer indication in terms of who in particular they have been (or where they have come from) and how in detail they may be characterized would seem indispensable both to a proper understanding of the precedential

---

ernment "took possession" of a railway previously nationalized by the Soviet Government (before Lithuania, Estonia, and Latvia proclaimed their independence from the Soviet Republic) and alleged subsequently to have passed into the ownership of the Estonian Government. The court did not consider the implications of these relationships however.

190 On "state trading" generally, see the enlightening symposium in "State Trading," *Law and Contemporary Problems*, xxiv (Spring 1959), 241, 367. For a more recent discussion, see David M. Cohen, "Some Problems of Doing Business with State Trading Agencies," *University of Illinois Law Forum* (Fall-Winter 1965), 520. See also Sigmund Timberg, "Expropriation Measures and State Trading," *Proceedings of the American Society of International Law*, LV (1961), 113.

value of past trends in decision and to a fuller appreciation of the significant factors that have shaped deprivee perspectives toward all other phases of the Process of Deprivation.

The deprivees in the century preceding World War I (primarily private individuals and business associations) emanated almost exclusively from the major economies of the West. This is not surprising. With the acceleration of industrialization, improvements in agricultural technology, faster means of communication and transportation, and an increasing number and complexity of business and labor techniques, Western capital began alone during these early years what is now by comparison a universal search for foreign markets and investments. This was especially true after about 1870, for it was during this later period that foreign investment first assumed truly international proportions, contributing as it did to the final dismantling of the old mercantilist structure.[191] It was, as Douglass C. North has succinctly remarked, "the era of the *Crédit Mobilier* and its imitators not only in France but throughout Europe and America."[192] For the most part, however—as past controversies bear out[193]—the deprivees throughout the 1815-1914 era came from Great Britain and the United States; from the former mainly because of Britain's unquestioned preeminence as a financial, industrial, and naval power, and from the United States (which, though generally a net capital importer, became increasingly a capital exporter on a large scale) primarily because of its proximity to "Middle America" where, as seen, most of the foreign-wealth deprivations of this period took place.[194] This is not to say that traders and investors from other economic centers such as France, Germany, or Belgium did not also sustain deprivations during this century. Rather, it is to observe that they did not do so until about 1880 when, following Great Britain and the United States, their economic outlook first began to expand beyond the familiar horizons of their European neighbors and their politically homogeneous foreign possessions.[195] Even then, however, their aggregate losses were small by comparison.

In broad outline, the deprivees of the interwar period differed but slightly from those of the preceding era. As before, they originated

---

[191] Of course, the earlier Age of Discovery and the period of colonization which followed greatly expanded Western horizons. Mercantilism marked national policy, however, and for the most part this meant that "foreign" investment was limited to colonial territories over which the investors' "mother countries" exercised both formal authority and effective control.

[192] North (fn. 38), 10, 15. See generally Feis (fn. 67).

[193] See authorities cited in footnote 36.

[194] See pp. 47-49.

[195] For helpful statistics, see *International Capital Movements* (fn. 40), 1-2.

principally in the major economies of the West. Also as before, they were mainly private individuals and business associations (though with increased emphasis on the latter). But at least three distinctions can be noted. First, traders and investors from Western countries other than Great Britain and the United States came to shoulder proportionately a greater share of the losses inflicted. Entrepreneurs from France, Germany, Belgium, the Netherlands, Switzerland, and from most of the Central European countries from the Baltic to the Aegean could now be counted as deprivees also. Partly the result of the extensive agrarian reforms undertaken by the European "Succession States" and of the major deprivations imposed by the Soviet Union, this trend was also the function of a dramatic but steady upturn in both public and private overseas initiative on the part of these countries (particularly those of Western Europe) since about the end of the Franco-Prussian War.[196] Second, while continuing to rank with British nationals as the major targets of Latin American (primarily Mexican) power, United States nationals found themselves within the focus of *European* deprivative policy as well. This can be generally explained by two major developments. Most obvious is that by 1919, mainly as a result of World War I, the United States had become a major creditor power.[197] Less apparent, but no less significant, was the great surge of migration to the United States in the years preceding and immediately following World War I (particularly from Eastern Europe);[198] in the process, immigrants left behind relatives from whom they might inherit and, in some cases, substantial possessions. Third, a visibly greater proportion of the deprivees during this period, in contrast to those of the pre-1914 era, sustained deprivations because they held foreign public and private securities. The principal immediate explanation was the swift repudiation of public and private debts by the Soviet Union in 1918,[199] a measure which affected foreign

---

[196] Thus, while the British remained the largest single group of foreign investors, by 1914 the French had invested some $9 billion abroad, the Germans about $5.8 billion, and the Belgians, the Dutch, and the Swiss between them about $5.5 billion, compared to little or no foreign investments in 1874. Same, 2.

[197] Not only had Great Britain, France, and Germany each lost between $4 and $5 billion of their prewar holdings (representing about half of the French and nearly the entirety of German foreign investments), but, in addition, the United States invested heavily abroad, publicly and privately. In 1913-14, for example, United States long-term foreign investments had an "approximate value" of $3.5 billion. By 1919-20 these investments were estimated to have reached $6.5 billion. Moreover, by July 1921 the United States had granted an aggregate of some $10 billion in intergovernmental credits. Same, 4-6.

[198] See U.S. Census Bureau, *Historical Statistics of the United States* (Washington 1960), 56-57.

[199] The Soviet Government repudiated the debts owed by its predecessors on January 28, 1918. For the text of the decree, see Bishop (fn. 44), 140.

(particularly French and British) interests on a vast scale.[200] More fundamentally, however, this third distinction reflected the unique character of much of the foreign investment of the preceding decades. From the mid-1870's until early 1928 (excepting a 1914-20 hiatus) public and private portfolio (as distinguished from direct) investments came to occupy an increasingly dominant position in the movements of the international capital market.[201] This, in turn, was a reflection of the growing sophistication and complexity of international financial techniques.

The deprivees of the post-1945 era have conformed in most respects to the pattern that existed before World War II. Still they come principally from the major economies of the West.[202] Still they include primarily private individuals and business associations, though with yet greater emphasis on the latter. But again at least three general distinctions can be seen. First, even more Western European traders and investors have sustained yet greater and more frequent wealth losses than they did in the past. Partly the result of the immediate postwar Eastern Europe nationalizations, this has also been due to the extraordinarily rapid dismantling of ancient empires and the complementary rise of Asian, African, and Middle Eastern elites whose resentment for their old colonial masters has been singularly noticeable in recent times. Second, while United States nationals earlier assumed a major share of the wealth losses in Latin America and

[200] Bishop has provided a helpful table of the major creditors affected:

Principal Debts of the Russian Governments

	Prewar Government	Industrial	War Debts
Great Britain	14%	25%	70%
France	80	32	19
United States	—*	6	7
Belgium	—	15	—
Germany	—	16	—

* Approximately $2,600,000 of "4% Rentes of 1894" had been purchased by Americans.

Same, 141. For a quantitative tabulation of public and private American claims against the Soviet Government pertaining to "losses from repudiation and confiscation," see same, 142. For the manner in which private claims were ultimately disposed of, see FCSC (fn. 115).

[201] See Feis (fn. 67), 3-80; *International Capital Movements* (fn. 40), 1-34; North (fn. 38), 17-28.

[202] At least two recent exceptions to this particular pattern should be noted however. Within the last several years, Burma and Tanzania have nationalized Chinese and Indian properties, respectively, mainly because these foreign minorities were said to have had an economic and financial "stranglehold" over the economic life of these two countries. See *Keesing's Contemporary Archives* (February 20-27, 1965), 20602, Pt. A, col. 1; same, May 22-29, 1965, 20754, Pt. A, col. 1.

Europe, since 1945 they have emerged as major deprivees throughout the world. A number of factors can be said to account for this development: the devastation inflicted by World War II upon all other major economies of the East and West; the comparative security and stability which blessed the American economy during the war years; the resulting unprecedented preeminence of the United States as an economic power thereafter; the nexus between the Eastern European deprivations of 1945-50 and the migratory patterns of a generation or more earlier. Perhaps above all, however, the development reflects the new awakening to overseas opportunity and responsibility which has greatly shaped American public and private policy in the last two decades.[203] Pressing ever outward beyond familiar (but not always friendly) Latin American and European economies, United States nationals have found themselves, rightly or wrongly, more and more the objects of sensitivities heightened by a "revolution of rising expectations." Lastly, in contrast to the deprivees of the interwar period and earlier, a significantly greater proportion have in recent years suffered losses because of their direct, rather than indirect, ownership and control of foreign-based assets. The reason lies mainly in the fact that the preponderance of foreign-wealth deprivations since World War II—indeed, the apparent totality since 1951—have occurred in the underdeveloped regions of the world[204] where in earlier decades direct, rather than portfolio, investments predominated, principally in the agricultural, extractive, and utility sectors.[205]

In any particular case, of course, just as it is important to identify all the significant characteristics that shape deprivor perspectives, so is it necessary to survey systematically all the significant characteristics that shape deprivee perspectives (with particular reference to the deprivation of foreign wealth, specifically, and to participation in the global wealth process, generally). Accordingly, questions similar to those deemed pertinent to the deprivors should also be entertained here. Framed now in terms of the most important deprivee identified (the private business association) they might include the following: How is it organized? For what purposes is it organized? What is the geographic compass of its operations? What is its size and economic strength? To what degree can it control the market to which it is spe-

[203] See Raymond F. Mikesell, "U.S. Postwar Investment Abroad: A Statistical Analysis," in Raymond F. Mikesell, ed., *U.S. Private and Government Investment Abroad* (Eugene, Ore. 1962), 44, 51-55.

"During the period 1946 through 1958 the United States' share of the net outflow of capital on an international scale amounted to two-thirds of the total." Mooney (fn. 5), 152.

[204] See pp. 51-52.

[205] See, e.g., *International Capital Movements* (fn. 40), 28-34.

cialized? With what other enterprises is it associated, both within and without the deprivor community, and what is the character of those associations? What relations does it maintain with what nation-states? To what extent can it influence national decision, at home or abroad? And so on.

Again, obviously, more detailed questions must await the particular case. Again, our emphasis must remain essentially suggestive and commendatory.[206]

Objectives

As should by now be obvious, the basic objective of the deprivee—actual and potential, manifest and associate—is, generally, to avoid the imposition of deprivations altogether (lawful or unlawful) or, failing that, to reduce their potentially severe consequences. In other words, the goal is to protect an existing and/or future foreign investment position either by way of safeguarding access to, use of and benefit from wealth processes and values or by way of assuring maximum security for all the values which support or derive strength from the investment position, or both. But however obvious, thus identified the objective is too broadly put to be analytically very helpful. A lower order of goal abstraction is therefore desirable. This can be both efficiently and realistically achieved by referring to a number of more particular demands which, when satisfied, may be said to have advanced (more or less) the basic objective of protection: prevention, deterrence, restoration, rehabilitation, reconstruction, and correction.[207]

Each of these more particularized protection objectives can be generally distinguished in terms either of the location of events in time or of the scope of demand which they entail. They may be briefly noted now, leaving detailed illustration to subsequent discussion.[208]

The goal of *prevention* may be seen to refer to all those protective demands which, over a varying range of time, would forestall the

[206] See Horowitz (fn. 51), 39-41), for a "digest" of economic, political, social, and military factors characterizing the essentially capitalistic, parliamentary-democratic, western and professional-military "First World" from whence, as indicated, most deprivees have originated. To the extent that deprivees may originate elsewhere, however, see the equivalent "digests" for the "Second" and "Third" worlds. Same, 41-46.

[207] In other words, deprivee objectives involve more than demands for "compensation" and "restitution," the traditionally limited focus of most writers in this field. For use of the six categories in analyzing participant objectives in other processes of interaction, see McDougal and Feliciano (fn. 14), 287-96, 309-33; McDougal, Lasswell, and Vlasic (fn. 14), 404-06, 416-36. See also Richard Arens and Harold D. Lasswell, *In Defense of Public Order* (New York 1961), 199-203.

[208] How these particular goals have been pursued in actual practice is suggested at pp. 117-65. Detailed illustration at this juncture would only make for unnecessary repetition.

initiation of deprivation or minimize its consequences well in advance of any expectation of imminent injury.[209] Its calculus pertains to possibilities rather than to probabilities, and emphasizes the long-range alteration of host community predispositions (from the deprivative redistribution of wealth and cognate values to the acceptance of a minimum respect therefor) as the fundamental precondition of international economic intercourse.

Demands for *deterrence*, on the other hand, involve estimates of shorter duration. Though like those for prevention they relate to deprivations in the future, they nevertheless differ in that they are concerned with deprivations that are clearly threatened or imminently promised. They pertain to probabilities rather than to possibilities and, as such, envisage retrenchment from a posture already manifest.[210] As has been stated elsewhere, albeit in a different conflictual context, demands for deterrence "seek to modify the calculations of the challenger as to the probable consequences of particular available alternatives—e.g. executing his threat or withdrawing it and making some other proposal—in such a way as to lead the challenger, in the light of his modified evaluations, to choose the alternative of abstention and withdrawal. . . ."[211]

But when the potential deprivor is not effectively deterred and when deprivations are in fact imposed, the goal of *restoration* assumes immediate relevance. The object, then, is to compel the rollback of measures already begun (perhaps even to the extent of wholly eliminating the existing deprivor elite) and/or to generate acceptance of demands for reducing the severity of loss to more tolerable proportions.[212] This is not to say that restorative demands relate only to specific past deprivations. To the extent that they seek the cessation of continuing or additional deprivative activity on the part of the immediate deprivor, or to the extent that they seek to thwart the imitative effect that the particular deprivations may have upon like-minded elites elsewhere (within and without the instant deprivor community), they may be seen to be concerned with the future also. In a substan-

---

209 For practical illustration, see pp. 118-35.
210 For practical illustration, see pp. 135-40.
211 McDougal and Feliciano (fn. 14), 291.
212 For practical illustration, see pp. 140-51. It should be noted, however, that if and when the elimination of a recalcitrant deprivor elite becomes the major concern, efforts at accelerating settlement may take a subordinate position. As Engler has written of deprived foreign oil interests in Mexico in the late 1930's: "Some unreconstructed oil men in the Shell and Jersey Standard organizations apparently were in no hurry for a settlement. Thoroughly misunderstanding the temper of the people, they were hoping and planning for a counterrevolution or collapse that would bring back the ousted companies." Engler (fn. 158), 195.

tial sense, demands for the restoration of "normal" economic relations represent a continuation of the demands which characterize the goals of prevention and deterrence: the prospective restructuring of the perspectives of potential deprivors, both proximate and remote.

The objective of *rehabilitation* typically applies to situations in which the deprivees and their associates either have been successful in winning acceptance of their demands for the termination, reversal, deceleration, or revision of deprivative policies and programs or have been shown more or less unbidden tolerance from the start. The primary focus is upon securing the reparation of values deemed to have been wholly or partially destroyed by deprivative devices.[213] Again, however, the focus is not altogether past-oriented. The ability to obtain reparation, whether in terms of compensation for damage done or in terms of the surrender of gains realized, has often depended on the capacity and willingness of deprivees to shape their reparative ambitions to the short- and long-term needs and demands of the deprivor community for "ordinary" and "proper" economic intercourse. and this, in turn, has involved calculations about the possibility of, and about ways of avoiding, future deprivative action. In other words, the goal of rehabilitation embraces more than simple reparation based on preexisting outcomes. It includes, as well, the attempted adjustment of future economic interaction on terms that are favorable to all the parties immediately concerned.

In a sense, the goal of *reconstruction* is like the goal of prevention. Both are long-term, future-oriented propositions. Both involve demands for protection against the occurrence or recurrence of deprivations long in advance of any specific expectation of injury. But reconstruction demands differ from those for prevention mainly in the scope of the goals sought. Whereas those for prevention are made primarily within and with reference to a preexisting public order context, those for reconstruction are more comprehensive in that they aim to transform the public order itself.[214] In short, demands for reconstruction purport to affect more basic predispositional and environmental change, by facilitating new techniques calculated to encourage the redistribution of wealth and cognate values more by consensual than unilateral means, and by accelerating the removal of underlying conditions which may be believed to contribute to the initiation of deprivative programs in the first place.

[213] It is upon this goal, as indicated in footnote 28, that most writers concentrate. For practical illustration of the manner in which this objective is pursued, see pp. 151-58.

[214] For practical illustration, see pp. 158-64.

A sixth and final objective is the goal of *correction*. In an important sense, it differs little from all the other protection objectives because, like them, it concerns demands for the reshaping of deprivor perspectives in terms calculated to cause abstention from deprivation. Like them, too, it looks beyond the particular identified deprivor to all potential deprivors. But it differs from the other protection objectives in that it contains an element of retribution, of punishment—usually the result of a desire to express disapproval of the deprivor's conduct and thereby to discourage similar conduct in the future.[215] This is not to say that other protection objectives—particularly those of deterrence, restoration, and rehabilitation—are not themselves sometimes marked by revenge or punitive considerations. It is simply to observe that punitive demands can and do reach proportions distinctive enough to merit separate notice.

In the particular confrontation, of course, these protection objectives may be sought in varying combination and sequence. It would be wrong to assume that they must be found in isolation or that in respect to a particular identified deprivor they will always be pursued in the order here presented. For example, deprivees may first seek simultaneously to bring about a reversal or revision of deprivations already imposed (restoration) and to press for the repair of values already injured (rehabilitation); then, perhaps faced with the probability of additional deprivation, they may seek to compel the withdrawal of threatened programs (deterrence); and all the while, they may hope to apply punitive measures for alleged wrongdoing (correction). Obviously, this possible (indeed, common) state of affairs greatly complicates the principal task of rational inquiry at this special juncture—the task of judiciously appraising the accuracy of deprivee perceptions about the kinds of protection that may be appropriately demanded in the concrete case. Moreover, the difficulty is compounded by the fact that these goals may change as the particular interaction progresses through time and that, like those of the deprivors, these goals are never so rationally conceived or pursued as the foregoing categorization might suggest. But the typology here employed does have the merit of calling attention to the significant components of deprivee demand (anticipatory and reactive) to which decision-makers have been customarily asked to respond. As with deprivor objectives, comprehensive appraisal would include careful assessment of the degree to which these objectives may be inclusively or exclusively demanded and of the extent to which they may involve the expansion, conservation, or destruction of other values.

[215] For practical illustration, see p. 165.

Situations

All the situational factors that were noted earlier as affecting the imposition of deprivations also affect the selection, intensity, and permissibility of responses thereto. Where the target of deprivation is located (space), whether the deprivation is temporary or permanent (time), whether special promises against deprivation have been expressly tendered (institutionalization), or the degree to which particular deprivations are part of wider conflict (crisis) are but some of the many questions that vitally affect these considerations. But certain other situational factors may be seen to be still more closely identified with, and hence more immediately qualifying of, deprivee response and policies related thereto. These other factors, too, may be organized with reference to the four basic situational dimensions heretofore mentioned.

Space. As noted, the geographic location (both physical and conceptual) of the target of deprivation before or at the time of the assertion of deprivative power has substantial bearing upon the extent to which deprivors can successfully impose deprivations and upon the intensity with which they may pursue their deprivative objectives. Obviously, the same observations apply when the question of deprivative competence is viewed from the standpoint of the deprivees. To speak of the possible success of *deprivor* policy is, after all, to speak also of its possible failure—in other words, of the possible success of *deprivee* policy in averting deprivation. And to speak of the intensity of *deprivor* interest in terms of geographic propinquity is but a complementary way of talking about the concentration of *deprivee* interest in the foreign wealth involved. The point has already been discussed and needs no further elaboration here.[216]

Noteworthy, however, is that these and other spatial considerations can also weigh heavily in the post-Outcome phase of the Process of Deprivation. That is, the location of all or part of the target of deprivation after it has been subjected to deprivation, as well as the location of the deprivees at this later time, also may be of critical importance. Foreign wealth that has been subjected to deprivation does not always remain within the exclusive dominion of the deprivor community. Sometimes in the course of resumed economic transaction appropriated "movables" and "choses in action" travel outwards to communities within which the deprivees and their associates have or are able to assert relatively greater and possibly effective authority and con-

---

216 See pp. 67-69. It nevertheless deserves mention that these particular spatial factors are appropriately considered within the pre-Outcome context, for upon them may depend whether or not there will be any actual deprivation at all.

trol. In this context, whether in terms of international community prescriptions or of prescriptions unique to a more parochial arena of decision, "title" or "ownership" may be contested and the extent to which particular deprivations should be universally honored or somehow endowed with "extraterritorial validity" opened to fundamental challenge.[217] It is, of course, the potential efficacy of these deprivee contests and challenges that is important for policy, in both absolute and relative terms. Though their success is never certain (as the well-known postdeprivative law suits in Aden, Italy, and Japan concerning the 1951 Iranian nationalization of the Anglo-Iranian Oil Company alone make clear[218]), their frequency or promise, the likelihood and intensity of complementary and alternative deprivee responses, the stability of third-party expectations in both specific and general context, the overall success or failure of deprivor policy itself—all of these and other policy-relevant questions are contingent upon this factor to some degree. What must not be forgotten is that it is the post-Outcome location of the wealth and of the deprivees involved that makes even consideration of this basic factor (and, hence, consideration of its related contingencies) a possibility in the first place.

Time. Supplementing the temporal features mentioned earlier[219] are at least four others which may be seen to have a more specialized impact upon the post-Outcome context of deprivee response. These may be quickly noted.

First, just as time may affect the location of the target of deprivation and, therefore, the competence to deprive, so may time affect the location of wealth already subjected to deprivation and, hence, the authority and control which deprivees and their associates can muster in pursuit of their protection objectives. It takes no pedant's footnotes to establish that deprivees will be in a more or less advantageous position depending on whether the wealth in question is within or without the deprivor community at the time of protective response; further,

---

[217] In this setting are found a variety of claims and counterclaims whose common concern is the extraterritorial honoring or dishonoring of the application of deprivative power. Examples are the claim that a deprivation is an "Act of State" which does (does not) require abstention from review, the claim that a deprivation by an unrecognized body-politic should (should not) be accorded "validity," and the claim that a deprivation contrary to "the public policy of the forum" may (may not) be denied effect.

[218] Anglo-Iranian Oil Co. v. Jaffrate and Others, *International Law Reports* (Supreme Court, Aden, January 9, 1953), 316; Anglo-Iranian Oil Co. v. *S.U.P.O.R.* Co., same (Court of Venice, March 11, 1953), 19; Anglo-Iranian Oil Co. v. S.U.P.O.R. Co., same (Civil Court, Rome, September 13, 1954), 23; Anglo-Iranian Oil Co. v. Idemitsu Kosan Kabushiki Kaisha, same (High Court, Tokyo 1953), 305. Anglo-Iranian was successful in only the first of these four cases.

[219] See pp. 69-70.

that the permissibility and success of particular types of deprivee contests and challenges are themselves usually dependent on the presence of such wealth within the "forum jurisdiction" at the time of suit. The significance this bears for all the policy-relevant questions just mentioned, especially the question of alternative deprivee response, should be apparent.

Next, considerations of time, whether in terms of statutory and other express limitations or in terms of such vaguer restrictions as "laches" and "prescription," can serve to preclude or at least to condition the justifiability of deprivee response. Typically such considerations have arisen within, or with exclusive reference to, domestic arenas of decision. But not invariably. Express temporal limitations have been many times stipulated, for example, in agreements concerning the international arbitration or conciliation of deprivative and other disputes.[220] And despite the traditional notion that nation-states are not barred by the "principle" of the limitation of actions in the absence of express agreement to the contrary it is apparent that inexplicit international limitations (whether or not derived from express or implied municipal law restrictions) have also served to check or modify deprivee demands at the international level of decision.[221] The concern, clearly, is to put an end to stale claims, to eliminate demands that are marked by "unreasonable delay." But what in fact constitutes an "unreasonable delay" is not so clear. The presence or

[220] Among numerous such provisions, Article VI of the General Claims Convention of September 8, 1923, between the United States and Mexico, 43 Stat. 1730, T.S. No. 678, is illustrative. It reads, in part: "Every such claim for loss or damage accruing prior to the signing of this Convention, shall be filed with the Commission within one year from the date of its first meeting, unless in any case reasons for the delay, satisfactory to the majority of the Commissioners, shall be established, and in any such case the period for filing the claim may be extended not to exceed six additional months."

On this particular provision Feller has written: "The period of one year for the filing of claims was lamentably short. Neither government had adequate opportunity to sort out the meritorious claims in its files. Since all claims, whether presented to the Commission or not, were to be considered as settled, the two governments proceeded figuratively to dump the contents of their claims files on the desks of the Commission." Abraham H. Feller, *The Mexican Claims Commission 1923-1934* (New York 1935), 57.

[221] For an example of the barring of a deprivative claim on grounds of "prescription" without reference to municipal law restrictions, see Gentili (Italy v. Venezuela), Jackson H. Ralston and W. J. Sherman Doyle, *Venezuelan Arbitrations of 1903* (Washington 1904), 720, U.N.R.I.A.A., x, 551. For an example of the barring of a deprivative claim based on a municipal statute of limitations, see Several Canadian Hay Importers (Great Britain v. United States) [1925], *American and British Claims Arbitration under the Special Agreement of August 18, 1910* (1926), 364, U.N.R.I.A.A., vi, 142. See generally F. V. Garcia Amador, "Third Report on Responsibility of the State for Injuries Caused in Its Territory to the Person or Property of Aliens," *Yearbook of the International Law Commission*, ii, 47, 67 (U.N. Doc. A/CN.4/111), 1958.

absence of crisis (conflictual and nonconflictual), the state of existing international relations (specific and general), the terms of the temporal limitation, the duration of the delay itself—these and other factors must be examined before a meaningful answer can be given. What matters is that we recognize that a lapse of time between outcome and response can have critical implications for policy. Even if by authoritative device it fails to thwart deprivee demands, it may have important bearing upon the character of those demands, the intensity with which they are pursued, and the means that are employed to satisfy them.

Even assuming the "timeliness" of deprivee response, however, time can serve to permit or preclude access to arenas of decision (organized and unorganized) in yet other ways. Time can be and often has been determinative of the nationality and other eligibility tests of a deprivee and, hence, of his (or its) competence to invoke international law norms and/or to obtain particular governmental assistance in the pursuit of one or more protection objectives. The "date of loss," the "date of claim," the "date of judgment"—one or all of these and other points in time have proved diacritical in this connection. This is so well known that it scarcely needs mention.[222] But it deserves emphasis that whatever temporal tests are applied (which, like the criteria for the "*punctum temporis*" of deprivation and because of the important consequences that hang in the balance, merit the most careful deliberation), they must be seen against the background of an increasingly mobile and increasingly complex international economic society.

Finally, questions about time have traditionally been of utmost relevance to the measure of reparation due deprivees, if any. Is reparation to be based on values current at the time of loss or at another time? Are relevant economic conditions at the time fixed for valuation temporary or permanent? Does it matter that the target of deprivation entered the deprivor community at a time when the risk of deprivation was or should have been known? Is denial of use between the time of loss and the time of settlement to be compensated? If past or future profits are to enter calculation, how long is "past" and how

---

[222] E.g., Nottebohm Case [1955], I.C.J., 4; Richard B. Lillich, *International Claims: Their Adjudication by National Commissions* (Syracuse 1962), 76-101; Lillich (fn. 182), 24-59; Lillich and Gordon A. Christenson, *International Claims: Their Preparation and Presentation* (Syracuse 1962), 26-39. For an indication of French international claims practice in this regard, see Burns H. Weston, "Postwar French Foreign Claims Practice: Adjudication by National Commissions—An Introductory Note," *Indiana Law Journal*, XLIII (Summer 1968), 832. For a complete overview of postwar French international claims practice, see Weston (fn. 133).

long is "future"? Do previous, concurrent, or future deprivations mitigate deprivor "responsibility" in any way? And so forth. Albeit impressionistically, the point is thus sufficiently demonstrated.

Institutionalization. All the institutional features that were noted earlier as potentially affecting the pre-Outcome stage of the Process of Deprivation are relevant here also.[223] But the situational factor having perhaps above all others the most important or at least the most pervasive influence upon the post-Outcome process of deprivee response is the overall paucity of highly developed or organized institutions (national and international) through which deprivee demands can be impartially and authoritatively considered.

This is most apparent at the international level, especially where permanently constituted arenas of decision are concerned. Concededly, a number of disputes involving wealth deprivation claims have been brought before the Permanent Court of International Justice and its successor, the International Court of Justice. But for a variety of technical reasons (including the well-known limitations upon jurisdiction and access) only a handful of these disputes have ever been adjudicated "on the merits."[224] Regrettably, little more can be said for the specially constituted international arena of decision in recent years. While ad hoc mixed-arbitral tribunals once provided a relatively frequent alternative to unilateral response, today their redressive role is hardly significant. This is not to say that mixed commissions, whether for single or multiple claim settlement purposes, have fallen into complete desuetude.[225] It is simply that owing partly "to the inherent defects and repeated failures of mixed claims commissions"[226] they are not as common as they once were.

---

[223] See pp. 70-72.

[224] Those adjudicated "on the merits" appear to be limited to the following: The S.S. Wimbledon [1923], P.C.I.J., Ser. A., No. 1; The Mavrommatis Jerusalem Concessions [1925], P.C.I.J., Ser. A., No. 5; German Interests in Polish Upper Silesia and the Factory at Chorzow [1926-28], P.C.I.J., Ser. A., Nos. 7, 13, 17; Appeal from a Judgment of the Hungaro-Czechoslovak Mixed Arbitral Tribunal [1933], P.C.I.J., Ser. A/B, No. 61; The Oscar Chinn Case [1954], P.C.I.J., Ser. A/B No. 63; Société Commerciale de Belgique [1939], P.C.I.J., Ser. A/B, No. 78; Case Concerning Rights of Nationals of the United States of America in Morocco [1952], I.C.J., 176. Those not adjudicated "on the merits" have included, among others, the following: Phosphates in Morocco [1938], P.C.I.J., Ser. A/B, No. 74; The Losinger and Co. Case [1936], P.C.I.J., Ser. A/B, No. 67; The Electricity Co. of Sofia and Bulgaria [1939] P.C.I.J., Ser. A/B, No. 77; Anglo-Iranian Oil Co. Case [1952], I.C.J. 93; Nottebohm Case [1955], I.C.J., 4.

[225] As White (fn. 60), 193, has noted, there have been six postwar agreements "which set up Mixed Commissions . . . entrusted with various functions concerned either with the interpretation of the agreement or with the determination of the compensation to be paid eventually by the nationalising State."

[226] Lillich, *International Claims: Adjudication* (fn. 222), 10.

Though less apparent, the same general point applies to national arenas of decision. To be sure, a number of foreign-wealth deprivations have taken place within communities having highly refined legal systems which afford a variety of general and special procedures for access to authoritative, and on the whole impartial, decision. But as was earlier observed, deprivations in this context—particularly since World War II—have been neither frequent nor of scope sufficient to cause much concern for the smooth functioning of international economic intercourse. Most have taken place, rather, within Communist and "veneer"[227] states where, for lack of legal skills, xenophobic-nationalistic motives, or other reasons, comparatively primitive, unorganized, or tractable legal regimes have often prevailed, with the result that remedial opportunities have sometimes been severely limited, if not wholly wanting.[228] And though more developed remedial institutions have from time to time been available to deprivees outside these communities, their utility has been limited by the practical and technical difficulties of obtaining "effective jurisdiction."

In sum, remedial opportunities open to deprivees and their associates have been and continue to be largely decentralized and unorganized, operating mainly from foreign office to foreign office, with claims adjudication limited to arbitral arenas within *deprivee* communities in a postdiplomatic setting.[229] The implications this bears for such questions as "the exhaustion of local remedies," specifically, and the collective resolution of deprivative disputes, generally, should be obvious.

Crisis. As should by now be apparent, responses to the deprivation of foreign wealth are affected by the same crisis situations that were discussed earlier as affecting the pre-Outcome stage of the Process of Deprivation.[230] These situations need not be reconsidered here. But at least one point already alluded to in a different context merits special mention at this juncture—more by way of re-emphasis than elaboration. It is, simply, that deprivations themselves, depending on

---

227 The term is used by Professor Carlston (fn. 15), viii.

228 See, e.g., John F. Everhart, "I Had My Property Grabbed by Castro's Men," *U.S. News & World Report* (March 7, 1960), 48; Allison (fn. 24), 48, 50-51. See also Richard B. Lillich, "The Effectiveness of the Local Remedies Rule Today," *Proceedings of the American Society of International Law* (1964), 101. The problem is not, of course, a new one. See, e.g., *International Law Association, Fortieth Conference Report* (Amsterdam 1938), 174-75: "Experience has taught that . . . the indispensable objectivity and impartiality [of national courts] are sometimes jeopardized by considerations of national interest; this occurs especially in cases in which considerable interests are at stake." See also Richard A. Falk, *The Role of Domestic Courts in the International Legal Order* (Syracuse 1964).

229 See the books and articles cited in footnote 222.

230 See pp. 72-75.

(among other things) the nature and degree of single or multiple value injury sustained by the deprivees and their communities, can and sometimes do provoke situations which can reasonably be characterized as "crisis situations," at least from deprivee perspectives. The point reflects, or is merely a different way of referring to, certain of the previously noted outcomes which deprivees and their communities may be required to suffer in particular encounters.[231] But it deserves further notice here because it serves to re-emphasize the potentially severe immediate consequences that deprivor activity can bring about, whether in terms of the importance and number of values affected, the extent to which they are affected, or the number of participants affected. In short, the consequentiality of particular deprivations may be so critical as to engage wholly different sets of community policies about the selection, intensity, and permissibility of deprivee response than might "normally" be the case. The aftermath of the Suez Canal Company nationalization in 1956, for example, might profitably be considered in this light.

Strategies

We come now to the heart of the post-Outcome process of deprivee response: the responses themselves (anticipatory and reactive). As previously elaborated, the concern of foreign deprivees—actual and potential, manifest, associate, and substituted—is the protection of existing and future investment positions or, more precisely, the prevention and deterrence of deprivation and, failing that, the restoration of some *status quo ante*, rehabilitation from loss, long-term reconstruction, and correction.[232] These protection objectives are pursued by deprivees and their associates through an array of strategies[233] which, to borrow from De Visscher's characterization of "the field of diplomatic protection," seem initially to exhibit a "disconcerting

[231] See pp. 80-98.
[232] See pp. 107-10.
[233] Most writers, when referring to the many techniques hereafter detailed, talk about "remedies." But the difficulty with this term is that it refers simultaneously to both operations and consequences (factual and legal). That is, it is defined by the answers to the very questions which may be at stake in the first place and in the process strikes a debatable note of permissibility, or lawfulness. *Black's Law Dictionary*, Rev. 4th edn. (St. Paul 1968), 1457, defines "remedy" as "[t]he means by which a right is enforced or the violation of a right is prevented, redressed, or compensated." In actual practice, however, many so-called remedies do not enforce "rights" or prevent, redress, or compensate the violation of "rights." Nor are they always permissible. In other words, by using the term "strategy" (or any other neutral and factually descriptive equivalent) we are in a better position to focus upon the operation of given techniques—"the means"—and thereby to appraise the factual and legal consequences which ensue.

medley of heterogeneous elements."[234] But however disparate they may seem or be, a certain homogeneity is nonetheless discernible. Like those of the deprivors, the strategies employed by the deprivees and their associates ("deprivee strategies" and "deprivee strategists," respectively) may be seen to involve all of the now familiar instruments of policy that are commonly employed in most global interactions: diplomatic, ideological, economic, and military. And when these strategic instruments are viewed as operating with reference to the specific protection objectives heretofore identified, the homogeneity is made doubly clear. This is not to say that deprivee strategies exhibit the same seemingly static quality that this categorization might suggest. To the contrary, like those of the deprivors they are found in constantly changing combination and sequence, with each strategy complementing and supporting every other. What may serve as a restorative strategy in respect of one deprivative encounter, for example, may at the same time constitute a deterrent to similar encounters in the future. Additionally, the strategies actually employed are not always limited, if even consciously specialized, to protection against wealth deprivations and no more; their uses are multifunctional. Further still, the particular strategies ultimately chosen are sometimes less the product of deprivee than of deprivor initiative, especially when, as in times of genuine economic reform, the deprivor community may be chary about scaring off the foreign commitment that may be indispensable to overall economic growth. But our homogenizing typology does have the advantage of permitting us to identify and describe protection strategies, by whomever inspired, in terms of the variables that do and should separate authoritative judgments about them through time and from case to case. As with deprivor strategies, the principal concern is with the permissibility and wisdom of the particular strategies employed, absolutely and in relation to each other; that is, with the degree to which deprivee strategies conform to the requirements of public order in this field.

STRATEGIES OF PREVENTION

Calculated to forestall or circumscribe the occurrence or recurrence of deprivations well in advance of any expectation of imminent injury, strategies of prevention are usually undertaken in an atmosphere of relative calm. Accordingly, they tend to emphasize more the persuasive instruments of policy than those of brute force.

Diplomatic. Diplomatic strategies of prevention have primarily involved efforts at securing restrictive promises in transnational agree-

234 Charles de Visscher, *Theory and Reality in Public International Law*, Percy E. Corbett, trans. (Princeton 1957), 275.

ments, both unconditional (absolute promises not to deprive, temporary and permanent) and conditional (promises not to deprive except under specially prescribed conditions).[235] These strategies, more than others, are sometimes the expression of deprivor initiative or at least deprivor-deprivee collaboration, and are found at both the "private" and "public" levels of negotiation.

At the "private" level they are seen principally in the making of two types of agreements: "concession agreements" and "special contracts of guarantee,"[236] among others.[237] An early and seemingly absolute prohibition is found, for example, in the famous 1933 Concession Agreement between Iran (Persia) and the Anglo-Iranian Oil Company:[238] "This Concession shall not be annulled by the Govern-

[235] It should be recalled that when these promises are in fact secured they serve as important features of the institutional environment of the pre-Outcome context. See pp. 70-72. Of course, the variety of unconditional and conditional promises tendered by way of municipal investment codes and official utterances must not be ignored. These, however, are less the product of deprivee diplomacy than of voluntary gestures on the part of the host community. Accordingly, they are not considered here as the product of deprivee strategy, though the strength of this conclusion will depend on the facts in each case.

[236] A "concession agreement" is defined by Professor Fatouros as "an instrument concluded between a state and a private person and providing for the grant by the state to the individual of certain rights or powers which normally would belong to and be exercised by the state." Fatouros, *Government Guarantees* (fn. 117), 125. As Professor Fatouros himself concedes, this is "a 'working definition' admittedly incomplete and vague." Same, 125, n.222. It merits emphasis at this juncture, however, that the word "person" should be read to include both individuals and groups and that the word "state" should be read to include any body-politic. A "special contract of guarantee" is defined by the same author as an "instrument by which a state gives to an investor, under certain conditions, certain guarantees or privileges, in the absence of a special statute regulating the granting of such guarantees." Same, 125-26. The same reservations and amendments apply here as well. It should also be noted, as Fatouros has done, that this latter type of agreement is less prevalent today than it was in the past, mainly "because it is being increasingly replaced by instruments of approval." Same, 128.

[237] While the two types of agreements mentioned are, as indicated, the chief vehicles of preventive diplomacy at the "private" level, a possible third type of agreement should not be overlooked. This is the so-called instrument of approval which Professor Fatouros defines generally as the "final instrument" by which "the state grants to the investor some or all of the assurances and privileges provided for in the original investment law, while the investor undertakes certain obligations with respect to the form, amount and other elements of the investment." Same, 123. Though usually the expression of investment laws previously and unilaterally enacted within the host community, these instruments are nevertheless "often preceded . . . by official or semiofficial negotiations and constitute, in fact and in spite of their form, a kind of agreement between the state and the investor, providing for the granting of guarantees to the latter and for his corresponding obligations." Same, 123-24. Accordingly, to the extent that these instruments may exhibit the securing of restrictive promises, they too should be seen as vehicles of preventive diplomacy.

[238] For the text of this agreement, see Jacob C. Hurewitz, *Diplomacy in the Near and Middle East* (Princeton 1956), II, 188.

ment and the terms therein contained shall not be altered either by general or special legislation in the future, or by administrative measures or any other acts whatsoever of the executive authorities."[239] A similar promise is found in the 1952 contract between the Government of India and the Standard-Vacuum Oil Company for the establishment of oil refineries in India which, says Professor Fatouros, is "a typical guarantee contract."[240] Here, Fatouros writes, "[t]he Government agreed not to expropriate the [Standard-Vacuum] refinery [sic] for at least twenty-five years."[241] Of course, the securing of either permanent or temporary prohibitions that are this absolute is not always possible. Accordingly, "concession agreements" and "special contracts of guarantee" often—indeed, usually—contain conditional promises of one sort or another which, though not prohibitive of deprivation as such, are nonetheless intended to minimize, if not to preclude entirely, losses resulting therefrom. In the Standard-Vacuum contract just mentioned, for example, the Indian Government agreed that if after twenty-five years it were to "expropriate" the oil refineries it would do so only upon payment of "reasonable compensation"[242] (thus demonstrating, parenthetically, the possibility of securing both unconditional and conditional promises within the same instrument). Still more specific is the 1960 concession agreement between the Government of Ghana and the Volta Aluminium Company (a consortium of American and Canadian firms), negotiated for the construction and operation of an aluminum smelter in Ghana.[243] By Article 38, according to one commentator, the Ghanaian Government agreed that if after thirty years it chose to "nationalize, expropriate or intervene in . . . any property, right or interest" of the

[239] Article 21, quoted in same, 194. Of course, this provision did not prevent the nationalization of the Anglo-Iranian Oil Company. But such provisions may still be deemed to have preventive value, even in Iran. See text and accompanying footnote 403. In this connection, it should be recalled that Articles 14 and 17 of the William Knox-D'Arcy Oil Concession of May 29, 1901 (predecessor to the 1933 Oil Concession) contained language similar to that found in Article 21 of the subsequent 1933 Oil Concession. See Hurewitz (fn. 238), 251.

[240] Fatouros, *Government Guarantees* (fn. 117), 127. The text is printed in India Ministry of Production, *Establishment of Oil Refineries in India: Text of Agreements with the Oil Companies* (Delhi 1953), 1-12. Fatouros adds that "[t]his booklet contains two agreements with other companies on the same subject which are similar in form and content to the one described. . . ." Fatouros, *Government Guarantees* (fn. 117), 228.

[241] Same, 128.

[242] Same. The words "reasonable compensation" are taken from the agreements.

[243] I have also been unable to locate a copy of this agreement. Nwogugu indicates, however, that the text is printed in "The Volta River Project: Statement by the Government of Ghana," February 20, 1961, W. P. No. 1/61 (a "white paper" of the Government of Ghana). I. Nwogugu, *The Legal Problems of Foreign Investment in Developing Countries* (Manchester, Eng. and New York, 1965), 170 n.4.

consortium it would make "payment of prompt, fair and adequate compensation 'in such amount or amounts as shall be determined by agreement or by award in arbitration as provided in this Agreement, and in currency or currencies originally laid out in acquisition of the property, right or interest, share or security so expropriated, nationalized or intervened in.' "[244]

Efforts along these lines have been more conspicuous and sometimes more detailed at the "public" than at the "private" level. But whatever actual or claimed success preventive diplomacy has had at the public level, it has been limited to restrictions in bilateral treaties,[245] and only a handful of these have provided for the complete prohibition of deprivation either temporarily or permanently. Illustrative are some of the peace treaties following World War I which contained numerous injunctions against deprivation by the so-called Successor States in their newly acquired territories,[246] several earlier treaties of commerce and navigation,[247] and, more recently, a Franco-Tunisian agreement of March 2, 1963, which, in providing for the ultimate transfer to Tunisia of certain French-owned farm properties, guaranteed undisturbed proprietorship for a five-year interim period.[248] The vast majority of restrictive promises secured at the "public" level have thus been conditional rather than unconditional, all of them bilaterally negotiated. Generally they are to be found in the scores of commercial and establishment treaties (e.g., treaties of "friendship, commerce, and navigation") that have been concluded over the last sev-

[244] Quoted in same, 171-72.

[245] All efforts at securing multilateral promises, though only of recent origin, have in most respects proved unavailing. See pp. 158-61.

[246] See Friedman (fn. 44), 185.

[247] E.g., Treaty of Commerce and Navigation between Great Britain and Japan, July 16, 1894 [1893-94], *British and Foreign State Papers*, LXXXVI (London 1899), 39; Treaty of Commerce and Navigation between Germany and Japan, April 4, 1896 [1895-96], same, LXXXVIII (London 1900), 582; Treaty of Commerce and Navigation between France and Japan, August 4, 1896 [1895-96], same, LXXXVIII (London 1900), 530. See Japanese House Tax Case, *Hague Court Reports*, I (Scott), 78, U.N.R.I.A.A., XI (Permanent Court of Arbitration, 1905), 51, wherein these treaties were construed by the Permanent Court of Arbitration to mean that lands and buildings held by French, German, and British nationals by virtue of "perpetual" leases granted by the Japanese Government were exempt from all imposts, taxes, charges, contributions, or other conditions except those expressly stipulated in the leases in question.

[248] For an account of this accord, see *Le Monde* (March 3, 1963), 16, col. 3-4. See also Agreement for Reparations and Economic Cooperation between Burma and Japan, November 5, 1954, 251, U.N.T.S., 215 (1956), Article III (2) of which stipulates that the shares of Japanese nationals in their joint ventures with Burmese nationals in Burma "shall not be expropriated by the Government of the Union of Burma for such length of time as that Government may respectively assure those Japanese people against expropriation at the time the individual contracts concerned are made."

eral centuries, especially in those to which the capital-exporting United States (and Great Britain, West Germany, and Japan as well) have been parties since World War II.[249] These treaties, commonly within a framework of "national" and "most-favored-nation" treatment and of general assurances regarding the "constant and complete" or "full protection and security" of alien persons and property, have thus most recently (though variously) provided that the "[p]roperty of nationals and companies of either Party shall not be taken . . . except for public purposes"[250] and/or "for reasons of social utility,"[251] typically upon "prompt payment of just compensation [representing] the full equivalent of the property taken [in] effectively realizable form,"[252] and sometimes subject to "due process" and judicial review.[253] An important exception to this general pattern are the less numerous agreements that have been negotiated by the United States and by the Federal Republic of Germany in connection with their post-World War II "investment guarantee" programs.[254] Typical (for it appar-

[249] On United States practice in this regard, see Robert R. Wilson, *United States Commercial Treaties and International Law* (New Orleans 1960), Chap. 4. Professor Wilson includes a detailed bibliography. It should be mentioned, however, that "underdeveloped countries" (the principal deprivors today) are *not* parties to a preponderance of these commercial and establishment treaties. For an indication of participation in connection with United States commercial treaties since 1949, see Fatouros, *Government Guarantees* (fn. 117), 97. This is to be contrasted with their lively participation in "investment guarantee" agreements. See footnote 254.

[250] See, e.g., Treaty of Friendship, Commerce and Navigation between the United States and Korea, November 28, 1956, Art. VI, ¶ 4, 8 U.S.T. 2217, T.I.A.S. No. 3947. Other expressions, such as "public benefit" or "public interest" are sometimes employed. See, e.g., Treaty of Friendship, Commerce and Navigation between the United States and Greece, August 3, 1951, Art. VII, ¶ 3, 5 U.S.T. 1829, T.I.A.S. No. 3057; Treaty of Friendship, Commerce and Navigation between the United States and Japan, April 2, 1953, Art. VI, ¶ 3, 4 U.S.T. 2063, T.I.A.S. No. 2863.

[251] See, e.g., Treaty of Friendship, Commerce and Navigation between the United States and Nicaragua, January 21, 1956, Art. VI, ¶ 4, 9 U.S.T. 449, T.I.A.S. No. 4024. Cf. Treaty of Friendship, Commerce and Navigation between the Federal Republic of Germany and the Dominican Republic, December 23, 1957, Art. VI, ¶ 4, 2 *Bundesgesetzblatt* 1468, which refers to "public utility or social interest."

[252] These requirements are contained in most of the treaties, though the precise language varies. For example, the Convention of Establishment between the United States and France, Art. IV, ¶ 3, November 25, 1959, 11 U.S.T. 2398, T.I.A.S. No. 4625, provides for payment "without needless delay." Similarly, the Treaty of Friendship, Commerce and Navigation between the United States and the Federal Republic of Germany, Art. V, ¶ 4, October 29, 1954, 7 U.S.T. 1839, T.I.A.S. No. 3593, omits the word "full."

[253] See, e.g., same, Art. V, ¶ 4. To similar effect, see the Treaty of Friendship, Commerce and Navigation between Federal Republic of Germany and Italy, November 21, 1957, Art. 6, ¶ 4, 2 *Bundesgesetzblatt* 949.

[254] For a description of these programs, see Staff Report of the International Bank for Reconstruction and Development, *Multilateral Investment Insurance*

ently serves as the model for others that have followed)[255] is West Germany's 1959 Treaty for the Promotion and Protection of Investments with the Government of Pakistan.[256] In addition to providing, *inter alia*, for the "protection and security" of guaranteed investments generally,[257] prohibiting "discriminatory treatment" of such investments and their related business activities,[258] and assuring

---

(Washington 1962), Annexes. The Japanese Government has also undertaken an "investment guarantee" program. Under the Japanese program, however, "[t]here is no requirement that the country of investment have entered into an agreement with Japan consenting to institution of the program." Same, 27. It also deserves mention that "underdeveloped countries" (the principal deprivors today) have been parties to a preponderance of the "investment guarantee agreements" negotiated with the United States and West Germany. See Walter S. Surrey and Crawford Shaw, eds., *A Lawyer's Guide to International Business Transactions* (Philadelphia 1963), 374-75. This is in distinct contrast to their heretofore limited participation in commercial and establishment treaties. See footnote 249.

[255] Unlike those of West Germany (which Fatouros says are "a sufficient substitute for the FCN treaties as far as the provisions on expropriation and exchange restrictions are concerned . . ." "The Quest for Legal Security . . ." [fn. 117], 257, 268), the United States guarantee agreements—usually in the form of an exchange of notes—do not generally provide for special treatment of the guaranteed investments. Promises secured from the host government are for the most part limited to assurances concerning (a) the right of the United States to be subrogated to U.S.-paid claims arising out of the deprivation of guaranteed investments; (b) the settlement of such claims by negotiation or, this failing, by arbitration; and (c) the favorable treatment of local currency acquired by the United States in the settlement of such claims. As regards payments for losses caused by "war," host governments commonly promise "national" and "most-favored-nation" treatment. For amplification of these points, see Fatouros, *Government Guarantees* (fn. 56), 104-06. On the United States "investment guarantee" program, see generally Marina von Neumann Whitman, *The United States Investment Guaranty Program and Private Foreign Investment* (Princeton 1959). See also Lawrence A. Collins and Aaron Etra, "Policy, Politics, International Law and the United States Investment Guaranty Program," *Columbia Journal of Transnational Law*, IV (1966), 240.

[256] November 25, 1959, 457 U.N.T.S. 23 (1963). Fatouros, writing in 1963, states that Germany has concluded similar agreements with Iran (1961), Greece (1961), the Federation of Malaya (1961), Togo (1961), Morocco (1961), Liberia (1961), and Thailand (1961). Fatouros (fn. 117), 266 n.45.

[257] Treaty for the Promotion and Protection of Investments with the Government of Pakistan, November 25, 1959, Art. 3, ¶ 1, 457 U.N.T.S. 23 (1963).

[258] Same, Art. 1, ¶ 2 provides: "Capital investments by nationals or companies of either Party in the territory of the other Party shall not be subjected to any discriminatory treatment on the ground that ownership of or influence upon it is vested in nationals or companies of the former Party, unless legislation and rules and regulations framed thereunder existing at the time of coming into force of this Treaty provide otherwise."

Art. 2 provides: "Neither Party shall subject to discriminatory treatment any activities carried on in connection with investments including the effective management, use or enjoyment of such investments by the nationals or companies of either Party in the territory of the other Party unless specific stipulations are made in the documents of admission of an investment." ¶ 2 of the Protocol annexed to the Treaty contains an inexhaustive list of what shall constitute "discrimination."

"consultation" or "arbitration" of relevant (including deprivative) disputes,[259] it lays down the following conditions:

> Nationals or companies of either Party shall not be subjected to expropriation of their investments in the territory of the other Party except for public benefit against compensation, which shall represent the equivalent of the investments affected. Such compensation shall be actually realizable and freely transferable in the currency of the other Party without undue delay. Adequate provision shall be made at or prior to the time of expropriation for the determination and the grant of such compensation. The legality of any such expropriation and the amount of compensation shall be subject to review by due process of law.[260]
>
> . . . .
>
> Either Party shall in respect of all investments guarantee to nationals or companies of the other Party the transfer of the invested capital, of the returns therefrom and in the event of liquidation, the proceeds of such liquidation.[261]

A final comment concerning these "private" and "public" efforts at preventive diplomacy is in order. Many, if not most, of the restrictive promises (unconditional and conditional) thus far secured pertain by implication and otherwise to all the strategies of deprivation, direct and indirect. Explicit statements to this effect—increasingly evident in recent years—speak for themselves. In the Protocol to the model German-Pakistan guarantee treaty just noted, for example, the term "expropriation" is expressly defined to include "acts of sovereign power which are tantamount to expropriation, as well as measures of nationalization."[262] And in the 1959 Treaty of Commerce, Establishment, and Navigation between the United Kingdom and Iran,[263] for another, "equitable treatment" is assured "in respect of any measure of requisition, civil or military, or of disposal, limitation, restriction or expropriation affecting . . . property, rights and interests. . . ."[264] But even when explicit statements do not obtain, general provisions promising "constant and complete protection and security" or pro-

259 Same, Art. 11. This includes submitting such disputes to the International Court of Justice.

260 Same, Art. 3, ¶ 2. For what is included in the term "expropriation," see footnote 262 and accompanying text.

261 Same, Art. 4. Articles 5 and 6 seek to regulate in detail the methods of such transfers as well as the eventual subrogation of the signatory governments to the claims of their nationals.

262 Same, ¶ 3.

263 March 11, 1959, Cd. 698, Iran No. 1.

264 Same, Art. 15. Cf. Cameroon-United Kingdom Agreement of July 29, 1963, Art. V (2) Cd. 2133, 478 U.N.T.S. 149, 152 (1965).

hibiting "unreasonable or discriminatory measures," as well as, or in conjunction with, more detailed provisions protecting against certain uses of monetary, fiscal, and other regulatory powers, would seem designed to serve the same ends.

Ideological. Ideologically oriented preventive strategies involve the selection and manipulation of verbal and nonverbal symbols for the purpose of shaping official and popular opinion (principally within host communities) in favor of unmolested foreign-wealth ownership. Seldom have these strategies been explicitly recognized by international law scholars. But they exist nonetheless and so give rise to important questions concerning their effectiveness, if not always their permissibility.[265] In a general sense, they may be said to be both positive and negative in character.

On the one hand, foreign entrepreneurs in particular have long sought, through a wide variety of "public relations" techniques, to foster sentiments of positive association between themselves and their host communities, presumably with the hope of "producing goodwill" and of exorcising the rapacious stereotype with which many of them have become rightly or wrongly identified.[266] Of course, it would be wrong to assume that foreign entrepreneurs alone are concerned with preventive public relations. All interested parties (especially the public agencies of deprivee communities) practice the "art" to a degree, sometimes on a vast scale. Still, commercial enterprise has traditionally been the "advance-man" in this special area. Indicative is the copiously illustrated *Aramco Handbook* of the Arabian American Oil Company.[267] Although "prepared primarily for the use of the Amer-

[265] Questions as to their permissibility can arise, for example, with reference to municipal laws regulating the use of the mails and communication media.

[266] As a one-time director of Latin American public relations for the United Fruit Company has put it: "Public relations is a preventive process, not a cure. It must operate on a base of long-established and persistent dissemination of correct information, through every possible medium. Every action of every employee of the company is a form of public relations, good or bad." Quoted in Stacy May and Galo Plaza, *The United Fruit Company in Latin American* (Washington 1958), 211. Accuracy compels us to acknowledge, however, that no matter how ancient propaganda practices may be, the "art" of public relations as expressed today is relatively new. Within the United States at least, modern public relations did not begin until about 1919-29 and was not an acknowledged and accepted part of general business activity until about 1929-41. See Edward L. Bernays, *Public Relations* (Norman, Okla. 1952), Chaps. 9, 10. And it is even more recent that foreign entrepreneurs have begun to take seriously the importance of coping with their "image" abroad. See Helen Dinerman, "Image Problems for American Companies Abroad," in John W. Riley, Jr., and Margerite F. Levy, eds., *The Corporation and Its Publics* (New York 1963), 137.

[267] Roy Lebkicher, George Rentz, and Max Steineke, *Aramco Handbook* (New York 1960). The authors emphasize that "[t]he opinions expressed are their own opinions and do not necessarily represent official views of Company management."

ican employees of Aramco,"[268] it acknowledges that such employees "represent America and Americans generally in the eyes of the people of Saudi Arabia" and that "[t]heir day-by-day conduct as members and leaders of an American-owned private enterprise is bound to have a more telling effect than any propaganda upon the manner in which the Arabs appraise free enterprise as a way of life."[269] The Introduction thus lays the foundation for, and heralds the importance of, cooperation and goodwill:

In the operations of the Arabian American Oil Company . . . modern industry with an American flavor has been introduced into Saudi Arabia—a country in which the advanced technology of modern industry was unknown until recent years.

Aramco is only one of several similar companies which are now converting the great underground oil resources of the Middle East into something of use and value in meeting the expanding oil needs of the free world. As such it typifies some developments in today's dynamic yet troubled world which are highly important now and can have the most vital consequences in the future.

The oil industry of today is representative of all modern industry. It utilizes some of the most advanced ideas of science and technology. It requires bold planning for the future, large outlays of capital, great construction projects, and complex coordination in the movement of its products in the avenues of trade. It brings together, in a united effort, large organizations of people representing almost all types and degrees of skill and professional knowledge. Hence, the extension of the oil industry into the Middle East has meant the commingling, in close working relations, of people from the West with people of the Middle East, of people who are schooled and

---

But they also point out that "[t]his and the previous editions have been prepared by Aramco employees who are not professional writers but have long been active participants in Aramco operations." Same, 3. Further, the *Handbook* is copyrighted in the name of the Arabian American Oil Company.

[268] Same, 2.

[269] Same. That the *Handbook* was written with more than Aramco's American employees in mind is further emphasized by the statement that

there has been no intention to underrate the importance of information and perspective among Saudi Arab and other employees who now play an influential role in Aramco operations. The kinds of information needed for the purposes intended, however, must depend on the background of the employees—the things they *ought* to know in relation to the things they already know. Much of the material in the Handbook will interest *and benefit* many employees regardless of their background. But other material, *particularly the facts about the Arab world* which the Arabs understand better than Americans do, is intended for the information of Americans. Same, 3 (emphasis added).

In this connection, see the discussion in footnote 266.

experienced in the techniques of modern industry with people who are learning these techniques.

Here is a great proving ground for the ability of people of widely different cultures and backgrounds, of different personal and national allegiances, to work together harmoniously in projects of great mutual advantage. It is a proving ground of the ability of people of the free world to rise above the common obstacles in human relations which have always hindered human progress—such obstacles as selfishness, prejudice, intolerance and misunderstanding.

Of these obstacles, misunderstanding is probably the most troublesome, if, indeed, it does not often encompass the others. Many, perhaps most, of our troubles in relations between people spring from ignorance of the facts, failure to understand the other person's viewpoint, and the human tendency to believe in fallacies propounded by misguided or self-seeking leaders.[270]

To be sure, company publications of this type are neither the sole nor necessarily the most important techniques employed. The *Aramco Handbook* itself makes this abundantly clear.[271] News releases, feature stories, product publicity, and institutional advertising in all the mass media,[272] as well as press conferences, public forums, plant tours, edu-

---

[270] Same, 1.

[271] Same, 189-221.

[272] A particularly vivid and enlightening illustration of the use of the mass media in this connection (and demonstrating other preventive techniques in the process) is a full page advertisement in the *New York Times*, March 28, 1966, p. 23, of The Mansfield Tire and Rubber Company of Mansfield, Ohio, "in collaboration with" The Madras Rubber Factory (MRF) of Madras, India, on the occasion of Madame Indira Gandhi's first official visit to the United States following her election as Prime Minister of India. Extending "A Warm Welcome from the People of the United States to Mrs. Indira Gandhi, Prime Minister of India and a Leader of Asia" and praising "[t]his gracious and talented daughter of the late Pandit Jawaharlal Nehru" and "worthy successor of the late Lal Bahadur Shastri," the advertisement goes on in some detail to applaud Mansfield's "association" with MRF as "an object lesson" of "technical collaboration between industries of friendly countries" whose "implications extend beyond the confines of the industry, deep into the aspirations of two people, separated by language, culture and continents, working within the framework of representative Government toward a common goal." The advertisement took pains to point out that:

1. Mansfield owns 20 percent of the capital stock in MRF.

2. Mansfield designed and set up the factory, trained Indian personnel and technicians.

3. Mansfield receives a royalty on sales in India against which Mansfield provides technical know-how and results of research. Mansfield bears the salary of American technicians sent to MRF and the expenses of Indians trained at Mansfield factories in the United States.

4. How has the collaboration paid dividends? MRF is the largest Indian licensed tire factory. It has an annual capacity of 360,000 tires and 7,500,000 pounds of tread rubber for retreading tires. The plant is operated entirely by Indian nationals and we are proud to say their efforts have met with real

cational training institutes, civic projects, and so forth—all must be counted.[273] Naturally, what particular shape they may take will depend on such factors as the availability of financial resources and the character of the foreign setting itself.[274] But all point in the same direction: the shaping of a favorable "image."[275] Arguably, the more

---

success—they have acquired skills, work in dignity and have self-assurance as security for themselves and their families.

It should also be noted that this advertisement was published at a time when Madame Gandhi was being criticized at home for pro-foreign-business policies. *New York Times*, March 6, 1966, sec. 4, p. 3, col. 3.

[273] There is remarkably little available information about the public relations techniques employed by investors abroad. But see David H. Finnie, *Desert Enterprise* (Cambridge, Mass. 1958), 182-92, who states that what happened at Abadan (Iran) represented a failure in public relations. See also the relevant chapters of the series of case studies sponsored by the National Planning Association on United States Business Performance Abroad. It is perhaps possible to analogize from the practices of firms within domestic settings, however. In this connection, see Frederic R. Henderer, *A Comparative Study of the Public Relations Practices in Six Industrial Corporations* (Pittsburgh 1956).

[274] "Factors which vary widely in each foreign setting, and which affect the businessman's planning" in this and other regards include, according to one writer, the following:

1. The degree of literacy of the population, the number and complexities of languages or dialects, the amount of education the population has had, and to what extent the population possesses skills of various kinds important in an industrial society.

2. The size of the population, with particular reference to the size and distribution of the consuming population; and the per capita income.

3. The prevailing type of economy, the degree of urbanization, and the existence of basic facilities necessary for industrialization, such as a transportation system and a communication system.

4. The type of leadership, the political orientation of government, and the political stability of government.

5. Cultural and religious traditions and beliefs.

6. Government policies with respect to providing hospitality or encouragement for foreign businesses, such as any incentives they may offer; the tariff policy; the policies governing the ownership of companies; regulations regarding employment policies; and regulations regarding the transferability of currencies.

7. The country's financial condition, the ease of obtaining credit, the trade balance, the availability of local capital, and other economic factors. Dinerman (fn. 266), 139.

Questions such as these are, of course, the kinds of questions that are relevant to the characterization or identification of particular deprivor participants. See footnote 51 and accompanying text.

[275] This, according to a corporate client of International Research Associates having a large number of foreign operations, includes the following:

1. The company is an integral part of the national economy.

2. The company is an important tax contributor to the national government.

3. The company puts the broad national welfare above immediate profits.

4. The company provides many jobs for local nationals.

5. The company gives local nationals opportunities for jobs with real responsibility and prestige.

favorable the "image" the greater the likelihood that deprivative action will not be taken.

As indicated, however, preventive ideology may be negatively as well as positively oriented. Rather than stress positively the values of economic and social cooperation, it may emphasize the short- and long-range disadvantages of noncooperation. Through the subtle (although sometimes not-so-subtle) manipulation of appropriate words and gestures, foreign interests—particularly those of large scale—are at all times and over the long term seeking to instill in others a recognition that they have the effective power to make good their demands should the need arise. For obvious reasons, specific examples are hard to come by. But a particularly vivid indication may be deduced from the activities of the foreign-owned oil enterprises in the Middle East where, according to one authority, it has been made abundantly clear that "[t]he major companies not only can refuse to accept oil offered by a producing country but they may also be able to dissuade others from doing so, thus barring markets and forcing oil operations to shut down: the country is unable to run the industry."[276] Of course, manipulations of this kind should be seen more as complements than as alternatives to the ideological devices first noted. Together they seek to insure that host community decisions will be based on more inclusive considerations than the parochial extremes of "national interest."

Economic. Economic strategies of prevention are directed against both the act of deprivation and its potentially ruinous outcomes. Like the diplomatic strategies mentioned, these strategies focus as much upon minimizing wealth and cognate value losses as they do upon forestalling the initiation of deprivation as such.

The economic strategies that aim to prevent the exercise of deprivation take many forms. This is the inevitable consequence of the truism that wealth is the key to the pursuit of most human activities. All pre-

---

6. The company does not interfere in any way with national political decisions.
7. The company takes a sincere interest in community problems.
8. The company's products are of high quality.
9. The company sells its products at a fair price. Dinerman (fn. 266), 157.

Of course, the success of any "image" must necessarily depend upon the extent to which these elements can be said to be actually true. As to the success in this regard of The National Cash Register Co., see Gilbert H. Clee and Alfred de Scipio, "Creating a World Enterprise," *Harvard Business Review,* XXXVII (November-December 1959), 77, 85.

276 Edith T. Penrose, "Profit Sharing Between Producing Countries and Oil Companies in the Middle East," *The Economic Journal,* LXIX (June 1959), 238, 250. It is of course possible that such long-term threats may become more short-term or may actually be acted upon, in which event they would take on the color of deterrence or restorative strategies.

ventive (as well as other) strategies depend on the economic instrument to some degree. But at least two techniques that are distinctively "economic" in their orientation are noteworthy in this special context. First is the use, either open or covert, of private or public financial resources to maintain or implant regimes friendly or otherwise sympathetic to foreign-wealth interests. The successful presidential campaign of conservative Joaquin Balaguer of the Dominican Republic in 1966, for example, was said to have been waged "American-style" and to have been "largely financed by U.S. businessmen with interests in the republic."[277] Elsewhere we are told (to demonstrate that these tactics are sometimes followed irrespective of the respectability of the elite involved) that "General Perez Jimenez's brutal dictatorship in Venezuela—with nearly a billion dollars annual oil revenue—long enjoyed [foreign] corporate support, as has an autocratic king in Saudi Arabia dependent upon his $300 million oil income."[278] Only the naive would deny that these practices exist. The second technique is exemplified by section 301(e) of the United States Foreign Assistance Act (otherwise known as the "Hickenlooper Amendment").[279] Enacted "at the urging of American oil companies among others,"[280] the amendment stands as a constant reminder that deprivations inconsistent with its provisions (failure to take "appropriate steps" within six months to provide "speedy compensation . . . in convertible foreign exchange, equivalent to the full value thereof" or such other "relief" as might be deemed suitable)[281] will trigger the suspension of American foreign aid.[282] To be sure, the legislation seeks to minimize loss

[277] *Newsweek* (June 13, 1966), 51, col. 3.

[278] Engler (fn. 158), 182.

[279] 76 Stat. 260 (1962), as amended 22 U.S.C. § 2370 (e) (1) (1965).

[280] Stanley Metzger, "Property in International Law," *Virginia Law Review*, L (May 1964), 594, 618. Among the "others" was the International Telephone and Telegraph Company, some of whose installations had recently been seized in the Brazilian state of Rio Grande do Sul. See footnote 27 and accompanying text. Thus, the president of IT&T at the 1962 annual meeting of the company's shareholders urged his listeners to "persuade our Government that its Alliance for Progress should not grant aid to countries that expropriate United States investments without fair and prompt compensation." *New York Times*, May 10, 1962, p. 52, col. 3. It should be noted at this point, however, that the late Kennedy administration did not originally support this legislation. See the statments of Secretary of State Dean Rusk in *Hearings on S. 2996 before the Senate Committee on Foreign Relations*, 87th Cong., 2d Sess., 1962, 27, 30-32, 557. See also the report of President Kennedy's news conference of March 7, 1962 in *New York Times*, March 8, 1962, p. 14, col. 8.

[281] 76 Stat. 260 (1962), as amended 22 U.S.C. § 2370 (c) (1) (1965).

[282] For a critical analysis of this amendment, see Richard B. Lillich, "The Protection of Foreign Investment and the Foreign Assistance Act of 1962," *Rutgers Law Review*, XVII (Winter 1963), 405. It should not be assumed, however, that formal legislation of this kind is a prerequisite of preventive strategy. For example, in 1964, without benefit of enabling legislation, France suspended economic

to American investors abroad. But it may reasonably be inferred that it aims to forestall the initiation of deprivation as well. As one writer has put it (although without this provision in mind), "[w]hen a country stands to lose more in future aid by confiscating private capital within its control than it stands to gain from the value of the capital at stake, it usually exercises a seemly caution and restraint in dealing with private interests affiliated with sources of potential largesse."[283]

Turning to the economic strategies whose function is more to lessen the impact of deprivation than to prevent its exercise, we find at least five techniques that have been employed with varying utility in the past. Common to all is an element of insurance planning well in advance of any threat of imminent loss—of long-term "risk-sharing."

Perhaps best known are the aforementioned "investment guarantee" programs that have lately been established by the United States, Japan, and the Federal Republic of Germany mainly to encourage private foreign investment in the less-developed regions of the globe.[284] An important correlative goal of these programs, however, is the prevention of deprivative loss. Under these programs, eligible nationals planning to make direct or equity investments abroad may purchase insurance from their own governments specifically to protect against the spoliatory effects of certain types of direct and indirect deprivation. Depending on the program and the investment involved, maximum recovery may be as high as 75 to 200 percent of the original investment plus net value appreciation.

To similar effect, but designed to stimulate "commodity" rather than "capital" flows abroad, are the government operated or controlled export credit insurance and guarantee schemes which are found in most of the major industrial countries and in some of the less-industrialized.[285] With varying specificity and comprehensiveness, these

---

aid to Tunisia following the latter's nationalization of French-owned agricultural lands. See *New York Times*, May 13, 1964, p. 17, col. 1. While undertaken in pursuit of restorative goals, the French action surely had also the correlative effect of putting would-be deprivors on notice as to the possible negative consequences of pursuing deprivative policies in the future. In other words, past practice itself, though primarily specialized to more immediate protection objectives, may have the same preventive effect as legislation.

[283] Bronfenbrenner (fn. 65), 201, 215.

[284] See footnote 254. It is reported that "Switzerland and Norway informed the O.E.C.D., in meetings of experts in 1963 at Paris, that they were moving toward the establishment of national programs of their own, and Denmark did so in 1964." Metzger (fn. 280), 625 n.75. For a list of the countries where U.S. investment guarantees were available as of February 23, 1966, see *International Legal Materials*, v (Washington 1966), 377-78.

[285] Further Report of the Secretary-General, *The Promotion of the International Flow of Capital* (U.N. Doc. No. E/3492), 1961, 82, n.1: "Among the countries in which export credit guarantee insurance schemes are known to exist are Australia,

schemes offer insurance to qualified private exporters to protect not only against "ordinary" default and insolvency ("commercial risks"), but, as well, against so-called political risks, among which are numbered a variety of deprivative and potentially deprivative measures.[286] For example, under one of the United States programs underwritten jointly by the Export-Import Bank and the Foreign Credit Insurance Association (a combine of more than seventy private American insurance companies), an exporter of goods or technical services can purchase as much as 85 to 95 percent coverage against such "political risks" as exchange convertibility or transfer restrictions, disallowance or nonrenewal of import and export licenses, and "[r]equisition, expropriation, or confiscation of, or intervention in, the business of the buyer or guarantor by a governmental authority. . . ."[287]

A third device calculated to prevent loss may be seen in the procurement of third-party guarantees: nationals of State *A* planning to invest in State *B* secure guarantees of indemnification from State *C* or some other third party. A familiar feature of international financial transactions, particularly before World War II, the technique has been largely limited to third-state guarantees of public securities floated in private capital markets.[288] That it might embrace other types of third-party guarantors and other forms of investment, however, is not impossible. For example, a provision of the Articles of Agreement of the World Bank, though apparently unexploited, authorizes the Bank to guarantee private loans "and other [private] invest-

---

Austria, Belgium, Canada, Denmark, the Federal Republic of Germany, France, India, Ireland, Israel, Italy, Japan, the Netherlands, Norway, Spain, Sweden, Switzerland, the Union of South Africa, the United Kingdom and the United States."

[286] For a detailed historical review of credit insurance in general, and export credit insurance in particular, see Hans Karrer, *Elements of Credit Insurance* (London 1957). See also "A Note on Recent Developments and Problems of Export-Credit Guarantees (with special reference to Western Europe)," *U.N. Economic Bulletin for Europe*, xii, No. 2 (Geneva 1960), 51, as updated by Further Report of the Secretary-General (fn. 285), 81-88.

[287] Foreign Credit Insurance Association: Export Credit Insurance Policy (Short-term—Shipment Form) (Form FCIA-100); Short-term—Political Risks Export Credit Insurance Policy (Form FCIA-300); Export Credit Insurance Policy (Medium-term—Shipment Form) (Form FCIA-200); Medium term—Political Risks Export Credit Insurance Policy (Form FCIA-400J). See also Marina von Neumann Whitman, *Government Risk-Sharing in Foreign Investment* (Princeton 1965), 218. For a synopsis of United States programs, see John E. Loomis, *Public Money Sources for Overseas Trade and Investment* (Washington 1953), 21-30.

[288] E. Borchard, *State Insolvency and Foreign Bondholders* (New Haven 1951), I, 103-11; W. H. Wynne, *State Insolvency and Foreign Bondholders* (New Haven 1951), II, 285-92, 317-20, 395-96, 617-20. For a brief summary account, see Nwogugu (fn. 243), 88-90.

ments" made in member countries.[289] But however restricted it is in practice, the technique remains a possible safeguard against the risk of debt repudiation, outright or surreptitious.

Still another preventive tactic, venerable to "private law" transactions, is the requirement of collateral security for hedging the risk of deprivative loss. Real property and chattel mortgages, pledges of tangible and intangible wealth, assignments of assets, or even mere assurances of the "full faith and credit" of the host community may serve the purpose. Like third-party guarantees, however, this technique has been limited, seemingly exclusively, to situations involving private loans to foreign public entities.[290] But like them, too, it might usefully be extended to other forms of investment. Attending a direct capital investment abroad might be, for example, an escrow assignment by the host community of certain of its revenues as security against any one or more types of deprivation. Of course, whatever the nature of the investment the efficacy of this strategy is going to depend in major part on the extent to which the designated collateral is placed outside the reach of the host community.

A fifth and here final, though wholly unilateral, economic strategy may be seen in those municipal laws which permit the treatment of deprivation losses as "deductible" for tax purposes.[291] It can fairly

[289] One of the "purposes" of the Bank as defined in Article I (ii) of the Bank's Articles of Agreement is "[t]o promote private foreign investment by means of guarantees or participations in loans and other investments made by private investors . . ." *The International Bank for Reconstruction and Development 1946-1953* (Baltimore 1954), 237. Professor Whitman explains the reason for the Bank's failure to give guarantees as follows:

> Even before the Bank had actually begun operations, it became obvious that the assumption of the Bretton Woods conferees ". . . that by virtue of the guaranties of the Bank's obligations provided by its capital structure, the Bank would have ready access to the private investment market" had been naively optimistic. Since the Bank itself was an unknown and untried quantity to investors, the securities it guaranteed would have sold at varying interest rates depending upon the credit of the borrower, which would have been a serious inconvenience and would have injured the Bank's own credit. In February 1946, American bankers informed the National Advisory Council that the Bank's own bonds would sell more readily than foreign bonds guaranteed by it. Since it was obvious that, for some time to come, the Bank would have to rely entirely on the U.S. investment market for private funds, this information made it clear that the Bank could help its borrowing members to acquire funds more cheaply and readily by selling its own securities and making loans to them from the proceeds. Accordingly, the Bank modified its view of its own primary function and began preparations for the marketing of its own securities. Whitman (fn. 287), 125-26.

[290] For a synoptic account, see Nwogugu (fn. 243), 90-95. See also Borchard (fn. 288), 81-100.

[291] See, e.g., *Internal Revenue Code of 1954*, § 165 (a); footnote 292; H. Gumpel and C. Boettcher, *Taxation in the Federal Republic of Germany* (Harvard Law

be argued, of course, that in their particular application these laws partake more of rehabilitation than of prevention. This was the obvious effect, for example, of a ruling of the United States Internal Revenue Service allowing the deduction of an estimated one billion dollars of American investments subjected to Cuban deprivation in 1959-60.[292] But this is the effect, after all, of the final fruition of any "risk-sharing" device, and so including those mentioned above.[293] The point is that the enactment of these laws long ahead of any actual injury, like the making of all "risk-sharing" arrangements, serves a distinctly preventive function.

Military. As indicated, preventive strategies do not normally entail use of the military instrument, generally because of the remoteness of deprivative threats in this strategic setting. But the accuracy of this statement necessarily depends on the techniques envisioned. For example, if use of this instrument, in conjunction with the use of the economic instrument, is to mean the supply of military assistance (in any one or all of its forms) for the purpose of maintaining or implanting regimes that can be trusted not to attack foreign wealth, we must concede that the military instrument has played not a small role among preventive strategies. If, on the other hand, it is to mean unilateral intervention by force—"gunboat diplomacy"—its preventive use is much less evident today than it was several decades ago.[294] Of

School World Tax Series 1963), § 7/2.10; M. Norr and P. Kerlan, *Taxation in France* (Harvard Law School World Tax Series 1966), § 7/2.8. But cf. same at § 11/2.6f. Cf. W. Brudno, C. Cobb and N. Palkhivala, *Taxation in India* (Harvard Law School World Tax Series 1960), §§ 7/2.7, 7/2.14; Cobb and F. Forte, *Taxation in Italy* (Harvard Law School World Tax Series 1964), § 7/2.7; Norr, D. Duffy, and H. Sterner, *Taxation in Sweden* (Harvard Law School World Tax Series 1959), § 7/2.8. But see Gumpel and H. Margain, *Taxation in Mexico* (Harvard Law School World Tax Series 1957), § 7/4.1.

292 Revised Ruling 197, 1962, *Cumulative Bulletin*, II, 66. The Ruling stated, in part, that "acts of confiscation, whether by way of seizure, intervention in, expropriation, or similar taking of property, by the Cuban Government constitute identifiable events which, in the light of all of the circumstances, have resulted in closed and completed transactions notwithstanding promise of indemnification," and held the resulting losses deductible under section 165(a) of the Internal Revenue Code of 1954. Same, 69. For relevant discussion, see Jay O. Kramer, "The Tax Effects of Cuban Expropriations," *Taxes*, XXXIX (April 1961), 309; William A. Patty, "Tax Aspects of Cuban Expropriation," *Tax Law Review*, XVI (1961), 415. For discussion of the United States income tax law in this regard after the Revenue Act of 1964, see Peter O. Clauss, "Foreign Expropriation Losses," *Taxes*, XLIII (March 1965), 201.

293 Of course, if and when "risk-sharing" devices do serve rehabilitative purposes they must be considered in that light as well. Otherwise, the whole question of "the measure of damages" cannot be realistically determined or understood.

294 This appears to be true at least of United States policy vis-à-vis Latin America generally, and the Caribbean area specifically, insofar as the long-term anticipatory protection of private American interests is concerned. Ever since the

course, the diacritical line between these techniques is sometimes exceedingly difficult to draw.

STRATEGIES OF DETERRENCE

Unlike the strategies of prevention, those of deterrence are concerned with forestalling deprivations that are clearly threatened or imminently promised. Unlike them too—truly, unlike most other strategies of protection—strategies of deterrence are above all communicative, only secondarily involving overt acts or undertakings. Indeed, deterrence strategies *are* communications (explicit and implicit). It is this distinction which invites momentary departure from the analytical typology thus far and hereafter recommended. Analysis in terms of the instruments of policy employed—paramountly diplomatic and ideological —seems neither the most efficient nor the most relevant for highlighting the variables that can and do affect decision in this area.

Serving almost always as the basis of deterrence strategy in this field, thus, are a variety of essentially verbal appeals aimed at dissuading the host community from pursuing the deprivative course it has already charted. These may be made either directly to the potential deprivors themselves or indirectly to third parties and wider audiences.

Surely the most obvious example of direct appeal is the practice of diplomatic protest itself. Remonstrances are habitually made by national governments to avert deprivative measures, either at their own initiative or at the request of their threatened subjects. If nothing else, they are part of the normal diplomatic routine. Recall, for example, the oft-cited diplomatic protests against Uruguay in 1911 and against Italy in 1912 relative to the proposed establishment in those two countries of state-owned life insurance monopolies (to the apparent exclusion of foreign companies engaged in that trade). In the first case, firmly worded British and French protests evidently impelled Uruguay to abandon her plans almost entirely.[295] In the case of

---

United States intervention in Nicaragua in 1926-27, United States policy has on the whole been marked by noninterventionist considerations. See generally Bryce Wood, *The Making of the Good Neighbor Policy* (New York 1961). The United States military intervention in the Dominican Republic in May 1965 is, of course, a notable recent exception. But on the basis of evidence presently available, it does not appear that this intrusion was prompted mainly out of concern for the long-term protection of private American commercial interests in that country, although one commentator, without giving authority for his opinion, has suggested otherwise. See *I. F. Stone's Weekly* (May 31, 1965), 1, 4.

[295] See Jèze, "Le Monopole Public des Assurances en Uruguay" (fn. 139), 12; Scelle (fn. 139), 637. Uruguay did establish a state-owned life insurance company to compete along with the private foreign companies, however. Albérich Rolin, "Les Droits des Sociétés Étrangères (A Propos d'une Consultation Récente de M. Clunet)," *Revue de Droit International*, XIV (2d Series, 1912), 82, 86.

Italy, protests by Austria-Hungary, France, Germany, Great Britain, and the United States were largely unavailing.[296] Of course, direct appeals such as these are not restricted to the highest levels of international communication. Protests by threatened owners themselves are commonplace and, when ineffective, usually precede official demurrers at higher levels.

Indirect appeals, too, are well-known. Involving communications to third parties (not necessarily unassociated with the challenging community) who in turn can exert pressure upon the potential manifest deprivor, these appeals seek to eliminate or somehow subvert the foundations upon which deprivative calculations are based. Illustrative are appeals (in accordance with or without benefit of explicit agreement) to presumed impartial mediators—adjudicative, parliamentary, or executive—for the purpose of securing authoritative declaratory or injunctive judgments forbidding execution of proposed deprivations. For example, in a 1926 declaratory judgment tantamount to a permanent injunction the Permanent Court of International Justice, upon submissions made by the German Government, held that an intended "liquidation" by Poland of certain German-owned rural estates in Polish Upper Silesia would be unlawful because it failed to conform to a convention concluded between Germany and Poland at Geneva in 1922.[297] But the arena of indirect appeal, whether adjudicative, parliamentary, or executive, need not be international. It is well-known that threatened foreign-wealth owners may in many host countries seek preventive "injunctive relief" from a number of different authorities, some of them sometimes quite disassociated from the challenging officialdom. An action brought in 1953 by the American-owned United Fruit Company in the Supreme Court of Guatemala for the purpose of enjoining the then Arbenz Government from appropriating the Company's Pacific Coast plantations pursuant to Guatemala's agrarian reform law of 1952, though unsuccessful, is exemplary.[298] Nor need the arenas of indirect appeal be restricted to organized forums. In some cases, strategists may seek to enlist third states to use their "good offices" or to express publicly a common front against the potential deprivor. At other times, through a variety of propagandist tech-

[296] It has been suggested, however, that "[p]ossibly because of the protests the enforcement of the law was postponed." Research in International Law, *Nationality, Responsibility of States, Territorial Waters* (Cambridge, Mass. 1929), 160. Katzarov notes that the law was repealed in 1923. Katzarov (fn. 44), 29. On this dispute, see generally Clunet (fn. 139); Audinet (fn. 139), 5; Jèze (fn. 139), 433.

[297] Case Concerning Certain German Interests in Polish Upper Silesia [1926], P.C.I.J., Ser. A., No. 7, 81-82. To similar effect, see *Czechoslovakia v. Radio Corp. of America* (fn. 140), 523, decided by the Court of Arbitration at The Hague.

[298] See *New York Times*, March 6, 1953, p. 6, col. 6; same, March 20, 1953, p. 47, col. 2.

niques, they may endeavor to rally popular support among persons within and without the challenging community who are potentially sympathetic to their cause.

There is, of course, far more to the making of these direct and indirect appeals than their mere transmission. This is not to say that they lack persuasive value in their own right. When made by parties representing or somehow associated with a major power, for example, they may and often do carry immense weight even in the absence of further gesture. But we should not overly romanticize their impact. Were foreign interests simply to rely on the good nature of the challenging community the probability of successful dissuasion would be slim indeed. Often complementing these appeals, accordingly, are a variety of threats (including bluffs) and warnings which, communicated singly and in combination, are calculated to impress upon the potential deprivor all of the uneconomic consequences, natural and otherwise, that are likely to follow should the deprivative challenge be carried out.[299] Expressive of the goal of deterrence, each seeks to constrain the challenger to change his expectations and to accept the alternatives of abstention or modification demanded by the imperiled foreign interests.

Of these complementary communications, *threats*—particularly when explicit or "unveiled"—probably are the most noticeable (though not necessarily the most common) mainly because they hold out the very real specter of "reprisal" and "retortion" through use of any one or all of the instruments of policy heretofore discussed. The classic though unavailing example in this field is the initial response of the British Government to the proposed grant by the Kingdom of the Two Sicilies in 1836 of a private sulphur purchase and export monopoly to the admitted detriment of British and other mining interests then operating. Chafing under unrelenting Sicilian insistence that the monopoly was necessary to protect "this especial benefit of nature" from "the shrewdness of some foreign speculators" and "the avidity of the proprietors . . . to realize a profit immediate,"[300] the

[299] For a discussion of the use of threats and warnings in the process of international negotiation, among other "moves," see Fred C. Iklé, *How Nations Negotiate* (New York 1964), 62-68. The use of these analytical categories in the present context is no less appropriate. As Schelling has pointed out, "[t]o study the strategy of conflict [of which deterrence-oriented situations are but a part] is to take the view that most conflict situations are essentially *bargaining* situations. They are situations in which the ability of one participant to gain his ends is dependent to an important degree on the choices or decisions that the other participant will make." Thomas C. Schelling, *The Strategy of Conflict* (Cambridge, Mass. 1960), 5. For a more elaborate treatment of these and other "moves" with emphasis upon formal game theory, see same, Chap. 5.

[300] Prince Cassaro to Mr. Kennedy [1839-40], *British and Foreign State Papers*, XXVIII (London 1857), 1187.

British Government felt compelled after long diplomatic correspondence to threaten "serious and unpleasant consequences."[301] This, as later became apparent, meant the dispatch of a British war vessel into Neapolitan waters.[302] But military countermeasures are only one of a number of possible consequences that can be threatened. Discontinuance of diplomatic relations, nonrecognition of the deprivor elite, the "freezing" or seizure of public and private assets and accounts, repudiation of existing debts, restriction or termination of business relations, cancellation of foreign aid—all have at one or more times been openly threatened. Of course, threats need not be nor are they always explicit. The subtle or "veiled" manipulation of appropriate words and gestures, at any given moment or over time, may serve equally well. This undoubtedly explains, for example, the otherwise inexplicable capitulation by "the weak State of Uruguay"[303] in 1911 to British and French insurance interests which were supported by the then incomparable strength of the British and French governments. In other words, just as foreign interests have traditionally sought over the long term subtly to instill in others the recognition that they have the effective power to make good their demands, so have they done also over the short term.

But threats are neither the sole nor even the most common levers of direct and indirect appeal. *Warnings* may also be dissuasive. They differ from threats, however, in that they contemplate no consequences attributable to any *special* effort on the part of the imperilled foreign interests. The party that warns simply points out to the potential deprivor what Iklé would call the "natural consequences" of his intended course—that is, all those consequences that "flow from the laws of nature, economic or technical developments, or because other parties, as well as the warner himself, simply pursue their own interests."[304] Thus have foreign interests commonly stressed what economists would call the "opportunity costs" of deprivation: loss of "face," "reputation," or "trust" resulting from the deprivative program in general, or from failure to abide by proscriptive judgments or promises in particular; deterrence of new, and perhaps voluntary withdrawal of existing, foreign capital and skills; retardation of resource exploitation and socioeconomic development; disruption of internal social and

301 Mr. Temple to Prince Cassaro, same, 1170.
302 See [1840-41], same, xxix (London 1857), 204.
303 Friedman (fn. 44), 54.
304 Iklé (fn. 299), 62. Iklé further explains: "In the warning, the prediction of the opponent's loss is an act of bargaining, but the action which causes the opponent's loss after he has made the unwanted move is independent of the bargaining; the action would take place whether or not it inflicted a loss on the opponent." Same, 63.

economic stability; deterioration of mutually friendly relations; and so forth. In the aforementioned Sicilian sulphur monopoly dispute, for example, the British Government repeatedly stressed the "serious injury" that the monopoly would cause to "commerce in general."[305] Likewise, upon learning that Algeria intended to nationalize all the remaining lands of the French "colons," the French Government, in addition to protesting the plan as "discriminatory" and contrary to the constitutive Evian agreements of 1962, warned the Algerian Government of "les conséquences qu'elles ne pouvaient pas ne pas entrainer sur les rapports franco-algérien si la sécurité de nos compatriotes n'était pas assurée," and of France's right "de prendre toutes les mesures qui lui paraîtront nécessaires."[306] The examples are many.[307]

Threats and warnings are not the only types of complementary communication, however. Still a third type—*promises of reward*—should be noted. Deterrence may be achieved as well by making abstention from, or modification of, deprivative policies seem highly attractive as by making such policies appear generally disadvantageous. This is, after all, no more than a reaffirmation of the metaphorical distinction between the inviting carrot and the menacing stick. When, for example, an explosives manufacturing concern operating in the Transvaal was in 1898-99 threatened with the loss of an alleged illegal concession, its foreign owners succeeded in persuading the then Republic of South Africa to forego cancellation of their "rights" by offering lucrative bribes to key governmental officials.[308] Unsuccessful, on the other hand, was the clumsy and belated attempt in early 1951 of the Anglo-

---

[305] Mr. Temple to Prince Cassaro [1839-40], *British and Foreign State Papers*, xxviii (London 1857), 1166. See text accompanying footnote 300.

[306] "Déclaration" by the Cabinet of the French Prime Minister, reprinted in *Le Monde* (October 3, 1963), 1, cols. 5-6.

[307] Seemingly successful, for example, was the United States protest to the Spanish Government in 1937 against the planned "collectivization" of certain American concerns, including a distributing agency of the Royal Typewriter Company of New York. Warned that Washington would pursue its own interests by demanding "the prompt and full compensation of all American nationals or concerns for any losses suffered by them as a result of the collectivization of businesses or concerns in which they are interested," Spain, with little or no apparent resistance (but undoubtedly influenced by its own internal strife at the time), "annulled" the decree in respect of "the agency in question." Green H. Hackworth, *Digest of International Law*, v (Washington 1943), 588. Ultimately unsuccessful, however, but demonstrating that these as well as other communications need not be made through official diplomatic channels, was United States Secretary of State Kellogg's warning to the Mexican Government in a statement to the press on June 12, 1925. Fearful that Mexico would cancel the land titles pursuant to which American and other foreign oil companies were then operating, Secretary Kellogg warned that "the Government of Mexico is now on trial before the world." Reprinted in Ernest H. Gruening, *Mexico and Its Heritage* (New York 1928), 601.

[308] Transvaal Dynamite Company Case, *Report of the Transvaal Concessions Commission*, Command No. 623 (1901), 69.

Iranian Oil Company to escape nationalization by offering a fifty-fifty profit-sharing arrangement to the then Iranian Government of Prime Minister Razmara.[309] One should consider here, too, the lure of continued foreign aid, implicit in the threat of its possible termination under such provisions as section 301(e) of the United States Foreign Assistance Act, mentioned above.[310] In short, strategies of deterrence need not emphasize the negative costs of noncompliance only. They may also stress the positive inducements to conforming conduct.

As we have seen, it is by no means certain that deterrence-oriented appeals will succeed even if complemented by threats, warnings, or promises of reward. Their efficacy is a function of many factors, some of which lie wholly outside the control of the appealing parties. Essential, for example, is that the appeals be (or at least give the appearance of being) in earnest and convincing—a necessity that may even require the undertaking of specific commitments (overt acts which make it difficult and usually costly not to keep one's promises),[311] such as the timely holding of naval demonstrations or other military exercises in areas proximate to the challenging community. It is also important that they be communicated clearly and precisely, ungarbled and undistorted. Moreover, the potential deprivor must be capable of receiving them with reasonable accuracy and efficiency and of assessing realistically the alternatives that are in fact available. And conditioning all of these factors, obviously, is the very ability and resolve of the potential deprivor to "follow through." To put it another way, there are limits to what Professor Schelling might call "the theory of interdependent decision."[312]

STRATEGIES OF RESTORATION

As suggested earlier, strategies of restoration are concerned with the retraction of deprivations already imposed and/or the acceptance of demands for reducing loss to more tolerable proportions. Traditionally conceived in terms of "reprisal" and "retortion," they involve the single and combined use by both public and private interests of all the instruments of policy heretofore noted. And while they range the full

---

309 For an account of the Company's maneuvers, see Walden (fn. 71), 64, 67.

310 See text accompanying footnote 297.

311 On "commitment" as a "strategic move," see Schelling (fn. 299), Chap. 3. See also Iklé (fn. 299), 66-68.

312 Schelling (fn. 299), 16: "If behavior were actually cool-headed, valid and relevant theory would probably be easier to create than it actually is. If we view our results as a bench mark for further approximation to reality, not as a fully adequate theory, we should manage to protect ourselves from the worst results of a biased theory."

gamut of a persuasion-coercion continuum, their historic emphasis has been and seemingly continues to be more coercive than persuasive —particularly when, as the British response to the nationalization of the Anglo-Iranian Oil Company makes clear, they are addressed to such broader goals as the total collapse of a recalcitrant regime.[313] It is this fact, indeed, which, given the crisis potentialities of our contemporary world, signals the need for the most cautious delineation of the policy-relevant variables that affect restorative activity.

Diplomatic. There are principally four diplomatic strategies of restoration. Though separately treated here, they are most meaningfully understood when seen as coordinates of economic and military policy.

Most prevalent are the direct appeals that are commonly lodged with deprivor governments by way of "informal representations" or "formal protests," the former often preceding the latter. Like their deterrence counterparts, they are frequently bolstered by threats, warnings, and promises of reward. Illustrative of the informal use of "diplomatic good offices" is the support that was extended by the United States in connection with the "cancellation" and "seizure" of certain interests of the Standard Oil Company of New Jersey by Bolivia in March 1937,[314] beginning with a "personal message" from Secretary of State Hull to Bolivian Foreign Minister Finot to be delivered in writing only upon request of the latter.[315] Through subsequent negotiations

[313] In this connection, see Ford (fn. 97), 119; Walden (fn. 71), 75. See also footnote 212 for an indication of some of the implications which this broader goal may have for deprivee settlement demands.

[314] Documents bearing upon this matter may be found in [1937] *Foreign Relations of the U.S.*, v (Washington 1954), 275-311; [1938] same, v (1956), 321-29; [1939] same, v (1957), 322-47; [1940] same, v (1961, 513-23; [1941] same, vi (1963), 464-77; [1942] same, v (1962), 586-91.

[315] . . . I am sure Dr. Finot will comprehend that this message is not to be construed as an official communication from one government to another, but solely as an expression of my personal concern by reason of the existence of a situation which may prejudice the steady growth of that confidence on the part of all of the peoples of the American republics one towards the other, to the value of which I know Dr. Finot, like myself, attaches the greatest importance.

. . . It is hardly necessary for me to add that the existence of these conditions are personally very distressing to me because of my confidence that both the Government of Bolivia and Dr. Finot personally are as anxious as we are in Washington to dispel any misunderstandings which today exist which would prejudice in any manner mutual confidence between our two peoples and between our two governments. I expressly refrain from dealing at this time with any questions of fact or law, but I do very earnestly desire to urge upon Dr. Finot the expression of my sincere hope that steps may be taken by the Bolivian Government at an early opportunity to make it clear that that Government has every intention of offering just and equitable compensation for the properties owned by nationals of the United States which may have been seized by the Bolivian authorities, or, failing an agreement between these nationals of the

a settlement of this controversy was eventually achieved.[316] Exemplifying formal protests, on the other hand, is the lengthy *aide-mémoire* of the United States Government handed the Ambassador of Guatemala on August 28, 1953 after Guatemala's "expropriation" of plantations belonging to the Compañía Agricola de Guatemala, a Delaware subsidiary of the United Fruit Company.[317] This and other protests brought no concessions from the Arbenz Government. But it is at least arguable that they did lend some encouragement to opposed internal factions which later, under the banner of Castillo Armas and with covert tactical assistance from the United States, succeeded in ousting the Arbenz regime and in bringing about a complete reversal of policy, including the forswearing of all such deprivations in

---

United States and the Government of Bolivia upon the form and amount of such compensation, that it will agree upon some method of adjudication of the rights and equities inherent.

In conclusion, Dr. Finot may be assured that I shall be happy in every appropriate and possible manner to cooperate with him with the hope that through negotiations, conducted in the spirit of friendship and fair dealing, between the Government of Bolivia and these nationals of the United States a fair and equitable settlement may be found. Telegram from the Secretary of State to the Minister in Bolivia [1937], *Foreign Relations of the U.S.*, v (Washington 1954), 284-85.

[316] See [1942] same (1962), 586-91. According to one writer, the settlement "purported to constitute full compensation for the seizure but which was in fact quite inadequate, its function primarily being to preserve the principle of compensation." J. Gillis Wetter, "Diplomatic Assistance to Private Investment," *University of Chicago Law Review*, xxix (Winter 1961-62), 307, n.108.

[317] Full text quoted in *Department of State Bulletin*, xxix (September 14, 1953), 357-60. Concerned that President Arbenz Guzman was following Communist or pro-Communist policies, the United States warned: first, that it expected "not only that the law of Guatemala shall be applied fairly as to American nationals, without discrimination, but also that both the law itself and its application shall conform at least to minimum standards required by international law"; and second, citing U.N. General Assembly Resolution 626 (VII), relied upon by Guatemala in defense of its policies, that "the undermining of confidence on the part of foreign investors is a direct result of Guatemala's expropriation of foreign-owned property; the Resolution warned that this would be the result." Same, 358-59. The Resolution referred to, finally proposed by India, and accepted by the General Assembly on December 21, 1952, was the first such resolution to acclaim a nation's "sovereignty" over its "natural wealth and resources." In addition, it recommended that "all Member States, in the exercise of their right freely to use and exploit their natural wealth and resources . . . to have due regard, consistently with their sovereignty, to the need of maintaining the flow of capital in conditions of security, mutual confidence and economic co-operation among nations." Notwithstanding this recommendation, the United States (along with the United Kingdom, the Union of South Africa, and New Zealand) voted against the Resolution on the grounds that it did not provide for reciprocal responsibility toward private investors. In this connection, see Edward D. Re, "Nationalization and the Investment of Capital Abroad," *Georgia Law Journal*, xlii (November 1953), 44, 51-52.

the future and the restitution of all United Fruit holdings appropriated in the past.[318]

Appeals to both municipal and international arenas of decision, whether or not pursuant to explicit agreement, also serve restorative ends. The American-owned Hanna Mining Company, for example, for several years sought reversal in the Brazilian federal courts of a 1962 decree cancelling concessions privately (and therefore, according to Brazilian Attorney General Trigueiro, "irregularly" or "falsely") acquired by Hanna to vast iron ore deposits in Minas Gerais State.[319] In international arenas, the ultimately unsuccessful two-step maneuver of the United Kingdom to force Iran to rescind its nationalization of the Anglo-Iranian Oil Company, first before the International Court of Justice and then before the U.N. Security Council, is perhaps the best known recent demonstration.[320]

A third type of diplomatic strategy involves the mobilization of third-party support for common resistance to the programs of the deprivor community. Sometimes the aim is restricted to bringing about widespread moral or other censure of the deprivor in accordance with deprivee notions about proper behavior. Thus may be characterized, for example, the American, British, and French appeal, made one week after Egypt's nationalization of the Suez Canal Company, for a conference of "nations largely concerned with the use of the Canal"[321] (subsequently held in London between August 16 and August 23). As then United States Secretary of State Dulles put it in a radio and television address to the American people announcing the tripartite appeal, "most people pay decent respect for the opinions of mankind when these are soberly, carefully, and deliberately formulated. And because I believe that, I am confident that out of this conference there will come a judgment of such moral force that we can be confident that the Suez Canal will go on, as it has for the last 100 years, for the

[318] See *New York Times*, December 28, 1954, p. 3, col. 5; same, January 1, 1955, p. 4, col. 4. According to these reports, however, the United Fruit subsidiary was obliged to agree to the payment to the Guatemalan Government of 30 percent of its annual future profits.

[319] See *New York Times*, September 18, 1963, p. 51, cols. 2-4; same, October 18, 1963, p. 48, col. 4; same, November 7, 1964, p. 35, col. 1; same, March 19, 1965, p. 54, col. 5.

[320] See Note, "International Law—The Anglo-Iranian Oil Dispute at the International Court of Justice and in the Security Council," *New York University Law Review*, XXVII (April 1952), 329; B. Shwadran, "The Anglo-Iranian Oil Dispute, 1948-1953," *Middle Eastern Affairs*, V (June-July 1954), 193.

[321] Tripartite Statement of the governments of France, the United Kingdom, and the United States of August 2, 1956, reprinted in *The Suez Canal Problem* (fn. 78), 34-5.

years in the future to serve in peace the interests of mankind."[322] At other times, however, the support sought may be far more extensive. Nowhere is this better demonstrated than in the "active and whole-hearted co-operation" which the British were able to obtain from the United States "in pursuing a coercive policy that eventually brought the small nation of Iran to her knees" following the latter's national-ization of the Anglo-Iranian Oil Company in 1951.[323]

Perhaps most dramatic, though in a sense paradoxical, is the fourth and last principal example of restorative diplomacy: the severance of diplomatic relations (involving the recall of the key personnel of vari-ous diplomatic missions or the complete withdrawal of consular mis-sions, trade agencies, and other representative bodies stationed within the deprivor community), or its equivalent—usually in situations where a deprivor elite has but recently come to effective power—the nonrecognition of the deprivor "sovereign" and its decrees.[324] Thus did Mexico's 1938 seizure of British-controlled oil companies provoke a wholesale breach of British-Mexican diplomatic relations.[325] Simi-larly did Soviet deprivations of American interests in 1918 serve as the major justification for United States refusal to extend *de jure* recog-nition to the Soviet Union until 1933.[326] Like other diplomatic strategies, however, such measures are seldom persuasive in isolation. Indeed, they are usually conceived as threats of more severe response should compliance with deprivee demands not be forthcoming. In other words, it seems rather an overstatement to say that "[i]n dis-putes concerning private foreign investments, the discontinuance of diplomatic relations must be regarded as a serious step ranking almost next to armed intervention."[327] Nevertheless, these measures are important in their own right because they can and do register (like the mobilization of third-party support) a kind of moral indignation

[322] Quoted in *Department of State Bulletin*, xxxv (August 13, 1956), 259, 261.

[323] See the exhaustive and incisive discussion in Walden (fn. 71), particularly 77-88. Among other things, this included a "'settle or else' policy of the United States whereby foreign aid was refused Iran as a penalty for her intransigence in the oil dispute," a policy which "was one of the principal reasons for the sub-sequent downfall of the Mossadegh regime." Same, 81.

[324] This particular tactic has been explicitly advocated by the Institut de Droit International. Article 24 of its final Draft Resolutions on the international effects of nationalization as adopted in 1950 reads: "By virtue of their sovereignty, foreign governments may take recognition *de jure* or *de facto* or the breaking off of diplo-matic relations dependent on the withdrawal of nationalization in cases of abuse." *Annuaire de L'Institut de Droit International*, xliii (i) (Bath 1950), 132.

[325] See Great Britain Correspondence with the Mexican Government Regarding the Expropriation of Oil Properties in Mexico, April 8-May 20, 1938, Command 5758, No. 1.

[326] See the various references and quotations in Hackworth (fn. 307), 1. See also Bishop (fn. 44), 1-26.

[327] Wetter (fn. 316), 300.

which, when combined with other techniques and especially when directed against deprivors peculiarly sensitive to moral pressure, may have considerable impact in accelerating acceptance of deprivee demands.

Ideological. Ideological strategies of restoration are seen principally in those private and public acts and utterances which, communicated to large audiences both within and without the dominions of the immediate parties, seek to cast widespread opprobrium upon the policies of the deprivor for the purpose of psychologically pressuring the acceptance of specific demands. Strongly motivated to these ends, surely, was the above-noted radio and television address of United States Secretary of State Dulles. The "seizure" of the Suez Canal Company, he claimed, was "an angry act of retaliation against fancied grievances" whose "purely selfish purposes" could not be allowed "to encourage a breakdown of the international fabric upon which the security and well-being of all peoples depend."[328] Particularly trenchant was French Premier Guy Mollet's statement to the press on July 30, 1956 in which he attacked President Nasser as an "apprentice dictator" whose methods were similar to those used by Hitler —"the policy of blackmail alternating with flagrant violations of international agreements"—and whose tract, *The Philosophy of Revolution*, should better have been called *Mein Kampf*.[329] To be sure, the aims of these utterances differ little from those of some of the diplomatic tactics just considered. But ideological strategies may also serve more grandiose designs; for example, they may be utilized, employing all the tools of modern propaganda, to encourage internal counter-elites capable of capturing effective power and of reversing or substantially modifying deprivative programs already undertaken. Whatever their immediate purpose, however, ideological strategies in this context have been used only modestly in the past. Invariably they have been limited to situations exhibiting high intensities in crisis or to situations partaking of wider ideological conflict. And like their diplomatic counterparts, they are generally most meaningfully understood when seen as ancillary to the use and perhaps even the failure of other instruments of policy.

Economic. Turning to the economic strategies of restoration, we find a host of techniques that have commonly been employed both by the deprivees themselves and by their home governments, though mostly by the latter (measures which should be apparent even to the

[328] Quoted in *Department of State Bulletin*, xxxv (August 13, 1956), 259, 260.
[329] Quoted in *Keesing's Contemporary Archives* (July 28-August 4, 1956), 15003, col. 1.

most superficial student of international affairs). Designed to isolate the deprivor community from access to and use of outside markets and resources, to eliminate or inhibit its external economic influence, or to complicate severely the efficient exploitation of its own internal resources—all to coerce compliance with deprivee demands—they include most of the techniques that have been the traditional ingredients of "economic warfare" over the centuries.

Insofar as the deprivation of foreign wealth is concerned, however, their use has largely been limited to the last half-century and particularly to the last two decades, mainly because deprivations before World War I were seldom sufficiently provocative to call them into play. Among the more common: the "blocking" or "freezing" of deprivor assets and accounts (public and private), typically the practice in connection with the major deprivations in post-World War II Eastern Europe;[330] the imposition of selective or total boycotts and embargoes, as when in 1960 the United States first prohibited American purchases of Cuban sugar and later proscribed most exports from the United States to Cuba—each substantially in reply to Cuban seizures of American-owned properties;[331] the denial of various loans and credits, as exemplified by several of the early financial measures taken by Great Britain and France against Egypt in 1956 after the nationalization of the Suez Canal Company;[332] and the suspension of foreign aid, as when the United States in 1963 and France in 1964, because of the nationalization of their citizens' holdings, cancelled economic assistance to Ceylon and Tunisia respectively.[333] Of course, whether these and other economic strategies will be employed and to what extent they will be combined with each other or with noneconomic strategies in the particular case is going to depend on a variety of factors. Generally speaking, however, the more intense the deprivative encounter the greater their likelihood and complementarity. This is well illustrated by the many economic measures (among others) undertaken by Great Britain following Iran's arguably critical na-

[330] See, e.g., Nwogugu (fn. 243), 261.

[331] As to the sugar boycott, see Proclamation 3355, 25 Fed. Reg. 6414 (1960), acting pursuant to authority granted by Pub. L. No. 86-592, 74 Stat. 330. As to the trade embargo, see Proclamation No. 3447, 27 Fed. Reg. 1085 (1962), acting pursuant to authority granted by Pub. L. No. 87-195, 75 Stat. 445.

[332] *Keesing's Contemporary Archives* (July 28-August 4, 1956), 15002-03. See also *The Times* (London), July 28, 1956, p. 6, col. 1; same, July 30, 1956, p. 8, col. 1, p. 12, col. 1; *New York Times*, July 29, 1956, p. 1, col. 8.

[333] As to the United States suspension of aid to Ceylon, see *Department of State Bulletin*, XLVIII (March 4, 1963), 328. As to French suspension of aid to Tunisia, see *New York Times*, May 13, 1964, p. 17, col. 2.

tionalization of the Anglo-Iranian Oil Company.[334] The same may be said of the economic strategies undertaken by the manifest deprivees themselves, as exemplified by the countermeasures pursued by the personal representatives of the nationalized Suez Canal Company in 1956.[335]

Just how effective any one or more of these many economic strategies can be in given situations (whether or not combined with other strategies and whether or not employed by the manifest deprivees or their surrogates) is obviously a primary concern. The level of industrial achievement of the deprivor community, the extent of its dependence on foreign trade, the degree to which deprivee strategists can control relevant world markets, their ability to muster concerted third-party opposition—these and other considerations will be determinative. Perhaps more important, however, given the dispropor-

[334] Jerrold L. Walden has given us a singularly succinct portrayal:

Determined that once rid of Mossadegh their troubles would be at an end, the British resorted to every economic means possible to force the Iranian Government into insolvency. Iranian credits in British banks were frozen, thereby impeding the satisfaction of the country's financial obligations to foreign nations. Special financial and trading privileges previously accorded Persia were withdrawn, the effect of which was to deny to Iran virtually all of her dollar exchange and "to make it impossible for her to sell oil to most of her former customers, and to prevent her from getting scarce British goods."

Export licenses for scarce metals and other items destined for Iran were also revoked, and in September of 1951, 3,000 tons of railway track equipment and 2,000 tons of sugar enroute to Persia were "requisitioned" by the British Government, notwithstanding the fact that these goods were being delivered pursuant to valid commercial contracts. If Persia could violate its contractual bargains, the British were not to be outdone, particularly if they could thereby bring about the demise of the existing Persian regime.

The principal actions of the British were directed toward preventing Iranian oil from reaching interested purchasers and thus providing the Persian Government with a source of income to sustain its nationalization policy. The British oil tanker fleet was withdrawn from Abadan so that Iranian oil could not be transported to foreign ports. Public warnings were issued that legal proceedings would be instituted against any and all purchasers of Iranian crude or refined products. In fact, the British Chargé d'Affaires in Iran reportedly averred that the British Government would pursue the matter all the way to the North Pole if necessary in search of a court that would adjudicate such a dispute. Diplomatic pressures were also brought to bear upon foreign governments to discourage or prohibit sales of Iranian petroleum products. Finally, the British Treasury refused to permit any country to pay sterling for Iranian oil, "a ruling that . . . [eliminated] most of Iran's former customers." As a result of these and other embargo measures . . . only Idemitsu, an independent Japanese oil distributor, and two independent Italian companies exported any significant quantities of oil from Iran during the more than three-year span between nationalization and settlement. Walden (fn. 71), 75-76.

[335] *Keesing's Contemporary Archives* (July 28-August 4, 1956), 15004-05. See also *The Times* (London), July 28, 1956, p. 5, col. 3; same, July 30, 1956, p. 8, col. 2.

tionately counterdestructive potential of these strategies, we want to know which are permissible and which are not. It would seem too general (if at all helpful) to say that while "[t]he legality of some of these [economic] measures in international law is not wholly established . . . neither can they be regarded as unlawful, under existing international law"[336]—or, in other words, that they are more or less lawful. Rather than futilely to seek conclusions that may be said to be valid in all cases, it would seem best to recognize that what may be permissible in one context may not be permissible in another. This of course necessitates the identification and assessment of all the variables that may bear upon this question: among others, the consequentiality of the deprivation, the presence or absence of special commitments, the crisis level obtaining, the possible alternative courses of effective action, and the absolute and relative base value positions of the contending parties.

Military. "Individual [armed] coercive action," De Visscher has written, "frequently practiced in the last century by various great Powers, came to an end at the beginning of the twentieth century at the same time as the preponderance of the European Powers, and more particularly the double naval and commercial hegemony of Great Britain, was diminishing in the world."[337] It is difficult to read this statement without a certain skepticism. It is too conclusive. For example, one commentator writing in 1928 has recorded twenty-four "instances of protection by force" between 1899 and 1927 of the persons and property of United States nationals alone.[338] Most of these "instances," concededly, were born more of a desire to restore public order disrupted by civil and revolutionary disturbances than of demands for retrenchment from specific deprivative practices. But even as to the latter—our immediate concern—De Visscher's assessment is too final. The fact is that deprivee strategists have continued into the twentieth century and up to recent times to employ a combination of more or less severe military strategies—logistic support of internal counter-elite factions, "pacific" blockades, naval and air power demonstrations, troop deployments, and even armed invasion—to further their restorative goals.

The Anglo-Iranian and Suez crises of the last decade furnish ample evidence. Thus, following passage of the "Single Article Law" na-

---

[336] Fatouros, *Government Guarantees* (fn. 117), 356-57.

[337] De Visscher (fn. 234), 276.

[338] Milton Offutt, *The Protection of Citizens Abroad by the Armed Forces of the United States* (Baltimore 1928), 82-149. See also Memorandum of the Solicitor for the Department of State, October 5, 1912, *Right to Protect Citizens in Foreign Countries by Landing Force* (3rd rev. 1934).

tionalizing the Anglo-Iranian Oil Company and after a series of anti-British riots and demonstrations in Iran, but *before* having exhausted less coercive measures, the United Kingdom turned to military pressures:

> Initial reliance was placed by the British Government, which had promptly come to the aid of its embattled company, upon a concerted exhibition of force. As matters in Iran deteriorated, Britain displayed its military armor like a haughty peacock. As early as May 25, 1951, it was announced that 4,000 British paratroopers "carrying full fighting equipment" would leave for the eastern Mediterranean within ten days. These defenders of the Empire were warned by no less a personage than Field Marshal Viscount Montgomery to be "ready for anything." The renowned British naval forces were also called into play. On June 26, 1951, the 8,000 ton cruiser *Mauritius* was ordered to the vicinity of Abadan. Four days later, it was reported that two British frigates, the *Wren* and the *Flamingo,* were in the proximity of Iranian waters and that a third frigate, the *Wild Goose,* had left Malta to join the other ships in the area. By the end of July, at least four British destroyers were deployed off the coast of Abadan, "bringing British naval forces in the Persian Gulf area to their greatest strength since the end of the war—a total of nine ships."[339]

The history of Suez strikes an even more discordant note. Within a week after Egypt nationalized the Suez Canal Company, the British and French governments began a rapid buildup of "precautionary military measures" for the purpose of delivering "an energetic and severe counter-stroke" to Egypt's action.[340] Complementing other strategies,[341] these included the ordering of aircraft carriers, battleships, heavy and light cruisers, heavy and light destroyers, frigates,

[339] Walden (fn. 71), 73-74. Walden's use of the word "initial" is somewhat misleading. Before undertaking these military pressures, the British government made a number of diplomatic overtures to Iran for the purpose of achieving amicable settlement. See Ford (fn. 97), 55-58. It might also be mentioned, as Walden has done (fn. 71), 73 n.37, that similar military pressures met with success when the original D'Arcy concession of 1901 was unilaterally cancelled by Persia in 1912. Angus Sinclair, "Iranian Oil," *Middle Eastern Affairs,* II (June-July 1951), 213, 218.

[340] See *Keesing's Contemporary Archives* (July 28-August 4, 1956), 15002-03. For extensive detail, see Thomas (fn. 78), 63-77.

[341] On July 28, 1956, the British Treasury issued two statutory instruments, the first forbidding the transfer of any cash, securities, or gold belonging to the Suez Canal Company in Great Britain without the Treasury's consent (complementing the Company's own moves, noted in footnote 334), and the second forbidding transfers in respect of both private and public Egyptian accounts in the United Kingdom without the Treasury's consent. Identical measures were announced by the French Government on July 29.

submarines, and a number of smaller craft to nearby Mediterranean waters, the sending of jet bomber squadrons to within quick delivery range, the dispatch of ground troops to undisclosed proximate destinations, and the recall of a number of army reservists.[342] Whether the contemporaneous diplomatic strategies pursued by Great Britain, France, and others at the two London conferences, in the U.N. Security Council, and through direct negotiation would ever have alone averted the subsequent violence with Egypt in late October 1956 can only be conjectured. But there is no gainsaying that the hostilities, while the immediate result of Israeli "retaliation," were a denouement "certainly not unrelated to the Canal problem"[343] and, hence, to the militarily buttressed restorative demands of the British and French governments.

These and other recent examples notwithstanding, however, it is true that twentieth century use of the military instrument to coerce reversal or revision of deprivative programs has been neither as frequent nor as unreserved as in earlier times. With its prophet Rudyard Kipling, the era of "gunboat diplomacy" has largely passed. This is undoubtedly the real thrust of De Visscher's observation and reflects, seemingly, a growing skepticism about the permissibility—despite the effectiveness—of military strategies in the foreign-wealth deprivation context.[344] Still, it deserves emphasis that the question of permissibility cannot be so quickly resolved. If military strategies do not always hold out the tragic prospect of severe conflagration, surely they heighten the prolongation and intensification of conflict. On the other hand, it must not be forgotten that the world today lacks an effective policing mechanism at the supranational level and that nonmilitary measures often fail as viable alternatives. Particularly when vital in-

[342] *Keesing's Contemporary Archives* (July 28-August 4, 1956), 15002.

[343] Leonard C. Meeker, "The Middle East Crisis and Developments in International Law," *University of Chicago Law School Record No. 3*, VI (1957), 4, 26. This paper was delivered by Mr. Meeker at a time when he was Assistant Legal Advisor for United Nations Affairs in the U.S. Department of State.

[344] As De Visscher himself goes on to explain:

> In 1902 the Drago doctrine, combining the political substance of the Monroe theory with a legal thesis, emphasized the abuse of force to which armed coercive action lent itself. In 1907 the Second Hague Conference adopted the Convention on the use of force in the collection of contract debts. Making the resort to constraint conditional upon an offer of arbitration, the Convention subjected it to international control. Since then, and especially since the second world war, the elements of the problem have profoundly changed. The notion and the protection of private property have weakened almost everywhere; while the more and more extensive practice of nationalization has made this the instrument of a State policy which can no longer be considered peculiar to certain countries. These changes, which have made foreign investment more precarious, have reduced the scope of claims for compensation for expropriation, withdrawal of concession, or nationalization. De Visscher (fn. 234), 276.

terests are at stake, these are considerations which require the most cautious balancing.

Strategies of rehabilitation seek to repair values wholly or partially destroyed by the imposition of deprivations. Probably because they are most immediately associated with the final adjustment of clashing interests, they have received by comparison the lion's share of scholarly attention, sometimes even to the near total disregard of other protective strategies. Still it is surprising to discover how little comprehensive attention has been given to them. The books are replete with discussions about the admissibility and measure of "restitution" and "compensation." But little or nothing is said about the means by which these reparations are sought. As important as the former issues are, they are not all that is relevant.

As will be seen, the strategies employed in this setting stress once again the persuasive rather than the coercive modes of behavior. For all practical purposes, they are limited to the diplomatic instrument, sometimes in conjunction with economic measures.

Diplomatic. Indeed, the use of diplomatic strategies is almost by definition indispensable to post-Outcome rehabilitation. In this setting one or both of the contending parties and/or their surrogates have calculated the costs of continued unyielding to be too high or, for whatever countervailing reason, indicated a willingness to reach some accommodation. Accordingly, tensions have subsided (at least temporarily) and the broadest of conciliatory "working principles" agreed upon. Here, in brief, the need for resolving outstanding differences generally, and such difficult questions as the admissibility and measure of reparation specifically, have been mutually recognized. Traditionally and preeminently, though not always successfully from the standpoint of deprivee strategists, this has been done by resorting to the essentially persuasive techniques of negotiation and adjudication, singly and in combination.[345]

Isi Foighel and Gillian White have suggested several helpful cate-

[345] This is not to suggest that conflicts (as represented, for example, by a "breakdown in negotiations") do not arise in the process of rehabilitative settlement itself. Nor is it to suggest that these conflicts never provoke resort to more coercive devices. When this happens, however, we find ourselves once again—at least from an analytic standpoint—in the restorative phase of post-Outcome interaction. This is a point which deserves emphasis not only because it signals a further approximation to reality but also because it reminds us of the highly fluid character of the events which we seek to cast into a categorical mold and, hence, of the absolute necessity of approaching this and all other categorizations with the highest degree of flexibility.

gories which, when consolidated, modified, and supplemented, form a meaningful typology by which most of these techniques can be conveniently tallied and assessed:[346] (a) the making of agreements *not* calling for immediate reparation, and (b) the making of agreements calling for immediate reparation. A third, obvious category will be mentioned below.

The first category of techniques—the making of agreements *not* calling for immediate reparation—may be seen to refer to three principal types of accords. All are commonly negotiated on an interstate basis, the manifest deprivees themselves playing but a minor role.

First, there are the agreements which look to single- or multiple-claim settlement by resort to variously structured permanent and ad hoc international arenas of decision, often multinational in character.[347] Thus have special *compromis* been drawn summoning decision-makers variously to decide "every matter of dispute, both facts and law"[348] or to "determine what sum *if any* shall be paid in settlement"[349] or "to pronounce as [they] shall deem most just, upon the amount of the indemnity due."[350] Likewise illustrative have been mixed claims conventions which typically confirm the compensatory or restitutive liability of a defendant High Contracting Party as to "all claims" (deprivatory and otherwise) previously "presented" to the plaintiff government "for its interposition" and adjudged by the appointed arbiters to warrant reparation.[351] For reasons indicated earlier, however, neither of these types of agreements are as commonly negotiated today as they once were.[352]

Second are the accords that contemplate settlement by resort to decision processes internal to the deprivor community. In these agreements, deprivee strategists secure pledges of reparation in both broad and specific terms subject to the requirement that individual deprivees

---

[346] See Foighel (fn. 64), 194-214; White (fn. 60), 193-231.

[347] Foighel (fn. 64), 202-205; White (fn. 60), 193-97.

[348] Protocol of an agreement between His Royal Highness Prince Devawongse Varopraker, Minister for Foreign Affairs of His Majesty the King of Siam, and John Barrett, Minister Resident and Consul-General of the United States, July 26, 1897, Art. I [1897], *Foreign Relations of the U.S.* (Washington 1898), 479; governing Marion A. Cheek (United States v. Siam) [1898], Moore, *Arbitrations*, v (Washington 1898), 5068; La Fontaine (fn. 36), 580.

[349] Agreement with Norway, June 30, 1921, Art. I, Stat. 1925 (1921), T.S. No. 654 (emphasis added), governing Norwegian Shipowner's claim (Norway v. United States), Hague Court Reports (Scott), II, 40, U.N.R.I.A.A., I (1922), 309.

[350] Protocol between the United States, Great Britain, and Portugal, June 13, 1891, Art. III, Malloy, II (1910), 1460, governing Delagoa Bay Ry. (United States and Great Britain v. Portugal) [1900], *Foreign Relations of the U.S.* (Washington 1902); La Fontaine (fn. 36), 398.

[351] E.g., Convention with Mexico, September 8, 1923, Art. I, 43 Stat. (1923), 1730, T.S. No. 678, governing the U.S.-Mexican General Claims Commission.

[352] See p. 115.

themselves press their claims directly with the deprivor authorities in accordance with prescribed municipal procedures.[353] Drafted mainly in connection with the Eastern European deprivations of the immediate post-World War II period, they are seldom written today largely because of the obvious burdens that individual deprivees may be made to suffer in enforcing compliance.[354]

Finally, there are the agreements which manifest no expectation of adjudicated settlement of any sort, but which nevertheless contain broad pledges of future reparation.[355] It is their generality, indeed, that largely explains why they have been attempted infrequently in recent years. Resulting in no commitment as to the timing, amount, and form of reparation to be had, as to the means by which these elements are to be determined or as to the specific interests to be rehabilitated, the negotiation of these agreements, like the second type noted above, has been confined mainly to the years immediately following World War II.

The second category of techniques—the making of agreements calling for immediate reparation—refers to two types of accords. Each are by and large creatures of the post-1939 period and each have in a major sense helped to transform the art of rehabilitative diplomacy in this field.

The first type, the product of interstate bargaining, usually anticipate future adjudication before a national commission within the deprivee community. These are the so-called lump-sum, *en bloc*, or global settlement agreements whose use in the foreign-wealth deprivation context has risen sharply in recent years, partly because of the inadequacies of other diplomatic techniques and partly because of the large number of major and minor losses spawned since World War II by the emergence of Communist regimes in Eastern Europe and by the xenophobic nationalism of much of the underdeveloped world.[356] The negotiation of these accords is by far the predominant rehabilitative technique employed today, with the deprivor community agreeing to pay a specified sum, *in money and/or in kind*, to the deprivee community forthwith (though nearly always by way of initial and install-

[353] See Foighel (fn. 64), 198-202; White (fn. 60), 197-201, 204-05. For a clear-cut example of this kind of agreement, see the Accord between France and Czechoslovakia of August 6, 1948, reprinted in G. Viénot, *Nationalisations Etrangères et Intérêts Français* (Paris 1953), 147-48, and discussed in Weston, *Indiana Law Journal* (fn. 222), 832, 838.

[354] But see footnote 405 and accompanying text.

[355] Foighel (fn. 64), 194-198; White (fn. 60), 201-03.

[356] Foighel (fn. 64), 207-214; White (fn. 60), 205-26, 230-31. See also Fouilloux (fn. 89), 444-48; Richard B. Lillich, "International Claims: Their Settlement by Lump Sum Agreements," in Pieter Sanders, ed., *International Arbitration—Liber Amicorum for Martin Domke* (The Hague 1967), 143.

ment payments) in exchange for the latter's release of the outstanding claims of its nationals.[357] Thereafter, it is for the deprivee community to adjudicate the individual claims and to distribute the available funds as it sees fit.[358]

The second type of agreement in this second category is significant because it confirms that rehabilitative diplomacy is no longer (if it ever was) the exclusive province of *interstate* dealing. Within the last three decades, individual deprivees themselves, often with the diplomatic "good offices" (if not the complicity or encouragement) of their own governments and frequently on a collective basis through what the French call "les groupements de défense," have begun to negotiate settlement agreements calling for immediate reparation (though again by way of initial and installment payments) directly with the deprivor community.[359] To date, all have involved publicly and privately controlled business associations of considerable economic size and strength. The earliest known to this author, both emanating from the Mexican oil seizures of the interwar period, are

[357] As Foighel has put it, their "characteristic feature is to be found rather in the 'balance receipt' given against payment covering a number of known and unknown claims, than in the estimate of the amount of the compensation [due as to each claim] . . ." Isi Foighel, *Nationalization* (London 1957), 97. A useful working definition has been given by a former chairman of the United States Foreign Claims Settlement Commission: "[A] 'lump sum,' 'en bloc' or 'global' settlement involves an agreement, arrived at by diplomatic negotiation between governments, to settle outstanding international claims by the payment of a given sum without resorting to international adjudication. Such a settlement permits the state receiving the lump sum to distribute the fund thus acquired among claimants who may be entitled thereto pursuant to domestic procedure." Edward D. Re, "Domestic Adjudication and Lump-Sum Settlement as an Enforcement Technique," *Proceedings of the American Society of International Law*, LVIII (1964), 39, 40. Compare Murray I. Litmans, *The International Lump-Sum Settlements of the United States* (Ann Arbor 1962), 1-2. A study of the lump-sum settlement process is a current major project of the Procedural Aspects of International Law Institute. The final product, to be published by the Syracuse University Press in 1970, will be a treatise entitled *International Claims: Their Settlement by Lump-Sum Agreements*. Working on this project, besides the author, is Professor Richard B. Lillich of the University of Virginia School of Law.

[358] As to American and British practice in this connection, see Lillich (fn. 222), and Lillich (fn. 182). For a companion volume to these studies, concerning equivalent French practice, see Weston (fn. 133). For an introduction to the latter, see footnote 222.

A recent development in United States practice makes clear that adjudication need not necessarily follow the making of lump-sum agreements. Thus, the U.S. Cuban Claims Act of 1964, 22 U.S.C.A. § 1643 (Supp. 1965), amending International Claims Settlement Act of 1949, 64 Stat. 12 (1950), provides for the "preadjudication" of deprivation claims despite the absence of agreement. For discussion, see Richard B. Lillich, "The Cuban Claims Act of 1964," *American Bar Association Journal*, LI (May 1965), 445.

[359] See White (fn. 60), 226-30. For evidence that deprivee governments sometimes encourage at least large corporate claimants to negotiate settlements on their own, mainly to obtain larger overall returns, see Lillich (fn. 182), 139-40.

the compensation agreements negotiated between the Mexican Government on the one hand, and the American-owned Sinclair Oil Company and the British-owned Whitehall Securities Corporation, Ltd. (as agent for the Mexican Eagle Group) on the other, in 1940 and 1947 respectively.[360] More recent and perhaps better known examples are, among others: the 1954 Iranian Oil Consortium Agreement (Part II) which helped put to rest the rancorous dispute between the Anglo-Iranian Oil Company and the Iranian Government;[361] the 1958 Agreement between the Government of the United Arab Republic and the Compagnie Financière de Suez (successor to the nationalized Suez Canal Company);[362] three compensation agreements drawn up in 1965 between Caltex, Esso Standard, and Shell, on the one hand, and the Government of Ceylon, on the other—each settling the 1961 Ceylonese "requisitioning" of certain of the assets of these three foreign enterprises;[363] and a series of agreements during 1964-67 between the Government of Argentina and several foreign-owned petroleum companies relative to the settlement of claims arising out of Argentina's "annulment" of previously granted oil production concessions.[364]

Obviously, no accounting of the diplomatic strategies of rehabilitation would be complete without mentioning a third and here final category of techniques: the rehabilitative appeals that are from time to time made by manifest deprivees and their surrogates to both international and intranational arenas of decision *without* special prearrangement (except insofar as they may be made pursuant to long-standing interparty and interstate agreements providing for and/or regulating the conciliation or arbitration of transnational disputes generally). At the international level these appeals have been less than frequent, mainly because of the popularity of preliminary compromissory agreement and because of the well-known limitations upon international jurisdiction and access. Nor has their frequency been much greater at the national level. Within deprivor communities they have been limited either by outright prohibitions or by what are all too often illusory promises of "due process." Outside these communities

---

[360] See Friedman (fn. 44), 29. On the Sinclair Oil Company agreement, see Wood (fn. 294), 232-33, 244-45.

[361] The Agreement has been made public and is available from the members of the Consortium. For discussion, see Walden (fn. 71), 64, 88-114.

[362] Text reproduced in *Revue Egyptienne de Droit Internationale*, XIV (Alexandria 1958), 328; *American Journal of International Law*, LIV (April 1960), 498.

[363] Texts reproduced in *International Legal Materials*, IV (Washington 1965), 1074-89.

[364] Texts reproduced in *International Legal Materials*, II (Washington 1964), 1, 11-12, 292, 359; same, IV (1965), 463; same, V (1966), 103; same, VI (1967), 1, 19, 696, 1073.

they have been hampered by the obvious difficulty of assuring both effective and sufficient jurisdictional control. All of this was alluded to earlier.[365] Nevertheless, as an available and sometimes valuable technique for securing reparation, direct adjudication should neither be forgotten nor dismissed. This is especially true in the case of deprivative disputes arising in connection with concession agreements and investment guarantee treaties whose terms commonly provide for resort to third-party (usually international) adjudication.

Economic. The success that may be claimed by any of the foregoing diplomatic strategies is obviously going to depend on a host of factors, some of which may lie wholly outside the effective control of the deprivee strategists. Among them, for example, may be the ability of the deprivors (in terms of both economic and political feasibility) to accept deprivee demands. Another may be the willingness of deprivors to abide by rehabilitative judgments or promises previously made (a question of the enforceability of commitment that merits comprehensive functional analysis in its own right).[366] Often of greatest importance, however—because they tend to condition even these factors—are the capacity and inclination of deprivee strategists to induce deprivors to prefer the settlement being demanded.

In few ways is this better evidenced than by the fact that deprivee strategists are today increasingly required to sweeten the terms of settlement by way of special offer and compromise, chiefly through use of the economic instrument; by proposing or accepting "value-tying" arrangements. To be sure, this is a technique that has been common to the adjustment of a variety of international controversies throughout history (indeed, to the resolution of purely municipal conflicts also). But insofar as the settlement of international deprivatory disputes is concerned, it appears to have flourished only recently—generally since World War II—and then almost wholly in connection with the interstate negotiation of lump-sum agreements. Whatever its limits in time and focus, however, the "value-tying" technique has displayed some diversity in practice. As Foighel has shown,[367] it can be divided

---

[365] See pp. 115-16.

[366] For a statement of the kind of functional study that is needed, see W. Michael Reisman, "The Role of the Economic Agencies in the Enforcement of International Judgments and Awards: A Functional Approach," *International Organization,* XIX (Autumn 1965), 929.

[367] Foighel (fn. 64), 111-123. Foighel also lists "compulsion" as another inducement falling within the pale of this technique. But the example cited by the author (the release of Yugoslav gold reserves in the United States for the purpose of forcing Yugoslavia to agree to the U.S.-Yugoslav lump-sum settlement agreement of July 19, 1948) seems to belong to one or both of the first two types of inducements noted. It does not seem properly to be an inducement in its own right.

conveniently into three principal (and so not exhaustive) types of inducements (the first being often an outgrowth of restorative strategies previously undertaken): the release of "frozen" assets and accounts, the remission of debts earlier incurred, and the tender of commercial and other economic advantages. It is the last of these, however, that has been the most widely employed in recent years, the first two having thus far been used (as Foighel's own illustrations bear witness) principally in connection with the settlements which attended the post-World War II deprivations in Eastern Europe. This derives mainly from the fact that most deprivations have of late been imposed, as we have seen, by underdeveloped countries whose historic participation in the global wealth process has been highly circumscribed and whose need for commercial and other economic benefits has been singularly critical.[368] Thus, we may recall Bolivia's consent to reimburse United States nationals deprived by the 1952 nationalization of the Patino tin combine (among others) following United States pledges to purchase 15,000 tons of tin at world market prices, to double Point Four aid from $1.5 million to $3 million annually, and to provide new technical assistance to help Bolivia resolve its long-term economic problems.[369] A more recent example, noteworthy because it illustrates that value-tying inducements may be tendered by the manifest deprivees themselves, is found in the settlement negotiated between United States and Brazilian officials relative to the 1962 nationalization of International Telephone and Telegraph installations in Rio Grande do Sul. Brazil agreed to compensate I T and T in an amount equal to 80 percent of the estimated value of the utilities taken in exchange for I T and T's offer to reinvest the sum paid in one of its Brazilian manufacturing subsidiaries for the purpose of expanding its line of electrical appliances available to the Brazilian consumer.[370]

Of course, the capacity and inclination of deprivee strategists to strengthen their diplomatic hands by offers of economic indulgence will themselves depend on many factors. For example, nations that are highly developed industrially or individual firms that are financially and in other ways powerful are more likely to find room for maneuver than those that are not so situated. From the standpoint

[368] Of course, this is not to suggest that the release of "frozen" assets and accounts or the remission of debts earlier incurred cannot be effective insofar as the less-developed countries are concerned. Nor is it to suggest that the tender of commercial and other advantages would not serve as inducements to more industrialized nations.

[369] See A. J. Thomas, Jr., "Protection of Property of Citizens Abroad," in *Institute on Private Investments Abroad*, Southwestern Legal Foundation (Albany, N.Y. 1959), I, 417, 437-38.

[370] Brazilian Embassy Press Release of June 6, 1962, on "Protection of Foreign Investments in Public Utilities."

of community policy, what must be stressed is that these and all other relevant variables may condition not only the ultimate effectiveness of rehabilitative diplomacy, but, as well, the permissibility of resorting to alternative and perhaps more coercive measures should such diplomacy fail.

STRATEGIES OF RECONSTRUCTION

Strategies of reconstruction, like those of prevention, focus upon the long-term avoidance of deprivative policies and programs and, as such are more persuasive than coercive. But they go further in that they seek (through mutually supportive instrumental combination) to affect more basic predispositional and environmental change. With modest exception, they are innovations of the post-World War II era, partly reflecting the shortcomings of other techniques of protection, partly reflecting a new-found urgency for genuine international economic cooperation.

Diplomatic. All the arts of diplomacy may be employed to bring about fundamental changes appropriate to peaceful and productive economic intercourse. Primary emphasis in the present context, however, has been upon the preparation, discussion, recommendation, and sometimes conclusion of a number of more or less formal arrangements tailored to these ends—through international governmental organizations, from foreign office to foreign office, by way of private and public conferences, among particular identified parties, and so forth. Most of this activity has been channeled toward the consummation of three closely related but nonetheless distinct types of multilateral agreements: conventions which would (a) prescribe the treatment to be accorded foreign-wealth owners under international law; (b) create an international investment fund; and (c) establish international machinery for the settlement of disputes between host countries and foreign investors. Though by no means limited to the Process of Deprivation, all three bear heavily upon it.

Before World War II, efforts to conclude a multilateral investment code were few and, at best, broad-gauged, restricted as they were to such proposals as were made in 1929 under the auspices of the League of Nations[371] and by the Harvard Law School Research in Interna-

---

[371] See League of Nations, *Draft Convention on the Treatment of Foreigners* (L.N. Doc. No. C.174.M.53.1928.II 14); *Basis of Discussion, Responsibility of States for Damage Caused in Their Territory to the Person or Property of Foreigners* (L.N. Doc. No. C.75.M.69.1929.V); John W. Cutler, "The Treatment of Foreigners in Relation to the Draft Convention and Conference of 1929," *American Journal of International Law*, xxvii (April 1933), 225. See also League of Nations, Committee for the Study of International Loan Contracts, *Report* (1939); League of Nations, Special Joint Committee on Private Foreign Investment, *Conditions of Private Foreign Investment* (1946).

tional Law[372] for the codification of "the law of State responsibility" generally. Since 1948, however, due mainly to an "increased consciousness of international economic problems along with widespread optimism as to the possibilities of international organization,"[373] more than ten major investment code proposals have been advanced,[374] beginning with the never-wholly-ratified Havana Charter of the International Trade Organization.[375] Most recent and therefore perhaps most important is the Draft Convention on the Protection of Foreign Property published in 1963 under the mantle of the Organization for Economic Cooperation and Development.[376] In essence, these many proposals would require that foreign-wealth deprivations be undertaken solely for reasons of "public purpose" and then only upon payment of "prompt, adequate and effective" compensation ("prompt" meaning payment at the time of deprivation or within a foreseeable time thereafter, "adequate" meaning usually the "fair market value" of the "property" lost, and "effective" meaning payment in the deprivee's currency or in currencies convertible thereto). Deprivations contrary to these strictures would be unlawful and, for this reason, ineffective to pass title and justificatory of a number of countermeasures. As is well known, however, none of these proposals have met with final success. Whatever real diplomatic achievement can be claimed in this area is limited to United Nations resolutions and declarations, the most noteworthy being provisions of the General Assembly's declaratory resolution on "Permanent Sovereignty over Natural Resources," adopted in 1962.[377]

[372] See Harvard Law School, *Research in International Law, Draft Convention on the Responsibility of States for Damages Done in Their Territory to the Person or Property of Foreigners* (Cambridge 1929), 131-239.

[373] Fatouros, *Government Guarantees* (fn. 117), 70.

[374] See Report by the Committee on International Trade and Investment Section on International and Comparative Law of the American Bar Association, *The Protection of Private Property Invested Abroad* (Chicago 1963), 19-23.

[375] See U.N. Conference on Trade and Employment, Final Act and Related Documents, Art. 12 (1948). For commentary, see Clair Wilcox, *A Charter for World Trade* (New York 1949).

[376] See O.E.C.D. Pub. No. 15637, December 1962, Appendix B, reprinted in *International Legal Materials*, II (1963), 241.

[377] 17 U.N. GAOR XVII (1962), 1194. The most favorable provisions, inserted at the urgings mainly of the British and United States representatives, are paragraphs 4 and 8:

4. Nationalization, expropriation or requisitioning shall be based on grounds of public utility, security or the national interest which are recognized as overriding purely individual interests, both domestic and foreign. In such cases the owner shall be paid appropriate compensation, in accordance with the rules in force in the State taking such measures in the exercise of its sovereignty and in accordance with international law. In any case, where the question of compensation gives rise to a controversy, the national jurisdiction of the State taking such measures shall be exhausted. However, upon agreement by sover-

A number of multilateral insurance schemes have also been privately and publicly proposed in recent years, in large measure because of the failure of codification. As of 1965, indeed, there were no less than a dozen such proposals, mostly from groups either affiliated with or otherwise sympathetic to private business interests.[378] Among the more important proposals—none yet being in effect—have been those of the Consultative Assembly of the Council of Europe in 1958,[379] the World Bank and the International Chamber of Commerce in 1962,[380] and the Organization for Economic Cooperation and Development in 1965.[381] While they differ in detail, nearly all exhibit a common format: an international agency (usually as an affiliate of the World Bank) of which both capital-exporting and capital-importing countries would be members; financing through paid-in and reserve subscriptions generally geared to national income; premium payment by the individual investor, sometimes shared by the host country; and protection of generally "new" direct and portfolio investments against both direct and indirect measures of deprivation (among other "nonbusiness" risks), with coverage ranging to as high as 90 percent for periods extending as long as thirty years.

Finally and likewise many have been the private and public proposals for international machinery designed to settle deprivative and other investment disputes directly between the immediate parties. Often featured as components of investment code proposals, the pre-

---

eign States and other parties concerned, settlement of the dispute should be made through arbitration or international adjudication.

. . .

8. Foreign investment agreements freely entered into by, or between, sovereign States shall be observed in good faith; States and international organizations shall strictly and conscientiously respect the sovereignty of peoples and nations over their natural wealth and resources in accordance with the Charter and the principles set forth in the present resolution.

These provisions were considered by the Bulgarian delegate to the Second Committee to be so favorable to foreign-wealth interests as to cause him to hyperbolize that the Resolution constituted "a charter of foreign investment." Same, 5. On this Resolution generally, see Stephen M. Schwebel, "The Story of the U.N.'s Declaration on Permanent Sovereignty Over Natural Resources," *American Bar Association Journal*, XLIX (May 1963), 463.

[378] For a synoptic statement, see Nwogugu (fn. 243), 79-88.

[379] See *Report on an Investment Statute and a Guarantee Fund Against Political Risks*, Consultative Assembly Doc. 1027 (September 8, 1959). Compare Council of Europe Opinion No. 39 (1953) or the O.E.C.D. Draft Convention on the Protection of Foreign Property, *International Legal Materials*, III (Washington 1964), 133.

[380] See Staff Report of the International Bank (fn. 254), 92; Statements and Resolutions of the Sixth Congress of the ICC, Brochure No. 230 (Paris 1963), 8-14.

[381] See Report on the Status of the International Bank Studies on Multilateral Investment Guarantees, Annex A, reproduced in *International Legal Materials*, V (Washington 1966), 92.

ponderance of these schemes have been independently urged in recent years. Most have called for the establishment of a new institution, notwithstanding existing adaptable machinery under the Permanent Court of Arbitration.[382] The most important proposal, however—because of its recent coming into force—has been the 1965 World Bank proposal for an affiliated but independent "International Centre for Settlement of Investment Disputes."[383] Substantially representative of other proposals, this multilateral convention makes conciliation and arbitration facilities available to individual investors without the assistance of their home governments—mainly to avoid the political and other difficulties inherent in the traditional state-espousal-of-claims system—with awards effective and enforceable in local jurisdictions.

Ideological. All communications that champion foreign enterprise —more particularly private foreign enterprise—as an important or even necessary ingredient in the global wealth process or which propagate symbols and practices otherwise conducive to the use of private wealth across national boundaries may be said to serve reconstructive goals, especially when they are directed at the suppression or elimination of patterns that have contributed to deprivations in the past. The myriad "public relations" techniques that were noted earlier among the preventive strategies daily employed by foreign entrepreneurs and their associates, for example, may be so viewed.[384] But the long-range shaping of popular and elite perspectives about the minimum conditions necessary for international economic intercourse may be seen to operate in still another connection: in the private and public preparation, discussion, and recommendation of the trilogy of multilateral conventions just described (among other international arrangements). As indicated, all but one of these proposals have thus far failed to secure complete and unreserved ratification. But the very proc-

[382] In 1962, the Bureau of the Permanent Court of Arbitration published rules of arbitration and conciliation for the settlement of international disputes between two parties only one of which is a state. See *American Journal of International Law*, LVII (April 1963), 500. See also Orman W. Ketcham, "Arbitration between a State and a Foreign Private Party," in *Rights and Duties of Private Investors Abroad*, Southwestern Legal Foundation (Albany, N.Y. 1965), 403, 406-07.

[383] See Convention on the Settlement of Investment Disputes between States and Nationals of other States, reproduced in *International Legal Materials*, IV (Washington 1965), 532. See also International Bank for Reconstruction and Development, Report of the Executive Directors on the Convention on the Settlement of Investment Disputes between States and Nationals of Other States, reproduced in same, 524. With twenty states having ratified the convention as of September 14, 1966, the convention entered into force on October 14, 1966, pursuant to Article 12 thereof. On the general advantages and disadvantages of this convention, see Note, "International Arbitration between States and Foreign Investors—The World Bank Convention," *Stanford Law Review*, XVIII (June 1966), 1359.

[384] See pp. 125-29.

ess of recommending them, whether through adversative negotiations or consentaneous deliberations, has had what Iklé would call an important "sounding-board effect."[385] At high-level conferences, in special publications, and elsewhere, deprivee views and policy goals have through this process received a breadth of exposure and consideration that would not have been possible had they been propounded by less conspicuous means. In short, irrespective of whether they have gained the adherences requisite for prescriptive purposes, the proposals themselves have had a profound impact upon all concerned and have themselves therefore served fundamentally to condition the total environmental context within which the Process of Deprivation takes place. This is a point which is too often ignored when strategic appraisals are made.

Economic. Like their diplomatic and ideological counterparts, the economic strategies of reconstruction are found in both the public and private sectors. Unlike those counterparts, however, they are seldom if ever actually conceived with an eye to the Process of Deprivation alone.

In the public sector, these strategies thus include most of the manifold programs that make up the economic policies of today's "mature" societies toward those that are less developed. As has been several times noted, most recent deprivations have taken place within those transitional communities that are presently emerging from colonial and semifeudal status, where the gap between demanded and actual levels of social and economic achievement is not only enormous, but widening. To be sure, there is no simple one-to-one correlation between this differential and the deprivations that have been imposed. Still, a nexus remains. For communities frustrated in their efforts to achieve "Fifty Years of Progress in Five Years,"[386] deprivative financing sometimes appears as a salutary, even if temporary, expedient. Accordingly, it is not unreasonable to suggest that international economic policies that are designed (whether for altruistic or self-serving reasons, or both) expressly to accelerate the fulfillment of these unsatisfied demands serve also to reduce the need for quick nostrums. Such international policies include, for example, programs for stimulating the flow of foreign capital and skills (from the public or private sector), schemes for stabilizing world trade and commodity pricing patterns, measures for alleviating imbalances in international payments, steps for curbing population growth, and so on. Of course, whether these policies do in fact contribute to the avoidance of dep-

---

[385] Iklé (fn. 299), 52.

[386] It was with this slogan that former Brazilian President Juscelino Kubitschek took office in 1956. See Szulc (fn. 167), 195.

rivations is another matter, one deserving of extensive study. Economic development does not of itself guarantee stability and may even bear consequences dangerous for foreign investment.[387] But if recent experience is any indication, there is reason to believe that the more developed the host community the less likely it is that deprivations will be imposed.

At least two principal types of economic strategy are pursued in the private sector. In a realistic sense, each may be said to be a part of that arsenal of "public relations" techniques which foreign entrepreneurs are ever-expanding.

The first type may be seen as counterpart to the public economic policies just mentioned and, as such, subject to the same qualifications. For obvious reasons, it has thus far been most notably practiced by the world's commercial and industrial giants—e.g., Royal Dutch/Shell and Aramco, Goodyear and Michelin, Unilever and United Fruit—mainly in the underdeveloped countries. Whether out of obligation or foresight or both, these great transnational enterprises have in many ways assumed the function of "miniature welfare states," dispensing all kinds of financial and technical aid under "private Point Four" programs to deal with the education, health, sanitation, housing, communication, transportation, and other "social overhead" problems with which their host communities are plagued.[388] As Standard Oil has put it, "Esso . . . has followed a policy of standing aside from purely Venezuelan affairs, while trying to fulfill in all respects its obligations as a good corporate citizen."[389] All this reflects, surely, that foreign investors have undergone a major change of attitude about their proper functions abroad and that they cannot be so easily depicted today as the unashamed profiteers they sometimes were. But apart from any genuine altruism that may cause them to pursue these

[387] Staley (fn. 177), 58: "For each of these objectives ('improved material livelihood,' 'freedom for the human spirit,' and 'peace and security') economic development of the underdeveloped areas is an essential condition. It is not, however, a sufficient condition for any of them, since economic advancement does not of itself guarantee the kind of society and government which will bring a wide distribution of economic goods, or freedom, or security and peace." See same, Chap. 4. See also Gabriel A. Almond and James S. Coleman, eds., The Politics of the Developing Areas (Princeton 1960), 536-44; Everett E. Hagen, A General Framework for Analyzing Economic Growth (Washington 1961); Charles P. Kindleberger, The Implications of Differential Economic Development (New York 1959).

[388] See, e.g., the relevant chapters of the series of case studies on, among others, the Creole Petroleum Corporation in Venezuela, the Firestone Tire and Rubber Company in Liberia, and the Standard-Vacuum Oil Company in Indonesia sponsored by the National Planning Association under the title United States Business Performance Abroad. In connection with the Middle East, see Finnie (fn. 273), 142-81.

[389] Standard Oil Co. of New Jersey, The Lamp (New York 1956), 4.

practices (for which, parenthetically, they are in some quarters given too little credit), it is difficult to explain their behavior other than that it is born of a belief that by reducing the elements of instability they can and do contribute to their own long-range and overall security.[390]

No less important and more widespread is the recent and growing practice of "internationalizing" foreign investments through "joint venture" undertakings, with and without benefit of express agreement.[391] Pursued both by investors already operating abroad and by investors anxious to develop yet unexplored markets and resources, these undertakings include such diversified "equity" and "nonequity" measures as combining risk capital on majority, fifty-fifty, and minority bases, establishing multinational participation in a single enterprise, opening share ownership to the public at large (local and foreign), arranging for the provision of technical services to indigenous firms, engaging in franchise and brand-use licensing, and entering into construction and job performance, management, and rental contracts.[392] The motives lying behind these undertakings are, as elsewhere, both complex and diverse and by no means limited simply to the avoidance of deprivations or other harsh treatment.[393] But there is no denying that when foreign entrepreneurs, large and small, either initiate or accede to requests for these transformative measures, the hope of avoiding deprivative treatment figures prominently in their calculations.[394]

[390] Summarizing the programs of the Firestone Tire and Rubber Company in Liberia and the Creole Petroleum Company in Venezuela, Bruce E. Clubb and Verne W. Vance, Jr., "Incentives to Private U.S. Investment Abroad under the Foreign Assistance Program," *Yale Law Journal*, LXXII (January 1963), 475, have stated: "The result is not only to create some measure of community dependence on the company, but also to generate a considerable reservoir of good will." Same, 503-04.

[391] For detailed analysis and a number of case studies, see Wolfgang Friedmann and George Kalmanoff, *Joint International Business Ventures* (New York 1961).

[392] Same, 84-124.

[393] "The motives of investor companies for participating in joint ventures in less-developed countries may be analyzed in various ways—usually with considerable overlap. The advantages usually mentioned are: 1) the achievement of capital savings and the reduction of business risks; 2) the obtaining of management skills and the maintenance of employee morale; 3) the facilitating of sales; 4) the improvement of governmental relations; and 5) the achievement of good public relations. There are additional miscellaneous advantages." Same, 134.

[394] "Reduction of risk as a motive [for joint venture arrangements] involves the notion that a company with a local partner is less subject to the danger of adverse action by the local government. If the government or a national development bank is the local partner, there is an added element of protection, not only against the gross risks of outright expropriation, but also against the often more dangerous risks of bureaucratic harrassment [sic] and gradual strangulation in red tape which sometimes afflict foreign investors who are out of favor with the governments of

STRATEGIES OF CORRECTION

Demands for punishment can be expressed in a number of ways, both conscious and subconscious. The more coercive strategies of restoration, for example—severing diplomatic relations, terminating foreign aid, imposing military blockades, and so forth—are not infrequently marked by more or less subconscious punitive considerations. Rehabilitative diplomacy, too, in the sense of intentionally inflated reparative demands, may be so influenced. An enlightened decision-maker would perceive this factor, however disguised, and assess the degree to which it should be allowed to affect deprivee response, if at all. On certain occasions, however, corrective demands may be asserted quite consciously indeed. This is ordinarily the case when the deprivation inflicted is presumed (if not already determined) to be unlawful, and then only when restorative strategies have succeeded sufficiently to permit either the exercise of unilateral control over the deprivor community or the intercession of appropriate third-party authorities. Thus have deprivee strategists, principally through litigative techniques, but sometimes through customary diplomatic channels, sought to win application of "punitive," "vindictive," or "retributory" damages for what Charles Cheney Hyde has called the "value of exemplary reparation as a deterrent of conduct otherwise to be anticipated."[395] It must be recognized, of course, that there is some difference of opinion about whether corrective damages may be awarded at all,[396] a debate that has obvious bearing upon the extent to which corrective demands have been pressed in the past and will be pressed in the future. But in a world that is badly in need of more persuasive techniques for assuring basic order, it is not untoward to suggest that corrective damages may have a proper and perhaps important role to play in this area.[397]

---

the countries in which they are operating." Same, 136. See also same, 141-42, wherein it is stated that "greater friendliness on the part of the government," providing an "incentive in the government to avoid actions damaging to the venture," and having a local partner as "an active agent to favorably influence government policies and treatment" are "three distinct ways" in which joint ventures can exert a "favorable influence on the local government." But see J. W. Sundelson, "The Case for One Hundred Percent Ownership in Foreign Investments," in John F. McDaniels, ed., *International Financing and Investment* (Dobbs Ferry, N.Y. 1964), 514.

[395] Charles C. Hyde, *International Law Chiefly as Interpreted and Applied by the United States* (Boston 1922), 515-16.

[396] See, e.g., Wortley (fn. 44), 138. See also Dunn (fn. 149), 172-87; García Amador, "Sixth Report on Responsibility of the State for Injuries Caused in its Territory to the Person or Property of Aliens—Reparation of the Injury," *1961 Yearbook of the International Law Commission* (New York 1962), II, 35-37.

[397] As Eagleton somewhat overzealously remarked several years ago: "It can no longer be argued that the sovereign state is above the law; and there seems to

Outcomes

One way to approach the Outcome phase of the subprocess of deprivee response would be to consider the impact of deprivee response (anticipatory and reactive) upon deprivor values. This is clearly necessary for proper appraisal in any given case, a point that is stressed below. But it seems neither the most efficient nor the most helpful from the standpoint of illuminating *all* the policy-relevant factors that pertain to deprivee response. More convenient and more meaningful is an assessment of the degree to which the specific protection objectives projected and pursued by deprivee strategists—prevention, deterrence, restoration, rehabilitation, reconstruction, and correction—are truly realized.

Of course, how effective or useful any one or more of the deprivee strategies may actually be, whether in the particular case or over the long haul of time and controversy, is a question that is neither easily nor quickly answered. More important, facile and hasty conclusions are usually dangerous, if not meaningless.

In the particular case, there are at least two dangers. First is the danger of premature judgment. What may at first appear to be an effective strategy (or outcome) may not be one in fact. Ostensibly resolving a number of diplomatic claims arising out of the deprivations in post-World War II Eastern Europe, for example, were many agreements which in a general way promised reparation to deprived aliens.[398] In many cases, however, the securing of these commitments proved futile, final rehabilitative settlements commonly not being won until several years later.[399] Second, and intimately related, is the danger of insular judgment. What may be supposed a generally ineffective tactic when considered alone may be rated more effective when seen in combination with other and especially more successful techniques. To put it another way, failure to recognize the complementary and cumulative impact of deprivee strategies can occasion inaccurate estimates. For example, it might be argued that the restorative economic strategies employed by the British against Iran following the nationalization of the Anglo-Iranian Oil Company[400] were generally without effect because "[w]hat they accomplished was to make Mossadegh a world figure and a symbolic champion of all Middle

---

be no reason why it should not be penalized for its misconduct, under proper rules and restrictions." Clyde Eagleton, *The Responsibility of States in International Law* (New York 1928), 191.

[398] See p. 153.

[399] Foighel (fn. 64), 194-214; White (fn. 60), 193-226. See also Weston (fn. 353), 838-40, 845-49.

[400] See footnote 334.

Eastern and Far Eastern countries which felt themselves to be down-trodden."[401] But can it be said with certainty that Britain's subsequent and seemingly decisive diplomatic efforts (mainly by way of enlisting American public and private support) would have produced a settlement quite so successful for British interests had these measures not been undertaken in the first place?[402] In any particular case, in sum, time and tactical relationships must be given their proper due before authentic conclusions can be reached.

When appraising the effectiveness of deprivee strategies over the long term, the danger is essentially one of unexplored judgment. To observe that restrictive promises in the 1933 Concession Agreement between Iran and the Anglo-Iranian Oil Company failed to prevent Anglo-Iranian's nationalization is not to say that the securing of identical or similar promises is without reward generally.[403] To point out that United States threats to suspend foreign aid to Ceylon did not deter the 1963 Bandaranaike Government from taking over certain American-owned petroleum installations is not to argue that like threats must always prove unavailing.[404] To stress with respect to

[401] Henry F. Grady, "What Went Wrong in Iran?" *Saturday Evening Post* (January 5, 1952), 30, 58.

[402] For details on the extent of British success in this regard, see Walden (fn. 71), 112-13.

[403] Otherwise it would be difficult to explain why the successor and still viable Iran Consortium Agreement of September 19-20, 1954, between Iran and eight foreign oil companies stipulates a similar, though more explicit, production of this type [Art. 41 (B)]; or why the Consortium Agreement prohibition is repeated almost verbatim in Art. 36(A) of the more recent Agreement of November 17, 1960, between the Government of Ghana and the Volta Aluminium Company (a consortium of American and Canadian firms) for the construction and operation of an aluminum smelter in Ghana. For the text of the former provision, see Hurewitz (fn. 238), 374. For the text of the latter see Nwogugu (fn. 243), 171.

[404] Cecil J. Olmstead, who has for several years been associated with Texaco, Inc., has addressed himself to this point specifically:

One hears that, since the Hickenlooper Amendment did not prevent the expropriation in Ceylon, it is not an effective means of obtaining compliance with international law in the area of private investment abroad. It is true that the Amendment did not prevent the seizure of United States-owned oil properties there but, for several reasons, I doubt that Ceylon should be selected as a test case. To begin with, the Hickenlooper Amendment was introduced in early 1962 and added to the Foreign Assistance Bill later in that year. Ceylon had determined to establish a government oil company in January 1961, when a bill was introduced in Parliament authorizing, *inter alia*, the requisition of certain assets of the private petroleum companies. Thus, Ceylon's program contemplating some nationalization was well under way before the Hickenlooper Amendment was even proposed, although United States-owned properties were not actually seized until February, 1963. "Foreign Aid as an Effective Means of Persuasion," *Proceedings of the American Society of International Law*, LVIII (1964), 205, 209.

In this connection, however, special attention should be given to the reasons lying behind the reluctance of the United States Government to apply vigorously

post-1945 Eastern Europe the bootlessness of obtaining promises of reparation requiring the manifest deprivees themselves to press their claims directly with the deprivor authorities is not to demonstrate that the winning of such rehabilitative commitments is necessarily worthless on other occasions.[405] The point is that the utility of deprivee strategies is a function of many variables (a number of which have already been mentioned in passing) whose accounting must be systematically undertaken before any realistic assessment can be expected. A meaningful answer about the effectiveness over time of any given deprivee strategy necessarily depends upon an exhaustive—or at least adequately representative—examination of the many or few specific past encounters within which it has been employed, referring to all the relevant features of the Process of Deprivation (retrospective and prospective as herein outlined), both before and after deprivation.

A survey of the effectiveness of deprivee strategies (and so of the attainability of deprivee objectives) as thus profiled, whether in the particular case or in all cases, is obviously beyond the scope of this essay. But it deserves emphasis that this issue has more than mere academic or tactical interest. For the extent to which particular strategies may be found effective, absolutely and in relation to each other, is bound to bear significantly upon one or all of at least three important and interrelated policy-relevant considerations.

First, and perhaps most important, their effectiveness may fundamentally condition the permissibility, or lawfulness, of the strategies actually employed in a given context. For example, if certain essentially persuasive techniques of restoration—say, diplomatic strategies of direct and indirect appeal—are found to have traditionally proved satisfactory in certain situations, the use, instead, of more coercive measures in like settings—say, economic boycotts or military maneuvers—may stand justifiably suspect. On the other hand, where certain techniques can be shown commonly ineffective in given situations, what would otherwise be held impermissible might be judged altogether appropriate. In short, considerations about the lawfulness

---

the provisions of the Hickenlooper Amendment against Peru following the latter's recent nationalization of the indirectly American-owned International Petroleum Company. For details see the *New York Times*, 1969: February 7, p. 10, col. 3; March 5, p. 46, col. 3; April 5, p. 3, col. 5; April 8, p. 1, col. 1; April 17, p. 9, col. 1. See also Richard N. Goodwin, "Letter from Peru," *The New Yorker* (May 17, 1969), 41-109; U.S., Congress, Senate, Committee on Foreign Relations, *United States Relations with Peru, Hearings before the Subcommittee on Western Hemisphere Affairs*, 91st Cong., 1st Sess., 1969.

[405] Those pertaining to the French nationalizations of foreign gas and electric holdings in 1946, for example, have been said to have been successful. See White (fn. 60), 204.

of particular strategies cannot be divorced from considerations about the availability of effective alternatives.

Second, the efficacy of specific protection measures is sure to influence the strategy choices that deprivees and their associates will make at a given time and in a given case. Obviously, strategies that seem to produce desired results are likely to command greater use than those that do not. What sometimes matters for policy, however, from the standpoint of basic world order, is less the effectiveness than the desirability (irrespective of the permissibility) of one strategy relative to another. If the more desirable strategy happens also to be the less effective, decision-makers may be concerned to strengthen its appeal in order to encourage its use. In any situation there may be a number of perfectly lawful alternatives, but the concern of policy may be to accomplish as much as possible with as little as possible. In a world that seems relentlessly to hold out the prospect of severe conflagration even from what may appear to be the most removed confrontation, this at the very least should be kept at the forefront of decision.

Finally, the effectiveness of particular deprivee strategies is likely to affect deprivor calculations about the immediate feasibility or advantage of given deprivative pursuits. As noted, some strategies may be so effective as to preclude or reverse deprivation programs altogether, or to otherwise render them sterile. This may or may not be the intended result. But whatever the goal, a question of desirability (if not also permissibility) arises again. It may be that a certain program—say, a much needed land reform or an ecological control plan—which necessitates even a large-scale deprivation of foreign wealth should not only *not* be discouraged, but positively encouraged. That is, deprivee strategies may sometimes serve essentially to frustrate legitimate demands and thereby, possibly, by circular causation to exacerbate a potential for truly remorseless deprivative action in the future. In such event the principal concern may be to eliminate the forces which hamper the realization of these demands, even if this means that foreign-wealth owners must suffer some loss. To put it another way, policy is as much concerned with the multivalued impact of deprivee response upon the deprivors as it is with the multivalued impact of deprivor activity upon the deprivees.

General Effects

Having thus seen (in broad outline only) who for what reasons and at what points of confrontation within the Process of Deprivation acts and reacts how and with what proximate results, *ex hypothesi* it is now possible to consider the general effects or long-term consequences which both the immediate parties and all who participate in the global wealth process may expect from deprivative activity. In contrast to the others, this phase of analysis is probably the most fundamental from the standpoint of policy recommendation and prescription. More than the others, it looks to the broad contours of transnational economic life that are likely to loom large (if not predominate) in the presence of the deprivative and counterdeprivative practices heretofore described and, hence, is the most closely related to the high-level policies which authoritative decision-makers reject and prefer and from which specific policies germane to concrete competing claims (arising out of each of the foregoing phases of interaction) derive.

Of course, any attempt to project the general effects of deprivative action is fraught with practical difficulty. In the first place, it is never exactly clear where short-term consequences end and long-term consequences begin. Moreover, no definitive conclusions are possible in the particular case until all the relevant facts are carefully marshalled and examined, no matter how identifiable and consistent general consequential patterns may be over time and controversy. But even when the temporal reference is established and when inquiry is limited to overall patterns, one is at once struck by the near total absence of in-depth analysis in this area, not only among international lawyers but also among international economists—a fact which, given the rudimentary relevance of long-term consequences to policy recommendation and prescription, raises obvious questions about the merit of past judgments. In short, no feature of the Process of Deprivation is more in need of comprehensive empirical study than this one. What follows here is a brief indication of the kind of appraisal that can and should be made both in the particular case and overall.

It is helpful to begin by acknowledging that there is a widespread tendency—principally in the capital-exporting world—to emphasize, if not sometimes to assume categorically, that foreign-wealth deprivations are more destructive than productive of economic and other values over the long run, not simply for the deprivees but for the deprivors and the rest of the world community as well. As the Chairman of the American Committee on Nationalization and Foreign Property put it to the International Law Association in 1958, "[w]e have interpreted the fact of many government takings, particularly since the Second World War, as in essence the frustration and failure of joint plans which had reached across national borders."[406]

---

[406] From the remarks of James N. Hyde, in *International Law Association, Report of the Forty-eighth Conference* (1959), 140. See also Department of State, Report to the President of the United States from the Committee to Strengthen the Security of the Free World [popularly known as the Clay Committee Report], *The Scope and Distribution of United States Military and Economic Assistance Programs* (Washington, March 20, 1963), 13: "Agitation for the expropriation of

This is a caricature to be sure. It is not an iron-clad proposition. But it is a caricature that is not too greatly exaggerated, especially when the focus is upon deprivations imposed by underdeveloped communities (as indicated, the primary deprivors today). The basic profile is familiar:

> A violent termination of foreign participation in the national economy does not necessarily come to grips with the real causes of the social tensions which brought about such a step. More than that, it may actually restrict the opportunity of the underdeveloped nation in question to make those advances toward economic growth which it hoped to achieve. The essential problem faced by the underdeveloped nation . . . is distributive justice in its own internal functioning. To deny justice to the foreigner by a violent expropriation of his property is not to solve the underlying internal maladjustments of the society. The foreigner made his investment on the basis of the current local conditions. When he entered the local society, he respected the cultural realities as they then existed. His skills and capital were contributed to the national system and enriched it in a measure not otherwise possible, if reliance for growth were limited to local capital. He was not a member or citizen of the state. The responsibility for local ills was not his. Injustice is only mounted on injustice when his property is expropriated without adequate compensation as a consequence of a failure of the domestic social system to achieve distributive justice in its functioning. To expel him from the national economy means that other actors in the international system will not be prone to make another contribution on similar terms. The national society will thus be thrust back upon its own resources as it seeks to achieve economic growth.[407]

It is not that this profile is wrong. To the contrary, it has much validity, particularly when the deprivations go uncompensated, as qualified above, and when the profile is itself given a limited temporal reference. It is simply that, even after putting aside the questionable assertion that there is no relation between local ills and past foreign participation, it is overly gratuitous in its twofold stress that foreign-wealth deprivations have the effect of deterring foreign capital and skills and retarding economic development—and so, by reasonable reduction, of contributing more to the destruction than to the produc-

---

foreign enterprises and for nationalization of private productive ventures is hardly conducive to the mobilization of private and foreign investment and is destructive to rapid economic progress."

[407] Carlston (fn. 15), 106-07.

tion of the values of international economic intercourse over the long run.

Consider, first, whether deprivations discourage foreign investment. According to the only known quantitative data on the subject, the deterrent effect may not be as great as it would seem popularly believed to be, at least not insofar as "direct" deprivations are concerned. A survey conducted by the National Industrial Conference Board of New York in 1950-51, for example, disclosed that of 107 American companies having direct investments abroad (the firms then representing about 54 percent of American direct private investment abroad) only 8 percent or less even mentioned "nationalization and expropriation" as an obstacle to direct foreign investment.[408] And in the aggregate tally this obstacle ranked only thirteenth among a possible twenty-one.[409] A Canadian survey conducted at about the same time indicated similar findings.[410] So too did surveys conducted by the United States Department of Commerce in 1952[411] and by Barlow and Wender in 1953-54,[412] the latter summarizing that "[i]t is possible that fear of expropriation has prevented companies from investigating foreign opportunity, but in such cases, we believe expropriation would be regarded as merely one of the many risks and uncertainties of foreign investment which combined to prevent companies from investigating opportunities."[413]

It should be noted, however, that all of these surveys were conducted over a decade ago and that, with nationalizations having intensified considerably in the interim, the risk of deprivation today may have greater deterrent effect than it did yesterday.[414] Furthermore, none of

[408] See J. Frank Gaston, *Obstacles to Direct Foreign Investment* (New York 1951), 17.

[409] Same, 8. Its rank was nineteenth in respect of direct foreign investment in Africa, fourteenth in Asia and Latin America, and eighth in Europe (where the memory of post-World War II deprivations was still fresh).

[410] See *Report of the Canadian Advisory Committee on Overseas Investment* (Ottawa 1950), 40-41, 60.

[411] See Department of Commerce Survey (fn. 152).

[412] See Barlow and Wender (fn. 152).

[413] Same, 210-12.

[414] That this may be so is suggested by another, more recent study conducted by the National Industrial Conference Board. Reporting on the "accumulated experience" of the investors of the twelve leading capital-exporting nations of the world in eighty-eight countries, the study states that a "*common* cause of hesitancy in committing funds is fear of expropriation or nationalization of the investment. Indeed, the 'fear' of expropriation is cited far more often as a deterrent to investment than are acts of actual expropriation. . . . While most acts of expropriation reported have been with compensation to the investors, companies are still reluctant to take all the risks of establishing a new business abroad, and fostering and developing it, only to have it taken over." (Emphasis added.) (Fn. 152, 14-15.) While not explicitly assigning any rank to "expropriation and nationalization" among the obstacles listed, it perhaps deserves note that the category was listed

these studies accounted explicitly for "indirect" deprivations which, as Rubin has suggested, may have greater deterrent effect than outright seizure itself.[415] And of course, overshadowing all such reservations is the truism that the effect is often the child of the thought, however unfounded the thought is in fact. In short, there is no blinking the fact that deprivations and threats of deprivation can and do have a deterrent effect overall. The experience of the last fifteen years especially makes it abundantly clear that a major determinant of private and public foreign enterprise is the attitude of host communities toward such enterprise; and in many ways indicative of that attitude, obviously, is the extent to which host communities have been or may be inclined to engage in deprivative practices. In other words, when contemplating an investment in a deprivation-prone community, the foreign investor is necessarily engaged in, and often put off by, considerations which go well beyond those of a purely commercial character.

But it does not follow that all or most foreign entrepreneurs will be thus deterred or that all or some foreign entrepreneurs should not be deterred, two assumptions which frequently tend to underlie the effects profile herein posed. The second is of course an assumption of preference—a policy judgment in itself, not a judgment about facts that may influence policy. If our observational standpoint is not to become confused, it must be given separate consideration elsewhere.[416] But the first assumption is not (being descriptive rather than prescriptive) and so is properly challenged here. Its difficulty inheres in the fact that it is predicated on a model of transnational entrepreneurial decision-making that is much less complicated than that decision-making process actually is; that is, on a model that treats as patently irrational any foreign investment decisions which *at first* appear inim-

---

eighth among a possible nine conditions "that generally distress investors and obstruct the flow of private foreign capital." Same, 1. See also Report of the Secretary-General, "Economic Development of Underdeveloped Countries—International Flow of Long-Term Capital and Official Donations, 1959-61," U.N. GAOR, XVII, 1962, 63. In 1961, Robert Garner, then President of the International Finance Corporation, made the point even more graphic by his statement that United States investors alone had held back an estimated $500 million in investments in Latin America generally, solely because of the Cuban seizures of 1959-60. Address to the Board of Governors of the International Finance Corporation, Vienna, September 21, 1961, 15.

[415] Seymour J. Rubin, *Private Foreign Investment* (Baltimore 1956), 37-43.

[416] The point is raised here principally to re-emphasize the importance of maintaining strict adherence to the separate undertaking of policy clarification and recommendation, as distinct from the performance of the other essential tasks of rational inquiry. In this connection, see pp. 181-82. As to the desirability of encouraging foreign investment, according to members of the "Pearson Commission," see *Partners in Development, Report of the Commission on International Development* (New York, Washington, and London 1969), Chap. 55.

ical to an entrepreneur's pecuniary best interests. Concededly, regrettably, and somewhat surprisingly, we know precious little about foreign investment decision-making, particularly in the underdeveloped world.[417] Nevertheless, and without going into all the acknowledged and unacknowledged factors that singly or in combination influence this practice, it is possible to conceive of a number of important situations in which foreign entrepreneurs may not be readily deterred by a host community's penchant for engaging in deprivative practices (at least not in any substantial sense).

Consider, for example, enterprises whose operations depend on the extraction or development of indigenous natural resources. Despite the possibility of exploiting other sources of supply or of purchasing the needed resources from others, despite the alternative of inventing or utilizing synthetic substitutes, and despite the fact that such enterprises may rank high among those most fearful of deprivative action, many will find themselves so "locked in" as to make it far less onerous to continue and perhaps even to expand the pattern of investment already established (though possibly in modified form) notwithstanding an ever-present risk of deprivation. Consider, too, those entrepreneurs (prevalent mainly at the individual and small corporate levels) who, usually uncommitted to any particular product or product line, are lured abroad by high profit potentials—by the possibility of reaping a handsome and quick capital gain on a modest capital outlay. They, too, are unlikely to be easily dissuaded, perhaps even if they have already suffered deprivations in the past. Still another example, closely related to the second, is the so-called promotional pacemaker, increasingly to be found in the underdeveloped world. Typically concerned with the development of enterprises for which there is little or no indigenous entrepreneurial experience—commonly in the manufacturing sector—he starts new ventures only to withdraw once the enterprise is under way and, as a consequence, is less likely than others to be put off by deprivative patterns. And of course, it by no means follows that deprivations imposed upon a particular nationality group or against a particular type of enterprise or by a particular subnational entity (and so forth), will deter investors who are not of such nationality or who are not engaged in such enterprise or who, though participating in the national economy, have no substantial interests in the narrower subnational entity. This is especially likely when it can be shown that they have excess capacity relative to the demand they can create for their products in already familiar markets and/or that they possess the potential for so controlling the local and international

417 But see, e.g. Aubrey (fn. 153), 397; Charles P. Kindleberger, *American Business Abroad* (New Haven and London 1969), 145-78.

markets to which they are specialized as to render major interference with their operations a hollow, if not counterproductive, exercise.[418] Other such situations are undoubtedly to be found.

But consider now the second emphasis commonly profiled: that foreign-wealth deprivations have the long-term effect of retarding economic development. Using arithmetic models based on reasonably well-refined patterns and relationships, economists can show that this need not be the result. Indeed, they can demonstrate that in purely economic terms economic growth can be significantly accelerated by deprivative practices.[419] The economists differ, however.[420] Perhaps, as one commentator has recommended, "it behooves laymen not to try to challenge the validity of such demonstrations."[421] Yet implicit here are at least two assumptions that are not beyond the reach of some lay consideration.

First is the assumption that foreign-wealth deprivations leave deprivor communities without financial resources sufficient to meet their economic growth requirements. Does this make sense? In many respects, yes. In most countries, particularly the underdeveloped, the scale of available financial resources has been far too low to bring about sustained and vigorous economic growth. And even if this were not so, most are faced with the need for some foreign exchange to purchase the goods and services their development demands. On the whole, foreign entrepreneurship helps to reduce the shortage of domestic savings and to increase the supply of foreign exchange—and, so, contributes to a recipient country's development. Cutting off this external supply, it follows, spells a generally corresponding restraint on development.

Notwithstanding, there exist a number of significant factors which, when added to this equation, must be seen as qualifying. In the first place, the proposition is itself premised on the notion that deprivations deter foreign investment. This, as we have seen, is not necessarily accurate, there being a variety of situations in which foreign capital

[418] In this connection, consider Cheddi Jagan, *The West on Trial* (London 1966), 397, wherein the author, citing and quoting from an alleged "confidential report" from "special advisor" Nelson Rockefeller to President Eisenhower, ruefully recounts that "[a]fter the overthrow of the Mossadegh government in Iran in 1953 [which Government had recently nationalized Iran's oil industry] through CIA subversion and intervention, the U.S. obtained a 40 percent share in Iran's oil industry."

[419] E.g., Bronfenbrenner, "The Appeal of Confiscation in Economic Development" (fn. 65), 201 (emphasis given to the Soviet and Chinese experiences).

[420] E.g., Garnick (fn. 65), 353; Benjamin H. Higgins, *Economic Development* (New York 1959), 472; cf. Bronfenbrenner, "Second Thoughts on Confiscation" (fn. 65), 367.

[421] Karst (fn. 167), 327, 361.

will probably continue to flow despite a deprivative climate. Secondly, it is by no means a foregone conclusion that foreign enterprise is in all cases more beneficial than detrimental to overall economic development, even in the purely economic sense. When it is not, its elimination may serve more a positive good than a net harm. Thirdly, in many countries (most notably in Latin America) it is less the domestic resources themselves than the capacity to tap those resources effectively that has been lacking. Aside from the use of disguised unemployment, controlled inflation, "pump-priming," and the deprivation strategy itself—what Benjamin Higgins calls the "primrose path of development"[422]—deprivor communities may be expected increasingly to cast about for more remunerative programs of voluntary and compulsory saving and for more gainful techniques of taxation and tax administration in the process of liberating themselves from what they may perceive to be an excessive dependence on foreign entrepreneurship. True, these programs may not be locally popular, particularly among the wealthy classes who (by chicanery or otherwise) have in many places long reaped the benefits of past exemption. But it should not be forgotten that deprivor elites may find themselves in a significantly stronger position to undertake such measures simply because of the solidifying psychological benefit which can attend assaults upon foreign capital. Lastly, deprivor communities need not and do not rely upon foreign entrepreneurship alone. The fact that private foreign capital contributes less than 10 percent of net investment within the developing countries and that future projections indicate no major change in this regard is at least partly confirmative.[423] Deprivor communities may look instead to foreign governments and international organizations for assistance. To be sure, the extent to which they can do so is limited. For a host of political and other reasons, there is a remarkable lack of public funds to go around, especially on an unfettered basis (a fact which some deprivation-prone communities are all too quick to forget). But in a world in which the powerful and wealthy are each day competing for cold-war allegiances the alternative is obviously not without significance. Illustrative is the hastily but worthily conceived Alliance for Progress through which public (and private) capital has been summoned to the task of development in precisely those areas where the risks of deprivation are extremely high.

The second assumption underlying the notion that deprivations retard economic growth is that foreign-wealth deprivations leave

[422] Higgins (fn. 420), Chap. 19.

[423] P. N. Rosenstein-Rodan, "International Aid for Underdeveloped Countries," *The Review of Economics and Statistics*, XLIII (Cambridge, Mass. 1961), 107, 127-29, 134-35.

deprivor communities without the enlightenment and skills they need for development. This has much validity also. Foreign entrepreneurs bring not only physical and financial resources to host communities but, as well, what economists call "external economies"—technological knowledge, innovations in products and production techniques, marketing information and experience, managerial and supervisory know-how, and organizational expertise—all of which are in themselves and because of their "demonstration effects" essential to real economic progress, but most of which are often in critically short supply. It follows that a deathblow to the goose that knows how to lay the golden egg should result in a generally corresponding slowdown in development. When in 1937 Bolivia nationalized properties belonging to the Standard Oil Company of New Jersey, for example, she was obliged to divert important developmental resources to the importation of oil from abroad (as it happened, from Standard's subsidiaries in Peru) because she lacked the know-how for continuing the Standard operations.[424]

But this assumption, too, is subject to important qualification. First, it presupposes that it is a direct rather than indirect investment that is being charged and that the investment in question manifests measurable "external economies" which in turn contribute significantly to the economic growth of the host community, conditions which surely are not always present. Also, the Bolivian experience is not inevitable. Egypt, for example, has defied all the "prophets of doom" by successfully operating the Suez Canal as an important source of revenue to help in the financing of the nearly completed and developmentally important (but ecologically controversial) Aswan Dam.[425] Still further, direct foreign investment is neither the sole nor necessarily the most important provider of economic enlightenment and skill. With the proliferation of "know-how contracts" and licensing agreements, the growth of firms engaged in the selling of technical and managerial services (through which, parenthetically, foreign experts can be re-

[424] Cleona Lewis, *The United States and Foreign Investment Problems* (Washington 1948), 155.

[425] *New York Times*, November 6, 1966, sec. 3, p. 1, col. 3: "The Egyptian operation of the canal since its seizure on July 26, 1956, has been the United Arab Republic's greatest success story. The canal has become a model of Egyptian efficiency and the 1956 clash with the West no less than a national epic. . . . Since 1956 . . . none of the calamities so arrogantly predicted in London and Paris have occurred." See also, to similar effect, the *Wall Street Journal*, January 26, 1967, p. 1, col. 6, wherein it is reported that the success of Pemex, the government-owned oil company which has been running Mexico's oil industry since Mexico "expropriated" foreign-owned petroleum properties in 1938, is worrying private oil company executives because, "[a]s a successful government venture, Pemex is the model for other countries wanting to nationalize their oil."

tained to assist in the operation of appropriated enterprises), the expansion of public and private "Point Four" programs, the increasing education and training of personnel abroad, and so forth, deprivor communities are continually becoming less and less hamstrung by knowledge and skill deficiencies. And to all these factors can be added, of course, the accumulation of transferable experience which deprivor communities gain over time from those undeterred by the risks of deprivation.

So much for the imperfections of the basic profile. Suppose, however, we were to accept the profile—that deprivations deter foreign investment and retard economic development—without reservation or qualification. Could it then be said that foreign-wealth deprivations are more destructive than productive of the values of international economic intercourse over the long run? Obviously, this is a question that cannot be satisfactorily answered—no more than can the basic profile be adequately appraised—without first heeding the characteristics of the participants involved, the purpose and scope of the deprivations imposed, the manner and intensity of their execution, the kinds of adjustments subsequently made between the contending parties (if any) and any number of other variables which sophisticated analysis would recognize as conditioning. But it is raised here nonetheless because if complete objectivity is to be achieved we must recognize that even (and perhaps especially) when it is directed to the most "violent" confrontations the question cannot be answered unhesitatingly and categorically in the affirmative. To do so, we can argue, is to impose an impossible rigidity upon the processes of historical change. Worse, it is to visualize the optimal requirements of international economic interaction in narrow, if not biased, terms. From such a perspective, the *desiderata* of international economic order become equated with the stabilization (or, at most, the gradual alteration) of existing structures and patterns. It is more painful to transform, so the argument runs, than it is to maintain or modify. But stability (often a euphemism for perpetuating the status quo) can be costly too, and not simply in economic terms nor, indeed, in terms of the host community alone. The traditional system may foreclose participation and so, arguably, preclude greater productivity and reward in the broadest sense. By tearing that system apart, however—whether in major or minor degree—a more inclusive shaping and sharing of economic and other values, and consequently a more enduring stability, may ultimately be realized.[426] This is saying no more, of course,

---

[426] The view that foreign investors will derive few benefits from deprivations has much validity over the short run. A long-range view recognizes, however, the basic and growing interdependence of the global wealth process, an interdepend-

than that revolution, for all the havoc that it wreaks, can spell a net gain to international society over the long run. This is neither new nor astounding. But it is a possibility with which many of us, in our failure to perceive all the dynamics of our revolutionary age, have failed to reckon.

To summarize, then, over the long term and depending on a wide range of variables, foreign-wealth deprivations may or may not deter foreign capital and skills, may or may not retard economic development and, thus, may or may not prove more destructive than productive of the values of international economic intercourse. And even if it is shown that they do discourage foreign investment and that they do check economic growth, it nevertheless remains that, over the longer term, they still may have a more productive than destructive impact. In few cases, of course, can our judgments be clear-cut; we must always assume a continuum of "more-or-less" rather than "either-or."

Clearly, all of this poses serious problems for policy. On the one hand, it may spell a need to improve or invent authoritative techniques (unilateral and plurilateral) by which deprivative incidents can be reduced (assuming that deprivations may themselves be deterred when it is recognized that they can have a deterrent effect): for example, the initiation of measures designed to decrease the flow of wealth (goods and services as well as capital) to deprivation-prone communities, or the creation of more effective communications about the long-term value of foreign enterprise to socioeconomic development. Those who accept automatically that deprivations have an overall deterrent effect (and, so, overlook creative ways to better the investment climate in a real sense) do foreign entrepreneurs and their governments an unwitting disservice in this regard. On the other hand, it may be that little or nothing should be done. Foreign entrepreneurs commonly adopt what are in essence schemes of self-insurance, with deprivative and similar risks being hedged by a reserve added to cost or a premium added to profit. Increasingly these schemes are being supple-

---

ence which tends to extend and share the benefits of the improved welfare of a deprivor community. The present beneficial economic relationship between Mexico and the United States may be a case in point. Total long-term United States private investment in Mexico had fallen by 1943 to $422 million from the 1914 total of $835 million and the 1930 total of $710 million (due to the agrarian and oil seizures, as well as to World War I and the subsequent great depression). Preliminary direct investment figures alone had risen to $1,177 million by year end 1965, however, and the majority of this investment was widely dispersed throughout the manufacturing sector in contrast to the primary resource concentrations of the earlier years. U.S., Congress, Senate, Subcommittee on American Republics Affairs, *United States-Latin American Relations*, Study No. 4, S. Doc. No. 125, 86th Cong., 2d Sess., 1960, 296; Samuel Pizer and Frederick Cutler, "Foreign Investments, 1965-66," *Survey of Current Business*, XLVI (September 1966), 30, 34.

mented by home government guarantees. Under such circumstances, and recognizing that resistance to deprivative programs may actually impede that enduring national and international stability which foreign investors agree is essential to successful enterprise, perhaps policy should favor foreign entrepreneurs and their home governments shouldering all or most of the burdens (admittedly often heavy) which they have sought in advance to offset or minimize. Manifestly, there are no easy answers. But it is clear that we negate all hope for any rational policy clarification if we ignore that there are, in fact, alternative long-term factual assessments to be made.

CONDITIONS

It must be recognized, finally, that there are many other factors, beyond those already noted, which condition policy and decision with respect to the Process of Deprivation but which, because of their more generally pervasive influence, defy our foregoing categorization. Of course, this should not preclude their being considered. Briefly, they include all those features (or conditions) which serve to characterize the wider world social process within which the Process of Deprivation operates.[427] Admittedly, this wider context is ever-changing. Furthermore, what may be relevant for one interaction may not be germane for another. Nevertheless, certain current conditions (some of which have already been alluded to) seem especially significant and, so especially deserving of attention—for example: the continuing territorial organization of the world community, increasingly within a framework of transnational ideological identification; the relatively recent multipolarization of world power, with different power blocs competing for different kinds of world economic order; the rising importance of transnational economic groupings and the consequent decline, albeit slow, of more parochial economic loyalties; the expanding interdependence of the peoples of the world in respect of all values and the growing recognition of such interdependence; the accelerating "revolution of modernization," particularly in the "Third World"; the widening economic disparity between the "haves" and the "have-nots"; and the increasing institutionalization, monopolization, and complexity of world markets and world market mechanisms.[428] Comprehensive appraisal of these and other conditions would seek richer indication of their relevance both to past and future expectations about the deprivation of foreign wealth and reactions thereto, on the one

[427] An efficient way to categorize these features, for purposes of specific inquiry (not undertaken here), is, of course, by value process and/or phase of value process. For illustration, see McDougal, Lasswell, and Vlasic (fn. 14), Chap. 1.

[428] For general discussion in this regard, see Baade (fn. 9), 3, 4-16.

hand, and to the fundamental policies that have been and are deemed controlling, on the other. It takes little imagination to see that if international law is to achieve "the reconciliation of basic divergencies" in this or any other area it must be made to account not only for the peculiar conditions of each case, but for the vicissitudes of the larger global context as well.

CONCLUSION[429]

As indicated earlier, reassessment of the objectives, or policy goals, sought by international law in respect of the deprivation of foreign wealth and responses thereto requires systematic description of more than the Process of Deprivation itself, the limit of our present inquiry. No less demanding of detailed description are the Process of Claim (within which deprivors and deprivees invoke authority in defense of claims and counterclaims arising out of the Process of Deprivation) and the Process of Decision (within which established decision-makers respond authoritatively to the deprivor and deprivee claims and counterclaims asserted). Obviously, systematic descriptions alone do not reconcile basic divergencies. To these tasks must be brought the continuous performance of all the essentials of rational inquiry: the clarification of goals, the description of past trends in decision, the analysis of conditions affecting decision, the projection of future trends in decision, and the invention and evaluation of policy alternatives. But the first requirement for any observer or decision-maker concerned with policy reassessment is at least a preliminary clarification of the general and specific policies he recommends.

It is this writer's conviction that conflict resolution in the present context, as in others, must favor the overriding goals of "an international law of human dignity"; or, as Professor McDougal has put it, "a world public order in which values are shaped and shared more by persuasion than by coercion, and which seeks to promote the greatest production and widest possible sharing, without discriminations irrelevant of merit, of all values among all human beings."[430] It is not enough to stop here, of course. The essential next step—concededly

---

[429] The discussion which follows is drawn in part, with the kind consent of the Ohio State University Press, from my essay, "Community Regulation of Foreign-Wealth Deprivations: A Tentative Framework for Inquiry" (fn. 9), 117. For further relevant details, consult the concluding remarks therein.

[430] McDougal and Associates, *Studies in World Public Order* (fn. 14), 987. To similar effect, but less comprehensively, Professor Fatouros has written: "The purpose of the international law norms on the matter is then to assure the optimal development of the world's natural resources consistent with the maximization of benefits to the state and the region in which the resources are located." Fatouros (fn. 11), 783, 810.

no easy one—is to relate this broad preference to the many concrete cases of competing claims which may and do arise. To take this step, it is necessary to engage in the kind of analysis that has served as the basis for this essay: systematic appraisal of all the relevant features in each of the various phases of the Process of Deprivation and the Process of Decision which may affect policy, and then, deliberate assessment of the potential significance of such features for the broad goals postulated. With a set of tentative formulations about the potential policy relevance of specific facts confronting him, an authoritative decision-maker will be in a better position to evaluate all facts and to make a more rational immediate choice.

It should not be assumed, however, that mere postulation of preferred community policy, in general terms (as above) or in utmost detail, can be regarded as an escape from that final creative choice that every decision-maker must make. There is not now nor is there likely to be, as Professor Falk seems to suggest, "a scientific alternative to human judgment" in the making of legal decision.[431] But conscious and enlightened commitment to truly genuine community policies which observers and decision-makers are willing to recommend and for which they will assume responsibility can illuminate the choices which *are*, in fact, open to them.

[431] Richard A. Falk, "The Adequacy of Contemporary Theories of International Law—Gaps in Legal Thinking," *Virginia Law Review*, L (March 1964), 231-32.

CHAPTER 3

Ocean Sciences, Technology, and the Future International Law of the Sea*

WILLIAM T. BURKE

INTRODUCTION

IN THE TWO decades since World War II, the international law of the sea has undergone careful reconsideration. National officials involved in maintaining the public order of the oceans have devoted serious attention to assessment and revision of this venerable body of law. Representatives of various private groups that share a common involvement in ocean exploitation, though they pursue numerous diverse objectives, have added their substantial efforts in appraisal and recommendation. Contributions of the same character may also be seen in the observations of individuals acting in a private capacity. The culmination of this enhanced activity came in 1958 with the adoption, as suitable for the demands of mid-twentieth century society, of the four Geneva conventions on the law of the sea.[1]

Accompanying, and outlasting, this recent revival of concern about the flow of decisions regulating interactions on the oceans has been an even more intensive upsurge in scientific inquiry into the complexity of oceanic phenomena.[2] This apparently sudden emergence of inter-

* This chapter was originally published in January 1966, as a part of the Pamphlet Series, The Social Science Program of the Mershon Center for Education in National Security, Ohio State University, and is reprinted here with the permission of the Ohio State University Press. The text has been slightly modified, the footnotes expanded and up-dated, and an Addendum appended.

The author is indebted to the Ohio State University Press for permission to republish and to the Mershon Social Science Program for support in aid of the original and continuing research which forms the basis for this paper. I am grateful to the following for permission to quote from copyrighted material: Dr. J. W. Clark, author of "Methods and Techniques for Sea-Floor Tasks," which appeared in *Ocean Science and Engineering*; the Marine Technology Society, publishers of *Ocean Science and Engineering*; the International Oceanographic Foundation, publishers of *Sea Frontiers*; and the editors of the *American Behavioral Scientist*.

[1] United Nations, First Conference on the Law of the Sea, *Official Records* (U.N. Doc. No. A/CONF. 13/38), Geneva, September 1958, 132-43.

[2] Speaking of the United States only, the Interagency Committee on Oceanography in 1963 noted "the recent growth in oceanography from a ten-million dollar enterprise involving only a few hundred professional workers in 1953 to one

est in scientific exploration and technological development rests primarily, no doubt, upon awareness of the high military value of expansion in knowledge of the sea,[3] but there is, equally clearly, a widespread realization that the ocean offers tremendous opportunities for realizing a great variety of important benefits for all peoples.[4] For a quick introduction to the potentialities in, and possibilities of, ocean exploitation, the following brief excerpts from recent authoritative studies are illuminating. An early study prepared for the Foreign Relations Committee of the United States Senate observes:

> In recent years, oceanography has received a great deal of attention. One reason for this is that the ocean has an important impact on world climate. To understand the factors controlling the atmosphere, a much better understanding of the effect of water movements and of transfers of energy between the boundary of sea and air is needed. A second reason is the potential wealth of the oceans and the fact that a new oceanic technology may provide new foods and mineral resources to mankind. A third and very important reason is military.
>
> Technological and scientific advances now permit us to consider more realistically the possibility of exploration and exploitation of vast ocean resources. Among these the possibility of developing revolutionary new techniques in the maritime and submarine arts opens wide vistas. For example, with nuclear energy new marine developments are feasible that use high-energy input, operate for long periods without refueling, and have the ability to operate the propulsion machinery without oxygen. Other developments with new engines and new ship designs may greatly change marine transportation technology, particularly the uses of submarines for nonmilitary activities.[5]

thirteen-fold greater in 1963 pursued by a few thousand." Interagency Committee on Oceanography, *Oceanography: The Ten Years Ahead: A Long Range Oceanographic Plan, 1963-72.* ICO Pam. No. 10 (June 1963), 7.

[3] U.S., Congress, House, Committee on Science and Astronautics, *Ocean Sciences and National Security,* 86th Cong., 2d Sess., 1960, H. Rep. 2078, 17.

[4] Same, 22-24.

[5] U.S., Congress, Senate, Committee on Foreign Relations, Study by Stanford Research Institute, *Possible Nonmilitary Scientific Developments and the Potential Impact on Foreign Policy Problems of the United States,* 86th Cong., 1st Sess., 1959, 23.

For a rapid introduction to achievements in scientific and technological efforts in the oceans, see the volumes containing the papers for the annual meetings of the Marine Technology Society, beginning in June 1965. See also generally Richard D. Terry, ed., *Ocean Engineering,* 4 vols. (Washington 1966). (A preliminary report submitted to the Chairman of the Interagency Committee on Oceanography by the National Security Industrial Association; originally completed in 1965 but available to the public beginning in 1966.)

More general indication of the vast potential benefit is to be found in the introduction to the National Oceanographic Program for the United States, as conceived by the Interagency Committee on Oceanography. Speaking of the need for long-range planning for oceanographic work, the ICO declared:

Such planning is all the more important in terms of making most effective use of research resources when considering that oceanography is small with respect to some indices of its practical importance. The burgeoning world population, particularly in the underdeveloped areas, makes the oceans with their huge and inefficiently exploited food resources of inevitable and increasing value to humanity as a whole. . . .

Other indices of the strategic importance of the oceans are becoming ever more clearly recognized. The cloak of concealment provided by a medium which is virtually opaque to all forms of energy except sound is of immense military significance. . . .

Other aspects of the oceans affecting all or large numbers of us in common include the health hazard posed by pollution from industrial wastes such as oil, chemicals, sewage, etc. and from radioactive substances; danger to life and property from waves and flooding; risk to shipping from floating ice, storms and navigational hazards; and threats to resources such as the recreational value of the seas which should be common property.[6]

That technological conditions no longer present an overwhelming obstacle to extension of significant activities to all parts of the sea is evident from the following observations in a report prepared by Dr. Edward Wenk, Jr., for the Committee on Science and Astronautics of the United States House of Representatives:

The barrier which has historically restrained man from submarine operations at all depths in the ocean now shows promise of being dissolved by technological advancement. High-strength steels, high-strength aluminum alloys, fiberglass reinforced plastic, titanium, and beryllium as engineering materials show the promise of producing structures whose strength-to-weight characteristics will permit their use in submarine hulls for operation 10 to 20 times deeper than the depth cited for the Nautilus. Exactly what will be the scientific as well as practical benefits are unpredictable, but recent experience has dramatically shown the advantage of priority in scientific achievement. Vehicles in increased number, either self-

[6] ICO Pam. No. 10 (fn. 2), 4. See, generally, Seabrook Hull, *The Bountiful Sea* (Englewood Cliffs, N.J. 1964).

buoyant as are submarines, or bottom crawlers, and even fixed underwater stations in which men may live and work safely, constitute some of the emerging realities that now make possible an attack on the entire ocean.[7]

Unfortunately, together with these optimistic accounts of realistically anticipated advantages are to be noted other statements indicating considerable disquiet about the legal arrangements established or available for permitting realization of the estimated gains. As early as 1959, even before the final failure at Geneva of the second multilateral effort to resolve some critical international legal problems involving the sea, Dr. Columbus Iselin, a widely known American oceanographer, is reported to have expressed this judgment: "The economic and social problems that will be encountered as we begin seriously to exploit marine resources seem to me to be formidable, much more formidable than the remaining unsolved scientific problems. Some very wise agency needs to be developing the ground rules within which the vast marine resources can be developed in an efficient and safe manner for the benefit of all mankind."[8] And only six years after the considerable labors of eighty-seven nations at the 1958 Geneva Conference on the Law of the Sea and four years after the 1960 Geneva Conference on unfinished business on the same subject, Dr. Athelstan Spilhaus, then dean of the Institute of Technology at the University of Minnesota, declared:

We need, for example, a new look at the law of the sea as it relates to the emerging exploitation of mineral resources, aquaculture, and the uses of the sea to promote national economic well-being and strength.

This is perhaps one of the most important and difficult of the marine problems to be tackled. Somehow we must bridge the dichotomy of preserving the traditional international freedom of the seas and making investment in the exploitation of the oceans feasible. It's an interesting thing that groups of distinguished lawyers were speculating and developing space law before the first Sputnik orbited; yet we merely whittle at the antiquated marine law when forced to by an item on the agenda of an international con-

[7] H. Rep. 2078 (fn. 3), 35-36. But see Don Groves, "Awake in the Deep," *Sea Frontiers*, x, No. 5 (Miami, Fla. Christmas 1964), 285, 294.

An authoritative examination of the types and design of undersea vehicles is contained in Richard D. Terry, *The Deep Submersible* (North Hollywood, Calif. 1966): another valuable compendium is U.S. Interagency Committee on Oceanography, *Undersea Vehicles for Oceanography*, ICO Pam. No. 18 (October 1965).

[8] Quotation contained in Cord C. Troebst, *Conquest of the Sea*, Brian C. and Elsbeth Price, trans. (New York 1962), 192-93.

gress or a crisis. People who deal with the sea should sit down with distinguished lawyers with a view to a complete overhaul in the light of the imminent occupation and exploitation of the oceans.[9]

Finally, the increase in scientific investigation into the ocean both stimulates the need for developing legal prescriptions applicable to previously unknown types of interactions on the sea and provides technical information indispensable for creating new legal provisions. The Interagency Committee on Oceanography offers a succinct statement of this perspective:

The "law of the sea" has historically been more conscientiously accepted as a code of international behavior than any other. Yet changes in prevailing rights of sovereignty, transit, and conservation increasingly depend on technological facts and scientific understanding. State as well as Federal legislators and policy makers must increasingly depend on oceanic science. When the interests of recreation, commercial fishing, sport fishing, oil exploration, and waste disposal compete for use of the same coastal resources, wise decisions that extend beyond preservation of the status quo can only be based on the fullest knowledge of the properties of the sea and its coastal areas. International disputes on defense aspects and fishing rights, which now occur with greater frequency, and matters of ownership of undersea mineral resources, sovereignty of straits or restricted waters or of strategically located sea mounts are a potential source of tension, and must be subject to agreements based on better data than now available.[10]

It is, thus, apparent that in spite of the considerable work lately devoted to clarification of, and agreement on, the law of the sea, persons closely associated with recent developments in ocean use, such as scientists and government officials, are disturbed about the capacity of the international legal system to deal with impending changes in exploitation of the ocean. Uneasiness exists both about the adequacy and availability of the legal tools that must be employed if grave and disruptive international controversy is to be avoided or minimized and about the level of attention devoted to emerging problems. It is

[9] Athelstan F. Spilhaus, "Man in the Sea," *1st U.S. Navy Symposium on Military Oceanography* (Washington 1964), ix-x. And see statements of Dean Athelstan F. Spilhaus, Dr. John C. Calhoun, Jr., and Representative Richard T. Hanna in U.S., Congress, Senate, Committee on Commerce, *Hearings on S. 944*, 89th Cong., 1st Sess., 1965. See also Wilbert M. Chapman, "Potential Resources of the Ocean," same, 132, 137.

[10] ICO, *National Oceanographic Program, Fiscal Year 1965*, ICO Pam. No. 15 (March 1964), 2-3.

not necessary to share fully the pessimism of some of these observers in order to find substance in their strictures about the lag in the evolution of legal prescriptions and structures appropriate to the needs of the new ventures upon the ancient resource that is the sea.[11]

This discussion does not propose to offer suggestions for immediate remedies for the difficulties that can be anticipated.[12] The objectives are rather to offer a preliminary, and necessarily brief, examination of the changes in the age-old process of interaction on the ocean that account in some measure for the emergence of novel problems by speculating about the types of future claims and counterclaims which will differ from those encountered in previous experience; and to make a short, rather general, survey of the broad outlines of the legal technicality inherited from the past that modern decision-makers might adopt, wisely or not, as useful for resolving disputes in the future. No systematic effort is made to clarify community policies at stake in the emerging struggle over the sea, though brief suggestions are made about the direction of further research on some problems.

SIGNIFICANT FEATURES OF THE PROCESS OF INTERACTION

A. Participants

In past centuries, states have played a familiar and important role in the exploration and utilization of the ocean and its resources; in view

[11] One point worth some emphasis in this connection is that scientists and engineers may not be the best source of legal advice about the sea. Despite the cogency of their admonitions about emergent legal problems, specific legal pronouncements from such sources should perhaps be scrutinized with care. To mention but one of several questionable instances that could be cited, one expert observer reports that "whale hunting is now rigidly controlled by international agreement." Athelstan F. Spilhaus, *Turn to the Sea* (Washington 1959), 29. This will come as something of a surprise to the International Whaling Commission which may yet come to be the model for ineffectual management of international resources. The Commission has hardly rigidly controlled anything and the valuable blue whale is now almost nonexistent.

[12] Nor does it seek to predict when grave difficulties will be encountered. The Report of the Panel on Oceanography of the President's Science Advisory Committee offers appropriate words of caution in this respect: "The frequency and gravity of possible legal problems are now difficult to project, since much depends upon the type, scope, and timing of ocean operations which may be undertaken in the future by this and other countries and upon attitudes and practices of other nations. However, there is realism in present concern about these possibilities, because the existing international legal structure was largely developed under conditions that differed greatly from those that are likely to prevail in the foreseeable future. The task of adapting this legal structure to rapidly changing conditions can quite conceivably generate stress in relations between nations in the form of lively, perhaps dangerous, controversy." Report of the Panel on Oceanography, President's Science Advisory Committee, "Effective Use of the Sea" (Washington 1966), 91.

of trends in scientific inquiry and technological development, their activity will probably be of even greater future significance. This development seems likely to eventuate no matter how a particular state arranges its internal social processes. For example, even in the United States, where considerable emphasis is placed upon private initiative, it is amply clear that the federal government will continue to occupy the dominant position in probing new ways and means of using the sea for national objectives.[13] Among the several, interdependent reasons for the special role of the state are the relative paucity of knowledge of the ocean, the critical strategic character both of the oceanographic sciences and of the information sought in and of the oceans, the costly technology involved in the study and use of the sea and particularly of its more inaccessible parts, and the fact that much of the projected activity in the sea does not immediately promise sufficient monetary gain to motivate consequential efforts by private groups. In combination, these factors suggest that comprehensive and sustained measures for developing new knowledge and uses of the sea require, and are likely to receive, an increasing level of support from the immense resources of the state, a level far above that available to, or reasonably expected from private resources.[14] Available data disclose that the major industrial states of the world are greatly enlarging their commitment to oceanographic exploration and research.[15]

At the same time, it should occasion no surprise in view of the vastness of the ocean and the range of even its known resources that international governmental organizations are engaged with increasing intensity in exploratory work, partially in direct scientific inquiry, but

[13] H. Rep. 2078 (fn. 3), 25-29; ICO Pam. No. 10 (fn. 2), 15-16. A representative of a private group, the National Association of Manufacturers, asserts that over half of "current expenditures" in the United States for ocean uses comes from private sources. Statement of John W. Clark on behalf of the NAM, in U.S., Congress, House, Committee on Merchant Marine and Fisheries, *Hearings Concerning National Oceanographic Program Legislation before the Subcommittee on Oceanography*, 89th Cong., 1st Sess., 1965, 347. In any event, insofar as the oil industry is concerned, contribution to new ocean uses is likely to be incidental to technological developments directly useful to the industry. There is, of course, no reason to expect the oil industry to play a major role in disseminating hard-won, profitable scientific information.

[14] H. Rep. 2078 (fn. 3), 110-15.

[15] ICO Pam. No. 10 (fn. 2), 39-41, offers appraisal of oceanographic efforts in the U.S.S.R., Japan, the United Kingdom, and Canada. See also U.S., Congress, House, *Report on the Soviets and the Seven Seas, Report of a Congressional Delegation to Poland and the Soviet Union*, 89th Cong., 2d Sess., 1966, H. Rep. 1809. Soviet work and facilities are examined in more detail in H. Rep. 2078 (fn. 3), 103-09. The increasing but still inadequate American involvement is partially chronicled in the annual projection of a National Oceanographic Program by the Interagency Committee on Oceanography.

mainly in coordination of numerous other activities in use of the sea.[16] The Intergovernmental Oceanographic Commission of UNESCO, among the newest of these organizations, is organizing many co-operative activities in the study of the sea.[17] Two of the most recent and ambitious projects operating through the IOC are the International Indian Ocean Expedition and the Tropical Atlantic Investigation. Other international organizations with wide-ranging interests that also are concerned with important aspects of oceanography include the Food and Agriculture Organization, the Intergovernmental Maritime Consultative Organization, the International Atomic Energy Agency, the World Health Organization, and the World Meteorological Organization. Numerous regional and functional organizations might also be mentioned.[18]

Private associations, national and international, specializing in achieving a variety of goals have, for centuries, occupied a prominent position in ocean interactions. Groups devoted to production of wealth are most obvious, of course, though even the nature of these groups is altered as we discover new uses for ocean areas. For example, the investment of the oil companies in ocean-centered activities, including shipping and oil production, virtually unknown a few decades ago, now is the largest by any single group of private organizations. Among private international groups, those interested especially in enlightenment appear to have become unusually active recently, including the International Council of Scientific Unions, the Special Committee for Oceanic Research, the Special Committee for Antarctic Research, the International Geophysical Co-operation, 1959, the International Union of Biological Sciences, the International Union of Geodesy and Geophysics, and the Pacific Science Association.[19] Within particular states, a very large number of private groups, such as universities and laboratories, are active in study of the oceans.[20]

Private individuals are, in any case, the principal actors in interactions on the sea and have multiple interests in its use. In the field of science, the role of the individual acting wholly in his own behalf is reduced for the reasons mentioned above, which are responsible for the increasing scope of state participation. Yet on a global basis the

[16] See generally the various numbers of *International Marine Science* (Section h), the newsletters prepared by the UNESCO Office of Oceanography, Paris, and the Reports on Activities of the Biology Branch of the FAO Fisheries Division; H. Rep. 2078 (fn. 3), 101-03; ICO, *National Oceanographic Program, Fiscal Year 1966*, ICO Pam. No. 17 (January 1965), 34-37.

[17] *International Marine Science*, Section d, reports on various international programs.

[18] Same, I, No. 3, Section b; same, II, No. 2, Section b.

[19] H. Rep. 2078 (fn. 3), 102-03.

[20] Same, 58-70, lists U.S. institutions, including governmental.

individual, without identification with other groups, is still a primary participant as he functions in a variety of roles including fisherman, sailor, swimmer, diver, researcher, businessman, and miner.

B. Objectives

Participants have for ages pursued all their values in and upon the sea, but the recent upsurge in interest in this area appears to be primarily concerned with increments in power, wealth, and enlightenment.

Everyone knows that states have continually resorted to the sea in many ways for promoting power objectives. Traditionally, the movement of ships, military and private, has been the chief form of exploiting the sea for power purposes, and states have engaged in frequent violent struggles to preserve or to acquire control over the ocean or strategic parts of it. And still today prominent observers emphasize that freedom of the sea includes, most importantly, the capacity to control the use of the sea by naval vessels.[21] But in the past decade or so, the opportunities for enhancement of power have involved methods of use greatly differing from the traditional, and these methods will undoubtedly undergo further changes as inquiry and exploration proceed. The major change, at least the one now discernible, arises from the advances in propulsion and in associated complex technology, which dramatically alter the conditions of access to the ocean.

Enlightenment is, in recent years, perhaps next only to power as the goal of participants, both public and private, in interactions on the sea. It has become a common activity for statesmen, politicians, and others to pronounce, with alarm, that knowledge of this vast domain is extremely limited and to forecast dire consequences if ignorance is not swept aside. Ever alert to sources of support, badly needed as it is, those who (in the United States at least) are aware of the shortage of knowledge and know-how relating to the sea and who are in a position to recommend appropriate action have energetically, and often successfully, promoted substantial increases in government support of basic and applied oceanographic research. Scientists themselves have, as noted above, organized on an international scale, as the vastness and complexity of the subject demands, so that comprehensive and systematic achievement can be brought within reach.

The pursuit of wealth by exploiting the sea is ancient, and the traditional practices aimed at this objective are familiar. But, as new opportunities are made available, the means for achieving wealth in the sea are being transformed. Within the past two decades, even

21 See, e.g., same, 12-13.

within the last five years, wholly new industries and enterprises have emerged for exploitation of the wealth and potential of the ocean. Technological development permitting drilling on the ocean floor from platforms designed to be supported by the sea bed and, more importantly, from floating platforms is responsible for the spectacular spread of the oil industry to offshore areas of the United States, England, Saudi Arabia, Nigeria, Kuwait, and elsewhere.[22] The total investment in these ventures must be measured in the billions.[23] It seems certain that similar activity will be extended to areas beyond the geological continental shelf that are still shallow enough to permit economic operations. In addition, it is probably reasonable to speculate that some time in the future, engineering techniques and facilities will be sufficiently developed to permit oil exploration and exploitation activities to be divorced completely from surface installations.

Other types of minerals are also present in great abundance in and under the oceans, including the deeper areas beyond the continental shelf. Estimates of the economic feasibility of exploiting the deeper ocean-floor resources are not immediately promising, but the day will surely come when the resources will be sufficiently scarce and costs of the necessary technology low enough to make ocean mining a viable enterprise for private groups.[24] Even before then it is likely that governments will begin extraction of minerals from these inaccessible areas, perhaps to develop techniques useful for military purposes or to acquire prestige from the achievement.

C. Situations

The principal changes to be expected in the situational characteristics of ocean use pertain to the rapid expansion of interaction to parts

[22] A recent survey noted exploratory or exploitation activity in the above areas and in Canada, Mexico, Trinidad, Peru, Brazil, British Honduras, Guatemala, Surinam, the United Kingdom, Germany, Norway, Denmark, France, Spain, Italy, Ethiopia, Tunisia, Senegal, Pakistan, various Persian Gulf locations, Egypt, Gabon, Dhofar, U.S.S.R., Libya, Japan, Borneo, Australia, and Papua. *Offshore*, xxiii, No. 6 (June 21, 1965), Annual Marine Drilling and Producing Edition, Conroe, Texas.

Some notion of future expansion in this activity is indicated in the following: "This year-by-year rise in volume of offshore activity throughout the world tends to bear out often-expressed belief of informed geologists that our industry has so far only figuratively scratched the surface of the vast offshore areas that await testing. One authority recently said that the industry so far has explored a mere five per cent of the world's known sedimentary basins lying within the 600-foot depth contour." Bauer, "High Rate of Offshore Drilling Activity to Continue," *Offshore*, xxvi, No. 6 (December 1966), 44.

[23] Estimates of yearly expenditures for United States offshore exploitation are reported at $2 billion and for the world at $5 billion. *Geo-Marine Technology*, I, No. 5 (April 1965), 22.

[24] See notes 60-62 and sources cited.

of the sea beyond previous access and the beginnings of institutional practices in certain types of use of the ocean.

1. Degree of Institutionalization in Use

All participants in interactions concerning the sea have pursued their objectives in substantial independence of each other largely because the sea is so huge in relation to the technology of use that consequential interference with others is rather easily avoided. Even the largest-scale single use of the sea, now illustrated by hydrogen bomb testing, which is by necessity exclusive of any other simultaneous use of the relatively immense area affected, could be and was carried out with very slight impact on other activities.[25] It may be doubted that this state of affairs will prevail much longer.

Beyond the need of cooperation for physical accommodation, the first area in which a considerable degree of organization in peaceful use has developed is, not unexpectedly, in scientific inquiry, the pattern of practices serving as the essential condition for development of wider uses of the ocean. Within a decade after World War II, recognition was general that to press an effective attack on the formidable barriers of ignorance about the sea, it would be necessary to act in concert. Although this realization was not entirely novel (the International Council for the Exploration of the Sea was formed a half-century earlier), it was the first time that a global effort was made to coordinate individual national scientific projects and to cooperate actively in specific multilateral projects. The initial framework of cooperation constructed for the International Geophysical Year was not allowed to wither; since that great achievement, states have provided a permanent mechanism for governmental cooperation in the Intergovernmental Oceanographic Commission. Numerous private groups, noted above, provide other structures for cooperation in activities aimed at the common goal of better understanding of the sea.

2. Locations of Interactions

A major consequence of the expected discoveries about the ocean will be the expansion of human activities to vast areas of the earth hitherto unavailable except for the most indirect, fleeting, and fragmentary observation. The increased sophistication of submarine technology, the present potential and virtually certain future development of

25 See Myres S. McDougal and Norbert A. Schlei, "The Hydrogen Bomb Tests in Perspective: Lawful Measures for Security," *Yale Law Journal*, LXIV (April 1955), 648, 682-84; but see Emanuel Margolis, "The Hydrogen Bomb Experiments and International Law," same, 629.

desirable resources in the deeper ocean areas beyond the shallow continental shelf, and the elaboration of the current tentative steps in developing underwater structures for human habitation will all contribute to the eventual spread of consequential interaction to the previously inaccessible depths of the sea. A few brief comments about each of these factors seem worthwhile in anticipation of subsequent reference to legal controversies.

Formerly, of course, man was limited in direct access to the ocean to the surface and to submarine areas very near the surface, and, in the latter case, this access was temporally severely limited. During both world wars and for a considerable period after the second, the major moves of antagonists on the sea occurred either on the surface or only a relatively few fathoms below. For subsurface operations, vessels were tied closely to the surface environment by the physical necessity of maintaining the necessary atmosphere. Both these limitations upon access to the sea, restrictions on depths and time, are and have been undergoing major alterations. Now a most significant element of military force moves at depths greatly exceeding those previously considered possible for submarines.[26] Moreover, these movements are, by virtue of new propulsion sources, divorced almost completely from the surface for very considerable periods.

This transformation in military craft is accompanied by spectacular developments in other types of submersibles. Though not a real submarine, the underwater vehicle "Trieste" enables scientists to extend their range of direct observation to the deepest known parts of the ocean, at least for short periods.[27] In addition, other large submersible vehicles, which will permit access to depths of 15,000 feet, are now available or are under development, enabling direct exploration and observations of the sea and the bottom for over one-half its area. Smaller submersibles capable of operation at useful depths, down to several hundred feet, are also engaged in significant exploration and investigation.[28]

Still another development in technology permitting expansion of access to the sea is that of remote-controlled vehicles utilizing external

[26] This does not necessarily mean, of course, that submarines operate at great depths, as indicated by the following: "Today's large submarines can operate in only the relatively thin upper part of the ocean, or less than ten per cent of the ocean's volume; consequently, there is an urgent need for smaller, deep-diving research-type vehicles—as precursors to larger military and commercial deep-diving vehicles—to perform countless experiments, to test materials and components, and to study the environment and many other technological facets." Terry, ed. (fn. 7), viii.

[27] H. Rep. 2078 (fn. 3), 79ff.

[28] See, generally, same; it is estimated that at the end of 1966 a total of twenty small manned submersibles were in operation "in the Free World." *Ocean Science News*, VIII, No. 52 (December 30, 1966), 1.

manipulators which can be designed for a variety of particular tasks in the deep sea. This technique of working on ocean tasks has been called a "telechiric" system, from the Greek words for "distant hand."[29] A recent description of these systems indicates the potential for the future use of this family of vehicles:

Telechiric systems are considerably less familiar than divers and DSV's (deep submersible vehicles). However, enough experience with their practical operation has been obtained to demonstrate that they are feasible in an engineering sense and in a psychological sense. . . .

The most significant point which has been gained by experience with telechiric systems is psychological. It was necessary to demonstrate by experiment that these systems can be learned, that no unusual operator skill is required, and that adequate speed and precision can be attained with a reasonable period of operator training.

The principal advantages of the telechiric system derive from the separation of operator and vehicle. The operator is in a safe, normal environment; when necessary a group of experts can be assembled to work with the operator and advise him in some complex procedure. The telechiric vehicle can be designed to suit a particular group of tasks; it can be made large or small, fast or slow, versatile or simple, as required. There is no engineering limit to the working depth for which telechiric vehicles can be designed.

The disadvantages of the telechiric system arise from its complexity. The telechiric vehicle must include a manipulating system; a sensory system; a command system; and a locomotor system. Even though it can be made small, it cannot be made extremely simple. Due primarily to the lack of experience with these vehicles they are quite costly and will remain so until the applications have developed to a point that will support a reasonable number of telechiric vehicles.

Like the other manual techniques, telechiric vehicles are tool using vehicles. It is usually desirable to make the integral manipulators as simple as possible and to furnish the telechiric vehicle with a variety of tools adapted to particular tasks. These may be similar to the tools used by divers and by DSV's but adapted to the special needs of telechiric manipulators.[30]

29 J. W. Clark, "Methods and Techniques for Sea-Floor Tasks," *Ocean Science and Engineering* (1965), 1, 267, 270. (Transactions of joint meeting of the Marine Technology Society and the American Society of Limnology and Oceanography, Washington, D.C., June 14-17, 1965.)

30 Same, 271. See also Clark, "Application of Modern Remote Handling Techniques to Oceanography," *Marine Sciences Instrumentation*, 1 (1962), 294. (A Collection of Papers Presented at the Marine Sciences Conference, Woods Hole, Mass., September 11-15, 1961.)

One kind of telechiric vehicle (called the Remote Underwater Manipulator) has been designed for operation directly on the ocean floor.

It resembles a tank and is powered and controlled remotely by means of lightweight coaxial cable. Mobility is achieved on tracked wheel assemblies to which is affixed a mechanical arm similar in most respects to the type of manipulator used for remotely handling radioactive substances. The RUM vehicle can carry a payload of 1,000 pounds per square inch. It can maintain a speed of 2.6 knots and will travel to the limits of its five-mile-long cable. Its total weight —24,220 pounds. Guidance and control are accomplished from a shore-based operating station, and through the use of underwater television and illumination the operator will be able to view operations of the vehicle so as to make effective use of the prosthetic arm.[31]

Robot systems differ from the telechiric in that the latter are controlled from a distance, whereas the robot is designed to perform tasks without continued direction. Such devices are now in use by industrial enterprises at depths of 1,000 feet and below.[32]

Lest it be mistakenly believed that science fiction is swiftly becoming reality only in the regions of outer space and not in the area of inner space, attention is due the recently expressed views of the former Oceanographer of the United States Navy, Rear Admiral E. C. Stephan: "The future for development of manned and unmanned exploratory and instrumented undersea craft seems unlimited and will be dependent only on the speed with which manpower and resources are made available."[33]

In evaluating the prospects for realizing resource potential, two factors of location must be considered: relationship to land masses and, particularly, depth of the area involved. The first relates more significantly to problems of legal control, but the second directly affects the prospects for exploration and, ultimately, for exploitation. Recognition of the importance of depth is necessary as an antidote to undue optimism. It is, of course, widely known that numerous valuable minerals are now taken from the sea bed or subsoil or the water itself, but none of the present ocean mining efforts occurs in deeper water, i.e., in depths much below the continental shelf. The intense attention being devoted to deep sea mining by business enterprise

[31] H. Rep. 2078 (fn. 3), 136; and see Clark (fn. 30), 302-03.

[32] Duane Valentry, "Robot Diver," Sea Frontiers, XII, No. 6 (Miami, Fla. Christmas, 1966), 322.

[33] As quoted in interview with Murray Smith, Data, VII, No. 4 (April 1962), 29.

suggests, however, that economic exploitation of this area may not be so far away as many believe.[34]

A final important condition affecting expansion of access involves the emplacement of structures, manned and unmanned, directly on the sea floor. This is one of the "emerging realities"[35] of oceanographic research and exploration, and it seems obvious that marked technological advance in developing underwater installations will have spectacular, if unforeseeable, effects upon the ways in which the sea is employed.[36] Perhaps a goodly portion of the relevant research is classified for military reasons and hence unavailable, but some information is in the public domain and it indicates the potentialities and problems involved.

The initial efforts are limited to relatively modest depths as would naturally be expected given the hostile character of the environment and the numerous problems of adapting human habitation to it. Even so, however, the depths in which experimenters are working are impressive. Thus, Jacques Cousteau and several associates remained 30 feet below the surface for one month, while others in his group dwelt for one week in a structure 90 feet down.[37] In June 1964, Robert Stenuit and Jon Lindbergh remained for forty-nine hours at a depth

[34] See notes 60-62.

[35] The words are those in the quotation from H. Rep. 2078, cited in footnote 3.

[36] One of the leading innovators in this field, Dr. Edwin A. Link, anticipates that within twenty years man "may live for days and weeks at the site of his labours" in the deep sea. See Edwin A. Link, "Working Deep in the Sea," in Nigel Calder, ed., *The New Scientist: The World in 1984* (Baltimore 1965), I, 103, 104.

"For the greater portion of the continental shelf (o to 3,000 feet) the economic use of man and machines for extensive and prolonged engineering operations is virtually assured in the next decade. The magnitude of national effort devoted to this technology is still contingent upon the assessment of the military significance of the continental shelf, and the assessment of its resources and of its scenic and recreational potential. For the next geographic areas of interest, the ocean ridges and sea mounts (6,000 to 8,000 feet), the capability to deploy vehicles and to mount installations is virtually assured within the next decade. In the next two decades, the commercial deployment of vehicles and machines in these areas is highly probable; and by the end of the century, the economic use of men and machines in these areas is not inconceivable. The magnitude of national effort in these areas is again contingent upon an as yet unassessed military, economic, and cultural potential. For the final areas of interest, the broad ocean basins (12,000 to 20,000 feet), within the next decade, the capability to visit selected areas of the bottom and to perform scientific and light engineering missions is virtually assured; within the next two decades, deployment of vehicles and machines in these areas is highly likely; and by the end of the century, the extensive economic deployment of a wide class of commercial and military vehicles is a distinct possibility." John P. Craven, "Sea Power and the Sea Bed," *U.S. Naval Institute Proceedings* (April 1966), 48-49.

[37] James Dugan, *Man Under the Sea*, rev. edn. (New York 1965), 402-03; Jacques Cousteau has discussed his earlier work in his book with James Dugan, *The Living Sea* (New York 1964).

of 430 feet in a structure designed by Edwin A. Link.[38] In July 1964, United States Navy divers occupied a specially constructed undersea shelter, placed on the sea floor 192 feet below the surface. The experiment was designed to last for three weeks; but bad weather required earlier termination, and the men had to come to the surface after eleven days. Despite the early ending, it is reported that the experiment was most productive, the most important result being the demonstration that divers could exist at such a depth and for such a period without serious physiological harm. The same study offered this appraisal of future work:

> Incidentally, exploration of the abyss appears not *now* to be limited by the tremendous hydrostatic pressures encountered but rather by our present lack of knowledge of various human responses to the environment. For example, the phenomenon of inert gas narcosis (often called "Rapture of the Deep" when applied to nitrogen narcosis), is not yet understood in detail by underwater physiologists. The effect of inert gas narcosis can produce a virtual state of "drunkenness" when a diver is exposed for appreciable periods of breathing gas under high pressure. At present, helium is used, to a large extent, instead of nitrogen since it does not display any appreciable narcotic effect. However, possibly at some depth helium will cause narcosis.
>
> Still another potential limitation exists in the increased breathing resistance that takes place when a diver breathes gas under pressure. This is due to the increased density of the gas. The gas mixture used in SEALAB-I increased the breathing resistance to approximately 1.6 times that of air at the surface. This effect causes some degree of lung fatigue which should increase with increasing depth.
>
> In spite of the known and unknown obstacles in the way, many problem areas are soon to benefit from the recent SEALAB effort. Among these are those of salvage, submarine rescue, underwater construction, underwater inspection and repair (cables, pipelines, etc.), strategic applications (ASW warning installations, coastal defenses, submarine bunkering stations) ocean floor mining, fish and underwater crop farming and oil drilling.[39]

Operation Sealab II took place during the summer of 1965. In this more ambitious experiment, or cluster of experiments, the Sealab was placed a depth of 205 feet off the coast of La Jolla, California, and was occupied by succeeding teams of aquanauts for a total stay of forty-

[38] Robert Stenuit, *The Deepest Days*, Morris A. Kemp, trans. (New York 1966); see also Groves (fn. 7), 285, 286-87.
[39] Same, 294.

five days. One aquanaut, Commander Scott Carpenter, occupied Sealab for the first thirty-day period.[40]

D. Base Values

Power, wealth, enlightenment, and skill appear certain to be most potent among the many values (or assets) that states and other participants will employ in attaining their goals in the ocean. It is traditional to note the special importance of the ocean in the aggregate power position of some states. In very recent times, in fact in the last decade, the historic role of the sea as a power base has altered greatly; with the completely new weapons systems created by both the United States and the Soviet Union (i.e., the Polaris-type nuclear submarine, carrying nuclear missiles), the sea is no longer significant only as a medium for transport of troops and goods vital to war efforts. It now serves as the location for powerful offensive weapons systems capable of reaching into the interior of major land masses and possessed of the crucial characteristics of great mobility and concealment. The attribute of concealment has thus far, in the opinion of many, offered mutual advantage to the major opponents since, by permitting each side to possess an unvulnerable deterrent to comprehensive nuclear attack, it has stabilized an extremely dangerous military confrontation.

It merits special emphasis that one critical effect of expanded oceanographic research may be to disturb the stability hitherto associated with submarine missile-launching systems. At the present level of knowledge, the ocean is regarded as largely opaque—only the transmission of sound permits the detection of submerged vehicles and objects, and thus far, such detection is reliable only within limited distances.[41] Should long-range detection devices emerge as a result of expanded research efforts, the consequences could be dangerous, though, to be sure, the significance of this development, when and if it comes, depends upon the total military-politico-scientific context in which it occurs. At present, the known acquisition of this detection capacity by one of the cold-war antagonists might have an alarming impact on expectations concerning the use of violence. Perhaps it is not too far-fetched to imagine that successful achievement in long-distance detection by one cold war antagonist might deliberately be

[40] For a variety of reports on this experiment see *Man's Extension into the Sea, Transactions of the Joint Symposium, 11-12 January 1966*, Washington, D.C. (A joint symposium sponsored by the Marine Technology Society and numerous other organizations.)

[41] H. Rep. 2078 (fn. 3), 17. In September 1965, it was reported that since 1963-64 the United States has been operating an underwater detection system effective for submarines approaching to within a few hundred miles of the Atlantic Coast. *New York Times*, September 14, 1965, p. 3, col. 1.

shared with the other, lest the ensuing instability in the power structure lead to costly adventures by one or another of the opponents.

It is to be expected when one views wealth as a base value that those with high positions in respect to this value are favored in achieving access to the expanding oceanic environment; and those already relatively well off in this respect are, not unexpectedly, more likely to gain in wealth position than are others. This feature, certainly not unique to this particular process of interaction, may, of course, lead to initiatives by those in a less favorable wealth position to subject some ocean resources to organized inclusive use, thus hopefully providing for augmentation of the basic wealth position of states generally, rather than just of a relative few.[42] The prospects for the success of such proposals are not sanguine; the degree of success attending them will depend upon numerous factors in the future. We know, of course, that the major resources of the continental shelf were allocated according to territorial notions, with each coastal state receiving exclusive rights of use, and that no serious attention was ever given to the thought of providing for organized international control of, and benefit from, the area.[43]

Enlightenment promises to be a more significant base value in the future than it has in the past, perhaps becoming more important than any other value. The scientific study of the sea is a relatively new enterprise, and because of this, in part, no participant as yet has acquired an outstandingly advantageous position. Nonetheless, only a relatively few states and very few private groups possess much knowledge of the sea, its processes, and its resources. For the vast majority of states in the world, the ocean is a body of water over which ships can move and from which fish can be taken, and it is no more than that. Among a handful of states, the scientific investigation of the sea has, on the other hand, a longer history; and for two, the Soviet Union and the United States, the pursuit of such an inquiry is a strategic enterprise the neglect of which could impose drastic disadvantages in their power position. If understanding of the complexities of the ocean environment continues to be a critical component of total strategy,

[42] Proposals to this effect are already being seriously recommended. See White House Conference on International Cooperation, Report of the Committee on Natural Resources, Conservation, and Development (November 28-December 1, 1965), 4-7; 17th Report of the Commission to Study the Organization of Peace, New Dimensions for the United Nations, Clark M. Eichelberger, chm., The Problems of the Next Decade (Dobbs Ferry, N.Y. 1966), 41-46. See also the discussion of these proposals by William T. Burke, Francis T. Christy, Jr., and Clark M. Eichelberger in Lewis M. Alexander, ed., The Law of the Sea: Offshore Boundaries and Zones (Columbus 1967).

[43] See Myres S. McDougal and William T. Burke, The Public Order of the Oceans: A Contemporary International Law of the Sea (New Haven 1962), 631-42.

it seems probable that the benefits, actual and potential, of new information about the ocean will be limited severely. The result may be to foreclose or greatly hamper the employment of presently available resources by states generally, as well as the acquisition and enjoyment of new base values.

Availability of reservoirs of special skills pertaining to the sea is a traditional asset in making use of the area; and as the world looks with increasing attention to the ocean, this value becomes correspondingly magnified in importance. An enormous range of skills is, of course, relevant in connection with such complex phenomena as the ocean, including those in a great many areas of the natural and physical sciences, engineering, communications, navigation, and propulsion. The state or other participant that may command or enlist such a varied group of skills as these and others is able to seek and attain a substantial increment in its total value position and is able, further, to enlarge the store of assets upon which it may draw in employing the ocean and its resources. Unfortunately for the community as a whole, the distribution of skills is not adjusted to the need for drawing upon ocean resources. For example, the areas having the greatest need for new sources of food are the same areas that suffer most from a lack of the skilled personnel that could contribute significantly to meeting the need.

E. Strategies

All available strategies will continue to be employed by all participants as the future importance of the ocean to mankind unfolds, but certain changes are reasonably foreseeable in the way certain of the policy instruments are wielded. Since agricultural productivity of land cannot be increased enough to meet the needs of swiftly increasing populations, observers and policy-makers are expanding their interest in the sea as an important source of food, and more specifically protein, for millions of deprived people around the world.[44] Fish already furnish a significant part of the diet of people in many countries; perhaps more importantly animal protein from the sea has proved very useful as food for land animals that provide a more desirable form of food than fish. So useful is fishmeal for chicken feed

[44] Wilbert M. Chapman, "Ocean Fisheries—Status and Outlook," *Transactions of the Second Annual Marine Technology Society Conference and Exhibit,* Washington, D.C., June 27, 1966, Supplement, 15; Chapman, "The Ocean and Human Food Needs," paper delivered at Gordon Research Conference, Colby Junior College, New London, N.H., June 21, 1966; Chapman, "Fisheries," in Terry, ed. (fn. 5), IV, 5-62; Milner B. Schaefer, "The Potential Harvest of the Sea," *Transactions of the American Fisheries Society,* XCIV, No. 2 (April 1965), 123-28; Schaefer, "Ocean Engineering—Economic and Social Needs for Marine Resources" (mimeo. paper, n.d.).

that Wilbert Chapman has observed that "it is chickens, rather than humans directly, that are stimulating the important part of the increase in the world fish production."[45] And the evidence is that the fish productivity of the sea is now relatively untapped.[46] In these circumstances it would be surprising if there were *not* optimistic statements about the desirability and possibility of more intensive efforts to utilize ocean fisheries.

For present purposes, the realism of the more optimistic estimates of the provender present and within reach in the sea need not be appraised. Though the difficulty of the task of exploiting these resources in helpful ways is probably grossly misperceived by many,[47] it is likely that some substantial increase in food productivity can be achieved. And no matter how great the increase may or can actually be, planners and policy-makers in needy states and communities will probably proceed on the assumption that a larger proportion of investment resources ought to be allocated to this sector of the total economy. The extent to which these planning decisions are made and effectuated and the degree of success achieved may depend, in large measure, on the continued study of the ocean in all its aspects, including, but not limited to, the role of the marine biologist and ecologist. It may be added separately, for appropriate emphasis, that national planning in the direction of increasing man's dependence on the sea also requires inquiry into the social sciences, including all of the complex factors affecting our varying perspectives about the ocean.

Among the sociological factors perhaps worth inquiry are the various cultural characteristics that may influence perceptions about the ocean and its resources. Religious beliefs, for example, may be important for their impact upon the nature and scope of fishing operations by certain groups.[48] Considerations of status in the community are known to have affected willingness to venture out into the farther reaches of the sea.[49] An indication of the potential research in this area is contained in the following excerpt from a report of an imaginary conference held to consider the relationship of man and the sea:

The Panel on Marine Agriculture suggested that several research tasks in comparative analysis of maritime communities might shed

45 Chapman (fn. 9), 132.

46 See the sources cited in footnotes 44 and 45.

47 Letter from Giulio Pontecorvo, *Bulletin of the Atomic Scientists*, XXI, No. 5 (May 1965), 33-34; Francis T. Christy, Jr., "Efficiency in the Use of Marine Resources," *Resources for the Future*, Reprint No. 49 (September 1964).

48 Robert Morgan, *World Sea Fisheries* (London 1956), 86.

49 Same, 175.

light on the problem of "cultivating the cultivators." One recommended study was analysis of ethnological data (beginning with the Human Relations Area Files) to determine the critical variables accounting for differences and anomalies in cultural attitudes toward fishing and fish consumption. (Related to this, the Committee on Marine Concepts was charged with gathering and classifying the concepts involved in acquiring and utilizing all forms of marine life as food in various languages, cultures and subcultures.) Numerous maritime societies and cultures have had what appears to be the same economic need and physical opportunity to use marine food resources. Some have developed the attitudes, skills, and social structure to permit at least partial exploitation of these resources; others have not. Analysis of such contrasts, it was felt, might provide a more solid foundation for creating the requisite skills and conditions among various populations.

Attention was directed to important cultural variations not only in the technology of fishing, and the degree of exploitation of marine resources, but also in the social functions of these activities. Comparative study of fishing and fish consumption from the perspective of cultural dynamics might lead to understanding the kinds of obstacles that exist, even in modernizing maritime cultures, to a rational exploitation of oceanic food resources.

Central to this kind of research would be a study of social change as it relates to fishing and fish consumption. Several historians were invited to begin scrutiny of available data to determine the social factors at work in the waxing and waning of fishing and fish consumption in various eras and civilizations. Studies of fishing communities and of fishermen, it was noted, had pointed to a sort of "fishing weltanschauung"; the fisherman has often seemed embedded less in an economic or occupational pursuit than in a way of life. In the traditional fishing community, requisite skills and attitudes are transmitted almost as esoteric lore from generation to generation, and observers have often remarked the tenacity with which fishing communities resist forces that might change their pattern of life. (They hold this tenacity in common with sailors; both groups tend to ignore or resist either marked deprivation or reward as incentives for occupational change.) This raised questions relating to the necessary and sufficient conditions for introducing modern technology into the world's fishing industries on the required scale. Would enough change-minded individuals emerge among traditional fishing and diving groups to carry out the transformation? Or would a virtually new class of marine workers be required? If so, how would they be recruited and from what population groups?[50]

Part of the point of calling attention to this proposal here is that, if it should be acted upon and deliberate manipulative techniques were employed to create and to stimulate increased use of ocean resources, it might be possible, or, indeed, imperative, to anticipate the emergence of controversy regarding access to particular resources and thus avoid serious strife.

Turning from cultural to material considerations, one finds that the more specific techniques for increasing the oceanic contribution to world food resources embrace refinements and imaginative developments in detection and location of fish, harvesting methods, environmental modifications, communications, materials, propulsion, and processing.[51] The new procedures, already under development or envisaged as technologically feasible, profit from research into military and space problems and seek to adapt to the above-mentioned phases of fishery exploitation such diverse modalities as radar, infrared procedures, laser beams, underwater acoustics, artificial methods of fish aggregation (including electrical, optical, olfactory, and chemical, as well as the use of air bubbles and remotely controlled self-propelled gear and underwater vehicles), fish farming and fertilizing, satellite communication (including television), improved navigation systems, materials technology, engine and ship design, nuclear radiation, refrigeration, and finally, but by no means least, computer technology. An imaginative projection of future world fishing methods has been offered by American and Canadian fisheries experts, who regard the eventual occurrence of these anticipated changes as "undebatable":

A fictional picture of fishing in the future might run along the following lines:

A net of unmanned buoys has been established for several years in the sea and the patterns of occurrence and distribution of natural resources have been determined and plotted. The buoys are interrogated at regular intervals through satellite telemetering and from their surface transmitters by pulse-coded sonic means to instrument heads at various depths in the sea. Transmission redundancy is reduced to a minimum as only points of parameter change

50 Clark Cameron, "Ahoy, Marine Sociology," *The American Behavioral Scientist,* IV, No. 7 (March 1961), 3, 4-5.

51 See Dayton L. Alverson and Norman Wilimousky, "Prospective Developments in the Harvesting of Marine Fishes," *Modern Fishing Gear Of The World,* II (London 1964), 583-88. (From paper presented at 2d FAO World Fishing Gear Congress, London 1963.)

are telemetered. As the data come in to "hydro-central" . . . computers reduce the mass of informational bits to contoured plots of biological oceanographic and meteorological parameters. By facsimile techniques, these data summaries are transmitted to the research laboratory and fishing centers of the world. When a biological parameter anomaly occurs, the nearest buoy would automatically be instructed to assess the nature of the instance with high-resolution sonar and autospectrophotometric methods. These data would be transmitted back to hydro-central for computer and human interpretation. The movements of the identified resources would be plotted.

In some instances it might be necessary to verify the nature of the resource or an anomaly by an on-the-spot check using aircraft perhaps equipped with Laserscopes or hydro-foil research craft equipped with high-speed self-propelled submersible television vehicles. Depending on the species, the main fishing fleet could be deployed into the path of the fish, or conversely, suitable deterrents could be placed in the sea to guide the fish to the catcher. Aircraft could disperse the necessary chemical pellets to olfactorily guide the fish, or remote-controlled underwater vehicles would produce the necessary electrical-sonic or bubble barrier to perform the same function. Depending on the depth of harvest, catches would be performed by catcher boats assigned to permanently anchored factory ships or by automated underwater vehicles operated from ship or shore stations.

Surveillance of the main plotting board in hydro-central would allow detection of weather conditions and precursors of El Nino type shifts in advance. Similarly, areas of high or low basic nutrient production could be watched and, with broad environmental limits, spawning populations deflected accordingly.[52]

That the ocean has always had a profound impact on military strategies hardly needs prolonged examination or explanation. With the establishment of submarine missile systems as a major, perhaps the chief, component of military power, the dimensions of military operations at sea have undergone considerable change. The ocean today clearly has greater relative importance for the world than it has had in all human history, for ocean-based weapons systems may now be employed either for threatening global destruction or for

[52] Alverson and Wilimousky (fn. 51), 588-89; see also Sir Alister Hardy, "New and Richer Marine Harvests Forecast," in Calder, ed. (fn. 36), I, 100-03, for reference to use of "tractor-trawls" for fishing. For contemporary techniques see Dayton L. Alverson and Edward A. Schaefers, "Methods of Search and Capture in Ocean Fisheries," in *Transactions of the Second Annual Marine Technology Society Conference and Exhibit*, Washington, D.C., June 27-29, 1966, 319.

preserving the world from indescribable devastation. The suddenness of this awesome addition to the strategic nature of the sea illustrates what can happen as a result of scientific developments, perhaps initially unrelated to the ocean, and suggests the wisdom of anticipating future changes in military policy as a result of the new emphasis on ocean sciences.[53]

Among all the available strategies open to the participants, it has long been apparent that in time of "peace" the principal mode of operation has been noncompetitive, with each participant in very substantial degree engaging in its own strategies irrespective of those employed by others. It definitely seems possible that this procedure will terminate in the not-too-distant future. The reason is simply that the conditions of use of the sea may undergo such change that explicit coordination of strategies becomes necessary. In respect to the exploitation of resources, for example, it seems more than likely that it will be necessary to join in cooperative activity, utilizing the resources of a variety of participants and excluding or limiting the competing activities of others.[54] In the case of fisheries, more specifically, the necessary condition for increasing productivity may be the initiation of joint efforts in estimating the size, location, and temporal duration of certain stocks; in determining the amount of effort that should be devoted to particular stocks; and in providing for the ways in which the yield can be limited and shared. Without joint decisions on matters affecting access and use, the benefits of an enlarged potential gain may be frittered away.

This same possible need for explicit coordination of strategy may also, someday, be accepted in manipulating military instruments. There is already, as noted below, explicit mention of joint strategies on employment of submarines.[55]

F. Outcomes

The question here is what effect the new interest in the sea, evidenced by intensified scientific and technological research, may have upon the shaping of values from interactions on the ocean. That value production will increase seems certain, as even the brief discussion below suggests, but it also seems likely that the distribution of values among

[53] See, generally, Craven (fn. 36).

[54] James A. Crutchfield and Giulio Pontecorvo, "Crisis in the Fisheries," *Bulletin of the Atomic Scientists*, XVIII, No. 9 (November 1962), 18-20; Christy (fn. 47); Christy, "The Costs of Open Access to Fishery Resources," in *Proceedings of the Fifth Meeting of the Governors' Advisory Commission on Ocean Resources*, Monterey, Calif., September 29-30, 1966, 50. But see Chapman, "On the Management of Ocean Fisheries" in same, 77.

[55] See p. 216.

participants may, for the short run at least, become more restricted. The process is likely to be a selective one, with some values becoming more widely held and others relatively less so.

1. Power

Historically, the ocean served to enhance the power of some states far more than others, even though the technology and skills necessary for access to the sea seem primitive by modern standards and hence rather generally available. It will be no great change, therefore, if increments in power resulting from new forms of employing the sea accrue to very few participant states. It seems amply clear that some of the new methods for achieving access to, and control of, the sea will not be widely available, at least in the first years of this modern effort at conquering the sea. The emerging discoveries in many scientific areas relating to access to the ocean will be too heavily imbued with military applications and connotations for their general dissemination. Moreover, the new technology of the sea promises to be both costly and much more difficult to develop than the vehicles and instruments customarily employed in traversing the sea. The development of deep-sea vehicles and structures, an obvious illustration, appears to be an expensive and complex undertaking, and its results may not be widely shared for decades.[56]

2. Wealth

The potentialities in greater productivity of wealth are beyond realistic measurements at this time. Outcomes that have significance for wealth include increased fishery production, production of gas and oil, the discovery and exploitation of other minerals, improvements in surface navigation systems, development of submarine navigation, utilization of the sea as a source of power, improvements in meteorology, and possible capacity to modify climate and weather.[57]

[56] It is reported, however, that "there are at least two dozen companies in the Free World producing non-military dry submarines." E. W. Seabrook Hull, "World Ocean Market Report," *Geo-Marine Technology*, 1, No. 5 (April 1965), 7, 23. Nonetheless the larger deep submersibles come high, the *Auguste Piccard* cost $1.5 million to build in Switzerland. And Hull reports that "The 1,000 foot, two-man Cousteau-Westinghouse diving saucer *Soucoup* and its support ship and crew, for example, leases to Scripps Institution of Oceanography for $70,000 per month plus an extra charge for each dive." See also Clark (fn. 29), 271.

[57] For analysis of benefits for the United States alone see National Academy of Science-National Research Council, *Economic Benefits from Oceanographic Research*, Pub. No. 1228, 1964. Excluding some very productive resources, such as petroleum, this report declared: "Our estimates indicate that a continuing national investment in oceanography of approximately $165 million a year (not counting the part for national defense) will be an essential component in bringing about savings of nearly three billion dollars a year, plus added annual production worth

Even with current technology, some estimate that fishery yield can be expanded five times over without danger to continued productivity, and one expert has declared that "If this renewable source of food is harvested properly, we might steadily take from five to perhaps a hundred times the present amount out of the sea."[58] As mentioned above in brief summary, improvements in gear, more efficient designs in fishing vessels, better underwater sound detection, sophisticated techniques for detection of commercial quantities of fish, and more adequate management policies and procedures can be expected to lead to high levels of productivity. It should be emphasized that all this activity aimed at improvement in yield must also be accompanied by efforts to stimulate demand for, and consumption of, fish and by resort to methods for encouraging allocation of labor and resources to this form of enterprise. Moreover, if the increment in wealth from the sea is to be distributed properly, all these factors affecting increased fishery yield must be brought to the attention of, or made available to, policy-makers in the less-developed states of the world.

Mineral resources of the ocean are most commonly thought about when attention is turned to wealth production from the sea. The high promise of this aspect of ocean use has already, of course, been realized in part with important and lucrative oil production now in operation off the coasts of a growing number of countries. Very recently the search for oil and gas has been extended to the North Sea, where a find of commercial quantities would be significant, perhaps as much in terms of political transformation as in dollars and cents. Some notion of the possibilities of this area is evident both in the large number of companies involved in the North Sea search and in the heavy expenditures, several hundred million dollars, that will be disbursed for exploration in the next several years.[59]

With respect to other minerals one authoritative source has summarized the situation as follows:

> Diamonds are recovered along the coast of South Africa, tin is dredged from shallow waters off the Indonesian Archipelago, Japan mines iron from its coastal waters, and heavy minerals are taken from beaches and near beach areas of the United States, Australia

---

almost as much. Ten to 15 years will be needed to achieve these gains, and other expenditures in addition to those for marine research will be required if they are to be realized." Same, 1-2. See also *National Security Industrial Association: A National Ocean Program* (1964), 9-48.

For a critical examination of the NASCO report see Report of the Panel on Oceanography (fn. 12), 55ff.

[58] See sources cited in footnotes 44 and 45.

[59] See, generally, *Offshore*, XXIII, No. 6 (fn. 22).

and India. Sulfur is recovered from beneath the Gulf of Mexico. Coal has been mined from tunnels extending from land to points under the sea in Canada and England, and bromine, magnesium, iodine and common salt are recovered commercially from sea water.

However, all present marine mining is in relatively shallow waters less than 400 feet in depth, and the equipment employed is generally the conventional hydraulic or bucket dredge. Normal evaporation, chemical precipitation, and ion-exchange procedures are applied to the removal of compounds and elements from salt water. Thus, there is no true deep-sea mining industry today.

The major deterrent to further extension of even the shallow-water mining, to say nothing of deep-sea mining, is cost. But there is also lack of a clear picture of where and what the resources are. The problems of investigation are formidable. At present, the industry lacks efficient methods and equipment either for prospecting or mining the sea bottom, it lacks knowledgeable marine scientists and engineers, and it lacks incentive since present sources are adequate to satisfy present markets.

It has heard the reports of manganese, phosphorus, gold, platinum, tin, and a host of other minerals found on the continental shelf or the deep-sea floor; but looking at the cost-benefit relationships, the mining industry is apparently obliged to wait until there has been a large-scale, long-range, comprehensive program of exploration before venturing very far into this difficult region. In the national interest, the initial exploration may be the role of government.[60]

The difficulties emphasized by this report may be somewhat less than overwhelming, and perhaps its cautious tone should be viewed with some skepticism. It is not, however, necessarily inconsistent with this caution to find it reported within two years of issuance of this statement that "An American shipbuilding company is financing the first commercial attempt to mine the manganese nodules scattered over wide areas of the Pacific bottom."[61] And shortly thereafter it was announced that the United States Bureau of Mines, in collaboration with two commercial enterprises, was undertaking an underwater mining research venture.[62]

[60] ICO Pam. No. 10 (fn. 2), 20-21. See, generally, John L. Mero, *The Mineral Resources of the Sea* (Amsterdam, New York 1965); David B. Brooks, *Low Grade and Non-Conventional Sources of Manganese* (Washington 1966); Terry, ed. (fn. 5), IV, Pt. I: "Mineral Exploitation."

[61] *New York Times*, January 30, 1965, p. 41, col. 3.

[62] Private concerns have been working in this new activity for some time. The President of Alpine Geophysical Associates, Inc., has written that ". . . since 1959 Alpine has conducted a number of ocean mining exploration programs and has

Perhaps reports about these ventures stimulated the declaration from a Soviet source that "Available data indicate that the USA has already begun to exploit these truly untouched reserves."[63] In this same Soviet study, reserves of raw manganese on the floor of the Pacific Ocean alone were estimated at ninety trillion tons.

Surface transport over the sea has long benefited from oceanographic research; hence, further contributions are merely a continuation of previous trends. The forms of the new assistance from science are, however, likely to appear very exotic to many people, such as provision for more precision in navigation by use of space satellites, the aid of satellites in regular communication, and the selection of more economical routes as a result both of better understanding of the physical movements in the sea and of more adequate weather predictions.[64]

Subsurface transportation may offer great potentialities for wealth production since it would permit year-round use of ice-bound waters and hence afford much shorter routes between major centers.[65] In addition, and no less important, movement below the ocean surface does not have to contend with the vagaries of weather or even the normal operation of wind and wave. The development of subsurface transport systems will bring with it requirements for facilities and equipment not now devised or, perhaps, even conceived.

Another potentially large contribution to wealth may come from the effect of better knowledge of the ocean upon meteorology. There is an intimate relationship between the ocean and the atmosphere; therefore, scientific study of the one is useful also for the understanding of the other. The benefits to be gained may be enormous if the new knowledge being generated can be employed to protect man from the tremendous losses inflicted annually as a result of the violent storms born in the ocean. Beyond this protection against large-scale catastrophe, there are many more or less mundane benefits that might be

---

outfitted and operated the requisite 'Ocean Mining Research Vessels.' These programs have included surveys for tin offshore Thailand, coal offshore England, Scotland, Wales, Japan, and Australia, iron ore offshore Japan and Canada, undisclosable natural resources offshore New York, New Jersey and Florida, and diamonds offshore South Africa." *Geo-Marine Technology*, 1, No. 6 (May-June 1965), 39.

63 Stuart R. Kaplin, "Underwater Geology," Series XII: *Geology and Geography* (All-Union Society for the Dissemination of Political and Scientific Information). Excerpts translated by Joint Public Research Service (Moscow, June 27, 1963), 19, 908.

64 NAS-NRC (fn. 57), 28-36. See, generally, Terry, ed. (fn. 5), II, "Navigation."

65 ICO Pam. No. 10 (fn. 2), 22; Link (fn. 36), 105; H. Rep. 2078 (fn. 3), 52.

within reach, such as prevention of erosion and of tidal and wave damage.[66]

The control of climate and weather obviously would have a great impact upon wealth positions, among others; and in a project for climate control, knowledge of the ocean would be a critical factor. A report of the House Committee on Science and Astronautics declares:

> Eventually, man desires to control climate, to enjoy the salubrious effect of mild and predictable weather. It would seem that the sheer mass of this natural phenomenon would defy adjustment. On the other hand scientists are confronted with many processes in which a condition exists of incipient instability. Like sitting on a fence, only relatively small forces or investments of energy are necessary to cause the process to swing radically from one side to another.
>
> If these processes could be controlled, the impact for constructive purposes by their application to marginal lands, thus to feed an increasing population of the future, will be significant. The military use of climate control carries with it more sinister implications. The nation that could influence the rainfall of another might well control the destiny of the world.[67]

3. Enlightenment

It is, perhaps, testimony of the long history of disregard for comprehensive efforts at scientific study of the oceans that the outcome most likely to be promoted in highest degree as a result of the recent intensification of interest in the ocean is the enhancement of knowledge. In part, the additions to knowledge may appear great because the fund now on hand is so relatively slight. Yet, in another more vital sense, the increment in enlightenment will loom large because much of what is to be discovered is of fundamental importance for so many areas of human interaction. Thus the significance of scientific inquiry into the sea in all its many phases relates, *inter alia*, to discoveries about the origins of the planet and the life inhabiting it, about the origin and location of the major continents, about the origin of the oceans themselves as the largest physical feature of our planet, about the relationship between this planet (as well as of certain particular features of it) and other planets in our universe, and about the com-

---

[66] See, generally, NAS-NRC (fn. 57), 36-39. See, generally, *Weather and Climate Modification*, Report of the Special Commission on Weather Modification to the National Science Foundation (NSF 66-3), (Washington 1966); Howard Taubenfeld, *Weather Modification: Law, Controls, Operations*, Report of the Special Commission on Weather Modification (NSF 66-7), (Washington 1966).

[67] H. Rep. 2078 (fn. 3), 52.

position of and processes occurring in the planet. These matters touch upon and may illuminate questions that have perplexed mankind for centuries. Numerous, more specific discoveries, of course, remain to be made—the import of which cannot now be anticipated.

PROCESS OF CLAIM

By far the most significant changes to be anticipated among the salient features of the process of claim are in the types of claims that are likely to be advanced as controversies arise concerning the exploration and enjoyment of ocean areas and resources.

In a previous inquiry into the law of the sea Professor Myres S. McDougal and I found it convenient to employ a structure of claim and counterclaim designed to call attention to the concentrations of inclusive and exclusive interests in the ocean and to aid in the identification of special interests.[68] One consequence of this method of inquiry was to focus attention more upon geographical areas than upon functional uses of the sea. In the following section, the system of organization adopted is one that seeks to place greater emphasis upon the kinds of uses and competences that could become the subject of controversy.[69]

A. Claims Relating to Access

1. Claims to Inclusive and Exclusive Access

Traditionally, states have sought to protect the movement of the manned vehicles that, for many different purposes, they have sent out upon, over, and under the oceans. Future conflicting claims to access may arise in connection with the movement, or emplacement, of novel types of manned and unmanned vehicles and objects. Such types include telechiric systems, operating either as a bottom-crawler or through the water as "conventional" submersible, robot systems, various inhabited submersibles capable of operating at continental shelf depths and deeper, special structures developed for prolonged habitation in submerged regions, and various types of unmanned buoy systems that are either inert in the water or self-propelled.

Among the manned vehicles, the eventual employment of telechiric systems, including bottom-crawlers, for exploration and exploitation may lead to controversy over the rights of access. The principal claim

[68] McDougal and Burke (fn. 43), 29.

[69] The structure of claim projected for the purposes of this paper is not completely comprehensive. It is realized, for example, that the section on resources is focused rather narrowly and that the claims to competence to prescribe and apply policy could be expanded. We have also omitted, intentionally, any consideration of claims associated uniquely with periods of active violence or very high expectations of violence.

here will probably center about the traditional doctrine of freedom of the seas. Not only may efforts be made to secure free access for these vehicles to all areas of the sea floor outside the territory of a particular state, but free-access claims also will be advanced as these vehicles have occasion to enter the submarine areas of another state. Differences about rights of access, if any arise, are likely to be sharpest in connection with the use of the state territory within the limits of the territorial sea. Coastal states may contend, for example, that coastal authority over access is not limited by the doctrine of innocent passage and that the coastal state may, if it chooses, completely exclude such vehicles from passing on or over the ocean floor within the territorial sea. And even if a state were to concede that the community of states should be permitted to have some access, under a right of innocent passage, it might still claim a greater scope of authority to designate telechiric systems, including bottom-crawlers, as offensive to particular coastal interests than was, or would be, claimed with respect to conventional surface vessels.

Beyond the territorial sea, but within the adjacent area of the continental shelf, coastal states might also seek to deny access to telechiric vehicles employed for exploration or exploitation. Since the floor underlying the oceanic part of the planet was not, until recent years, open to direct access by man, there is an understandable lack of customary or conventional international-law prescriptions upon which to base claims to exclusive control over access to interactions there. Beyond the territorial sea, at least, the only use of the ocean floor as a spatial extension resource has been for the purpose of laying cables to establish communications between the continents and islands. It was universally agreed that access to this area for this purpose was inclusive—that each state had authority to engage in cable-laying and that no state could exclude any other from engaging in this activity. But the development of a technology permitting drilling for oil in areas beyond the territorial sea, led states to claim an exclusive competence over the sea bed and subsoil for this purpose. So widely were these claims pressed that international agreement was rather quickly obtained making it explicit that each state has "sovereignty" over the continental shelf for purposes of exploring and exploiting its mineral and certain animal resources. The agreement, the Continental Shelf Convention of 1958, also sought to provide for accommodation of the authority of coastal states for this purpose with other actual and potential activities in this area, including those undertaken for cable communication and scientific investigation.[70]

[70] *Official Records* (fn. 1), 142-43; see generally McDougal and Burke (fn. 43), 691-724.

But the existence of the Continental Shelf Convention, with its provisions seeking to accommodate exclusive access for limited purposes with inclusive access for others, does not necessarily preclude conflicting claims to access as new techniques in exploration and use of the sea emerge and become refined. Thus it seems possible, though how likely cannot be determined, that coastal states may seek to exclude access by bottom-crawlers, for example, engaged in certain types of activities, including scientific, either completely or on condition that detailed accounts of the locations and projected work are furnished the coastal state in advance. The Convention already contains certain limitations on access for oceanographic investigations; as new techniques are developed, states might claim extension of the scope of their exclusive controls.

When bottom-crawlers and other remotely controlled vehicles become available for military purposes, if such operation proves useful, the possibility of conflicting claims over access by this type of vehicle might be heightened by grave apprehensions of threat to adjacent land and sea areas. In conjunction with the development of deep submersibles, the operation of bottom-crawlers may add new dimensions to the range of undesirable impacts of operations at sea upon coastal interests. Indeed, the possible uses of surface vessels, perhaps considered inimical to the interests of adjacent states, may be expanded by the coordinated operations of inhabited submersibles and telechiric systems, including bottom-crawlers, not to speak of aircraft, missiles, and satellites. The result may be that states adjacent to an area of such use might claim to exclude all of the associated equipment, including the submarine devices, from the region involved. Support might be sought in asserted authority over contiguous zones for security or over the use of the continental shelf for military purposes. Counterclaims asserting free access may be expected to emphasize, not surprisingly, the traditional doctrine of freedom of the seas, contending that inclusive access to ocean areas, historically protected through invocation of this principle, extends to protect not only craft moving through the water or on the surface but also vehicles traveling or positioned on the bottom.

As the employment of remotely controlled vehicles, including bottom-crawlers, becomes more commonplace, the demands for exclusive control by one state may arise also from inconsistent uses of the submarine regions, in addition to demands stemming from anticipated detrimental impact on land-based interactions. Presently, for illustration, some states use limited areas of the ocean bottom for the storage of low-level radioactive waste materials. Although these areas are small, it is clear that the demand is for exclusive use since there is always the possibility of some contamination as containers deteriorate under the physical and chemical actions of the sea. If the amount of these wastes is enlarged, the areas for disposal may have to become larger and, thereby, increase the chance that storage may occur in locations considered desirable for other uses. Attempted entry by bottom-crawlers or submersibles into such disposal areas might very well generate conflicting claims.

Beyond the continental shelf, in the area of the deep ocean floor, the use of telechiric craft by one state or group associated with a state could also lead to claims to exclusive authority. Although it is difficult at this stage to anticipate and to describe the context in which this might occur, some speculation suggests possibilities. Thus, if one state were to carve out an area of the ocean floor for exclusive use for a particular purpose or for all purposes, it might assert the claim to exclude any form of foreign intrusion, including various types of telechiric craft, for any, or any inconsistent, purpose. The doctrines available for asserting exclusive authority might derive, for example, from analogous claims to limited exclusive authority over high-seas areas for military maneuvers, nuclear testing, and missile experiments. Counterclaims would contend, more or less familiarly, that inclusive access is protected by the doctrine of the freedom of the seas. The emplacement of submarine installations, manned or unmanned, on the ocean floor could stimulate similar controversies. It is already well known that underwater structures have been adapted to human habitation for brief periods. As technology increasingly improves and as physiological and psychological obstacles are surmounted, the prospects for locating these structures on the ocean floor for extended occupation for a variety of purposes will also improve.[71] Again the major claim is likely to be inclusive, urging that all are free to place these structures on the bed of the sea for whatever purposes believed desirable and that no other state may seek to exclude them. Potential counterclaims here will arise from alleged authority by coastal states over the territorial sea, contiguous zones, and the continental shelf, alleging that permanent installations in such areas are incompatible with coastal interests.

The desirability of installing submarine structures on a particular part of the floor of the sea could conceivably also lead to opposing claims of free access. It may be speculated, for example, that one state might seek to "occupy" a sea mount of limited area by emplacing a submarine dwelling and then contend that access to such a sea mount was limited to the first group establishing an installation there. Such a contention might be advanced even if the surface of the sea mount

[71] See quotation from Craven in footnote 36.

could accommodate another installation since it may be thought desirable to preclude the surveillance made possible by close association. It is not known why such a localized area could come to be regarded as so strategic or critical as to justify emplacing a habitable dwelling, but the possibility that preclusive access might thus be asserted, limiting the otherwise acknowledged free access of others, seems worthy of mention.

The operation of conventional military submarines has been suggested as a potential occasion for certain claims to control access even in areas outside the comprehensive authority of any single state. It is common knowledge that both the United States and the Soviet Union maintain large fleets of submarines continuously deployed at sea and prepared for instant military action. Suggestion has been made that these states might wish to establish a submarine surveillance system by which the location of submarines could be plotted as means of increasing their mutual security as, for example, in connection with controls over delivery vehicles for nuclear weapons. Presumably this system would operate not merely within designated areas contiguous to both states but over entire oceans. Anticipation of this possibility has been expressed as follows:

> Under present international law, a submerged submarine outside territorial waters in peace time is not violating any law or amenity, and is not subject to attack. Thus the probability will become steadily greater in the future that an international mischief-maker will be able with impunity to initiate a nuclear holocaust.
>
> It may then become necessary to make a change in international law which would require a submerged submarine to surface and identify itself on demand or be subject to attack. For enforcement of such an international agreement a submarine surveillance system might be essential throughout the high seas.[72]

When nuclear weapons proliferate, as now appears a near certainty, and the two superpowers more clearly perceive the common danger, proposals of this kind might become more attractive to both. Perhaps an announcement regarding development of a Chinese Communist submarine fleet will provide impetus to more serious exploration of the possibility of joint action against clandestine methods of delivering weapons.

The placing of objects in the water, unmanned but either free-floating or self-propelled, might cause controversy over access. Pres-

[72] NAS-NRC, *Oceanography 1960-1970* (Washington 1959), Chap. 10, "International Cooperation," 4-5.

ently, this claim may be illustrated by the use of buoys for various scientific purposes, such as current measurements. This network of buoys would be employed to ascertain, record, and communicate information from widely scattered areas of the globe.[73] Since, for scientific purposes, political boundaries are irrelevant, inquiry into the properties of the ocean may make it desirable or even essential to place buoys within areas generally conceded to be within some degree of control by a particular state, as in internal waters, territorial sea, contiguous zones, or over the continental shelf.[74] Coastal states might seek to exclude such objects completely from these areas or perhaps establish acceptable conditions of access that fall short of complete denial. Counterclaims might rest upon a variety of possible propositions, including assertions that buoys designed to gather information about the sea are unique subjects and ought to be given preferred position with respect to access, that buoys in the territorial sea should be treated as analogous to ships in passage and accorded a right of visitation or stay so long as they are not shown to be offensive to coastal interests, and that anywhere beyond the territorial sea a right of access for scientific buoys is fully established under the general rubric of freedom of the seas. The factors suggesting potential difficulty here are that buoys are not ships, hence are not, arguably, entitled to the rights of access accorded ships and that if construction, design, and instrumentation are not properly conceived, buoys might be a navigational hazard in some places.

Even beyond areas within the comprehensive or more limited authority of a single state, i.e., in the high seas proper, exclusive claims are conceivable. Where very large objects, or groups of objects, are employed as buoys or drifting scientific stations, the claim might be made that the area occupied by them plus a surrounding zone is subject to the exclusive authority of the sponsoring state and that intrusion into the zone or deliberate interference with the objects may be proscribed, and sanctions attached, by national prescriptions. The

[73] See Report of the Panel on Oceanography (fn. 12), 26 and App. II, 112; see also Staff Report on Ocean Buoys, *Geo-Marine Technology*, I, No. 3 (February 1965), 31.

[74] See, generally, UNESCO, Intergovernmental Oceanographic Commission, *Preliminary Report of UNESCO and IMCO on the Legal Status of Unmanned and Manned Fixed Oceanographic Stations* (Doc. No. NS/IOC/INF-34), 1962; same, *Report of the Director-General of UNESCO in Consultation with the Secretary-General of IMCO on the Legal Status of Oceanographic Research Stations* (Doc. No. UNESCO/IOC/INF-60), 1964. The author is grateful to Commander Larry Parks, Office of the Navy Judge Advocate General, for supplying these documents and relevant unclassified sections of the U.S. delegation reports to IOC meetings.

claim is surely to be anticipated with respect to buoys, of whatever size, that no other state is authorized to interfere deliberately with their operation or hinder the sponsoring state's control over them for the purpose sought.

A final problem about buoys concerns the participant entitled to claim rights in connection with their use. Assuming the nation-state is in some measure protected in location and use of buoys, are international organizations entitled to the same rights of access and enjoyment?

A further source of controversy could reside in the use of self-propelled objects made to move about in response to stimuli from particular characteristics of the environment, thus permitting continuous plotting of various features of the ocean. Since these objects may be free-floating, the potential for conflict lies in the possibility of excluding or interfering with other uses of an area, as for fishing and navigation. Or the devices might intrude into areas alleged, or actually, within the exclusive authority, comprehensive or limited, of another state.

2. Claims to Accommodate Inclusive and Exclusive Access

Another category of claims concerns the chief methods by which states have sought to accommodate their inclusive and exclusive claims to control access to the sea. These have been through the device of establishing boundaries in the ocean, either a boundary fixed in relation to a particular sea area or a boundary enunciated in relation to certain activities occurring there. In some instances, the boundary projected in the past, such as that of the continental shelf, has made reference to both criteria.

The problem to be assessed is whether states will or should seek to alter previously delimited boundaries in response to the new instrumentalities for exploiting the oceans. States might seek, for example, to widen their previously claimed, if not accepted, width for the territorial sea or even internal waters, either in order to achieve exclusive control over newly perceived benefits from the ocean or to seek to minimize newly perceived threats from that source. States might also, in more likely speculation, seek to extend authority for limited purposes beyond state territory as in creation of contiguous zones for objectives not previously considered important. The possibilities with respect to the continental shelf boundary, as with other potential boundary problems in the regions beyond the continental shelf, will be mentioned in connection with the claims about enjoyment of resources.

B. Claims Relating to Competence to Prescribe and to Apply Policies for Craft Making Use of the Sea

The subject matter of these claims is usually called "jurisdiction," by which is here meant the competence to prescribe regulations that determine the consequences of interactions and the competence to apply a regulation to a set of events.[75] For the most part, the claims to be made to authority will be with respect to conventional sea-going craft, and therefore inherited jurisdictional principles will provide ready guides for responding to such claims. In the following brief discussion, we speculate on possible new claims to competence to prescribe, accompanied by summary statements of the general consensus regarding authority over conventional vessels. There is no discussion of competence to apply since claims to this competence will probably either parallel the claims to prescribe or remain the same as in the past.

1. Claims Relating to Competence to Prescribe

a) Claims Relating to Interaction of Vehicles and Objects Using the Oceans

Prevailing expectations about authority over vessels have been summarized as follows:

> For centuries it has been common statement in the authoritative literature that each state has competence to prescribe regulations for its own vessels and that no state may, save in accordance with specified exceptions in international law, prescribe regulations for the conduct of ships of other states. All the traditional sources from which customary and international law is inferred . . . yield an abundance of decision and expression to establish the very high authority of this principle.[76]

With the exceptions noted below, the new types of submersible vessels being developed, or already in use, will probably not give rise to new problems in conflicting claims to competence. Whether non-military or military, these vessels can be, and no doubt will be, identified with a particular state in the normal ways, as by registration (attribution of national character) for nonmilitary vessels and by entry on the naval list for military craft.[77] The national character thus impressed upon them will then serve the traditional pur-

---

[75] See, generally, Myres S. McDougal, Harold D. Lasswell, and Ivan A. Vlasic, *Law and Public Order in Space* (New Haven 1963), 656-748.

[76] McDougal and Burke (fn. 43), 498.

[77] Same, 1057-61, 1113.

poses of such attribution that encompass, in brief, all the procedures that states employ for maintaining shared access to, and productive use of, the sea.[78] In important, if partial, detail, the state whose national character is impressed upon a vessel is regarded as solely competent, in most circumstances, to control its activities and to serve as the principal (but not sole) protector of the craft against abuses of authority by other states.

With respect to at least three of the newer instrumentalities conflicting claims to competence to prescribe might develop: the establishment of installations on the ocean floor to be inhabited for varying periods; the employment of small submersibles for exploration on continental shelves; and the use of large, uninhabited surface-buoy systems for various purposes, including scientific, military, and commercial.

Underwater stations resting on the ocean floor can be mobile or immobile, but in either event, disputes over competence to prescribe could arise in particular contexts. Even if coastal states do not object to emplacement of stations beneath adjacent waters outside the territorial sea but on the continental shelf, or even outside the continental shelf but still in adjacent waters, there might be demand for compliance with coastal regulations regarding the nature, scope, and duration of the activities to be carried out by the station in the surrounding waters. The sponsoring state might respond, and very probably would in the case of a mobile station, such as a submarine resting on the floor, that the structure or craft falls in the same category as conventional vessels over which the state of national character has sole competence to prescribe while the station is in a high-seas area. The potential use of stations for scientific purposes in connection with the continental shelf raises questions of the applicability of the 1958 Continental Shelf Convention, and disputes might turn on interpretation of that instrument.[79] Even more likely to be productive of disputes, however, are the use of underwater stations for direct, if "peaceful," military operations.

[78] See, generally, same, Chap. 8.

[79] Presumably the argument would be made that scientific investigation, no matter how conducted, was permissible only with coastal consent. It might also be contended that *a fortiori* any submerged station could be excluded by the coastal state no matter what its use.

It is quite possible that claims to control the use of installations on the shelf for scientific or other purposes may rest, not upon the Continental Shelf Convention, but upon an asserted or alleged principle of customary international law. The latter is the basis for the recent Netherlands claim to control installations on the continental shelf. See H. F. van Panhuys and Menno J. van Emde Boas, "Legal Aspects of Pirate Broadcasting," *American Journal of International Law,* LX (April 1966), 303; for critical comment upon the Dutch claim see Burke, "The International Law of the Sea and New Technologies," in Alexander, ed. (fn. 42).

Very similar competing claims might be raised in connection with the operation of small submersibles, inhabited or not, in connection with ocean floor exploration. Here, again, demands for coastal competence might be based upon the Continental Shelf Convention. It is possible, too, that new prescriptions might be promulgated in the form of a submerged contiguous zone designed to extend limited authority, even extending to denial of access, for protecting a real or imagined coastal interest from deprivation by the activities of these submersibles. The counterclaim here could be put most strongly, perhaps, in terms of the general expectations, summarized above, concerning the sole competence of the state of registration to control its vessels.

Conflicting claims in regard to buoy systems may arise, initially, because these objects are not inhabited and may not be within the physical control of the sponsoring agency and therefore are susceptible to pilferage, sabotage, or other deliberate destruction. Since the buoys, though perhaps very large, are not considered to be vessels and are not, therefore, registered with a particular state and endowed with a national character, it is possible (though perhaps not likely) that they would be regarded as without protection from interference. Nonetheless, it is reasonable to speculate that the state placing such buoy systems in the water, or whose nationals did so, might seek to prescribe for the protection of such systems, including stipulations about the inviolability under normal circumstances of the buoy, its instrumentation and associated gear, provisions for responsibility for avoidable but inadvertent damage (as well as for deliberate harm), and sanctions for violation of the regulations so prescribed. Counterclaims might contend that when these objects are placed in water beyond the physical control of the sponsoring state or group they are, in the absence of agreement among the states concerned, beyond the protection of exclusively prescribed rules. This contention could be coupled with the assertion that protective regulations must be inclusively prescribed, so that the conditions of liability for damage or destruction are established by states generally rather than by the sponsoring state alone. It seems probable in view of the difficulties of detecting offenders, and of applying sanctions to them, that states will seek general explicit agreement on the protection of these systems.

b) *Claims Relating to Competence to Prescribe for Events on Board Craft or Objects in the Sea*

(1) *Events Affecting Public Order*

The new scientific and technological developments in ocean exploitation do not now appear to suggest any need for claims differing from those made to authority in conventional and familiar situations of ocean use. This allocation has been described as follows:

> In matters relating both to the discipline to the crew and to control of the passengers, it is imperative that the state of national character should have competence immediately to apply its authority. It is the current fashion to refer to the metaphor of the ship as a "floating bit of territory" as outmoded fiction, but as in the famous aphorism, a "fiction feigned is very near the simple truth." The very real community on board a ship is as much in need of the unified prescription and application of authority for the maintenance of public order as a community on land. Every state demands this competence with respect to its ships and in turn recognizes similar competence in other states.[80]

The new generations of submersible craft appear very similar to traditional ships in this respect, and the prospective use of fixed underwater stations inhabited for varying periods is certain to require a similar arrangement for controlling events threatening disruptions of public order. The problem is not too dissimilar to that presented by the communities living aboard surface drilling platforms engaged in exploiting the continental shelf. Coastal states have acted to extend some, at least, of the land-based legal system to events on such platforms.[81] It is, hence, less than prescient to anticipate that states will claim a competence to extend relevant legal prescriptions to such corresponding events in the new installations.

(2) *Events Not Directly Affecting Public Order*

When and if underwater installations become commonplace and are inhabited by relatively large groups for prolonged periods, there will be occasion to provide for the legal consequences of normal day-to-day interactions as deprivations (torts and crimes), agreements, dispositive acts, and changes of status (births, deaths, marriages, etc.). Although these events may occur in the exotic environment of a building hundreds of feet below the surface of the sea, the problems of legal competence are not likely to present particular difficulty. Many different states may make claim to competence to prescribe the consequences of such interactions, but the established allocations of competence for dealing with these problems in more conventional surroundings will probably provide satisfactory accommodation of conflicts.[82]

80 McDougal and Burke (fn. 43), 1092.

81 For the U.S. see 43 U.S.C. § 1333, for the U.K. see the *Continental Shelf Act*, 1964, S. 3.

82 McDougal and Burke (fn. 43), 1094-95; McDougal, Lasswell, and Vlasic (fn. 75), 674-704.

C. Claims to the Enjoyment of Mineral Resources

1. Claims Relating to Whether Resources Are
Subject to Exclusive Appropriation

As with potential resources in outer space, presently even more inaccessible than those of the ocean floor, three major types of claims can be envisaged with respect to the mineral resources of the sea.[83] The first, in time, if not in eventual importance, is the assertion by a state that certain resources of an area or *all* resources in a particular area are subject to exclusive appropriation by a single state and that no other state or group may, without consent, have access or even seek access to the resources or area involved. Support for this demand for exclusive access and control will perhaps stem from previous decisions allocating sea resources, notably those underlying the territorial sea and continental shelf. The claim most likely to be contraposed to the demand for exclusivity, though it may be advanced as a primary claim and not merely as a counterclaim, is that the mineral resources of the sea, either all or certain of them, are open to free access by all who may wish to benefit from them and that no single state or group is authorized, or should be authorized, to acquire exclusive power and dominion over all or any of the mineral resources of the sea. Justification for this position will probably be found in appeals to the ancient doctrine of freedom of the seas under which, it may be urged, animal resources of the sea have largely been left open to exploitation by all comers. The third type of potential claim is also inclusive, as was the second mentioned here, but demands organized inclusive exploitation or regulation of exploitation. Such claim could take a variety of forms, but all would share the common feature of a community enterprise engaged either in direct exploitation or in allocating rights to such exploitation.

Claims to exclusive access will probably, in more detail, be limited both geographically and temporally. The ocean is a vast area, and with the sizable quantities of some minerals on the ocean floor, the claim to exclusive use might include only a relatively small area and only for a term of years. One suggestion is that a 100 mile square area might be large enough to provide adequate return on investment, if uninterrupted exploitation can thereby be secured. Since minerals are found in areas far more expansive than this, there would appear to be no necessity for conflict between exclusive claims. In other cases, however, where minerals are located in a small, uniquely advantageous area, not duplicated elsewhere, there would be potential for controversy in the absence of agreed upon criteria for exclusive appropriation.

[83] The categorization of claims here is the same as that employed for space resources in McDougal, Lasswell and Vlasic (fn. 75), 770-74.

For completeness of reference, if not for cogent speculation, it is necessary to mention the possible claim that the mineral resources of the deep ocean floor have already been allocated by the Continental Shelf Convention of 1958.[84] This claim might contend that the definition of the shelf incorporated therein is flexible and that the area of exclusive coastal control extends outward to the limits of all exploitation, including the mining of surficial sea-floor sediments. The counterclaim in reply could concede that the shelf is defined by treaty in terms of the depth at which exploitation is possible, but would observe that the situation envisaged at Geneva did not include the possibilities now emerging in deep ocean-floor mining. Furthermore, the reply could continue the policies that supported the allocation of the adjacent shallow submarine regions to the adjacent state for certain purposes are not, at least not obviously, pertinent to allocation of the deep ocean floor to states adjoining on that ocean. Hence, there is no reason to regard the broad language of the Continental Shelf Convention as necessarily incorporating the general expectation that the deeper areas are to be allocated to adjoining, but nonadjacent states. All this could be buttressed by attempts at persuasive demonstration that the policies at stake in allocating the minerals of the deep sea bed are very different from those involved with the adjacent shallow areas.

2. Claims with Respect to Modality of Establishing Exclusive Appropriation

Although it may be agreed that certain resources may be regarded as subject to exclusive appropriation, controversy may still be engendered by conflicting claims concerning the modality by which a claim may be established. Claims to exclusive appropriation may rest upon discovery or symbolic acts, effective occupation and use, or contiguity. Claims on the first of these grounds have not been frequent recently with respect to any resource and have never been accepted in practice. Claims to land resources put forward on the basis of effective occupation and use are, of course, very familiar and constitute the chief method by which exclusive appropriation of such resources has been established. Contiguity, as the foundation for a claim to exclusive appropriation, has also been advanced without marked success in ac-

---

[84] But see Mero (fn. 60), 289: "Presumably also, the continental shelf can be extended by the coastal nation out over the edge of the geologic shelf, down the continental slope and on out over the deep ocean floor to whatever point a commercial minerals dredge can operate. Such an extension was probably not the intention of the Conference, but the wording of the articles of the Fourth Convention is so clear as to leave little room for maneuvering on this point."

quiring land resources but has been honored in somewhat greater degree for ocean resources.

D. Claims to Enjoyment of Animal Resources

1. Claims to Inclusive and Exclusive Access

The advancement of demands for use of marine animal resources range from complete exclusivity, rejecting any exploitation of a particular area or resource by nationals of another, to the polar extreme of complete inclusivity, asserting commonly that all peoples may share in exploitation without limitation. Within these extremes, states assert claims with varying degrees of inclusivity and exclusivity.[85]

Claims to exclusive access are made in terms both of areas and of particular resources. Each coastal state lays claim to exclusive access to all adjacent animal resources by reason of its more comprehensive claim to the territorial sea. Beyond the territorial sea, exclusivity is sometimes also demanded in the establishment of a contiguous zone for fishing purposes. In the submarine regions, states seek exclusive access to the animal resources of the ocean floor by assertion of authority over continental shelf resources.

Demands for sole exploitation of a particular animal resource or resources take the form of an outright claim to ownership, as in the United States assertion regarding fur seals in the nineteenth century, or as a preferential position in an international conservation scheme. This latter claim is illustrated by the International North Pacific Agreement concerning the exploitation of halibut and salmon. The same type of claim is more generally made in the demands for preference or priority for a coastal state when multistate exploitation of a particular fishing stock or stocks is subjected to regulation.

Inclusive access to marine animal resources is urged in terms of the doctrine of freedom of the seas. The common assertion of claim is that the nationals of each state must be permitted free access to fishing resources and that they cannot be forbidden such access, nor can it be qualified, without the agreement of the state excluded.

Accommodation of access concerns both exclusive and inclusive claims. In the first instance, states must seek to reconcile claims to exclusive access with claims to inclusive. This is sought chiefly by the method of establishing various boundaries in the sea. Thus the claims to delimitation of the areas of internal waters and territorial sea, by providing for the base line for the territorial sea and by setting a width for the latter, are a method for determining both the areas within

---

[85] See, generally, Douglas M. Johnston, *The International Law of Fisheries* (New Haven 1965); McDougal and Burke (fn. 43), 923-27.

which the coastal state claims exclusive disposition of resources and the areas within which the general community may have uninhibited access. Beyond the territorial sea, but similarly affected by delimitation of the base line inclosing internal waters, the establishment of a certain contiguous zone may also delimit areas of inclusive and exclusive access. Finally, the areas asserted to be part of the continental shelf may be alleged to determine the sharability of certain animal resources connected with the shelf or in the water above it. And in this special instance of shelf animal resources, claims to exclusive access are also made in terms of the definition of the animal resources that a state claims to be in a certain relationship with the shelf. Illustration of this claim may be seen, for example, in the United States contention that king crabs are a shelf resource exploitable solely by Americans and in the claim by Brazil that lobsters on its shelf area are exploitable solely by Brazilians.

Necessity for accommodation between conflicting claims may also arise from common insistence upon inclusive access to a resource. The problem occurs, as is well known, because free entry to a fishery has the effect of permitting virtually unrestrained exploitation by all participants. If fishermen cannot be assured that their own restraint in exploiting a resource will achieve any proposed goal of limitation since others may enter the fishery at will, there is no incentive to accept limitations on fishing effort. This situation may lead either to demands for sole use by one participant, as some states allegedly seek through widening of the territorial sea, or to the creation of a contiguous zone for fishing, or to efforts for establishing a regulatory scheme binding on all actual and potential participants. As part of this scheme some states have demanded a priority in access for themselves.

2. Claims to Competence over Access to Fishery Resources

Claims to competence to decide who gets access to what fishery resources are also both exclusive and inclusive. Some states, for example, assert not only a demand for sole access to a particular fishery but also contend that such access can be established unilaterally. In this view, the decision about the permissibility of unilateral enjoyment is also unilateral.[86]

Most claims are, however, that decisions about access must be made inclusively, i.e., that unilateral enjoyment can only be established in accordance with a general consensus in the community. The most important demands in recent years for enlarging the area of exclusive

[86] McDougal and Burke (fn. 43), 486-87.

fishing have incorporated also the claim that the permissibility of en-largement is decided by an inclusive process of decision.

That most claims to prescribe and apply policy to fishery activities are inclusive, and that each state commonly asserts sole authority over its own vessels, are, however, the occasions giving rise to the most in-tractable problem involving ocean resources. How does the commu-nity or an individual state establish a system for regulating exploita-tion if no one state has any authority over all those involved? The problem, in other words, is to create a structure of authority that will assure orderly, peaceful, and economical use of the resources of the sea.

A principal goal of the present discussion is to seek an approach to this problem by suggesting a fruitful means of describing previous efforts at establishing international organizations concerned with fishery conservation and of indicating some factors that might be taken into account in future efforts.

E. Claims Relating to the Administration of Shared Use

Since the new practices in exploring and exploiting the oceans will continue to permit a significant degree of sharing in participation with others and yet have a high degree of collective impact, it can be expected that demands will be forthcoming for explicit multilateral agreements establishing the conditions and consequences of inter-action. Among the activities that seem likely to call for an accommoda-tion demanding multilateral prescription are the employment of buoys of different kinds for various purposes; the establishment of com-munications between surface objects and others (including those in the space above and both surface and subsurface objects); the establish-ment of underwater communications conducted for underwater opera-tions (including navigation); the disposal of wastes; the conduct of scientific experiments; the operation of subsurface installations; the pursuit of scientific investigations; and the acquisition and manage-ment of sharable and nonsharable resources. A brief summary of these possibilities seems warranted.

The major legal problems about buoys that calls for explicit regula-tion, other than the claims about access already mentioned, include access to the equipment on the buoys and to the data collected by it, protection of the buoy system and shipping through appropriate notices, markings, and lights, and liability for interference with the buoy system and for harm caused by it.[87]

The communications networks required for the newly intensi-

[87] See sources cited in footnote 74.

fied use and study of the sea must, of course, be meshed with other demands for space in the radio spectrum. The international procedures for dealing with this problem area are already well established and in frequent use, so that this is not a novel difficulty nor one that should require the development of new institutions or practices.[88] In one aspect, however, the ocean communications problem may be unique; that is in the development of entirely submerged communications systems. Whether or when this type of communication becomes an international problem perhaps depends primarily upon the emergence of submarine transportation as an economic mode of commercial transport. Should this occur, it would then probably be necessary to arrange for allocations of the frequencies, stations, and, perhaps, depths that will be used by the participating states in establishing a communications and navigation system for the submerged vehicles.

Problems of waste disposal, especially of radioactive materials, are and have been under constant scrutiny in the international arena.[89] States have already joined in efforts to eliminate one of the major sources of pollution, that caused by oil.[90] If the ocean becomes a more inviting place for storage of radioactive wastes, concerted action to minimize undesirable effects may be widely demanded. Insistence on inclusive regulation of this form of interaction may be intensified when participants widen the range and form of their multiple uses of the sea. The widely expected, or at least hoped for, increase in food productivity, for example, will surely focus increased attention on possibilities of contamination from radioactive substances, as would, also, of course, successful establishment of human habitations under the sea.

Mutual accommodation by explicit agreement would appear necessary in providing for the safety of underwater installations which states and private associations employ for pursuing their objectives in the sea. In the beginning, at least, subsurface structures may require attendance or surveillance by observers on the surface; hence navigation problems may revolve around the conventional necessity for avoiding collisions. But as more sophisticated equipment and procedures are devised and surface assistance can be eliminated, protection may

[88] See Gerard E. Sullivan, "International Regulation of Communications for Oceanographic Equipment," in Alexander, ed. (fn. 42).

[89] See, generally, International Atomic Energy Agency, *Radioactive Waste Disposal into the Sea* (Vienna 1961); Convention on the High Seas, Article 25.

[90] Convention for the Prevention of Pollution, United Nations Legislative Series, *Supplement to Laws and Regulations on the Regime of the High Seas, Vols. I and II, and Laws Concerning the Nationality of Ships* (U.N. Doc. No. ST/LEG/SER.B/8), January 1959, 33.

require the use of large surface buoys or other means of signaling the presence of underwater objects. It is perhaps not beyond the realm of probability that a system of registration will be devised as a means of disseminating information about the location of underwater buildings.

At present, scientific cooperation in carrying out study of the sea is largely organized through private associations of scientists, but in the future it could be desirable to provide a more formal organization. In fact, of course, the beginning of such a mechanism exists in the form of the Intergovernmental Oceanographic Commission. The newly created Committee on Fisheries of the Food and Agriculture Organization is an embryonic effort at more formal organization in the important area of fisheries research and regulation.

The management of sharable and nonsharable resources is an area in which it is already quite clear that explicit inclusive arrangements are a critical requirement. For resources that are sharable, the problems of economic use are abundantly illustrated by the difficulties encountered in fishery exploitations. We have already had some experience in attempting to resolve these problems, though it would be a gross overstatement to say that the efforts have met with a great measure of success. Even resources to be regarded as nonsharable, meaning those in which some measure of exclusive right to access is honored, will very likely require multilateral agreement. Thus, it seems probable that there will be some, perhaps even many, ocean resources that can be exploited economically only on condition of recognizing a degree of exclusive appropriation. Even if simple priority in time is recognized as decisive of who may appropriate resources, there will probably still be a need for agreement on how to accommodate exploitative operations with other, potentially conflicting, uses of the sea.

PROCESS OF DECISION

The two types of decision comprising the total flow of decisions called international law, the constitutive and the particular, appear certain to undergo varying degrees of change in response to innovations in the specific processes of interaction and claim concerning the ocean. The constitutive process of decision, the process by which the general community establishes the basic structure for international decision-making, embraces all phases of the decision process including decision-makers, objectives, base values, arenas, strategies, and outcomes.[91] The particular decisions made are those in response to spe-

[91] For comprehensive discussion see McDougal, Lasswell, and Vlasic (fn. 75), 94-137.

cific controversies over exploration and use of the sea.[92] The following discussion attempts brief preliminary speculation, seeking both to identify potential changes in some aspects of the constitutive process of decision as it pertains to events on the ocean and to recall the principles and techniques inherited from more conventional periods in the history of ocean exploitation, which decision-makers have in the past employed for resolving some disputes about particular claims and which they might use, rationally or not, in the future.

A. Constitutive Process of Authoritative Decision

1. Authoritative Decision-Makers

Nation-state officials have long been the most important decision-makers in the law of the sea; and, barring major change in prevailing expectations, they will continue to be of the most consequence in performing critical decision functions. It seems probable that even if the new possibilities of intensified ocean use are limited initially to a relatively few states, the representatives of all states will expect to have a voice in projecting new legal prescriptions, or altering the old, to deal with emerging problems. Nonetheless, special influence on choice will reside in the few states whose capabilities in exploitation are most advanced.[93]

International governmental organizations are the more recent participants in authoritative decisions and have already had significant roles to play.[94] The existence of the United Nations was probably indispensable to the formulation of the Geneva Conventions on the law of the sea, for without the focus and continuity provided by such a forum it is doubtful that the outcome could have been realized against the inertia of numerous states. And, of course, it was a subsidiary organ of the General Assembly of the United Nations, the International Law Commission, whose extensive efforts produced the drafts that formed the basis of discussion for the conference convened in Geneva in 1958. Other specialized agencies, particularly the FAO, also contributed to the background work of the 1958 Conference in addition to their continuing role as collectors and disseminators of information useful for legal purposes. One specialized agency, the Intergovernment Maritime Consultative Organization, is devoted wholly

[92] This aspect of the decision process is more fully examined in McDougal and Burke (fn. 43).

[93] Observers frequently emphasize this factor in recommendations urging greater support for ocean science and technology. See, e.g., *Hearings* (fn. 9), 137.

[94] One prominent observer estimates that the need for cooperation on the ocean is alone sufficient to require an organization such as the United Nations and the specialized agencies. Chapman, same, 137.

to certain maritime matters; others, including UNESCO, ITU, and WMO, have limited competences in connection with the oceans.

Among the less universal international organizations prominent in the decision process relating to the ocean are the various conservation organizations established to deal with marine fisheries. Only relatively few states belong to one or another of these groups, and, in general, the decision-making competence conferred upon them is minimal.[95]

Private associations, national and international, have specialized in achieving wealth and enlightenment or in representing certain skills and interest groups, and they have long been active in influencing various official participants. Like similar groups in space exploration, scientific bodies concerned with the ocean will have a continually stronger role as the ocean becomes more evidently a critical area of interaction for a variety of endeavors.

Even the private individual, who only exceptionally has significant influence in the decision process, may occasionally, by force of personality or intellectual contribution, have impact on the flow of decisions.

2. Objectives

There is no indication that decision-makers will discontinue their efforts to achieve common interests as activities in exploitation of the oceans are intensified. Moreover, there is nothing in the perceivable future to indicate that recognition of interdependencies in use of the ocean will be obscured; indeed this recognition is much more likely to become clearer as the conditions of ocean exploitation are more intimately affected by each participant's activities. Nevertheless, the degree or extent to which decision-makers can act to achieve their recognizable common interests in peaceful and productive uses of the sea depend on many factors, particularly those pertaining to expectations of violence prevalent at critical times. The fact of the matter is that, at least in the intermediate run, the ocean is too critical and strategic in calculations of relative strength to permit full or even substantial deference to the accomplishment of some common objectives. In short, effective realization of common, widely recognized interests in the use and control of the sea depends on a much wider constellation of factors than those immediately concerned with this area.

[95] See FAO, *Comparisons and Abstracts of Selected Conventions Establishing Fisheries Commissions* (FAO 1962); Jean Carroz, *Establishment, Structure, Functions, and Activities of International Fisheries Bodies,* I—Indo-Pacific Fisheries Council (FAO Doc. No. FIb/T57), 1965; same, II—Inter-American Tropical Tuna Commission (FAO Doc. No. FIb/T58), 1965; same, III—Regional Fisheries Advisory Commission for the Southwest Atlantic (FAO Doc. No. FRm/T60), 1966; *International Fisheries Bodies* (FAO Doc. No. FI/T64 (En)), 1966.

3. Arenas

Whatever the impact of expectations of violence on wider perspectives about authority over the ocean, the experience of even the past few years established that more organized inclusive arenas of decision can be, and will be, employed for making decisions about relatively important disputes over access to, and enjoyment of, the sea. In the past, the vast majority of important decisions responding to controversies over use and control of the sea were made in totally unorganized arenas. What we call international law consisted (and, for the most part, consists to this day) of inferences of legality drawn from uniformities in the behavior of states and other participants.[96] As noted above in relation to participants, the establishment of the United Nations and its subordinate organs and components, especially the International Law Commission, has already provided a somewhat more highly organized arena for making decisions. The work of the specialized agencies, the FAO, the ITU, the IMCO, and UNESCO, though they have not exercised any comprehensive competence with respect to the sea, does provide some experience with inclusive, organized structures of authority. Tentative beginnings, and no more than that, have been made in the marine conservation field toward establishing inclusive arenas of decision. It seems eminently safe to assume that the competences of all these groups in regulating events on the oceans will either be enlarged, or, perhaps in addition, new organized arenas will be devised for facilitating performance of various decision functions.[97]

4. Bases of Power

Since the most important decisions about the oceans are still made by states in a decentralized arena of decision, it should occasion no surprise to find that state officials retain exclusive control over the most potent bases of power and, except sporadically, have been reluctant to confer significant values on international organizations.

The extent to which organized structures of authoritative decision are deprived of support for decision-making is indicated both by the minimal formal authority usually conferred upon them and, in those cases where ample authority is conferred, by the minimum effectiveness that they can exercise. Not a single organization, including the United Nations, possesses, in prevailing expectation, any significantly comprehensive competence to prescribe or apply policy. Indeed, very

96 See McDougal, Lasswell, and Vlasic (fn. 75), 115-19 for discussion of the requirements for establishing customary international law.
97 See, generally, FAO Committee on Fisheries, *Report of the First Session,* June 13-18, 1966, FAO Fisheries Rep., No. 33 (FAO Doc. No. FIp/R33 (En)), 1966.

recent experience indicates a diminution in the capacity of the U.N. for effective action regarding vital problems.

It would, however, be clearly inaccurate to conclude that organized arenas of inclusive decision are devoid of bases of power, including formal authority. Authority conferred does include, in relation to the oceans, important roles in the performance of the decision functions of intelligence, recommendation, and appraisal. Moreover, with respect to other values, the international organizations with responsibilities relating to the sea are sometimes able to use control over enlightenment and skill as potent bases of power. The task of collecting and analyzing data regarding social, economic, and scientific problems of international significance and of disseminating information can serve to focus the attention of effective power-holders upon problems of legal significance and might have a measurable impact upon the decision-makers charged with recommending, prescribing, applying, or terminating regulations.

It remains to record the hypothesis that if contemporary trends in ocean use make for greater interdependency among participants, the tendency will be to confer more assets upon the international organization that will be found necessary for effective regulation.

B. Particular Decisions

1. Claims Relating to Access

a) Claims to Inclusive and Exclusive Access

The substantive law relative to specific claims and counterclaims, the general principles established in past experience that could possibly be employed for resolving future problems, can be briefly summarized. It is evident that the principles accommodating inclusive and exclusive access are largely those applicable to areas near land masses, a feature due principally to the fact that most disputes over access have arisen in the more restricted water areas bordering coasts. Beyond these adjacent seas, the predominant principle has been expressed in the venerable doctrine of freedom of the seas, which both enjoins that all states are entitled to free access to the sea with sole control over vessels allocated to the state of its nationality and prohibits any comprehensive exclusive authority over access to any other state. It is true, of course, that even in noncontiguous high seas, states have sought and, in the view of some, have obtained the authority to exclude access by foreign vessels to particular water areas. Illustrative of these decisions are the demands by the major powers (the United States, the Soviet Union, and the United Kingdom) for exclusive use of huge

ocean areas for the testing of nuclear weapons, and the response re-
vealed by the behavior of other states.

In waters most immediately adjacent to the land, the part called
internal waters, states in their traditional practice have honored a completely exclusive and comprehensive authority in the coastal state to
forbid the entry of foreign vessels at the discretion of the coastal state.[98]
In very recent times, as the area of internal waters has been expanded
by international agreement, there has also been explicit agreement
that in certain parts of internal waters, namely the high seas and territorial sea inclosed as internal waters by a newly established straight
baseline system, foreign vessels are protected in a right of access, the
same right as that honored by the doctrine of innocent passage previously associated with the territorial sea.

This general recognition of a right of passage through the territorial
sea, if innocent, has been the chief doctrinal method by which states
have sought to accommodate the common inclusive interest in a free
movement on the oceans with the common exclusive interest in protecting each state from sea-based deprivations.[99] All states have thus
been enabled to make efficient use of the sea for transportation and
communication, while the coastal state could preclude access when
threats of harm to important coastal interests appeared. The recent
authoritative formulation of doctrine in the Territorial Sea Convention of 1958 expresses this balance of interests by first acknowledging
a right of innocent passage and then defining "innocent" to mean passage which "is not prejudicial to the peace, good order or security of
the coastal State."[100] In confirmation of the special weight that this
rather vague language appears to place on coastal interests, a subsequent section provides that under certain limited conditions, involving demands of military security, the coastal state may suspend all
passage through a specified part of the territorial sea.[101] Since this
article provides that such portions may not include areas of the territorial sea forming a strait,[102] it seems clear that inclusive interests
in free access were not disregarded.

Submarines are especially provided for in the Convention in regard
to access to the territorial sea. Apparently reflecting the practical cir-
sumstance that historically submarines have always been military instrumentalities, it is stipulated that such vessels must travel on the surface when transiting the territorial sea.[103] Presumably, a submarine

[98] See, generally, McDougal and Burke (fn. 43), 99-126.

[99] Same, at 187-269, examines community policy and the trend of decisions regarding this problem of access.

[100] Article 14 (4).

[101] Article 16 (3).   [102] Article 16 (4).   [103] Article 14 (6).

making a submerged passage would not be considered innocent and could be excluded from passage or, perhaps, even destroyed, if exclusionary measures were of no avail. Contemporary events suggest that discovery of an unidentified submarine in national waters can occasion drastic measures by the coastal state.

In the surface waters immediately adjacent to the territorial sea, coastal controls honored by international law have historically included some measure of authority over access by foreign vessels,[104] in recognition of the common exclusive interest in protection of internal social processes of the coastal state. Although not without controversy, coastal states have often asserted a competence, limited in both duration and purpose, to control access to waters variously distant from the land and beyond the territorial sea. But recent decision, embodied in multilateral international agreement, appears to have placed stringent, and in the view of some, undesirable, restrictions on coastal authority to limit or condition access to contiguous zones. Thus, the 1958 Convention on the Territorial Sea and Contiguous Zone, in Article 24, seems largely, it not completely, to preclude consequential coastal competence to prescribe or apply policy in contiguous zones. The dimensions of the authority remaining in states are not entirely clear, and it appears uncertain whether the limitation on authority embodied in Article 24 will survive the legitimate demands of states in protecting their common exclusive interests.

Also, beyond the territorial sea and overlapping the regime of contiguous zones as envisaged by the 1958 Convention, the waters superjacent to the continental shelf have recently become subject, in accordance with widely accepted principles of international law, to a measure of exclusive authority over access. The more precise content of these prescriptions was the subject of debate at the 1958 Geneva Conference and was clarified in some detail in the Convention on the Continental Shelf produced at the conference and now in force between states parties to it, including the United States. It was, of course, obvious (though not without controversy) long before the Geneva Conference met in 1958 that if the general community was to honor any access to the mineral resources of the continental shelf that required structures extending above the surface, that some, perhaps substantial on occasion, restriction on free access to the surface of the sea must be conceded.[105] Moreover, since the pattern of claim after the initial United States proclamation in 1945 quickly established that coastal

104 McDougal and Burke (fn. 43), 582-607 discusses community policy and decisions.
105 See, e.g., H. Lauterpacht, "Sovereignty over Submarine Areas," *British Yearbook of International Law*, XXVII (1950), 376, 402-03.

states were to be conceded their demand for exclusive access, it became recognized that restrictions on inclusive access were to be determined exclusively, i.e., by each state acting unilaterally with a minimum of review by other states or the organized community of states. Hence, it caused no surprise when the Geneva Conference concluded with almost universal support that on the continental shelf each state has "sovereign rights for the purpose of exploring it and exploiting its natural resources."[106] This means, clearly, that even substantial interference with inclusive access to the area for purposes of movement may be justified on occasion in carrying out exclusive activities on the shelf.

Beyond these rather general references to "sovereign rights" for specified purposes and the more specific accommodation in later provisions of the named rights in navigation, fishing, and scientific investigation,[107] the convention does not deal directly with future conflicting claims to access, but it is certainly implied, and no doubt did not seem worthy of mention, that access to the ocean bottom for whatever purpose would be subject to a measure of exclusive coastal authority similar to that honored over the indicated surface operations.

On the high seas, beyond territorial sea, contiguous zones and continental shelf, states enjoy the greatest measure of freedom of movement, although even in these vast expanses some exclusive restraints on inclusive access are honored in exceptional instances. Here again, as in contiguous zones, the extent of exclusive authority is not beyond controversy. There remains, however, a considerable record of acquiescence, not accorded merely as a matter of courtesy but in recognition of legal requirement, in assertions by states of authority to control access by foreign vessels to these areas of the high seas.[108]

b) *Accommodations of Inclusive and Exclusive Access*

The final set of doctrines that decision-makers use to resolve controversies over access are concerned with delimitation of the familiar "zones" of authority: internal waters,[109] territorial sea,[110] contiguous zones,[111] and continental shelf.[112] It is familiar history that the response by decision-makers to controversies about access have sometimes been framed in terms of principles for the delimitation of various zones of authority. For example, the Anglo-Norwegian Fisheries Case was essentially concerned with the issue of access to fishery resources, rather than with use of the sea as a spatial extension resource; but

106 Convention on the Continental Shelf, Article 2 (1).
107 Article 5.
108 See McDougal and Burke (fn. 43), 751-94.
109 See, generally, same, 305-445.   110 Same, 446-564.
111 Same, 597, 605-06.   112 Same, 663-91; 724-30.

the International Court of Justice (in addition to others) also approved the Norwegian straight baseline system (creating new areas of internal waters) on the grounds that factors relating to movement and navigation may warrant the inclosure of certain areas within internal waters. And, of course, some demands at the Geneva conferences of 1958 and 1960 for a wider territorial sea rested upon assertions of a need to control the access of vessels to and aircraft over the waters adjacent to a state.

2. Claims Relating to Competence to Prescribe

a) *Claims Relating to Interactions of Vehicles and Objects Using the Oceans*

In previous discussion, it was convenient to make a quick summary of the inherited jurisdictional principles that are probably suitable for most of the claims to prescribe regarding new kinds of vessels and instrumentalities; hence, only brief mention will now be made of treaty provisions and certain customary prescriptions to which decision-makers could, or might, turn in seeking guidance for resolving controversies about more difficult problems. The 1958 Continental Shelf Convention, the Convention on the Territorial Sea and Contiguous Zone, and, perhaps, customary prescriptions concerning authority over contiguous zones, all might be thought relevant to claims about underwater stations or the new types of submersibles. In the following discussion, it is intended only to note that these various prescriptions could be employed by decision-makers seeking to resolve controverted claims. It is not now sought to clarify policies for their application, nor to present detailed descriptions of apparently analogous previous decisions, nor to attempt predictions of detailed application in specific contexts.

Certain of the general provisions of the Continental Shelf Convention, as well as more specific articles, are relevant in connection with claims over activities on the shelf and in the waters above. Of the general provisions, the most important is Article 2(1), which confers upon coastal states "sovereign rights" over the continental shelf "for the purpose of exploring it and exploiting its natural resources." Article 2(2) confirms the exclusiveness of the rights involved by explicitly declaring that if the coastal state does not explore or exploit the shelf, no one else may do so without coastal consent. The significance of these provisions is in their potential for authorizing interference with exploration of the shelf, including activities of substantial scientific merit as well as of commercial or military value. The form and nature of such restrictions cannot, of course, be identified in detail, but it is possible to envisage conditions or limitations with undesirable effects such as, for example, excessive license fees, unreasonable stipulations about permissible areas of work, and onerous regulations concerning time of work, equipment, and personnel. Moreover, the breadth of Articles 1 and 2 might even be used to justify restraints upon activity in the waters above the shelf.

Subsequent provisions in the convention deal more specifically with the relation between coastal authority over the shelf and certain critical activities, namely, navigation, fishing, conservation, and scientific research. With respect to the former three operations, "interference," apparently referring to physical obstacles, is permissible if it is not "unjustifiable." But with respect to scientific research, no interference is permissible, subject to the condition that the research is "carried out with the intention of open publication." It is somewhat difficult to understand what this latter prohibition on interference might mean, especially in light of still another provision dealing expressly with research. Article 5(8) states:

> The consent of the coastal state shall be obtained in respect of any research concerning the shelf and undertaken there. Nevertheless, the coastal state shall not normally withhold its consent if the request is submitted by a qualified institution with a view to purely scientific research into the physical or biological characteristics of the continental shelf, subject to the proviso that the coastal state shall have the right if it so desires, to participate or be represented in the research, and that in any event the results shall be published.

Apparently this provision is intended to have a limited application, i.e., only to "research concerning the continental shelf and undertaken there" and not to research concerning the waters above. Unfortunately, if this supposed distinction is not an operational one, and it seems suspiciously neat considering the physical and biological interdependencies involved, the result could be that decision-makers might feel inclined to extend coastal competence to prescribe to all research in the shelf area, including that carried on by submersibles and other instrumentalities in the waters above the floor.[113]

Potential authority for extending coastal competence to prescribe for interactions involving foreign craft and stations in areas adjacent to the territorial sea might also be sought, and perhaps found, in the customary prescriptions on contiguous zones.[114] Here, however, as

---

[113] This important area has been examined further in Burke, *A Report on International Legal Problems of Scientific Research in the Oceans* (1967).

[114] Discussion of these prescriptions and citations of literature are in same at 584-603.

noted above in connection with decisions about access, the Convention on the Territorial Sea and Contiguous Zone in Article 24 appears to limit coastal competence severely. Despite the restriction, it is worth recalling that states are still authorized to extend authority beyond state territory for security purposes, and future decision-makers perhaps would look to this authority to establish coastal competence with respect to certain military activities in nearby sea areas. It may be added also that the traditional flexible concept of the contiguous zone, apparently interred by Article 24 of the Territorial Sea Convention, may suddenly be revived to cope with demands created by hitherto unimagined uses of the sea.

3. Enjoyment of Mineral Resources

It has been over fifteen years since lawyers interested in the law about exploitation of marine oil deposits were reminded that the process of decision, even in the traditional international law of the sea, contained two parallel streams of principles by which controversies over access to such marine resources might be resolved.[115] The first, usually considered the predominant principle, emphasizes freedom of access for all who wish to compete in exploitation. Formulated in terms of the doctrine of freedom of the seas, this principle would, if projected into the future development of ocean resources, honor inclusive and unorganized access to resources. The sharing of use protected by international law would emerge from the unpatterned joint activities of many different entrepreneurs acting on the ocean. The similarity to the regime for exploitation of fishery resources is obvious.

The second set of principles, more recently evolved but no less authoritative, is designed to honor exclusive (though common) interests of coastal states and would, in the context of mineral exploitation, concede exclusive access to a certain area to one state, whether coastal or not. It is now familiar to all that despite some challenge to the allocation of exclusive access to coastal states, the general community has adopted this principle for allocating many, though not all, of the mineral and animal resources of the continental shelf by conferring on the coastal states "sovereign rights" for exploration and exploitation of such resources. Moreover, the definition of the continental shelf for the purpose of this allocation was left open-ended so that it might be expanded outward as exploitation became feasible in deeper waters.

The primary question posed by these alternatives in inherited principle is not hard to perceive. It is whether either of these sets of prin-

115 See Lauterpacht (fn. 105), 403-08.

ciples, establishing patterns of exploitation in certain contexts, will serve community policies when new areas or new resources are opened to exploitation by advancing technology and, if not, what other principles and procedures can be devised or adapted as practicable and desirable courses of action. The suddenness with which exploitation possibilities are being surveyed in the deeper ocean beyond the continental shelf, coupled with the contributions of those interested in opening undersea areas to direct human access, quite clearly call for more intensive examination of this problem than has been deemed desirable or useful in the past.

In addition to examination of previous experience with ocean resources, inquiry should include a comparative survey of the principal techniques employed by the major legal systems for allocating mineral resources on land.

It is not now intended to attempt a detailed clarification of the community policies at stake with respect to mineral exploitation. Some comment should, nevertheless, be made concerning principles available from past experience. It seems clear that similarities and dissimilarities between previously exploited ocean resources and those yet to be exploited will be critical in evaluating the usefulness of previously accepted principles for allocating rights of exploitation. Mineral resources existing on the ocean floor, such as manganese nodules, can both be compared with and contrasted to fishery resources.[116] The latter occur in tremendous numbers and are mostly self-replenishing. The manganese nodules also are found in vast quantities, estimated in the trillions of tons, distributed rather thinly over large areas of the ocean floor. These nodules are as a whole probably self-replenishing, since the rate of exploitation will most likely be exceeded by the rate of formation. But the nodules are not in movement and the costly equipment to take them must, even if mobile, be concentrated on the resources of a relatively fixed area. Fishing vessels, of course, are required to be highly mobile, at least under present technology, in order to fit the characteristics of the prey. The same stock of fish can be, or has been, fairly regularly, subjected to simultaneous fishing by vessels of different states in the same ocean as well as in different parts of the sea, and fishing so conducted can still be a profitable enterprise. But this same arrangement might not work for the ocean mining industry. Mr. John Mero, a leader in the study of the feasibility of ocean mining, has emphasized that a major feature distinguishing mining from fishing is that the miner has an investment

116 Mero (fn. 60), is a comprehensive account of these resources and the technology and economics of their exploitation. See especially 284-93 for reference to legal problems and information relevant thereto.

in the mineral deposit he is working or even proposing to work;[117] this is not usually the case with fishermen though it sometimes can be. The occasion for the investment in the potential mine is that the feasibility of mining various deposits differs greatly, dependent on a considerable number of factors, and very careful studies must be made to determine which of several sites should be worked. The mining system employed will then be designed for efficient operation at the site chosen.[118] It is, hence, easy to see that the mining operator has an interest in securing exclusive access to a particular location. Without more, these considerations appear to mean that provision for free access to ocean mineral resources must be accompanied by a system for recognizing exclusive rights in limited areas. Such recognition would, presumably, permit profitable operation at the same time that it affords virtually unlimited access to the same or similar resources elsewhere.[119] It is, of course, possible that for the initial mining ventures, the need for international legal protection will be minimal. If exclusive access is needed, it may be assured by virtue of the unique technological capabilities of the new enterprise as well, possibly through control over, or access to, markets.

4. Enjoyment of Animal Resources

The bitterest peacetime controversies about the sea have focused upon conflicting claims to access to fishery resources. Here, again, decisions over the centuries have sought to protect the interests of both coastal and noncoastal states (so termed in relation to the fishery resources concerned). Some degree of exclusive access has been protected through recognition of exclusive authority over access to certain waters adjacent to the state. Traditionally these were the areas of internal water, such as bays and gulfs of certain dimension and size, and the territorial sea of modest width, usually about three miles. More recently exclusive access has been permitted increasingly in larger areas as international law comes to recognize new methods of delimitation of sea areas. Illustrative are the employment of the

[117] Same, 291-92.
[118] Same.
[119] Gain would perhaps continue to be achieved so long as excessive entry into exploitation is avoided. If entry is open and easily effected, the same problems experienced by fishermen would apparently soon develop. See Christy (fn. 47), 6. This means that the recognition of exclusive access to the mineral resources of particular areas is not a sufficient method of protecting exploiters. So long as a new venture may be undertaken in any area of the ocean other than that in which exclusive rights have been recognized, the threat remains of bankruptcy for the initial entrepreneur. In these terms, exclusive rights of access to mineral resources underlying the ocean are simply not relevant to the problem of those who wish to undertake such enterprises.

straight baseline system that has become widespread since the Anglo-Norwegian Fisheries Case and since its inclusion in the provisions of the 1958 Convention on the Territorial Sea and Contiguous Zone as well as through the creation of new areas of exclusive access through use of the venerable contiguous-zone concept.

At the same time that these various devices and principles were molded as a means of adjustment to the pressure for more extensive fishing rights, the hoary doctrine of freedom of the seas, connoting in this context free access to the fishery resources of the high seas, continued to be invoked to permit anyone who wished to enter into exploitation. The prevalence of this general principle about access to fisheries occupies a central place among the factors contributing to the difficulties of establishing and maintaining a regime of rational exploitation of these resources.[120] For whatever expansions have occurred in areas of exclusive fishery rights, or in techniques for securing such rights outside exclusive areas of the sea, the regions generally accepted as open to unrestricted entry by fishermen are still very large and offer great potential for increasing future fishery productivity. In this vast area, states and other participants still consider freedom of the seas a doctrinal means of claiming an unrestricted right to participate in a fishery and, as a principle, commanding decision-makers to concede such right.

It is still unclear whether the grave difficulties attending this relative anarchy in exploitation will be resolved by the recent agreement directed toward that end. The details of the Convention of the Conservation of the Living Resources of the Sea, adopted at Geneva in 1958, are not here relevant, but it should be noted that the important provisions of this treaty seek both to allocate competence to coastal and noncoastal states to prescribe conservation regulations and to provide machinery for third-party settlement of disputes over such asserted competence. No experience has been gained with the operation of these provisions, and observers vary considerably in assessing its prospective effectiveness in moderating, or avoiding entirely, the bitter disputes so frequently erupting over access to fishery resources. Some express the sanguine view that the 1958 Convention provides the necessary objective standards to which states can look to obtain relief. Others are less than optimistic and call attention to a major defect in the 1958 Convention, namely, the absence of any criteria for allocating a common resource that, by hypothesis, must be placed under a regime of limited exploitation. In this view, it does not seem likely that major disputes over division of a resource can be avoided by an agreement that ignores that problem entirely. Whatever the ac-

120 Same, generally.

curacy of these opposing prognoses, observers should keep the situations supposedly subject to this agreement under close appraisal.

As with mineral resources, the problems for the future are whether principles developed in the past, including the recent 1958 treaty, may serve community policies in fishery exploitation under new conditions and, if the inherited prescriptions are inadequate to meet emerging needs, what practicable and desirable alternatives can be devised.

An assessment of experience indicates that one of the major neglected areas of inquiry has been the structure and functioning of the established fishery conservation organizations.[121] It has, of course, long been evident that unrestrained access to marine fisheries might create special problems for those engaged in exploitation. For a very long time, and to a considerable extent even today, the critical problems for conservation regimes were thought to be those of preserving from complete extinction the animal resource that was being exploited, and of maintaining the greatest physical yield that the particular resource was thought able to sustain on a year-to-year basis.[122] The focus in such efforts was, at least formally and perhaps also effectively, upon the means by which these objectives could be reached. In more recent times, these objectives have been criticized as being too limited, as overemphasizing the biological condition of the resource to the exclusion of other considerations; and recommendations are increasingly offered that more sophisticated objectives must be conceived so that the entire social context of fishery exploitation can be taken into account in regulating access to the resources. In whatever way the objectives have been expressed, states have had recourse to special organizations through which they have sought their aims. It appears to be worthwhile, if more effective efforts at management are to be made in the future when increased pressure on international fishery resources seems virtually inevitable, to undertake a detailed inquiry into the structure and functioning of these beginning endeavors at regulat-

---

121 Apparently the only systematic study is Kline R. Swygard, "The International Halibut and Sockeye Salmon Fisheries Commissions: A Study in International Administration" (Ph.D. thesis, University of Washington, 1948). Because the Salmon Commission was just beginning operations, Professor Swygard's inquiry centers upon the Halibut Commission, but within this scope the study is both superbly detailed and comprehensive.

It should be noted that the Food and Agriculture Organization now has under way studies mentioned in footnote 95. In addition, see J. E. Carroz and A. G. Roche, "Proposed International Commission for the Conservation of Atlantic Tuna," *American Journal of International Law*, LXI (July 1967), 673.

122 Swygard (fn. 121), 4; Van Cleve and Johnson, *Management of the High Seas Fisheries of the Northeastern Pacific* (University of Washington Publications in Fisheries, New Series, Vol. II, No. 2, 1963), 24-25.

ing international resources.[123] The object, as with any legal study, is to attempt to clarify goals, to observe trends in decision, to identify factors affecting decisions, to appraise the impact of decision in terms of the fulfilment of goals, and to offer recommendations to maximize the chances of achieving goals.

In organizing such an inquiry, observations of detail about a particular organization should be made in ways that permit a comparison with other groups over an extended period. One particular scheme, adapted from another study into the use of enterprisory organizations in the development of outer space, appears in the following outline.[124] In slight departure from outline form, brief statements or questions are included to indicate the possible direction of inquiry into past experience.

a) *Features of Internal Constitutive Process*[125]

(1) *Establishment of the Organization*

(a) *Constitutive Grant of Capacity*

The grant of legal capacity is not unusual even for international organizations, and it is of interest whether the charters of the fishery conservation bodies contain provisions for this, and, if so, whether the form of stipulation is general or specific. It is possible that provision might be made for subjection of a member to the local law either by incorporation or by subjection to its supervision.

A separate but related question is whether occasion has arisen for nonmembers to recognize the capacity of the organization or to refuse to do so, either with respect to the "internal affairs" of the group or to relations with nonmembers.

(b) *Membership*

It may be useful, especially in comparing various organizations, to observe whether original membership in a group is dependent upon exploitation of a particular area or a particular resource and to note the varying effects upon identity of members. Additionally, membership may be limited to states alone or widened to include other entities. On occasion, degrees of association are established with other entities admitted to one of these categories. Subsequent members may be subjected to different qualifications and sometimes provision is made for original members to later assume a different status.

---

[123] See sources cited in previous footnote and literature there cited.

[124] McDougal, Lasswell, and Vlasic (fn. 75), Chap. 8.

[125] For an elaboration of points 1, 2, 3, and 6 of the following outline see Burke, "Aspects of Internal Decision Processes in Inter-Governmental Fishery Commissions," *University of Washington Law Review*, XLIII (1967), 115.

Termination of membership may be critical, and it is important to inquire into provisions for withdrawal, suspension, and expulsion, particularly examining both the conditions and limitations under which such actions can be taken and the procedures employed.

(2) *Structure of Organization*

The principal inquiry here is into the internal bodies or organs, their composition and method of establishment. It might be especially useful to note specific qualifications for membership in particular internal bodies. Revealing insight could also be possible by investigating the identifications of individuals serving on the component organs, i.e., whether they are industry representatives, government scientists, trade unionists, lawyers (and principal clients), or affiliated with a university. Effort should be made to analyze in terms of skill as well as interest categories.

Within a particular organ it is of interest whether particular states are afforded any special position with respect to certain kinds of decisions, as, for example, whether members especially affected by a decision are granted a special competence with respect to that decision.

A decentralization of function may be sought as a means of engaging unique interests of some members, as, for example, the use of panels for geographical subareas by the Northwest Atlantic Fisheries Commission. Experience with this device should be carefully appraised for the contexts in which it has been found useful.

Obviously attention should be devoted to changes that occur in structure through time, including the addition or elimination of various organs and committees.

(3) *Objectives*

Special attention to this aspect of the constitutive process is justified since the efficacy and desirability of the objectives of established organizations should be subject to constant appraisal. Moreover, there appear to be substantial differences of opinion about the appropriate goals of marine conservation. For these reasons, if none other, scholarly inquiry should not only note the general and specific statements of formal objectives, but also seek to discover the goals sought in effective operations. Where there appears to be a discrepancy in formal and effective objectives, investigation can then proceed to examination of conditioning factors.

(4) *Bases of Power*

It is unlikely that study will disclose that substantial assets have been conferred upon conservation organizations, but it is nevertheless of considerable importance to determine how the values at the disposal of the group are controlled by internal organs. The questions here are: who within the organization controls the wealth, enlightenment, skill, loyalties, and other assets; and how is such control exercised.

(5) Strategies

The most important inquiry here relates to the allocation of authority within the group over diplomatic, ideological, and economic strategies. For appropriate emphasis in connection with diplomatic strategy, separate attention could be given to the voting provisions and practices of the organization, including provisions for weighted voting, the criteria for determining weight, the kinds of questions on which votes are weighted, the majority needed for various types of decisions, and the varying effect to be given to different types of decisions.

(6) Outcomes

Although it would be surprising if these international organizations were granted any comprehensive competence to make decisions, especially in the prescription and application of policy, useful analysis would extend to discovery of the internal distribution of such competences as are conferred. It seems probable that intelligence-serving is the single most important function of these groups, and comparative study to determine who performs this function might lead to valuable generalizations to add to those already advanced by observers.

(7) Modification and Termination

The potentially drastic impact upon fisheries from recent developments in scientific research and technology may make it imperative to make careful provision for amending the instrument establishing the conservation regime and for terminating the entire enterprise. Previous experience in this regard should be examined for the aid it may give future endeavors.

b) External Interactions

(1) Participation

A useful indicator of the scope of participation by these organizations in the more general constitutive process is to be found in their interaction with other participants. Nation-state relationships, especially between members, are most noticeable, but relationships with other entities are probably of no less importance. The international governmental organization, because of its pivotal role in intelligence-serving as a global enterprise, occupies a most critical position in interactions with these less universal marine conservation bodies. Even private groups and individuals are, in sum, virtually as important as states in terms of their interactions with conservation organizations.

(2) *Situations*

(a) *Geographical*

Sometimes states establish a conservation regime designed to operate in a particular part of the sea. Provisions for this purpose, and the assumptions underlying them, should be noted. In addition, it can be important to observe whether any limitations are placed upon access by the organization to particular ocean areas. Generally speaking, territorial waters of member states are not excluded from permissible access by conservation organizations, nor have other areas of claimed exclusive fishing rights. It remains to be seen whether the recent tendencies toward exclusive fishing zones beyond the territorial sea have an impact on conservation activities.

(b) *Structures of Authority*

The matter for study under this heading includes the provisions and practices concerning access to the decision processes of other participants. With respect to member states, it is probable that most attention should be directed to intelligence and recommending functions. In addition to assessing the situation in regard to nonmember states, note should be taken of provisions for coordination of activities with other international governmental groups, such as joint research work, interchange of observers, and exchange of information and advice.

Special care should be taken in observing relations between the conservation organizations and nongovernmental groups. Frequently, the charter provides for the appointment of advisory groups or committees; and interest here centers upon the exact functions performed by such advisers, their terms of reference, the composition of the group, and the degree of influence they possess. Among other outside groups, relations with affected elements in the community are noteworthy, such as the various segments of the fishing industry and associated industries.

A final point for inquiry slightly alters the focus, examining access by other groups to the organization, including those mentioned above. Access by communications media merits particular attention in view of the suspicion that conservation organizations have deliberately sought to operate free of consequential public scrutiny of their activities.

(3) *Acquisition and Control of Base Values*

(a) *Formal Authority*

The reference is to the specific competences that the states concerned have agreed to confer upon the organization. In addition, examination of the charter provisions and subsequent practice should include the privileges and immunities, if any, of the personnel and resources belonging to the organization.

(b) *Effective Power*

Financial underpinning of the organization is a fundamental component of effective power. Study should disclose the various sources of funds, the methods for deciding allocation of expenses, the criteria for determining obligation, the methods to be used in collection, and the sanctions available for assuring collection.

(4) *Strategies*

Focus here is, again, both upon provisions of the charter authorizing the organization to engage in specific strategies vis-à-vis other participants and upon the applications of these provisions in practice. The nature of the conservation organizations is such that diplomatic and ideological strategies may be most significant. In connection with the latter, it would be of particular interest to discover the nature and scope of efforts, if any, to communicate with mass audiences and with special segments of the public, such as labor unions, industry groups, and scientific organizations.

(5) *Outcomes*

A most vital task involves detailed scrutiny of the charter provisions for, and the implementation of, performance of the decision functions of intelligence, recommendation, prescription, invocation, application, appraisal, and termination. With respect to each of these, the broad inquiry is: who, seeking what goals, has done what, under what conditions, utilizing what base values, pursuing what strategies, with what effects?

(6) *Effects*

Effort should be made to discover what long-range impact the organization has had upon the values of all participants.

5. Regulation of Shared Use

The inherited prescriptions available for regulating sharable uses of the sea are not conspicuously available. It seems apparent that both decision-making structures and substantive policies and principles will have to be created to meet the new problems. As indicated above, certain structures of authority for decision-making are now established that may be put to use, but they are not now afforded any comprehensive competence and will have to be reconstituted if new difficulties in shared use are to be met properly.

CONCLUSION

However misguided the foregoing speculation about the concrete shape of future controversies may prove to be, new sources of dispute undoubtedly will emerge from conflicting claims over the ocean and its resources. Assuming that it is useful to anticipate these possibilities, an important question concerns the steps that influential participants can take to avoid or minimize seriously disruptive conflict. Reference can be made to what is generally the most effective power-holder, the nation state, both as individual actor and as member of an alliance or coalition.

Of immediate interest are the alternatives either available to the United States or actually being undertaken. The first measure that comes to mind, one indispensable to other efforts aimed at avoiding anticipated difficulties, is that of undertaking the necessary studies for determining as carefully as possible the inclusive and exclusive interests that states generally, and the United States in particular, should seek in interactions with others. Fortunately, individuals in the government and interested private groups seem fully aware of this need and are sponsoring meaningful action. The first session of the Eighty-ninth Congress had before it legislation embodying provision for studies of certain aspects of sea law,[126] reflecting the concern expressed

[126] U.S., Congress, House, H. 5175, introduced by Congressman Lennon, provides for a study of the legal problems of management, use, and control of the natural resources of the oceans and ocean bed. With respect to this legislation, the State Department is reported to have stated that it was unaware of the need for any such study from the standpoint of international law or relations. See U.S., Congress, House, Committee on Merchant Marine and Fisheries, *Legislative Calendar*, June 15, 1965, 49. In contrast the Office of Science and Technology is reported to have observed that such studies "could well serve to consolidate the applicable existing federal and international statutes and may highlight unsuspected legal programs [sic] arising from new activities of the national oceanographic program." (Same.)

by individual congressmen that research be undertaken as a means of avoiding disputes.[127] Among private groups, the Committee on Oceanography of the National Academy of Sciences has established the Panel on Law, Uses of the Sea and Technology, which is charged with examination of important problems. The academic community, too, has begun to take initiatives in promoting inquiry into the law of the sea. The University of Rhode Island, for example, through its departments of oceanography and geography has created a Law of the Sea Institute that seeks, among other goals, to facilitate communication among scientists, engineers, businessmen, and lawyers concerned with sea problems. Members of the faculty of the University of Washington have been notably active in interdisciplinary studies in the fishing aspects of ocean exploitation.[128]

Use of diplomatic strategies would gain in effectiveness and, perhaps, acquire impetus from the studies and actions just mentioned. Indeed, one area of fruitful inquiry, perhaps urgently needed, is that of examining the process of multilateral agreement-making by which the world community has sought to reach explicit agreement on the law of the sea. Experienced individual participants in international negotiations and observers of this process warn that, from an American perspective, multilateral diplomatic initiatives for agreement about phases of ocean exploitation must be undertaken cautiously and that careful attention must be devoted to a considerable range of problems if general agreement is sought only on one of them. It is said that the 1958 Geneva Conference on the Law of the Sea dealt with issues other than those of primary interest to the United States and that it was necessary to take and defend a position on these issues even though the real American interest was focused on the need for agreement on other problems. Assuming, for present purposes, the validity of this view of the events at Geneva in 1958, it could be very helpful to study the Geneva conferences from this perspective to learn what can be done to create more favorable conditions for resolving widely controverted issues. It does not seem necessary to conclude that the Geneva experience must inevitably be repeated and that modification of the process is impossible or not worth the effort. The problem thus posed is that of planning the presentation of proposals and their consideration and disposition in ways that permit focus on relatively narrow issues involving selected problems. The suggestion is that study

[127] Statement of Congressman Hanna in *Hearings* (fn. 9), 89.

[128] See, e.g., Van Cleve and Johnson (fn. 122); Royce and others, *Salmon Gear Limitation in Northern Washington Waters* (University of Washington Publications in Fisheries, New Series, Vol. II, No. 1, 1963); James A. Crutchfield, ed., *Biological and Economic Aspects of Fisheries Management* (Seattle 1959).

of the Geneva Conference and the events leading to it may provide important clues to improved diplomatic strategies.

It might be helpful in this connection to recall that important agreements about international resources can be reached without the participation of every single state in the world. For example, radioactive waste disposal and fishery problems might be handled with most efficiency in less than universal arenas.

Beyond implementation of desirable policies through carefully designed and executed negotiations on selected problems—selected, it may be emphasized, without awaiting the confrontation of a crisis— the United States can utilize a variety of other assets in a program that hopefully will help to avoid serious conflicts over the ocean. The available store of enlightenment would seem to be especially valuable and might be managed in several relevant ways. One major, relatively untapped method would seek to harness persons with specialized skills to shed light on anticipated problems. The economic aspects of fishery exploitation have attracted concern only within recent years, and the level of this concern is probably still inadequate for the scope of the problem. Whatever the merits attending positions adopted by contestants in argumentation about appropriate objectives for management of fisheries, a major program of economic study could provide information essential to resolution, or at least clarification, of disputes. The value of investigation into these economic aspects of exploitation is, of course, not limited to fishery resources in which the United States has a direct interest. For numerous reasons, study of this type should probably proceed under the auspices of international institutions.

The influence of a particular state upon decision outcomes dealing with specific legal issues may be intimately affected by the timing, as well as the substantive content, of its own initial claims to authority. It may be recalled, for example, that the United States Proclamation concerning the continental shelf had an undeniable impact on the ultimate decision by the general community about allocation of resources in this area. On one of the substantive problems alluded to above, the United States may again be in a position to play a critical role through assertion of unilateral claim or, at least, influential pronouncement. Thus, as noted earlier, the mining of ocean floor surficial deposits may become a reality in the foreseeable future. From present indications, it seems most likely that United States nationals will take the lead in entering upon this form of exploitation and that the United States government will be called upon to take a position about the scope and substantive details of claims to access. The opportunity thus presented is that of taking the lead in establishing a pattern of responsibility and restraint in the assertion of claim to newly available resources. To be sure, past experience has been that restraint in assertion of claim has not prevented others from making extravagant demands. Nonetheless, it merits emphasis that these demands, though still not wholly effectively refuted, have never commanded wide assent and, indeed, have been categorically rejected by most states. At the very least, it seems evident that the United States could, by suitably limited claim or announced position, promote policies directed at maximizing inclusive benefit from the vast storehouse of resources in and under the sea.

The latter point can be generalized, of course, though perhaps not too helpfully, to the effect that all assertions of claim regarding access to, and authority over, the oceans should be designed to serve the common interests of states both inclusive and exclusive. The task of appropriate specification of such interests, and their accommodation, is a separate task not assayed here.

Turning the focus of attention from the state as an individual participant to the state in the wider setting of an alliance or coalition may disclose new requirements for appraisal and action. Specifically it may be time for members to devote systematic attention to the impact on relations with each other of scientific and other developments involving the ocean. Already, of course, stress from intra-alliance conflicts over fishery exploitation has occasioned multilateral efforts at alleviation. But these were more or less familiar controversies, with backgrounds as ancient as the fishing grounds themselves. The point now is that there may be new, perhaps unexpected, pressures from wholly new directions unless some effort is made at anticipation. Suggestive in this connection is the burgeoning activity in the North Sea directed at oil and gas exploration. Perhaps the discoveries there will be so immense that boundaries can be established in amicable fashion, but perhaps the resource may be so limited that locations of productive areas might engender serious divisiveness among allied states.

Valuable discoveries in the North Sea might have effects elsewhere too, for example, upon alliances in the Middle East. The Arab world now appears to be in some disarray, and the cessation of European dependence upon Middle East oil could conceivably add to the difficulties or, perhaps, even lessen them.

In the even wider perspective of relations between the highly industrialized and the less-developed states, the discovery and exploitation of marine mineral resources may have important impact. A tendency toward reliance upon the raw materials exported by less-developed states may cease or change direction, with unknown effects upon political relationships.

Within the Communist bloc, or blocs, where dissension is noticeable, relationships can be influenced by ocean developments. Earlier, for example, it was speculated that employment of submarines by Communist China could conceivably lend some enchantment to agreement by the United States and the Soviet Union on armament control.

In sum it seems apparent that the protection of common interests calls for continued appraisal and study by all participants, but particularly by the nation-state, of the processes of interaction, claim, and decision involving the ocean.

ADDENDUM

The preceding essay was completed in September 1965 and originally published in January 1966. A few interpolations were made in the text in January 1967 when the manuscript was forwarded to the editors for this book. This Addendum was written in October 1969. In view of the time elapsed since the original composition, some comments might usefully be added in order to place the objectives sought in the perspective of events since 1965 and now to be expected.

The intervening events of major importance pertain primarily to the process of decision by which controverted claims are resolved, but it is also noteworthy that the types of claims being advanced have emerged somewhat more clearly in some instances. We comment on the latter first.

PROCESS OF CLAIM

Claims Relating to Access

Interestingly enough the major conflict for the future regarding access, i.e., movement or emplacement of objects, may well come not from the exotic vehicles which move about by remote control and perform many difficult undersea tasks, but from the old and familiar problem of transit through straits. A number of factors bear on this, including recent developments in the construction of extremely large bulk carriers, the discovery of potentially enormous reserves of oil in the Arctic, the emerging capability of transiting the Arctic ice pack, the relatively sudden debut of the Soviet Union as a world sea power, the continued interest of the United States in ease of movement for its naval vessels, and the possible insistence by coastal states of an enlarged control over vessels passing in the territorial sea (for example, by levying charges for general navigational assistance). This volatile mix could produce near-violent controversy and, in any event, is virtually certain to loom as a crucial issue should states seek to renegotiate the Convention on the Territorial Sea and Contiguous Zone.

Claims to portions of the ocean floor stemming from emplacement of an installation do not now appear likely to be asserted as a claim to acquire territory. Although it is now clearer than it was in 1965 that such installations are both useful and technically feasible, the claim made for such access will probably be restricted to that form of jurisdiction and control which may be required for safety and efficiency of operation. It is now even likely that claims to emplace certain things on the seabed will not be honored at all.[129]

The whole spectrum of potential claims about access of buoys and other unmanned platforms is now far more sharply focused than it was a few years ago, including especially the prospect that coastal controls may be asserted even beyond the territorial sea. It is now plain that very large numbers of these platforms, or Ocean Data Acquisition Stations (ODAS) as they are now called, will be required when the Integrated Global Ocean Station System, presently in the advanced planning stage, is implemented during the 1970's. As noted below, measures for disposing of these legal issues are also at an advanced stage.

As of this writing only two states appear to have advanced a claim to acquire specific mineral resources of the seabed beyond the continental shelf, and these claims (by Saudi Arabia and Sudan) are to supposed deposits in locations contiguous (about 50 miles) to the coasts concerned.[130] Apart from this unique situation there are no claims to deep seabed resources and no actual mining activity involving any such resources although some exploratory work is under way.

The situation has, however, clarified somewhat since 1965 even though it is generally conceded that our knowledge of deep ocean mineral resources (particularly surficial deposits) is still quite limited. First, it seems even clearer than before that states are not willing to accept the notion that the entire ocean floor has already been allocated to the coastal states by the Continental Shelf Convention. This conclusion appears evident in, and anticipated rather clearly by, the deliberations of the Sea-Bed Committee of the United Nations. It

[129] The reference is to the agreement recently reached between the Soviet Union and the U.S. to prohibit the installation of certain military weapons on the ocean floor. Details of this agreement, and even whether it is acceptable to other states in the Eighteen Nation Disarmament Committee, are not available at this writing.

[130] Apparently only Saudi Arabia has adopted legislation on this, but a Saudi representative is quoted as stating that it intends to propose joint exploitation with Sudan. *Middle East Economic Survey*, XI, No. 50 (October 11, 1968), 1.

does not follow, so far as this writer is concerned, from the application of any "natural equilibrium" or "balance" which Professor Goldie somehow manages to construct by a woeful misreading, or curious interpretation, of the passages in the above essay which dismissed the idea that the Shelf Convention disposed of the seabed.[131]

Second, claims to eventual exploitation of deep sea mineral resources are very likely to be subjected to some form of international machinery but this machinery will probably not be granted any extensive competence of a regulatory nature, at least in the beginning.[132] It appears improbable now that states will succeed in establishing an effective international agency which will itself monopolize all deep sea mineral production. This does not exclude, of course, the formation of intergovernmental groups for the purpose of combining resources to engage in such production. It is not very profitable here to speculate about the details of the authority states may demand for the prospective agency beyond noting that what seems likely to emerge is a modified flag-nation system involving registration of claims by states. It seems likely too that this system will produce a very modest revenue for expenditure on some international projects.

Claims to Competence to Prescribe

One set of claims which has come into particular prominence since 1965, beginning in 1967 in fact, are those that require the consent of the coastal state to scientific research conducted in areas alleged to be subject to coastal jurisdiction. Traditionally scientists had moved about on the ocean without much regard for political boundaries, but this happy situation suddenly began to change in the late 1960's.[133] Coastal states began both to deny permission for research or entry into ports and to establish administrative obstacles in their consent procedures that threatened to bring research in some ocean regions virtually to a halt. At this writing it is still unclear whether procedures may be implemented successfully by which scientific research and data acquisition may continue as effective operations. Recent steps to alleviate this situation are noted below in discussing particular decisions.

131 See L.F.E. Goldie, "The Exploitability Test—Interpretation and Potentialities," *Natural Resources Journal*, VIII (July 1968), 433, 440-42.

132 An excellent survey of the issues involved is in Report of the Secretary-General, *Study on the Question of Establishing in Due Time Appropriate Machinery for the Promotion of the Exploration and Exploitation of the Resources of the Sea-Bed and Ocean Floor beyond the Limits of National Jurisdiction and the Use of These Resources in the Interests of Mankind* (U.N. Doc. No. A/AC.138/12), June 18, 1969.

133 As late as the summer of 1967, U.S. officials expressed little concern over this matter, an attitude that changed drastically by the spring of 1968. With respect to the former time period see, generally, Burke (fn. 113).

Claims to Enjoyment of Animal Resources

Perhaps the most striking development of the past few years is the number of states that are claiming either a 12-mile territorial sea or exclusive fishing zone,[134] which means, in either event, that the living resources within this area are regarded as subject to the exclusive disposition of the claimant state. Accompanying and stemming from this development, which no doubt reflects an insistence, suitably modest, upon the "special interest" of the coastal state in adjacent living resources, is a proliferation of bilateral agreements by which the claims of noncoastal fishing states are recognized, accommodated, and mutual adjustment made in competing interests.[135]

Scarcely less noticeable in the behavior of the developing states is the pronounced concern for claims to mineral resource development in comparison to living resources. Most observers regard exploitation of the former of less significance to developing states generally than development of the latter, having in mind both the need for protein foods and the enormous difficulties involved in realizing any appreciable net yield over the medium term from exploitation of deep sea mineral resources. Although a good deal of activity is apparent concerning claims to exclusive access to fisheries, the major political emphasis has obviously been upon mineral resources. Perhaps the principal motivation for this emphasis, which can only be mistaken unless a quick breakthrough somehow develops in exploitation of mineral resources, is political in nature, with little if any relationship to a realistic assessment either of the benefits available from living resources or of the many obstacles to efficient development of mineral resources.

The modest expansion in claims to exclusive access to living resources underscores the continuing failure of the western South American states, the so-called CEP states, to secure support outside Latin America for their demands for control over resources for at least 200 miles from their coasts. At the same time and despite the near universal expectation that such claims offend against international law, the states affected thereby have been unable either to persuade these states to moderate their demands in accordance with law or to apply the power necessary to discourage the unlawful application of coastal regu-

[134] As of August 1969, a total of 69 states had either a 12-mile territorial sea or exclusive fishing limits.

[135] See, generally, the testimony of Ambassador Donald L. McKernan in *Activities of Nations in Ocean Space*, U.S., Congress, Senate, Subcommittee on Ocean Space of the Foreign Relations Committee, *Hearings on S. Res. 33*, 91st Cong., 1st Sess., July 25, 1969, 49-62.

lations within the 200-mile zone. The reasons for these failures quite plainly lie in the political hazards involved and not in any notion that the CEP claims have even the color of law.

PROCESS OF DECISION

Constitutive Process

Activities in the international decision-making structure since 1965 are barely short of remarkable and offer, over the long-run, a genuine basis for hope that states can act to clarify important common interests in ocean use.[136] Whether this clarification can be achieved depends not only on the institutional structures devised for making decisions but also and primarily on the wisdom and moderation of the states participating in the process—most particularly the developing states.

On the international level both the United Nations and the specialized agencies have taken express cognizance of the need for improvement in international procedures and have acted to set up new institutional structures for coping with some of the problems. For present purposes the major importance of these actions is in their suggestion that the organized international decision-making structure is sufficiently imaginative and flexible to create the new organisms that may be required to confront the novel problems posed by more intensified ocean usage.

Within the United Nations the major innovation has been the creation at the Twenty-third General Assembly in 1968 of the Committee on the Peaceful Uses of the Sea-Bed and the Ocean Floor beyond the Limits of National Jurisdiction. Although the Committee has a rather restricted mandate, it nonetheless can serve the vital function of providing a sound informational basis upon which debate and discussion might proceed. In addition it may be expected that the Committee's deliberations could serve to identify important issues, to focus attention upon the range of alternative solutions, and to survey the factors that bear on choice. A Committee performing such functions could make an invaluable contribution to a sound and equitable legal framework for development of the seabed and ocean floor beyond national jurisdiction.

It remains to be seen whether the Sea-Bed Committee approaches its task in the manner mentioned, but the fragmentary materials avail-

---

[136] It is appropriate to emphasize the reference to "the long-run." Attempts to reach precipitate decisions are very likely to prove counterproductive. My views on this are expressed in Burke, "Law, Science and the Ocean," Occasional Paper No. 3, Law of the Sea Institute, University of Rhode Island, August 1969.

able at this writing suggest that the Committee sees its task as laying a solid foundation for later action rather than as frantically developing solutions in the absence of an adequate basis therefor.[137]

The Sea-Bed Committee certainly should not lack for ample preparatory studies. In other actions the General Assembly and the Economic and Social Council called for studies that would provide a substantial input for the decision process. Thus in Resolution 2172 the General Assembly endorsed ECOSOC Resolution 1112(XL) of March 7, 1966, which requested the Secretary-General to make a survey of the present state of knowledge of the resources of the sea beyond the continental shelf, excluding fish, and of the techniques for exploiting these resources.[138] In addition the Assembly requested the Secretary-General, in cooperation with numerous agencies and organizations, to make a "comprehensive survey of activities in marine science and technology, including that relating to mineral resources development, undertaken by members of the United Nations family of organizations, various Member States and intergovernmental organizations concerned, as well as by universities, scientific and technological institutes and other interested organizations." For present purposes it is also important to emphasize the accompanying request that the Secretary-General, in cooperation with UNESCO and FAO, "formulate proposals: (a) ensuring the most effective arrangements for *an expanded program of international cooperation to assist in a better understanding of the marine environment through science and in the exploitation and development of marine resources, with due regard to the conservation of fish stocks . . .*" (emphasis added).

As noted further below, these Resolutions have had a very considerable impact on international marine science affairs in addition to leading to the production of the studies requested which are themselves quite valuable contributions.

Further preparatory work for the Sea-Bed Committee took place in connection with the agenda item introduced by Ambassador Pardo of

137 See *Interim Report of the Economic and Technical Subcommittee of the Committee on the Peaceful Uses of the Sea-Bed and Ocean Floor beyond the Limits of National Jurisdiction* (U.N. Doc. No. A/AC.138/S6.2/6), April 1, 1969; *Report of the Legal Subcommittee of the Committee on Peaceful Uses of the Sea-Bed and Ocean Floor* (U.N. Doc. No. A/AC.138/18/Add.1), August 29, 1969.

138 Resolution 2172 is reproduced in *Marine Science Affairs—A Year of Plans and Progress: The Second Report of the President to the Congress on Marine Resources and Engineering Development* (March 1968), 192-93. All other General Assembly resolutions referred to in this Addendum are in *Marine Science Affairs —A Year of Broadened Participation: The Third Report of the President to the Congress on Marine Resources and Engineering Development* (January 1969), 233-41.

Malta in August 1967, which eventually led to the adoption of Resolution 2340(XXII) in December 1967. The Resolution established an *Ad Hoc* Committee to Study the Peaceful Uses of the Sea-Bed and the Ocean Floor beyond the Limits of National Jurisdiction. In discharging its functions the *Ad Hoc* Committee succeeded in demonstrating the difficulty and complexity of the issues involved and in revealing the wide divergences in the views of the numerous states concerned. After consideration of the *Ad Hoc* Committee's Report[139] at the Twenty-third Session, the General Assembly proceeded to create the permanent Sea-Bed Committee as noted above.

Activities outside the U.N. itself but within the specialized agencies are hardly less notable and no less important than these actions by the General Assembly. One result of Resolution 2172(XXII) was the Report of the Secretary-General entitled *Marine Science and Technology: Survey and Proposals*[140] in which he called for an expanded program of international cooperation in marine science and proposed that "the General Assembly recommend to Member Governments, UNESCO, FAO, WMO and such other organizations of the United Nations family as may be concerned that they agree as a matter of urgency to broaden the base of IOC so as to enable it to formulate and co-ordinate the expanded programme."[141] At about the same time this recommendation was made in the spring of 1968, the United States announced its proposal of an International Decade of Ocean Exploration and issued a White House paper in support of the concept.

In response to these actions, and having well in mind the political overtones of the suddenly intense involvement of the General Assembly in ocean affairs, the specialized agencies began to coalesce in support of an expanded Intergovernmental Oceanographic Commission and to prepare the basis for an expanded program in marine science. At its June 1968, meeting, the IOC Bureau and Consultative Council endorsed the concept of the International Decade of Ocean Exploration. The following December the General Assembly adopted Resolution 2467D(XXIII) which endorsed the Decade and an expanded program of international cooperation and which called upon the IOC to prepare a comprehensive outline of such a program in which the Decade would be an important element.

[139] *Report of the Ad Hoc Committee to Study the Peaceful Uses of the Sea-Bed and the Ocean Floor beyond the Limits of National Jurisdiction* (U.N. Doc. No. A/7230), 1968.

[140] This Report was made to the Economic and Social Council as U.N. Doc. E/4487, April 24, 1968.

[141] Same, p. 77.

Subsequently at its sixth session the IOC, after an enormous amount of preliminary work by the national and international scientific communities, both public and private, agreed upon such a comprehensive outline. Perhaps of greater importance, the IOC adopted recommendations for revision of its governing statute (which must be approved by the UNESCO General Conference) in order to strengthen the IOC and formed an interagency committee composed of representatives of UNESCO, FAO, and WMO to provide stronger and more effective support for the IOC as the leading international agency in coordinating an expanded program.

Elsewhere within the U.N. family the most notable action in altering the decision process was that taken by the FAO in amending its Constitution to establish a Committee on Fisheries. This move was part of a more general reorganization intended to afford greater recognition within FAO to the unique importance and urgency of international fishery problems. Among other tasks the Committee is to: "(d) consider the desirability of preparing and submitting to Member Nations an international convention under Article XIV of the Constitution to ensure effective international cooperation and consultation in fisheries on a world scale . . ." In implementation of this charge the Committee agreed to review the "terms of reference, composition, and activities of existing bodies and to draw from that review suitable conclusions with regard both to the need for further action by the Committee and FAO and also regarding steps that the bodies concerned, or their members, could take in order to ensure their greatest possible success." For the first time, then, an authoritative international group aims to appraise the effectiveness of existing decision-making bodies and to make recommendations for improvement.

Within the United States easily the most important events in marine science affairs since the reconstruction of NASCO in 1957 are the passage of the Marine Resources and Engineering Development Act of 1966 and the results spawned thereby. The Act established the National Council on Marine Resources and Engineering Development, a cabinet-level body chaired by the Vice-President, and the Commission on Marine Science, Engineering, and Resources, a group composed primarily of private individuals. The Report of the Commission, entitled *Our Nation and the Sea* and issued in January 1969, could well be a vital turning point in marine affairs since it proposes a sweeping reorganization of the executive branch of the government which would permit far more rational and productive decision-making in this area than is possible under the present extremely fragmented structure of the federal government.

Both the Council and the Commission have emphasized the legal problems of the sea, the former through contract studies[142] and the latter by devoting very substantial attention to a number of problems in its report.[143] The combined efforts of the Council and Commission have thus served to highlight the need for confronting issues of law and policy as part of the drive to conquer the ocean frontier.

The United States nonetheless still suffers a severe handicap in coping with the whole field of international affairs in the marine science field. The fact is that the organizational framework within the executive branch is still highly fragmented, with responsibility divided between various departments and further subdivided within the individual departments. It is thus very difficult and sometimes impossible for the United States to speak effectively and with one voice on the international scene, and it is next to impossible at this time for the U.S. to direct its numerous ocean policies toward an overall plan or goal. Until this defect is remedied the U.S. will continue to endure a loss in influence and prestige in international affairs.

In a summary comment on the constitutive process of decision, it may be useful to note that current topics of debate concern the wisdom of convening a new conference on the law of the sea (on the model of the Geneva conferences of 1958 and 1960) and of seeking to negotiate on various issues such as the shelf limit, the regime beyond, fishery limits, territorial sea limits, coastal authority over the territorial sea, and so on. As noted above the U.N. Sea-Bed Committee is addressing at least the second of these issues and may also be asked to consider the first. The other issues are not presently being similarly debated but they would certainly be ventilated if a new general conference on the law of the sea were convened.

Leaving aside the question of whether a general conference must be convened (or whether certain issues may be isolated for negotiation and disposition), the principal differences of opinion presently concern the consequences of negotiating sooner rather than later. One body of opinion, apprehensive about the strong nationalistic trend noticeable in the past decade in extending coastal authority farther into the ocean, holds that an agreement reached now will result in less such intrusion than would result either from an agreement negotiated in the more distant future or from the interaction of states dur-

---

[142] *Marine Science Affairs—A Year of Broadened Participation* (fn. 138), 195, lists these contract studies.

[143] Report of the Commission on Marine Science, Engineering, and Resources, *Our Nation and the Sea* (1969), 135-37, 141-57, 201-05. The three volumes of the Commission's Panel Reports contain discussions of a great variety of legal issues, from local to international.

ing the delay. The premise of this group is that the nationalistic trend is not going to abate very soon, but will intensify and demand even greater deference to supposed coastal rights.

A contrary view is that negotiations soon will have highly undesirable results in terms of impacts on freedom of use of the ocean for a variety of purposes including transit, fishery exploitation, military use, and scientific research. In this view there is no need to attempt now to negotiate all these issues and if there must be negotiations they would better be delayed until we have better information about ocean resources and environment. The passage of time will, it is thought, allow coastal states to moderate their demands as some of the newer states mature and begin to realize how difficult and costly it is to wrest benefits from the sea.

Obviously these different views share the same concern, namely, to avoid undue interference by coastal states with those freedoms mentioned above. In the hope of achieving this avoidance, an intermediate position is urged by some, namely, to seek to negotiate about ocean problems issue by issue, thereby fostering informed resolution of these issues without regard to extraneous factors. Some success has attended this approach in recent years but it remains to be seen whether the states most concerned about the oceans can agree to this method in the context of consideration within the United Nations. The means chosen for disposing of these matters may well have grave import for public order during the decade of the 70's.

PARTICULAR DECISIONS

Claims Relating to Access

Although there is not a great deal of evidence for support, the conclusion is quite commonly reached that transit through areas subject to coastal authority is likely to be unduly circumscribed in the future unless positive measures are taken to avert this eventuality. A good deal of this apprehension undoubtedly arises from recent events such as the seizure of the *Pueblo*, the Soviet Union's refusal of passage of the U.S. Coast Guard icebreakers through the Vilkitsky Straits, and continued seizures of U.S. fishing vessels by some South American states. Perhaps another major factor contributing to this general impression are the numerous statements by representatives of developing states emphasizing the "rights" of coastal states in adjacent water regions.

Unease concerning traditional rights of freedom of movement undoubtedly stems also from the very strong movement toward expansion of the territorial sea to 12 miles. Information available as of

August 1969, disclosed 46 states claiming 12 miles as against 33 claiming 3 miles, and extensions to the former distance seemed to be occurring almost weekly. There is no longer any doubt whatsoever, if any existed even as long ago as 1958, that a 12-mile territorial sea is completely in accord with international law. Perhaps it is for this reason that there is so much present concern over the rights of passage through these regions and particularly through straits. It is safe to predict that considerable agitation and turmoil will attend this issue in the decade ahead.

Claims about access of buoys to waters adjacent to coastal states and elsewhere are now under active consideration within the Intergovernmental Oceanographic Commission, and it now appears that a treaty on this topic may be concluded early in the 1970's. On issues such as this, perhaps more technical than political, it is plain that intergovernmental institutions in ocean affairs are extremely useful. As noted below this same comment may also be made in connection with matters tinged heavily with politics.

Claims Relating to Competence to Prescribe

The sudden increase in difficulties over scientific research in the continental shelf area and elsewhere stimulated a similar increase in activity within the organized decision process. In 1967, at the request of the Soviet Union, the 5th session of the Intergovernmental Oceanographic Commission established a working group on the legal problems of scientific investigation, and the work of this group still continues. At the 6th IOC session, in September 1969, the Commission adopted a Resolution establishing a procedure for facilitating the process of securing clearances for investigations within areas over which national jurisdiction is exercised. Essentially the procedure calls for notice to a coastal state as soon as the early tentative decision is made to undertake an inquiry, and for a later, more detailed description of the program to be submitted to both the coastal state and the IOC. The purpose of these notices is to alert the coastal state early enough to permit it to plan participation by its own scientists if they wish to do so and to allow sufficient time to check on the authenticity of the project. The IOC role is to forward the description to the coastal state, requesting favorable consideration, together with "a factual description of the international scientific interest in the subject prepared by the requesting state, supplemented, if he considers this desirable, by the Secretary."

The significance of this IOC action, beyond its potential value for removing an impediment to ocean research, is in its demonstration of the capacity of the institution to respond quickly to perceived problems of an intensely political nature. Still it is fairly clear that the success of the new arrrangement depends, in the end, on the reactions of the states and other groups concerned, both those who request clearance and those with the authority to decide.

Enjoyment of Mineral Resources

Seeking to deal with this issue is responsible for a great deal of the agitation and excitement within international institutions, especially the United Nations, and it is this matter alone which accounts for the many and varied developments within the national and international decision process referred to earlier. Some of this focus represents undue attention to a single issue since there are good grounds for believing that its importance has been grossly exaggerated and that the haste to deal with it may have unfortunate repercussions on far more important matters. Be this as it may, it appears now that the initial decisions to be made will represent some modest new development in international law, with heavy emphasis on maintaining easy, though not unrestricted, access to the ocean for exploitation of these resources. It is hardly useful or wise to speculate much about this matter since it seems probable that the decision process will be involved with this question well past the decade of the 70's.

CHAPTER 4

The Relevance of International Law to Emerging Trends in the Law of Outer Space

IVAN A. VLASIC

INTRODUCTION

IN THE twelfth year since the launching of Sputnik I and after man's landing on the moon it may be appropriate both to appraise past trends in the legal regulation of outer-space activities and attempt to outline some of the major problems that will require legal controls in the years to come. One can think of no other period in human history before the advent of nuclear energy and space technology when a span of eleven years could provide a sufficient body of experience for a meaningful reflection upon the past on the one hand and an adequate basis for a consideration of the future on the other. It is eloquent testimony to the current tempo of technological and social change that such a short period of time can now telescope as many events of surpassing importance to the development of international law as only a century could in another era.

At the outset it is necessary to state that this study is based on the assumption that the evolution of a public order in space will continue to be in large measure affected by the developments in the arena of terrestrial politics. The experience of the past decade suggests that it would be unrealistic to expect any major or unique developments in the law of outer space which would not reflect and incorporate the trends characteristic of power politics on the earth. The two regions are, notwithstanding many distinctive features of the space environment, politically, militarily, and legally integral parts of the wider earth-space arena and will so remain in the foreseeable future. This unity should not, however, preclude the possibility of certain initiatives, which were originally conceived for and tested in outer-space interactions, to influence developments on earth.

Yet it would be a serious error to view outer space as merely another dimension of international politics. Outer space is not only a new environment, vast beyond comprehension and scarcely known to man, but a wholly new experience in human endeavor. The attraction it holds in equal degree for the scientist, government official, industrialist, the military, the mass media, and for the proverbial "man in the street" is quite unprecedented. If an historical parallel is sought, it could only be compared with the prevailing attitudes toward the exploration of distant continents during the golden age of discovery. The fact that the great powers continue to allocate vast resources to the conquest of this new frontier, while a large segment of mankind suffers chronic hunger and the opportunities for the beneficial exploitation of the more accessible riches of the oceans are only beginning to attract attention,[1] offers compelling evidence of the special significance attached by the governing elites to outer space.[2] Unless some dramatic changes occur in the order of these nations' priorities, prospects are that outer space will continue to exert a most powerful attraction for an ever-increasing number of states.

It has become commonplace to assert that recent advances in science and technology, culminating in the opening of outer space, inaugurated what is probably the most revolutionary period in the entire course of man's history. Unfortunately, the rapid pace of research and development in science and technology has not been paralleled by equally creative efforts in social sciences, including law. "No great institutes," complains one critic, "have devoted themselves to a many-sided study of legal, political, intellectual, economic and other impacts, actual and potential, of the new era."[3] Far too much contem-

[1] For recent authoritative survey of the economic potentialities of the world's oceans, see *Resources of the Sea (Beyond the Continental Shelf): Report of the Secretary-General*, U.N. Docs. E/4449, February 21, 1968; E/4449/Add. 2, February 7, 1968; E/4449/Add. 1, February 19, 1968. See also special issue of *Scientific American*, (The Ocean), ccxxi (September 1969).

[2] For example, according to the President's report to Congress, total U.S. expenditures for space activities up to January 1, 1969, have amounted to almost $57 billion. Of this sum, $17 billion was spent by the Defense Department, $38 billion by NASA, and the rest by other governmental agencies. *New York Times*, January 18, 1969, p. 21, col. 2. Of the civilian funds, about $26 billion has been spent on manned space flight, including about $24 billion on the Apollo moon-landing program.

The Soviet Union is believed to have expended on space projects during the same period in terms of its gross national product an even larger amount.

Some members of the U.S. Congress are reported to be "increasingly concerned that space may be obscuring, and interfering with, the important and rewarding benefits to be realized in civil aviation of the future." U.S. Congress, Senate, Committee on Aeronautical and Space Sciences, *Policy Planning for Aeronautical Research and Development*, 89th Cong., 1st Sess., 1966, 1. Their concern stems primarily from the contrast that emerges "when research and development program for aeronautics is compared with the total NASA appropriation ($124 million out of $5.102 billion or about 2 percent for fiscal year 1967.)" Same, 3.

[3] Harold D. Lasswell, "The Social Consequences of the Space Age," in NASA, *Fifth National Conference on the Peaceful Uses of Space* (Washington 1966), 194, 197. For additional perceptive comments see Earl Warren, "Science and the Law: Change and the Constitution," *Journal of Public Law*, xii, No. 1 (1963), 3; C. Wilfred Jenks, "The New Science and the Law of Nations," *International and Comparative Law Quarterly*, xvii (April 1968), 327; Oscar Schachter, "Scientific

porary legal thinking suffers from lack of imagination, concern for the peripheral, and status-quo bias. In a period of spreading and increasingly divisive confrontations as well as the proven inadequacy of the inherited institutions to cope with the urgent problems of the present, let alone of the future, the overwhelming majority of the international legal community shows concern primarily for problems that are essentially of marginal relevance, no matter how limited their impact may be upon world public order. There is little evidence of a major and concerted effort to relate law constructively to the new technology and to the new sociopolitical conditions that are largely brought about by that same new technology. Particularly noticeable is the absence of imaginative plans for meeting anticipated contingencies of the future before crisis erupts. Yet the importance of anticipating future developments for purposes of providing rational policy alternatives for decision-makers in an era of swift scientific, technological, and social change cannot be overstated. Perceptive observers continue to warn of a "tremendous imbalance—the mismatch between [the] rapidly accelerating scientific and technological advance on the one hand and lagging social advance on the other," a mismatch which is "widening at an alarming rate."[4] In earlier periods, failure to engage in the critical examination of existing institutions and refusal to think contextually of the future, while harmful, probably would not have resulted in calamity. The penalty for the same omission in the nuclear-space age could be incalculable.

One cannot but contrast the great caution in thinking about and planning for the future, so characteristic of many politicians, lawyers, and social scientists, with the aggressive boldness consistently displayed in that regard by the defense planners. The managers of the military establishment and their associates in industry and the academic world never seem to tire of long-range planning, even to the point of "thinking about the unthinkable," and of devising various new martial uses for fresh scientific discoveries.[5] Within the restricted con-

Advances and International Law Making," *California Law Review*, LV (May 1967), 423.

[4] Simon Ramo, "Space and the Automated Society: 1980-2000, Decades of Dichotomy," *Aerospace Historian*, XIII (Spring 1966), 18.

[5] "The dynamism of the defense establishment and its culture," Gen. David M. Shoup, former Commandant of the U.S. Marine Corps, wrote recently, "is also inspired and stimulated by vast amounts of money, by the new creations of military research and matériel development, and by the concepts of the Defense Department-supported 'think factories.' These latter are extravagantly funded civilian organizations of scientists, analysts, and retired military strategists who feed new militaristic philosophies into the Defense Department to help broaden the views of the single service doctrinaires, to create fresh policies and new requirements for even larger, more expensive defense forces." David M. Shoup, "The New American Militarism," *The Atlantic Monthly*, CCXXIII (April 1969), 51, 56.

text of the arms race, they show considerable imagination in this effort, as will be demonstrated below. It seems rather obvious that those concerned with the maintenance and promotion of international public order can afford to do no less. This need is made more urgent by the continuing ascendancy and the growing power of the military in an increasing number of nation-states.

Alongside the already stereotyped transnational confrontations between the totalitarian and democratic societies, between the "Communist world" and the "free world," and between the affluent and underprivileged communities, one can observe today within many countries an equally significant though less publicized confrontation, that between the "military-industrial complex" and the citizenry. Managers of this complex expend in the name of "security" increasingly vast amounts of national resources—in some instances 50 percent or more of a country's budget—which could otherwise be used for socially more beneficial programs, such as the elimination of hunger, disease, substandard housing, and illiteracy. As President Johnson remarked, "[r]esources continue to be diverted from critical human needs to the acquisition of armaments and the maintenance of military establishments that in themselves feed fears and create insecurity among nations."[6] Apart from being one of the major causes of world instability, this process, moreover, threatens to transform even traditionally democratic societies into garrison states. The influence of the security establishment has been exceptionally great in the domain of space activities, making pursuit of military objectives the dominant characteristic of space exploration and use to date.[7]

Because "security" considerations so profoundly affect decision-making processes both nationally and internationally, especially in regard to the politics and law of outer space, the feasibility of any major proposal for a more rational utilization of space science and technology is conditional upon the success in de-emphasizing the role of the military instrument as supposedly the most effective guardian of vital national interests and of world public order as well. But, as Ralph E. Lapp warns, "corrective measures will not be easy because the disease of our weapons culture has metastasized itself into the lymphatic system of our society."[8] Yet the disease must soon be cured for otherwise there may be little room for international law in outer space or, for that matter, in any other environment.

[6] Message of July 16, 1968 to the 18-Nation Committee on Disarmament. *Department of State Bulletin*, LIX (August 5, 1968), 137, 138.

[7] More than 50 percent of all the satellites launched since 1957 to date (mid-1969) by the United States and the Soviet Union have been designed for military uses. *New York Times*, June 29, 1969, sec. 4, p. 12, col. 5.

[8] Ralph E. Lapp, *The Weapons Culture* (New York 1968), 179.

This essay is to some extent a modest attempt to stimulate the search for such corrective measures. It is not, therefore, conceived as a comprehensive report on the developments to date in the legal regulation of outer-space activities or an analysis of certain specific problems such as the legality or illegality of space reconnaissance, the liability for damage, or the fixing of boundaries between airspace and outer space, all of which have received extensive coverage in the literature.[9] The principal purpose of the present inquiry is to focus upon a few broad areas which, it is believed, will be of major impact in the coming decades not only for the growth of space law but also for world public order and the well-being of mankind as well. Analysis of the relevant experience of the past decade, combined with the anticipated future uses of outer space, suggest that military activities in outer space, the use of space technology for hazardous experiments, and above all, the pattern of international cooperation in the conquest of outer space should be singled out for special scrutiny.

A convenient point of departure for the examination of these problems is a brief review of the major achievements to date in the legal regulation of space activities. Such a review, apart from its informational value, should provide a basis for a more balanced assessment of future needs and prospects.

I. SPACE LAW 1969—AN APPRAISAL

Assessment of the accomplishments in the legal regulation of outer-space activities since the advent of Sputnik depends on the observer's point of view. Quantitatively and qualitatively, the results to date may not appear impressive when compared with some other areas of international lawmaking, or with mature systems of law, abounding in statutes, judicial decisions, formal agreements, and custom, or with the early expectations of many countries and individuals. However, if one considers the unfavorable international climate under which the legal regime for outer space had to be built—the largely unknown space environment, the rapid rate of technological change, the military implications of astronautics, and the imperfect structure of decision-making processes in the contemporary world—progress so far achieved could be said to surpass what was reasonable to expect under

[9] For an account of these and other issues of the emerging space law see Myres S. McDougal, Harold D. Lasswell, and Ivan A. Vlasic, *Law and Public Order in Space* (New Haven 1963); Carl Q. Christol, *The International Law of Outer Space* (Washington 1966); C. Wilfred Jenks, *Space Law* (New York 1965); James E. S. Fawcett, *International Law and the Uses of Outer Space* (Dobbs Ferry, N.Y. 1968); John C. Cooper in I. A. Vlasic, ed., *Explorations in Aerospace Law* (Montreal 1968).

the circumstances. Nevertheless, even if one regards as successful the efforts made since 1957 to create within the shortest possible time a workable, although rudimentary, legal regime for outer-space activities, it cannot be said, as will be shown later, that the results adequately reflect either the existing potentialities of space science and technology or the basic political and social needs of the period.

The reasons which account for the failure of the world community to respond more fully to the pressing needs of our age seem, paradoxically, to be identical with those which have been primarily responsible for the relatively rapid development of space law: on the one hand, the existence of two hostile superpowers holding a virtual monopoly of new technology and apparently bent upon using it for further enhancement of their power and, on the other, the rest of the nation-states, lacking such capabilities and therefore apprehensive about their future in the realm of outer space and about their security as well. A combination of these factors led to the initiation of strong demands for prompt international action immediately after the launching of Sputnik.[10]

The fundamental principles of the future legal regime for outer space could already be clearly discerned at the thirteenth session of the U.N. General Assembly held in 1958. In the course of the debates a remarkable consensus emerged to the effect that access to the domain of space should be open to all states, regardless of their technical or economic capabilities. A Resolution, the Question of the Peaceful Uses of Outer Space,[11] adopted at the end of the session expressed the "common interest of mankind in outer space," urged "international co-operation in the study and utilization of outer space," called for the "fullest exploration and exploitation of outer space for the benefit of mankind," and pointedly emphasized the "sovereign equality" of all member states of the United Nations. A special *Ad Hoc* Committee on the Peaceful Uses of Outer Space, established by the same resolution and charged, inter alia, with the examination of legal problems posed by the advent of space exploration, was prompted to suggest in its report of July 1959, that the practice of states may have initiated a rule "to the effect that, in principle, outer space is, on conditions of equality, freely available for exploration and use by all."[12] The consistently permissive attitude of states toward orbiting spacecraft certainly allowed no other conclusion. For reasons which

[10] A more systematic discussion of these demands appears in McDougal, Lasswell, and Vlasic (fn. 9), 199ff.

[11] U.N. G.A. Res. 1348 (XIII), December 13, 1958.

[12] U.N. Doc. A/4141, Report of the *Ad Hoc* Committee on the Peaceful Uses of Outer Space, July 14, 1959, 64.

had nothing to do with the problem of access, a clear pronounce-ment by the United Nations on the status of outer space was post-poned until December 20, 1961, when by unanimously adopting Reso-lution 1721(XVI), the General Assembly enunciated the principle that "outer space and celestial bodies are free for use by all . . . and not subject to national appropriation," a principle which was fully reflective of the preexisting uniformity in the practice and expecta-tions of states.

To no one's surprise, the resolution further declared that the ap-plication of international law, including the Charter of the United Nations, extends also to outer space. In addition, it directed the Sec-retary-General to establish a public registry of objects launched into orbit and beyond, and states were invited to furnish the necessary in-formation for the registration of launchings. The registry commenced functioning in March of 1962, when first reports were filed, and since then it has recorded hundreds of launchings.[13]

The continuing accumulation of practical experience, the imminence of additional states entering the satellite-launching phase of space exploration, and the rapid advances in the range of space activities made it increasingly desirable and necessary to enunciate in one docu-ment certain fundamental principles which should guide states in the use of the new domain. Following lengthy negotiations, within and outside the United Nations, the General Assembly on December 13, 1963, adopted, again by a unanimous vote, Resolution 1962 (XVIII), the Declaration of Legal Principles Governing Activities of States in the Exploration and Use of Outer Space. This document was undoubtedly a landmark achievement in the continuing process of regulating space activities. Apart from reaffirming the essential free-doms of outer space, already asserted in a previous Resolution (1721), the Declaration prescribed that activities in outer space are to be conducted in the interest of maintaining international peace and security and promoting international cooperation; that states bear international responsibility for all national activities in space; that private activities in outer space require governmental authorization as well as supervision; that when activities are carried out by interna-tional organizations, responsibility shall be borne by them and by par-ticipating states; that states launching space vehicles are internationally liable for damage resulting from accidents on the earth, in airspace,

[13] The United States submitted its first registration report on March 5, 1962, and the Soviet Union on March 23, 1962. See U.S., Congress, Senate, Committee on Aeronautical and Space Sciences, *International Cooperation and Organization for Outer Space*, 89th Cong., 1st Sess., 1965, S. Doc. No. 56, 261 [hereafter cited as *International Cooperation*].

or in outer space; that "jurisdiction and control" over spacecraft and their crew, while they are in outer space, are vested solely in the state of registry; that ownership of spacecraft is not affected by their passage through outer space or by their landing beyond the limits of the state of registry; that states are to render all possible assistance to astronauts in distress and promptly repatriate them; and that the exploration and use of the space environment must be carried on in accordance with international law, including the Charter of the United Nations. Furthermore, by invoking in its preamble General Assembly Resolution 110(II), the Declaration condemned the use of outer space for "propaganda designed or likely to provoke or encourage any threat to the peace, breach of the peace, or act of aggression."

Although aside from this reference to harmful propaganda, the Declaration contained no other provisions specifically designed to prevent the use of outer space for activities potentially inimical to international public order, persistent demands to curb the extension of the arms race into this new region did yield in 1963 a measure of success. The success achieved has not been, unfortunately, commensurate with the expectations of the international community. The first concrete step in the prevention of the militarization of outer space was taken on August 5, 1963, with the signing of the (Moscow) Treaty Banning Nuclear Weapon Tests in the Atmosphere, in Outer Space, and Under Water.[14] This Treaty put an end to the testing of nuclear devices at high altitudes, a practice which had caused considerable radio-active contamination of the earth environment. The importance attached to this Treaty by the governments is best illustrated by the speed with which it secured the adherence of more than one hundred states, including all the actual and potential nuclear-weapon states except France and the People's Republic of China. These exceptions notwithstanding, the virtually universal acceptance of the Moscow Treaty and the proven harmful effects of nuclear testing on all states should soon give it the character of international custom, thereby making conduct contrary to its prohibitions a violation of international law.

The next step in the process of demilitarization of outer space was taken during the same session of the United Nations which produced the Declaration. As a result of an informal agreement between the United States and the Soviet Union, on October 18, 1963, the General Assembly through its Resolution 1884(XVIII) issued a call upon all states "to refrain from placing in orbit around the earth any objects carrying nuclear weapons or any other kind of weapons of

---

[14] For the text of the Treaty see same, 130. The Treaty entered into force on October 10, 1963.

mass destruction, installing such weapons on celestial bodies, or stationing such weapons in outer space in any other manner."[15] While this Resolution at the time of its adoption was not intended to create legal obligations, the subsequent incorporation of its substance in the Space Treaty makes it an important landmark in the continuing quest to control the arms race.

The field of telecommunications is one aspect of space utilization where international legal regulation during the last decade has largely kept pace with the technological developments. The finite nature of the radio spectrum on the one hand, and the vital role of radio communications in outer space activities on the other, are factors primarily responsible for the quick and willing response of states to the demands of urgent practical needs. Radio impulses are employed to track, guide, control and, if necessary, destroy space vehicles; scientific information about outer space collected by spacecraft is relayed back to earth by means of radio signals; astronomers study the distant reaches of the universe through signals originating in outer space and received by radio-telescopes located on our planet; and, finally, radio spectrum serves the needs of conventional and satellite communications. Given such critical importance of radio for space activities, it is not surprising that as early as 1959, the Administrative Conference of the International Telecommunication Union (ITU) decided to allocate 13 frequency bands for space and earth-space radio communications, to prescribe conditions for the use of these frequencies, and provide for a radio astronomy service.[16] Following this provisional arrangement, extensive studies were undertaken by various national administrations and ITU with a view to formulating technical principles upon which a more permanent allocation could be based. These studies made it possible to hold in the fall of 1963 the Extraordinary Administrative Radio Conference which agreed on the allocation of some 15 percent of the radio spectrum to various space services, including communications satellites, space telecommand, telemetry, tracking, meteorological and navigational satellites, space research, radio astronomy, and satellite identification.[17] Agreement incorporating these

15 An excellent account of this resolution appears in A. E. Gotlieb, "Nuclear Weapons in Outer Space," *Canadian Yearbook of International Law*, III (1965), 3.
16 The results of this Conference are discussed in U.S., Congress, Senate, Committee on Aeronautical and Space Sciences, Edward Wenck, Jr., *Radio Frequency Control in Space Telecommunications*, 86th Cong., 2d Sess., 1960, Com. Print, 79ff.
17 The decisions of the Conference were included in the "Final Acts of the Extraordinary Administrative Radio Conference to Allocate Frequency Bands for Space Radio Communication Purposes" (Geneva 1963). For details see International Telecommunications Union, *ITU and Space Radiocommunication* (1968), 7-10; N. Jasentuliyana, "Regulatory Functions of I.T.U. in the Field of Space Telecommunications," *Journal of Air Law and Commerce*, XXXIV (Winter 1968), 62.

and other measures designed to secure the orderly use of radio in space must be considered as being one of the most significant events in the legal regulation of outer space activities to date.

Without this agreement the practical utilization of communications satellites might have been either long delayed or perhaps made entirely impossible, because the risk of interference would be too great to warrant the costly investment. Thus, the decisions taken at the ITU Conference contributed directly to the establishment in August 1964, of the International Telecommunications Satellite Consortium (Intelsat), the first multinational enterprise for the commercial exploitation of space technology.[18] With the successful launching on April 6, 1965 of the "Early Bird" satellite, the Consortium commenced its business operations. Despite its patently undemocratic features, Intelsat has achieved great success in bringing the benefits of communications satellites to a large number of nations. From an original membership of 11 countries, it has grown by mid-1969 to 67 countries, 15 of which operate 25 earth stations.[19] The basic Intelsat treaty—Agreement Establishing Interim Arrangements for a Global Commercial Communications Satellite System—is of limited duration and must be replaced by 1970 with a new long-term treaty.[20]

At its 23rd session, held in May 1968, the Administrative Council of the ITU decided to convene another World Administrative Radio Conference in 1970 or early 1971. The Conference will be entirely devoted to problems of space radio services.

[18] On August 20, 1964, two interrelated agreements were opened for signature in Washington, D.C.—the "Agreement Establishing Interim Arrangements for a Global Commercial Communications Satellite System" and the "Special Agreement." The first is intergovernmental in character and prescribes the organizational and financial structure of Intelsat; the Special Agreement contains provisions relating to the commercial, financial, and technical operations of Intelsat. The text of these agreements is reproduced in U.S., Congress, Senate, Committee on Aeronautical and Space Sciences, *United States International Space Programs: Texts of Executive Agreements, Memoranda of Understanding, and Other International Agreements, 1959-1965*, 89th Cong., 1st Sess., 1965, 431. On June 4, 1965, a third related Intelsat treaty was signed in Washington—"Supplementary Agreement on Arbitration." Text in T.I.A.S. 5646, 77.

[19] *Air and Cosmos*, VII (May 24, 1969), 19.

[20] Article IX (a). Literature on Intelsat is already voluminous. Useful articles include: Richard R. Colino, "INTELSAT: Doing Business in Outer Space," *Columbia Journal of Transnational Law*, VI (Spring 1967), 17; Peter D. Trooboff, "INTELSAT: Approaches to the Renegotiation," *Harvard International Law Journal*, IX (Winter 1968), 1; Herbert I. Schiller, "Communications Satellites: A New Institutional Setting," *Bulletin of the Atomic Scientists*, XXIII (April 1967), 4.

For a critical review of the Intelsat arrangements, see Soji Yamamoto, "Agreement Establishing Interim Arrangements for a Global Commercial Communications Satellite System," *Japanese Annual of International Law*, IX (1965), 46; F. Batailler, "Les Accords Relatifs à l'Exploitation Commerciale des Satellites de Télécommunications," *Annuaire Français de Droit International*, XI (1965), 145;

However, until the definitive arrangements, currently in preparation, come into force, the original agreement of 1964 will remain in effect. The task of devising a durable organizational structure for the new enterprise which will adequately express the common interest of mankind in space telecommunications is one of the critical challenges confronting statesmen and international lawyers at this time.

Probably the most remarkable feature of the short history of space law, and one that could have far-reaching consequences extending beyond the immediate issues of outer space, was the emergence of the U.N. General Assembly as the principal world community organ for setting standards of conduct for space activities. Very soon after the advent of the space age it became apparent that for the overwhelming majority of states the United Nations was the proper forum to be entrusted with the formulation of the fundamental rules of behavior in the new environment. The fact that the Charter did not grant to the General Assembly the competence to legislate, except in matters of internal organization, was obviously considered not sufficiently compelling to bar the Assembly from enunciating certain basic principles and expecting the participants in space interactions to act accordingly. It appears that the majority of member states felt that the absence of any community-approved guiding policies would only serve to encourage conflict and the growth of vested interests, both posing a threat to the more immediate goals of space exploration and to the eventual establishment of an effective legal order in the new medium. Through its quasi-legislative intervention in the early stages of space exploration the General Assembly may be said to have laid the foundations of space law and thus created conditions conducive to peaceful utilization of the new environment.

The high mark of the quasi-legislative activities of the General Assembly was undoubtedly the adoption of the Declaration of Legal Principles. Because of its overriding importance, the authority of the Declaration has been the object of much comment.[21] Particular attention was accorded to the question whether or not it created binding obligations. The reason for asking that question was found in the Charter which, as previously noted, does not explicitly endow the

---

G. P. Zhukov, "World-wide Telecommunication System for Satellites" (London 1967), mimeo., memorandum submitted to the Space Law Committee of the International Law Association for the 1966 I.L.A. Helsinki Conference.

[21] The range of views expressed by officials and publicists can be found in I. Vlasic, "The Growth of Space Law 1957-65: Achievements and Issues," *Yearbook of Air and Space Law*, I (1967), 365, 374-79. See also D. Goedhuis, "Reflections on the Evolution of Space Law," *Netherlands International Law Review*, XIII (1966), 109, 111ff.

Assembly with legislative powers.[22] While the appraisals cover a wide spectrum of opinion, the view accepted by a majority of officials and publicists is to the effect that the Declaration stated obligations not unlike those under a formal treaty. The unique legal nature of this document was ably explained by the former chairman of the Legal Subcommittee of the U.N. Space Committee and now judge of the International Court of Justice, Manfred Lachs of Poland:

> . . . it can be said that almost all Members of the United Nations attached to it an importance similar to that resulting from a legally binding instrument, assimilating it, as it were, to the latter.
>
> Thus, by expressing their will to be bound by the provisions of the document in question, they consented so to be bound, and there is no reason why they should not be held to it, for their intention seems to be clear—the question of form ceases to be of essence.[23]

Whatever the ultimate characterization of the Declaration, its effect in practice did not materially differ from the effects that one would expect to result from a formal agreement: no state has either protested or, as far as it is known, acted in violation of its principles. But the true significance of the Declaration extends beyond the direct impact of its provisions; it is in the affirmation of the U.N. General Assembly as an indispensable and effective participant in the development of the law for outer space.

This quasi-legislative role of the General Assembly may have been to some extent undermined, and the authority of its future law-oriented space resolutions somewhat diminished, by the signing on January 27, 1967 of the Treaty on Principles Governing the Activities of States in the Exploration and Use of Outer Space, Including the Moon and Other Celestial Bodies.[24] If the text of the Treaty

22 For a more general inquiry into the lawmaking capacity of the General Assembly, see Richard A. Falk, "On the Quasi-Legislative Competence of the General Assembly," *American Journal of International Law*, LX (October 1966), 782.

23 Manfred Lachs, "The International Law of Outer Space," *Recueil des Cours*, CXIII (1964-III), 1, 98. For comparable views, expressed more recently, see Fawcett (fn. 9), 4-14.

24 The text of the Treaty was prepared within the United Nations and was unanimously adopted by the General Assembly as U.N. Doc. A/RES. 2222 (XXI), December 19, 1966. It was opened for signature on January 27, 1967 in Washington, Moscow, and London, the capitals of the countries whose governments are designated by Article XIV (3) as "depository governments." On that day representatives of 60 states signed the Treaty in Washington. *Department of State Bulletin*, LVI (February 20, 1967), 266. The Treaty came into force on October 10, 1967, and by mid-1969 has been signed or ratified by nearly a hundred nations.

incorporated provisions elaborating upon the principles enunciated in the Declaration, or covered important new ground, such anxiety would not arise. But the Treaty mainly reiterates, often verbatim, the provisions of the Declaration and only modestly expands the frontiers of space law. Even "its few provisions that are new," one commentator noted, "are so loosely drafted as to suggest that the authors did not expect them to be put to a real test of interpretation, but thought that as long as the instrument looked reasonably like a treaty, the main purpose was served,"[25] and that purpose was political expediency. In many instances the sole difference between the two documents is that where the Declaration speaks of outer space, the Treaty adds, somewhat redundantly, "the Moon and other Celestial Bodies." In this light, the adoption of the Treaty, while ending the not too serious uncertainty that existed in some quarters as to the rights and duties of states in outer space, may have strengthened the view, until recently of limited appeal, that even the most solemn outer space resolution of the General Assembly is merely a nonbinding expression of intent.[26]

The more important provisions of the Space Treaty which have no equivalent in the Declaration relate to measures designed to limit the militarization of outer space and celestial bodies. The Treaty thus stipulates in Article IV, in accord with General Assembly Resolution 1844(XVIII), that the contracting parties will refrain from placing into outer space or installing on celestial bodies any kind of weapons of mass destruction. The same article further prohibits "the establishment of military bases, installations and fortifications, the testing of any type of weapons and the conduct of military maneuvers on celestial bodies." However, the use of military personnel for nonmilitary missions is explicitly permitted. Article XII accepts a concept adopted in the Antarctic Treaty and provides for inspection on a basis of reciprocity of "[a]ll stations, installations, equipment and space vehicles on the moon and other celestial bodies" by the representatives

[25] Fawcett (fn. 9), 15. For other appraisals, see Paul G. Dembling and Daniel M. Arons, "The Evolution of the Outer Space Treaty," *Journal of Air Law and Commerce*, XXXIII (Summer 1967), 419; Vladimir Kopal, "Treaty on Principles Governing the Activities of States in the Exploration and Use of Outer Space, Including the Moon and Other Celestial Bodies," *Yearbook of Air and Space Law*, II (1968), 463; D. Goedhuis, "An Evaluation of the Leading Principles of the Treaty on Outer Space of 27th January 1967," *Netherlands International Law Review*, XV (1968), 17; Thomas R. Adams, "The Outer Space Treaty: An Interpretation in the Light of the No-Sovereignty Provisions," *Harvard International Law Journal*, IX (Winter 1968), 140.

[26] "It may even be that this ill-constructed and precarious instrument is a retrograde step." Fawcett (fn. 9), 16.

of the contracting parties. In contrast to the virtually unlimited right of inspection accorded the Antarctic observers,[27] before an inspection of outer space installations can take place a "reasonable advance notice" must be given of a planned visit "in order that appropriate consultations may be held" between the parties involved.[28] Such fore-warning, though admittedly for safety purposes, could conceivably frustrate the objective of the inspection by giving to the offender the opportunity to conceal the prohibited equipment or temporarily terminate activities which are banned by the Treaty. It must be noted that apart from the limitations just outlined, the Treaty places no restrictions on the military uses of the "void" of outer space. The obvious explanation for the omission is that this region is precisely the one currently being used by the great powers for military purposes.

Another new area covered by the Space Treaty relates to procedures whose objective is the promotion of safety in space exploration. Under Article V, the parties have agreed promptly to exchange or to provide the U.N. Secretary-General with information concerning any phenomena they have discovered in outer space which could endanger the life or health of astronauts. The contracting states have also agreed to notify the Secretary-General as well as the international community "to the greatest extent feasible and practicable, of the nature, conduct, locations and results" of their activities in outer space and on celestial bodies (Article XI). Prior to the Treaty's entry into force, reporting to the United Nations on national space activities was a voluntary undertaking; now the contracting parties have an obligation to provide such information. The decision as to the time and content of notifications is, however, left to each state.

Since the Space Treaty, in common with the Declaration, includes mainly general principles and breaks very little new ground, many urgent problems of space law remain unsolved. It is not suggested, of course, that the Treaty should or could have settled all or even most of the issues considered urgent. However, it was not unreasonable to expect in a document agreed upon in December of 1966, only a few years before the manned landing on the moon, to find, for example, more specific stipulations regarding the exploration of celestial bodies. Given the intense rivalry between the United States and the Soviet

[27] "Inspection teams despatched by a signatory of the Antarctic Treaty have complete freedom of access at any time to any and all areas of Antarctica. Inspection teams may be despatched by a signatory upon compliance with only one prior condition: the communication of the names of those on inspection teams to all other signatories to the Antarctic Treaty." James Simsarian, "Inspection Experience Under the Antarctic Treaty and the International Atomic Energy Agency," *American Journal of International Law*, LX (July 1966), 502, 503.

[28] Article XII, Space Treaty.

Union in the space race, omission from the Treaty of any provisions requiring the prelaunch coordination of national programs involving manned exploration of celestial bodies, especially in regard to the selection and use of the landing sites, might have caused this historic venture to begin in conditions of tension and conflict. The absence in the Treaty of any guidelines relating to the management and allocation of useful resources found on celestial bodies may turn out to be potentially disruptive of public order, since the prohibition against national appropriation contained in Article II is too general to be of much help in this respect.[29] Analogies to the regime of the high seas, while useful, nevertheless fail to answer the questions of who should reap the benefits of investment and effort and through what procedures these will be determined. The Treaty can also be criticized for having failed to provide for more direct and more comprehensive participation by the United Nations in the administration, exploration, and use of celestial bodies. Few states or individuals would disagree with the observation that "peace would have been better insured if the treaty had declared explicitly that the resources of space belong to all men and shall forever be administered for all humanity by the United Nations."[30] That no such provisions exist in the Treaty could be attributed to a desire on the part of the Soviet Union and the United States to "avoid too open commitments in this strange new region,"[31] as one commentator put it, particularly commitments in favor of the world organization.

Most of these, and many other, equally pressing, issues have received scant attention by the Legal Subcommittee of the U.N. Space Committee. Prior to and immediately following the conclusion of the Space Treaty, the Subcommittee's efforts were concentrated mainly on the preparation of the draft treaties on the rescue of astronauts and on liability for damage caused by space activities. The former, under the cumbersome title of Agreement on the Rescue of Astronauts, the Return of Astronauts, and the Return of Objects Launched into Outer Space, was successfully completed in December of 1967 and opened for signature on April 22, 1968.[32] The formulation of the liability convention, at the time of writing, still awaits completion.

---

[29] For a discussion of these provisions in the Treaty, see S. Bhatt, "Legal Controls of the Exploration and Use of the Moon and Celestial Bodies," *Indian Journal of International Law*, VIII (January 1968), 33.

[30] Editorial, *New York Times*, December 11, 1966, sec. 4, p. 8, col. 1.

[31] Fawcett (fn. 9), 15.

[32] The text of the Treaty was annexed to U.N. G.A. Res. 2345 (XXII), December 19, 1967. Reprinted in *American Journal of International Law*, LXIII (April 1969), 382. The Treaty entered into force on December 3, 1968. For commentaries see, Paul G. Dembling and Daniel M. Arons, "The Treaty on Rescue and Return of Astronauts and Space Objects," *William and Mary Law Review*, IX (Spring 1968),

The Rescue and Return Agreement is an elaboration of the provisions of the Space Treaty relating to astronauts and space objects. The most interesting aspect of the Agreement is the status it grants to astronauts as "envoys of mankind," a status that no other explorers or individuals, except accredited diplomats, enjoy under international law. According to American interpretation,[33] to some extent supported by the background and the wording of key Article IV, the contracting party on whose territory the personnel of a spacecraft have landed due to accident or emergency, must "safely and promptly" repatriate them to the launching authority, even if they have committed crimes, such as espionage, against the returning country. In other words, the duty of assistance and return is unconditional and applies without distinction to civilian as well as military personnel aboard spacecraft.

Among other legal problems awaiting authoritative decision in the more immediate future one should include the establishment of appropriate community procedures for the prevention of potentially harmful space programs; more effective control over military uses of space; the development of techniques for easy identification of spacecraft; improvement in the procedures for the registration of launchings with the Secretary-General to secure a comprehensive and up-to-date inventory of all spacecraft in orbit and beyond; regulations for national and international registration of spacecraft; clarification and elaboration of procedures for the settlement of disputes arising under the existing space-law treaties; solution of the probable future problem of transit privileges for spacecraft traversing foreign airspace on their way to or from outer space; the legal regime of vehicles such as "aerospacecraft" or "space shuttles," capable of operating both in airspace and outer space; the definition of permissible and impermissible activities; a more precise determination of principles and rules of general international law which apply to outer-space activities; the setting up of procedures for the avoidance of interference between spacecraft and aircraft in the region used for aerial navigation; the formulation of effective arrangements for global and regional programs of cooperation with special emphasis on projects specifically designed to assist the developing nations; the restructuring of the International Telecommunication Union and its endowment with policing powers over the use of radio spectrum; the establishment of

---

630; P.-H. Houben, "A New Chapter of Space Law: The Agreement on the Rescue and Return of Astronauts and Space Objects," *Netherlands International Law Review*, XV (1968), 121; R. Cargill Hall, "Rescue and Return of Astronauts on Earth and in Outer Space," *American Journal of International Law*, LXIII (April 1969), 197.

33 See, e.g., Dembling and Arons (fn. 32), 652-53.

effective international controls over direct broadcast via satellites; a rational and equitable allocation of radio frequencies and positions to communications satellites operating from synchronous orbit; and, of course, the completion of the work on the convention for liability for damage caused by space activities which has been in preparation since 1962.[34] Even this, by no means all-inclusive, summary of problems requiring legal regulation should suffice to demonstrate that despite some significant achievements to date, the process of building an effective regime of public order in the domain of space is still very much in its infancy.

II. MILITARY USES OF OUTER SPACE AND THEIR EFFECTS ON PUBLIC ORDER

It is probably not an exaggeration to assert that the future of legal order in outer space will largely depend on the degree of the militarization of the new arena. Despite a broad variety of scientific programs now carried out by means of space technology, one must not overlook the fact that the main driving force behind many contemporary advances in space science and technology has been and continues to be the quest for military supremacy, rather than the attainment of scientific, technical, industrial, or prestige goals. The realm of outer space from the very outset of the space age has been regarded by the space powers as an extension of the traditional theaters of military operations.[35] Since the potentialities of space for defense and offense were largely unknown, it was felt prudent to investigate its usefulness for various military objectives and employ any new discoveries well ahead of any potential enemy.

The all-pervasive fear of a militarily significant technological breakthrough which might upset the so-called balance of power has often been cited in justification of the continuing interest of the defense establishment in outer space. Following more than a decade of heavy financial and manpower investment in the examination of the military potentialities of outer space, it now appears that no major breakthrough has been achieved.[36] That, of course, does not exclude

---

[34] The Legal Subcommittee of the U.N. Space Committee has currently on its agenda, in addition to a draft liability convention, a study of the questions relative to the definition of outer space and the utilization of outer space and celestial bodies, including the various implications of space communications, the legal problems of direct broadcasting via satellites, and a draft convention on spacecraft registration.

[35] See, e.g., Thomas S. Power, *Design for Survival* (New York 1965), 228.

[36] Dr. Harold Brown, then Director of Defense Research and Engineering, made the following statement in the course of hearings before the U.S. Senate Committee

the possibility of some such breakthrough in the future, provided the same high level of interest and financing is sustained. What is, however, worth stressing, especially in the context of a discussion on international public order, is that the sum total of military space applications to date does not amount to the usefulness of a single major nonspace weapon system. By and large, the existing military space hardware serves as an auxiliary to the earth-based military systems. In some areas it has improved the performance of the military instrument without introducing any strategically significant innovations.[37] To illustrate, it may be useful to summarize the more important current uses of military space technology.[38]

Reconnaissance has been one of the earliest applications of space technology to military missions. Observational satellites are believed to provide today a comprehensive and continuous surveillance over wide areas of the globe, some of which are inaccessible by other means. One special type of satellite equipped with infrared sensors is used for detecting ballistic missile launches. "Ferret" satellites collect electronic intelligence by monitoring radio traffic and obtaining the operating frequencies of military radar over the territory of potential enemies. The most recent claim is that the efficacy of reconnaissance spacecraft has already reached the point where they could be used in

---

on Aeronautical and Space Sciences, held in August 1965:

> Because I judge that our expenditures are bigger here and that our programs are more varied, I think that we are at least as likely as the Soviets to find any such breakthrough, if it exists.
>
> I rather doubt that it exists. As I say, for 7 or 8 years we have been looking for something really new that space would show us that we could do that we can't do any other way. I don't think we have found it.
>
> We have found ways to do things better with space than we can do them in other ways. But the most generally mentioned ones, things like bombs in orbit, I think we have investigated the potential enough to know that it is a less effective way of doing what you can do from the ground or from the sea or from the air.
>
> So all I can say, Senator Symington, is that I don't see this breakthrough, but we have to keep spending quite a lot of effort, building technology, examining systems, to see that if it exists, we find it first, and I think we are doing that.

Asked to make an estimate of where such a breakthrough might occur, Dr. Brown replied: "I don't see it and so I can't make an estimate of where it would be." U.S., Congress, Senate, Committee on Aeronautical and Space Sciences, Hearings, *National Space Goals for the Post-Apollo Period*, 89th Cong., 1st Sess., 1965, 324 [hereafter cited as *National Space Goals*].

[37] The ICBM, which *was* a major strategic breakthrough, cannot properly be considered a space weapon. Even though a long-range ballistic missile in its trajectory penetrates outer space, it is at this time a land- or sea-based weapon.

[38] For some recent data, see *New York Times*, June 29, 1969, sec. 4, p. 12, col. 5; *Newsweek* (April 21, 1969), 62. Estimates of Soviet satellite reconnaissance activities are offered in *Aviation Week and Space Technology*, LXXXIX (December 9, 1968), 83.

many respects as a substitute for on-site inspection in an arms control agreement. Navigational satellites provide precise positioning data for submarines and other naval vessels which require accurate position fixing. Geodetic or mapping satellites supply exact information about the location of various points on the globe with relation to one another. Data thus obtained can be employed in the calculation of firing elements for ballistic missiles. The military are also relying upon satellites for securing a continuous flow of information concerning weather conditions around the world. In 1966 an experimental military communications satellite system was inaugurated by the United States to provide when perfected a worldwide emergency capability invulnerable to intentional jamming or blackouts due to natural causes. By January 1969, this system had grown to 22 operational satellites in orbit.[39] The United States also has in a 60,000-mile orbit several "Vela" spacecraft designed to detect, locate, and report on nuclear detonations from the distant reaches of space to the surface of the earth.

Two additional developments are worth mentioning because they are commonly regarded as falling within the category of space-oriented military systems. First, the United States in 1966 asserted that it possessed an operational antisatellite weapon capable of destroying orbiting hostile spacecraft.[40] Second, on several occasions in recent years the Soviet Union has claimed it possessed in its military arsenal a "global rocket" (or "orbital missile") capable of hitting from orbit any target on the earth.[41] Assuming that both claims are based on fact, it appears that neither system can be considered a true space weapon. The American antisatellite weapon is most likely ground-based and designed primarily as defense against incoming ballistic missiles rather than against hostile satellites;[42] the Soviet "global rocket," presumably the so-called Fractional Orbit Bombardment System (FOBS), is almost certainly an improved version of their intercontinental ballistic missile and also ground-based.[43] The fact that

39 *New York Times*, January 18, 1969, p. 21, col. 2.

40 *Report to the Congress from the President of the United States: United States Aeronautics and Space Activities 1965* (Washington 1966), 49-57; U.S., Congress, Senate, Committee on Aeronautical and Space Sciences, *Hearings on S. 2909*, 89th Cong., 2d Sess., 1966, 660 [hereafter cited as *Hearings on S. 2909*].

41 *New York Times*, November 8, 1965, p. 1, col. 6. See also Walter C. Clemens, *Outer Space and Arms Control* (Cambridge, Mass. 1966), 72ff (Center for Space Research, M.I.T., CSR TR-66-14).

42 Hanson W. Baldwin, "Space Holds High Military Potential," *New York Times*, November 20, 1966, sec. 12, p. 7, col. 1.

43 *Aviation Week and Space Technology*, LXXXVII (November 13, 1967), 30; same, LXXXVIII (June 10, 1968), 16; William C. Foster, "Prospects for Arms Control," *Foreign Affairs*, XLVII (April 1969), 413, 414.

the United States did not claim that its antisatellite weapon was space-borne on the one hand, and failed to protest the Soviet claim on the other, would seem to confirm this appraisal, especially in the light of Article IV of the Space Treaty which prohibits the stationing of weapons of mass destruction in outer space.

The space environment during the past decade has also been used for experiments related to devising a system of military communications immune to crippling interference, and, at the same time, making it possible to deny to the enemy the use of the radio spectrum. The best known instances of such experiments have been the notorious detonations of nuclear devices at high altitudes (up to 300 miles) and the launching into orbit around the earth of millions of copper dipoles (Project West Ford). A test involving a nuclear explosion high over the Pacific is known to have resulted in a virtual blackout of transpacific communications for several hours.[44] An unintended outcome of this experiment was the creation of a new region of radiation above the earth. Project West Ford[45] appears to have been an attempt to safeguard against man-made or natural disruptions of radio links by creating an artificial ionosphere in the form of a belt of tiny copper dipoles. While it succeeded in generating much hostility against its planners, this project failed to accomplish its mission and by all available indications it seems, at least for the time being, to have been abandoned.

The above catalogue is not a very impressive one, especially when compared with the enthusiastic predictions as to the defense potential of space technology made shortly after the launching of Sputnik by the advocates of military space programs. However, disappointments to date do not seem to have seriously affected the hopes of the military that some time in the future an effective space-based weapon system might be found. Regardless of the realism of such hopes, the military and their allies in industry and politics seem to act on the assumption that the current level of armed confrontation will continue for a long time and that the interests of national security will therefore require maximum effort in all environments, including outer space. In this respect, the following forecast of the future made in 1966 by Dr. Harold Brown, Secretary of the U.S. Air Force at the time, is illustrative:

44 For a revealing analysis of these texts, see John E. Mock, "High-Altitude Nuclear Effects," *Air University Review*, XVII (January-February 1966), 26.

45 For details about the West Ford experiment, see Leonard Jaffee, *Communications in Space* (New York 1966), 91-99. See also *International Cooperation* (fn. 13), 407; Patrick Moore, *Space in the Sixties* (Penguin Books edn., Baltimore 1963), 75-79.

In looking at the future, one cannot be completely confident of very many things. There are a few, however, that seem to me quite certain. I think the world will continue to be full of conflicting interests and that during the next twenty years our own national interests and objectives will have to be supported by military power, as they have been in the past. The security of many other countries, even if some peace-keeping functions should be assumed by international bodies, will depend fundamentally on US military power. . . . Twenty years hence, I expect it [USAF] will be performing new roles in space and in the atmosphere, as well as functions similar to those of today, though perhaps not in the way and certainly not with the same equipment.[46]

An important step in the continuation of the arms race in outer space was taken on August 25, 1965, when President Johnson approved the development of the Manned Orbiting Laboratory (MOL) program, a project long urged by an influential segment of the defense establishment. The officially announced objectives of MOL were "to improve knowledge of man's ability in space and its application to military purposes, to develop technology and equipment for the advancement of manned and unmanned space flight and to perform meaningful military experiments."[47] The concept of MOL was essentially a replacement for the costly Dynasoar program, canceled in 1963. The purpose of Dynasoar was to help design a manned orbital reentry vehicle that could operate in outer space and in the atmosphere and land as a conventional aircraft.

It was assumed that reconnaissance would be the most important function of MOL, at least in the beginning. There were those, however, who had hoped that it would eventually serve as a space-borne command center and even as a "floating fortress capable of intercepting and knocking down hostile spacecraft."[48] After expenditures of about $1.3 billion, the project was abruptly canceled in June 1969, reportedly for budgetary reasons. This decision does not necessarily mean that there will be no American military manned spacecraft in outer space. According to a leading aerospace journal, the MOL cancellation "underscores a significant Nixon decision to throw full support toward a civilian orbital station with enough flexibility to include covert manned surveillance only as needed."[49] The

[46] Harold Brown, "USAF's Foreseeable Future," *Air Force and Space Digest*, IL (May 1966), 43.

[47] Statement by Director of Defense Research and Engineering, Dr. John S. Foster, Jr., in *Hearings on S. 2909* (fn. 40), 656.

[48] *Time* (September 3, 1965), 57.

[49] *Aviation Week and Space Technology*, XC (June 16, 1969), 28.

same source asserts that the U.S. government has thus fully endorsed the rival plan of the National Aeronautics and Space Administration (NASA), which calls for building an orbital station capable of accommodating up to 100 astronauts. Whether there is, or was, in the Soviet Union a comparable program in the process of development is not known, but given the Soviet capability to orbit heavy payloads and the apparent determination of the U.S.S.R. to use outer space for the enhancement of its military power, such a possibility certainly exists. It is, perhaps, indicative of Soviet intentions in this respect that for some time the principal Russian effort in space has been toward the creation of large manned "spaceships" capable of operating in near-earth orbit for long periods of time.[50] Even though no reliable information is available as to the specific mission assigned to these spaceships, it is entirely possible that their intended role is similar to that of the much advertised MOL.[51] There is no way of ascertaining their real function short of on-board inspection, and the Space Treaty does not call for such inspections.

Irrespective of what the Soviet decision might have been prior to the announcement of the MOL, once the United States had publicly committed itself to this project the action-reaction phenomenon, assisted by the Russian defense establishment, may have left the Soviet government no choice but to follow the American example. The pressure by the same groups which had succeeded in making the United States government adopt the MOL project,[52] or for that matter, any

50 See, e.g., a series of articles on Soviet space plans translated in *Current Digest of the Soviet Press*, xix (October 25, 1967), 3-8.

51 Y. Zonov, a Soviet space engineer, wrote in *Pravda* (January 17, 1969, p. 3) that "the establishment of manned space stations in orbit around the earth is a task that stems logically from the whole development of research in terrestrial and outer space, and fulfillment of this task is essential to further successes in the study and exploration of space." Zonov goes on to explain the advantages of such stations for the performance of various programs, such as long-distance telecommunications, voyages to planets, medical research, chemistry, astronomy, etc., *Current Digest of the Soviet Press*, xxi (February 5, 1969), 5.

52 For example, without citing any hard evidence, the Military Operations Subcommittee of the House Government Operations Committee in advocating MOL contended that the Soviet Union is "substantially ahead of us in this field." *Aviation Week and Space Technology*, lxxxii (June 7, 1965), 16. A mass circulation periodical reported at the time on the "deep conviction of top U.S. Air Force leaders . . . that Russia is directing its main energies and resources not to the moon, but to mastery of space nearer earth. Some are convinced that Russia, far behind in the missile race, is now striving to leap-frog the U.S. and move ahead with manned satellite weapons." "The Real Story of the Space Race," *U.S. News & World Report* (April 5, 1965), 33, 34. Yet, a few months later, according to Hanson W. Baldwin, the military analyst of the *New York Times*, in "the race for space, the United States appears to hold a strong lead in military utilization and application." Baldwin (fn. 43). Even in late 1968, barely six months before the cancellation of MOL, Dr. Raymond L. Bisplinghoff, Dean of the M.I.T. School of

other new military aerospace program, may prove similarly irresistible within the U.S.S.R. and other countries. It is as pertinent as it is instructive in this connection to recall that many military hardware plans have in the past received governmental approval not so much on the basis of their proven utility or necessity as on the basis of claims, not always founded in fact or ascertainable, that "the other side" is apparently, or probably, already engaged in a similar program and that there is, therefore, a risk of a dangerous weapons "gap." The antiballistic missile (ABM) controversy, dealt with below, is the most recent illustration of this phenomenon.

The MOL (or its current equivalent) by no means exhausts the catalogue of advanced military space projects in the developmental phase or under consideration. In the continuing search of new roles for the military in outer space, it was reported some time ago that no less than 70 "detailed conceptual packages" have already been submitted to the USAF research and development office.[53] They range from "refined command and control and surveillance platforms, to some admittedly far-out possibilities, such as: a satellite interceptor system based in a C-5A aircraft, a variety of manned offensive and defensive systems powered by Van Allen belt radiation, nuclear-powered ferry vehicles, environmental-control and Earth-illumination satellites, orbital weapons programs, and even a 'Doomsday Machine' linked to an asteroid belt explosion."[54] Another report similarly outlines a variety of potential future military developments under scrutiny, including: "aerospace plane," capable of operating both in atmosphere and outer space; "satellite interceptor," for inspection and destruction of hostile satellites; "global surveillance platform," for improved reconnaissance; and "orbital weapons system," described as "rocket-driven dreadnoughts to carry super H-bombs or 'death rays' focused on earth targets."[55]

Only a few weeks before the Soviet Union and the United States reached agreement on the text of the Space Treaty, an eminent military analyst wrote about the future role of the military man in space as follows:

Engineering, argued for a "vigorous pursuit" of the MOL program and said that he "would be very unhappy to see MOL dropped." "What National Strategy for Manned Spacecraft Operations?" [an interview], *Astronautics and Aeronautics*, VI (October 1968), 58, 62. It is, perhaps, appropriate to add that Dean Bisplinghoff's School is one of the largest academic recipients of Defense Department funds.

[53] *Missiles and Rockets*, XVIII (May 30, 1966), 24, 28.

[54] Same.

[55] *U.S. News & World Report* (April 5, 1965), 35. See also Edgar E. Ulsamer, "The Ultimate in Hypersonic Flight—the Aerospace Plane," *Air Force Magazine*, LII (January 1969), 80.

He will pilot tomorrow's fighting machines in the cosmos. And in time he may actually be able, with a whole host of scientific aids, to control the weather with the tremendous military and social consequences this implies.

What form these manned fighting machines of tomorrow may take one can now only guess, but clearly one of the most important future military needs is for some sort of a manned and maneuverable space intercepting vehicle, which can close with, inspect, and, if necessary, capture, identify, or destroy orbiting bombardment missiles or enemy satellites.

In the more distant decades, when the biological hazards of space flight have been neutralized and when man is capable of achieving his full potential in a foreign and dangerous environment, it seems certain that military astronauts will be commonplace.[56]

These prophecies must be taken seriously not merely because they come from well-informed sources but more importantly because they reflect the current trends in the arms race in both the conventional and the nuclear-space fields.[57] The latest phase in this race which threatens to affect outer space relates to the construction of anti-ballistic missile (ABM) defenses.[58] This is not entirely an unexpected development since both the United States and the Soviet Union have been working on such a defense system for some years. What has given it special urgency was the alleged discovery that the Soviets have stepped up their efforts in building an ABM shield around strategically important areas of the U.S.S.R. While no knowledgeable expert has suggested that these efforts have made the U.S.S.R. invulnerable to a missile attack, the American proponents of ABM claim that the United States must embark without delay on a major antimissile program of its own if it wishes to continue its strategic superiority.[59] Directly related to the ABM developments is the immi-

[56] Baldwin (fn. 43). See also Power (fn. 35), 234-36.

[57] They apparently were taken seriously, at least in part, by the U.S. Defense Department which was reported as planning a space station in Australia "to explore the threat of nuclear launching pads and the defense against such an attack," *New York Times*, December 12, 1966, p. 51, col. 1.

[58] There is already in existence extensive literature on the ABM defense. The more recent useful contributions include: Andrew Stratton, "Contests in the Sky," in Nigel Calder, ed., *Unless Peace Comes* (New York 1968), 64; Lapp (fn. 8), 144-69; Lapp, "A Biography of the ABM," *New York Times Magazine*, May 4, 1969, p. 29; Hans A. Bethe, "The ABM, China and the Arms Race," *Bulletin of the Atomic Scientists*, xxv (May 1969), 41; D. G. Brennan, "The Case for Missile Defense," *Foreign Affairs*, xlvii (April 1969), 433; Abram Chayes and Jerome B. Wiesner, eds., *ABM: An Evaluation of the Decision to Deploy an Antiballistic Missile System* (New York, 1969).

[59] Yet, ten years of study, research, and development of ABM techniques costing $4 billion, made U.S. Secretary of Defense McNamara "convinced that the ICBM

nent deployment of Multiple Independently Targetable Reentry Vehicles (MIRV).[60] These new missiles, each capable of carrying several nuclear warheads, are regarded essential by the military to penetrate the enemy's ABM defenses, just as the ABM's are thought to be essential to defend against hostile MIRV's. Apart from adding a new extremely costly dimension to the existing arms race and placing agreement on the limitation and reduction of strategic weapons beyond reach, this trend, if allowed to continue, could directly affect the cause of public order in outer space in two ways.

First, since antiballistic defenses are designed to destroy or neutralize the hostile missiles through high altitude nuclear explosions, they may require before becoming fully operational additional testing involving the use of nuclear warheads in outer space. Such tests are now explicitly prohibited by the Moscow Test Ban Treaty. However, the Treaty confers upon each party the right to withdraw on three-months' notice "if it decides that extraordinary events . . . have jeopardized the supreme interests of its country."[61] The prospect of a major upset in the present "balance of power"—and the installation of an even partially effective ABM defense is widely believed capable of producing such a result—would certainly be considered a threat to the "supreme" national interests, justifying withdrawal from the Treaty and the resumption of nuclear tests at all levels, including outer space.[62]

Second, it is conceivable that in order to penetrate the ABM defenses, attempts will be made to develop nuclear-armed offensive systems permanently stationed in outer space and capable of hitting from there targets on earth. Even though such "orbital" weapons are presently considered not only less effective but also much more costly than the earth-based ballistic missiles,[63] this might not be viewed as a sufficiently compelling reason for the defense establishment to refrain indefinitely from experimenting. Think of the ever-changing and often contradictory justifications used by the military and their civilian allies to secure public acceptance for the ABM system, despite its highly doubtful usefulness. Activities along these lines, involving

offense has a sharp advantage over any anti-ballistic missile defense system." *Aviation Week and Space Technology*, LXXXVI (February 6, 1967), 27. The same opinion was expressed in 1969 by the majority of experts in the field.

[60] Harold Brown, "Security Through Limitations," *Foreign Affairs*, XLVII (April 1969), 422, 429.

[61] Article IV.

[62] According to a report published in the autumn of 1968, a contingency plan for the resumption of atmospheric tests was about to be submitted to the U.S. President. *Aviation Week and Space Technology*, LXXXIX (October 21, 1968), 107.

[63] *National Space Goals* (fn. 36), 304.

the placing of weapons of mass destruction in outer space, it will be recalled, would contravene the provisions of the Space Treaty.[64] The Treaty can be denounced, however, one year after its entry into force, such withdrawal to take effect one year from the date of receipt of notification to the depositary governments.[65] In contrast to the Moscow Test Ban Treaty, a contracting party wishing to withdraw from the Space Treaty is not required to give reasons for its decisions.

The preceding review of the existing and planned military uses of outer space is intended to illustrate several relevant points, including: the wide scope of the anticipated military activities in outer space; the implicit assumption that there will be in space hostile vehicles which will have to be destroyed, even though there are none there at the present time and no attempt has so far been made by any state to interfere with the space programs of another; and the lack of concern about the effects of these measures upon the cause of world public order and the maintenance of peace on our planet.[66] The review makes it obvious that the efforts made during the past decade to "avoid [in the words of a U.N. resolution] the extension of present national rivalries into this new field" of outer space have achieved only modest success. The Space Treaty, while prohibiting the stationing of weapons of mass destruction in outer space and on celestial bodies, does not preclude states from carrying on their current military uses of outer space or affect their immediate military interests and plans.[67]

[64] Article IV.   [65] Article XVI.

[66] This essentially militaristic attitude on the part of the major powers is not characteristic only of their outer-space politics. The scope of the malaise was succinctly and accurately stated by U.N. Secretary-General U Thant in his annual report of September 26, 1968, to the General Assembly:

> In the period under review, I regret to have to report that little progress, if any, has been recorded toward the growth of international order based on law and justice. On the contrary, there has been a serious decline in the standards of international ethics and morality, with states relying increasingly on force and violence as a means of resolving their international differences.
>
> This tendency to return to force as a means of national policy strikes at the very basis of the United Nations; just settlement is sacrificed to superior might, and international tensions are consequently heightened. If this trend is not reversed, and if the principle of nonintervention in the free destiny of nations is not reestablished, the future of international peace and security itself is indeed a very dark one. *New York Times*, September 27, 1968, p. 22, col. 2.

[67] In the harsh, though not entirely inaccurate, appraisal of the Space Treaty by a member of the Stanford Research Institute, the Treaty "may be a destructive diversion from the most serious arms control problems facing the United States and the world, that of the control, reduction, and eventual elimination of nuclear-tipped strategic missile delivery systems." Sidney J. Slomich, "Arms Control and Disarmament: The Great Evasion," *Bulletin of the Atomic Scientists*, XXIV (June 1968), 19.

To say that a continuation of the arms race in any environment and particularly in the common domain of outer space is inimical to the interests of all countries, including the superpowers, and that effective measures should be taken to reverse this trend states the obvious without enhancing the prospects for de-escalation. It would seem no more rewarding, at first glance, to suggest specific measures designed to achieve even a gradual demilitarization of outer space; consider the number and variety of ignored official and private proposals made in the last ten years. To expect decision-makers of major states to alter their policies in direct response to private pleas while they remain deaf to appeals emanating from far more influential sources would be naïve. An argument predicated on the self-interest of such states, could, perhaps, make some impression. The ensuing observations are made from this perspective.

It will be recalled from the preceding survey of military uses of outer space that not a single space-based *weapon* system has been developed to date (in contrast to weapons, such as the ICBM, which traverse outer space for brief periods of time). Furthermore, during the same period no militarily significant breakthrough has been achieved and, according to a most authoritative source, none is in sight.[68] It has been learned in the course of costly experiments that "such things as the bomb in orbit, for example, do not make much military sense as of now or for the foreseeable future."[69] In view of this record, one is bound to ask whether, on balance, the self-interest of the actors, and the interests of the world community as well, would not be better served by terminating any further militarization of outer space. The history of the arms race shows that modern weapons technology cannot be and never was for very long a monopoly of any one country. Even underdeveloped societies—as the examples of China today and of the Soviet Union in the past confirm—can, provided they have sufficient incentive, rapidly catch up in military technology with far more advanced countries.[70] It is virtually certain that every major innovation or breakthrough achieved by one country will soon be duplicated by others. Hence any gains accruing to the security of a particular actor will be at best of short-term significance; in the long run, the security of all is bound to diminish. No less an authority than the Director of the U.S. Arms Control Agency has publicly de-

---

[68] See footnote 36.   [69] Same, 304.

[70] U.S. government officials have since 1967 credited the People's Republic of China with having "more missile power than is needed to put an object into orbit." *New York Times*, January 18, 1967, p. 7, col. 3. On April 24, 1970, China became the fifth member of the exclusive spacepower club (after the U.S.S.R., U.S.A., France, and Japan) by launching a 381-pound satellite into earth orbit. *New York Times*, April 26, 1970, p. 1, col. 8.

clared that "with another round of strategic force deployments, we can expect to be less secure than we are today."[71]

Moreover, the arms race inevitably produces a destabilizing effect in the world arena by drawing an ever-increasing number of communities into the competition and thereby creating and augmenting suspicion and distrust. In President Johnson's words: "[the] fearsome engines of today are not mere symptoms of intention. Weapons have themselves become a cause of fear and a cause of distrust among other nations. As weapons become more numerous and more deadly, fear and tension grow."[72] The same point was made by Manfred Lachs, Judge of the International Court of Justice:

> More and better weapons of mass destruction as "deterrents" or means of "mass retaliation"—the search for a strategic breakthrough, far from increasing security, produce chain reactions, with the risks of conflict ever increasing. The fallacy of the assumption that armaments would help the solution of political differences has become manifest. Is it not true that the opposite is the case? By their growth armaments become a political problem in themselves; worse still, without solving any of the existing difficulties, they become sources of additional conflicts, increase suspicion, the feeling of insecurity, mistrust. They force us to move within a vicious circle, the dimensions of which are constantly increasing.[73]

The political, economic, and psychological cost of the arms race makes it almost impossible to initiate any major joint program of space utilization which would benefit the needy peoples of the world. Great powers still show no genuine awareness that "the real dangers of the 1970's and the 1980's lie not in Europe and the traditional conflict across the Elbe, but in the third world of Africa and Asia."[74] As the affluent countries continue to allocate increasing resources for armaments seeking "security" from one another, demographers and nutrition experts are warning that unless there is enough food to feed the world's expected population of four billion people in 1980, the impoverished nations may resort to force to acquire food or the land needed to produce it.[75] "Thus," one observer comments, "we pursue

71 William C. Foster, "More Weapons—Less Security," *Department of State Bulletin*, LIX (November 18, 1968), 526, 528.

72 Same, LII (May 27, 1965), 973.

73 Lachs (fn. 23), 88.

74 Lord Chalfont, "Prospects for Peace," *Bulletin of the Atomic Scientists*, XXII (May 1966), 2, 4 (Lord Chalfont, Minister of State for Foreign Affairs, U.K., with special responsibility for arms control and disarmament affairs).

75 *New York Times*, December 7, 1966, p. 3, col. 1. Vladimir Dedijer, himself a former Yugoslav guerrilla leader, puts forward the thesis—confirmed by recent experience—that guerrilla revolts, with only minimum outside support, are largely

the impossible goal of perfect security in response to not very acute threats, while the acute ones—worldwide hunger, poverty and discontent, racial injustice, and a poisoned environment—remain overshadowed."[76] Here again, the long-term effects of the arms race militate against the attainment of the desired objective—greater security.

The elite responsible for this trend often act as if it believed that military power was the most important factor in achieving respect in the world arena. While no one has as yet supplied a rational yardstick by which to measure the relative value of various elements contributing to respect, there is considerable evidence that such power generates fear and resentment more often than respect. That was true long before the advent of nuclear and space technology, of modern means of communication, and the "revolution of rising expectations." There is probably no other practice which has been more often and more widely condemned by the peoples of the world in recent decades than the relentless accumulation of weapons, reflective of the intent to use force for the achievement of national objectives. It would seem safe, therefore, to conclude that a pattern of behavior which, for example, promotes the common interest and reflects the humane aspirations of the world community is more likely to enhance respect than the pattern which suggests force as its main ingredient and as such can at best serve the interests of only one state or a small group of states.

All these considerations tend to confirm the belief that any gains in security achieved through the militarization of outer space have been outweighed by the negative effects of the arms race upon a number of other important policy objectives. There are convincing reasons to assume that the introduction of some novel systems into outer space, such as "bombs in orbit" or "satellite interceptors," would be similarly unproductive. When to these factors one adds the likelihood that a reasonable overall balance now exists between the armed forces of the United States and the Soviet Union, especially between their space segments, one can perceive a chance for putting an end to any further militarization of outer space and for a start in reversing the trend. As an initial measure, aimed primarily at creating a spirit of trust, it might suffice to limit the desired agreement to the cessation of any new military uses of space, leaving the questions of de-escalation of the existing uses and of inspection for subsequent negotiations.

---

immune to suppression by even the most advanced military technology. "The Poor Man's Power," in Calder, ed. (fn. 58), 18. The regions most vulnerable to guerrilla revolts are, of course, the poor regions of the world.

[76] Robert Gomer, "The ABM Decision," *Bulletin of the Atomic Scientists*, XXIII (November 1967), 29.

It would be too optimistic at this time to expect the superpowers to terminate the military uses of space—such as those for reconnaissance, communications, and navigation—which are already fully integrated with their military machines. In addition, such uses could, in any event, be distinguished from nonmilitary uses only through prelaunch inspection, and such inspection would be hard to get oustide a major disarmament agreement which is at present apparently beyond reach. As is well known, many space activities can serve both military and scientific purposes and the dividing line between them is often difficult to draw. This is particularly true of spacecraft equipped with cameras and other devices designed to record conditions existing in the surrounding and subjacent environment. Think, for example, of meteorological satellites, against which no objections have been heard. Even though their purpose is to take pictures of the underlying cloud cover, the cameras they carry do not stop recording when there are no clouds beneath. Hence they often supply clear pictures not only of the cloud formations but also of the surface of the earth. Or, consider the potentialities for observation by manned spacecraft. Both the Soviet and the American astronauts have been taking from orbit excellent photographs of the continents over which they were navigating. However, no one protested against their activities. Possibly nothing short of prohibiting photographic equipment in outer space could alter the situation. Similarly, satellites designed to aid civil communications and navigation are virtually undistinguishable from those used to serve identical military purposes.

For all these reasons the only rational measure at this juncture that can be recommended as having a reasonable chance of success is the one aimed at terminating further militarization of space. This step might eventually lead to a major disarmament program. The suggested moratorium, if accepted by the superpowers, would, like the Moscow Test Ban Treaty, almost certainly be endorsed by the overwhelming majority of states. The beneficial effects of such an agreement upon stability in the international arena, upon the development of world public order, and especially upon the future utilization of outer space would not be long in coming.

To convince the elites of the superpowers that it is in their interest to terminate further escalation of the use of space for military purposes before other states join in this futile competition and before the tensions resulting from the escalation lead to violence, presents probably the greatest immediate challenge to all those concerned with the maintenance of peace and the promotion of legal order in the earth-space arena. What is required is nothing less than a change in the basic orientation of the policy-makers, i.e., a change from narrow nationalism to a broad concept of the community of mankind. The interdependence between the attainment of such a change in the loyalties of the elite and the achievement of a disarmed world (the ultimate aim of every civilized government) was eloquently expressed by Lord Chalfont:

> It is true, however, that before effective disarmament on any large scale becomes a practical possibility there will have to be a revolution in political thought. There will have to be a full realization that the rule of law between nations is as basic to human existence as the rule of law between individuals. But eventually there will have to be something even more fundamental; no less than a revolution in the political philosophy that underlies the concept of the nation-state. We shall have to look again at the Hobbesian proposition that the natural state of man is a state of war; and that in this relationship society's overriding duty is to secure its own continued existence. From this derives the doctrine that governments are morally obliged to do everything to ensure the security of the state—that, as Spinoza has suggested, "a nation can lie, cheat, break its word, attack another nation if it seems to be in its own interest to do so." And those who insist upon the eternal validity of the concept of the sovereign state might do well to recall that Hobbes himself proposed a principle of limitation on the obligation of the subject. It was to last only as long as the sovereign state retained the power to protect the subject.
>
> It seems valid to ask whether, in the century of nuclear weapons, the state still, in every case, has that power. This is not to advocate any doctrine of anti-statism, but merely to suggest that it is time to look with a disenchanted eye at some of the dogma of nationalism and the more unthinking forms of patriotism.[77]

III. CONTROL OVER POTENTIALLY HARMFUL SPACE ACTIVITIES

Next to a global thermonuclear conflict, possibly the greatest threat to the integrity of our terrestrial habitat in the future may come from the indiscriminate application of the new technology and from uncontrolled scientific experiments, both upsetting the balance of nature.[78] The pace of man-induced changes in the earth environment, which began in 1945 with the nuclear explosions, is widely considered to be almost catastrophic by nature's standards. Admittedly, many of the discoveries responsible for these changes, such as atomic

[77] Chalfont (fn. 74), 4.

[78] For a concise and instructive discussion of these threats, see Barry Commoner, *Science and Survival* (New York 1966).

energy, synthetic detergents, insecticides, and weed-killers, have richly contributed to the living standards of men everywhere. However, the massive introduction of these technological innovations has seldom been preceded by a careful study of their long-term impact upon our environment. Responsible scientists continue to warn about the growing gap between the efforts to find the quickest possible application for the new scientific discoveries and the efforts to assess the hazards of such application.[79] The result of this disparity in effort has been, according to an authoritative report, that

> . . . new, large-scale experiments and technological developments of modern science frequently lead to unanticipated effects. The lifetime of the artificial belts of radiation established by the Starfish nuclear explosion was seriously underestimated in the calculations which preceded the experiment. Synthetic detergents were committed to full-scale economic exploitation before it was discovered that an important fault—resistance to bacterial degradation in sewage systems—would eventually require that they be withdrawn from the market. The hazards of pesticides to animal life were not fully known until pesticides were massively disseminated in the biosphere; the medical risk to man has hardly been evaluated. Nuclear tests responsible for the massive distribution of radioactive debris were conducted for about 10 years before the biological effects of its most hazardous component were recognized.[80]

These relatively novel products of modern science and technology are not, however, the only pollutants upsetting natural balance on our planet. Fire, for example, is threatening man's environment by augmenting at an alarming rate the carbon-dioxide content of the air which regulates the temperature of the earth. The internal-combustion engine is another offender. The noxious gases which the fuel in such engines emits contribute heavily to the creation of smog, that toxic umbrella covering an increasing number of the world's cities. The "ordinary" air inhaled nowadays by a dweller of a modern metropolis is "filled with tons of pollutants: carbon monoxide from gasoline, diesel and jet engines; sulphur oxides from factories, apartment houses, and power plants; nitrogen oxides, hydrocarbons and a broad variety of other compounds."[81] With accelerating urbanization,

[79] Same, esp. at 121-32. See also Gordon J. F. MacDonald, "Science and Politics of Rainmaking," *Bulletin of the Atomic Scientists*, XXIV (October 1968), 8.

[80] Report by the Committee on Science in the Promotion of Human Welfare of the American Association for the Advancement of Science (Washington 1965). The quotation is from Commoner (fn. 78), 62.

[81] President Johnson's message to Congress of January 30, 1967 on "Protecting our National Heritage." *New York Times*, January 31, 1967, p. 20, col. 1.

industrial growth and the rapidly multiplying number of vehicles, current efforts to control this process can do little more than keep the conditions from becoming unbearable. The areas of the globe still immune from contamination by man-made devices are rapidly shrinking. The process is truly ubiquitous; it affects our cities and countryside, our forests, lakes, and rivers, as well as our oceans and airspace.

These problems, like the biosphere on which man's survival depends, do not recognize local or national boundaries. A growing realization of the universality of these environmental and ecological conditions is at last beginning to stimulate international concern, which is hopefully a prelude to concerted international action.[82] Thus, on December 3, 1968, on the initiative of Sweden, the General Assembly of the United Nations adopted without a dissenting vote Resolution 2398(XXIII),[83] calling for a World Conference on Human Environment to be held in 1972. The great value of this Resolution must be seen in its all-inclusive approach to the destructive forces that are altering man's natural habitat and affecting his "physical, mental, and social well-being, his dignity and his enjoyment of basic human rights, in developing as well as developed countries." Although the Resolution does not explicitly mention space activities as a potential environmental threat, its scope is broad enough to encompass all present and future activities that may cause the impairment of the earth's system of life.

Advances in space technology have now created new opportunities for experiments which may considerably augment the risks to the integrity not only of our terrestrial environment but also of the realm of outer space. As one observer puts it, "[a]rmed with the great potentialities of modern science, men may be tempted to proceed to all sorts of experiments. Prompted by praiseworthy motives—mainly the urge for new discoveries—scientists are frequently unaware or disregard the consequences their experiments may bring about. . . . They 'may produce results from which there can be no return.' "[84] Among the activ-

---

[82] See, e.g., U.S., Congress, House, Committee on Science and Astronautics, Report of the Subcommittee on Science, Research, and Development, *The International Biological Program: Its Meaning and Needs*, 90th Cong., 2d Sess., 1968, Com. Print; Dean Rusk, "Science and Foreign Affairs," *Department of State Bulletin*, LVI (February 13, 1967), 238, 240-41; Rusk, "The Human Landscape," same, LX (February 10, 1969), 127; Abel Wolman, "Pollution as an International Issue," *Foreign Affairs*, XLVII (October 1968), 164; "Oil Pollution of the Sea," *Harvard International Law Journal*, X (Spring 1969), 316; *Problems of the Human Environment: Report of the Secretary-General*, U.N. Doc. E/4667 (May 26, 1969).

[83] Text in *Department of State Bulletin*, LIX (December 30, 1968), 711.

[84] Lachs (fn. 23), 71-72. As an illustration of the type of scientific project that could have catastrophic consequences, see P. M. Borisov, "Can We Control the Arctic Climate?," *Bulletin of the Atomic Scientists*, XXV (March 1969), 43 (the Soviet scientist proposes building a dam across the Bering Strait to increase the flow

ities which can at this time be identified as posing particular hazards to the earth-space environment the following merit special attention: the use of nuclear energy in outer space, voyages to celestial bodies which may result in biological contamination of the earth and/or planets, and large-scale weather modification. A brief examination of each of these hazards follows.

One of the most important requirements for space exploration is energy. It is needed both in propulsion for producing the required vehicle velocity and aboard spacecraft for the operation of various scientific instruments, for the execution of guidance and control commands, and for the transmission of radio signals. While for journeys of short duration with relatively light payloads, chemical propellants and conventional power plants (e.g., chemical fuel cells and storage batteries) will be adequate if not ideal, for journeys of long duration and for heavy payloads, more efficient and reliable sources of energy are necessary. Nuclear systems are generally considered the best answer to these needs. For example, the anticipated energy requirements for manned exploration of even the nearest planets to our earth—Mars and Venus—are so great that only nuclear energy can satisfy them.[85] Of more immediate interest is the prospect of a dramatic improvement in the cost-efficiency of future moon missions by the employment of a nuclear upper-stage which could increase the payload for a lunar landing by 60 to 70 percent on a direct launch. The use of nuclear power plants is also contemplated for the lunar stations which will house astronauts and their equipment.[86] Moreover, the functioning of satellites for direct broadcasting is believed almost impossible without nuclear reactors.[87] A wider application of nuclear power plants in outer space may be only a few years away; their use is planned in manned orbiting laboratories and in spaceships.[88]

These energy needs were foreseen very early and significant advances have been made to date in harnessing nuclear energy for space missions.[89] The United States and the Soviet Union are working on sev-

---

of warm Atlantic water across the Arctic Basin and reduce the access of the colder Pacific water).

[85] Glen T. Seaborg, "The Nuclear Path to Deep Space: A Report on Progress," *Air Force and Space Digest*, XLIX (April 1966), 69. See also "Electric Power Generation in Space," *NASA Facts* (NF-38/12-67).

[86] *Hearings on S. 2909* (fn. 40), 541-42.

[87] Jaffe (fn. 45), 166.

[88] *Hearings on S. 2909* (fn. 40), 670. Target date for the first flight of the NERVA nuclear rocket is 1976. *Aviation Week and Space Technology*, XC (January 20, 1969), 28.

[89] For a progress report on the U.S. space nuclear programs, see U.S., Congress, Senate, Committee on Aeronautical and Space Sciences, *Hearings on S. 1941*, 91st Cong., 1st Sess., 1969, Pt. 1, 368-79.

eral projects and both have already placed in orbit spacecraft carrying nuclear devices.[90] As these devices contain highly toxic substances (e.g., plutonium 238), they present a serious danger of radioactive pollution to the environment in which they operate—the area where the launching site is located, the atmosphere, the void of outer space, and celestial bodies.[91] The danger is not limited to accidental releases of radioactivity but includes also pollution caused by the exhaust from nuclear rockets. In this context it is important to appreciate that even low-level exposures to radiation may induce a variety of harmful somatic and hereditary effects. The anticipated increase in the number of space powers and the widening range of space missions will inevitably augment the risk of radioactive contamination.[92]

Another hazard facing the human race in the coming years (one which biologists are warning against) is the peril of interplanetary, or world-to-world, contamination. A possibility exists that astronauts and spacecraft returning to earth from journeys to celestial bodies will bring back microorganisms that could cause contamination of catastrophic proportions on our planet. The dimension of this hazard to man, animal, and plant life has been described as follows:

> Even if extraterrestrial organisms have a different chemistry, they may do incalculable damage on earth by multiplying wildly in com-

[90] At least four satellites launched by the U.S. Department of Defense since June 1961, have used electricity generated from the heat provided by radioisotopes. One of these units was still operating in 1966, after four and a half years in outer space. In April 1965, the U.S. launched into orbit a nuclear reactor which operated for 43 days, and during that period made 552 orbits around the earth. *Hearings on S. 2909* (fn. 40), 540-41. The Soviets are also reported to have launched into space two payloads containing radioisotope power supplies. Same, 558. NASA's meteorological satellite Nimbus-III, launched into orbit on April 14, 1969, carried aboard two SNAP-19 nuclear isotopic generators. Albert Ducrocq, "Au delà des 'Nimbus,'" *Air and Cosmos*, VII (April 26, 1969), 11, 13.

[91] As a result of a failure to achieve orbit, a U.S. Navy navigational satellite launched in May 1964 dumped into space 2.2 lbs. of plutonium 238. It was reported that this toxic material was "dispersed into fine particles suspended about 12,000 ft. above the West coast of Africa." *Missiles and Rockets*, XIV (June 1, 1964), 12. In May 1968, two nuclear generators carried by the Nimbus-B satellite, fell into the Pacific off the coast of California when the satellite was destroyed due to malfunction. The generators were recovered in October 1968. *New York Times*, October 11, 1968, p. 10, col. 1.

In the course of the second moon voyage, the crew of Apollo 12 deployed and activated on November 19, 1969, a so-called Apollo Lunar Surface Experiments Package (ALSEP). The ALSEP's energy source is a small nuclear reactor containing Plutonium 238. The package is expected to transmit scientific and engineering data to earth for at least a year. U.S., Congress, Senate, Committee on Aeronautical and Space Sciences, *Hearings on S. 3374*, 91st Cong., 2nd Sess., Pt. 1, 1970, 135-37.

[92] One should not forget the potential hazards of earth-based nuclear reactors. For a critical examination of these hazards and of the existing safety standards, see Sheldon Novick, *The Careless Atom* (Boston 1969).

petition with native plants. A more subtle danger is that they may upset the delicate chemical balance on which earthly life depends. An exotic organism living humbly in the soil might starve native plants by turning some vital nutrient, such as nitrogen, into a form they cannot use. If the earth's plants die of starvation, its animals, including man, will die too. Since the nature of extraterrestrial life is not known, the most farsighted scientists cannot imagine at present all the ways that it might affect earthly life.[93]

Concerned scientists caution that the threat of potential infection of our planet is not confined only to organisms brought back from celestial bodies believed to harbor life, such as Mars, for example; even on the seemingly lifeless moon there is at least a very remote possibility of finding in lunar soil and rock dormant forms of life that could be reactivated in contact with the earth with unpredictable consequences.[94] The immediacy of this threat is underscored by the fact that one of the most important scientific missions of the initial voyages to the moon is to bring back to earth samples of lunar materials. The point worth stressing is that the first manned lunar landing took place after only a most superficial instrumented investigation of the moon. Moreover, in May 1969, only two months before the moon landing, NASA announced that it had relaxed the original quarantine measures designed to prevent possible contamination of the earth's biosphere with substances brought back from the moon by the astronauts.[95] Since this decision was probably made on grounds other than impartial scientific advice, the episode provides an illustration of the somewhat casual attitude toward unknown biological risks. In this connection, it is instructive to remember that the Indians of North America were decimated by smallpox imported by European explorers, and that, in turn, Columbus's expedition brought back to Europe diseases which had not been known there before.

There is, however, an additional aspect of interplanetary contamination to consider, namely, the possibility of infecting celestial bodies with germs of earthly origin. Carelessly conducted planetary probes might forever remove a celestial body from use as a base for scientific investigation, for the search for extraterrestrial life, and for the collection of information that might lead to an understanding of the origin of life. With an eye to the planned instrumented and manned landings on Mars, a report prepared by an eminent panel of experts warned:

[93] *Time* (June 4, 1965), 52.
[94] Harold M. Schmeck, Jr., "Space Infection," in Walter Sullivan, ed., *America's Race to the Moon* (New York 1962), 117.
[95] *Aviation Week and Space Technology*, xc (May 26, 1969), 21.

Contamination of the Martian surface with terrestrial microbes could irrevocably destroy a truly unique opportunity for mankind to pursue a study of extraterrestrial life. Thus, while we are eager to press Martian exploration as expeditiously as the technology and other factors permit, we insist that our recommendation to proceed is subject to one rigorous qualification: that no viable terrestrial microorganisms reach the Martian surface until we can make a confident assessment of the consequences.[96]

Hence the conduct of interplanetary probes in the absence of appropriate safeguards and without the fullest understanding of the risks involved could cause incalculable damage to the scientific exploration of outer space.[97]

Programs designed to experiment with or alter weather patterns on our planet probably have the greatest potential for causing catastrophic deprivations to mankind. Man has been engaged in attempts to influence the weather since the beginning of recorded history, but only with the advent of space technology has he at last acquired the tools that promise success in this endeavor. Various proposed weather modification schemes assign artificial satellites a key role in the undertaking because they "provide an opportunity to conduct experiments that could not be performed by other methods, due to their unique position of being outside the Earth's atmosphere."[98] Such schemes in-

[96] Report by a panel on space research of the U.S. National Academy of Sciences. *New York Times*, April 27, 1965, p. 24, col. 4.

[97] A group of American scientists believes that the Soviet spacecraft which crashed on Mars and Venus have already transferred to these planets "a considerable number of viable terrestrial micro-organisms." B. C. Murray, M. E. Davis, and P. K. Eckman, *Planetary Contamination II: Soviet and U.S. Practices and Policies* (RAND Corporation paper, P-3517), March 1967).

That space-launching countries are not even complying with the modest sterilization standards prescribed by the Committee on Space Research [hereafter referred to as COSPAR], can be learned from resolution No. 21, adopted on May 21, 1968 by the Committee at its Tokyo meeting. In this resolution COSPAR's Assembly expressed "concern" about precautionary measures being taken by the launching nations to avoid biological contamination of the planets and noted that COSPAR's Panel on Standards of Space Probe Sterilization has not recently been active. *COSPAR Information Bulletin*, No. 45 (August 1968), 14.

[98] NASA, *A Survey of Space Applications* (Washington 1967), 102. The potentialities of satellite technology for inducing weather changes and the risks inherent in these activities are indicated in William J. Kotsch, "Weather Control and National Strategy," *U.S. Naval Institute Proceedings*, LXXXVI, No. 7 (July 1960), 74; Morris Neiburger, "Utilization of Space Vehicles for Weather Prediction and Control," in Simon Ramo, ed., *Peacetime Uses of Outer Space* (New York 1961), 153; Walter Orr Roberts, "Atmospheric Sciences for the Space Age," in NASA, *Fifth National Conference on the Peaceful Uses of Space* (Washington 1966), 40. A comprehensive account on weather and climate modification is offered in National Science Foundation, *Weather Modification* (Washington 1967).

clude artificially induced rainmaking over a limited area, the changing of the course or intensity of larger storm systems, increasing the amount of solar radiation received by portions of the earth's surface through the employment of orbital reflector satellites, and major alterations of climate over wide regions of the globe. Although no one can at this time predict with accuracy the date when large-scale modification of climate and control over precipitation will become feasible, few doubt that man will eventually develop this awesome power, perhaps to some extent in the present century.[99] The hazards inherent in such experiments are immense, more so if undertaken while fundamental knowledge about weather behavior is still inadequate and the effects of various technological applications on the balance of nature are largely unknown. According to an American authority:

> It is not certain that if we modify the atmosphere in one direction and initiate a chain of events leading towards a climatic change, we can then easily reverse the trend. It is also a fact of life today that man is, indeed, governed by his everyday operations—at least on a scale that makes it only prudent to investigate quantitatively by experiments of this kind. When we build great cities, like the megalopolis that stretches from New York to south of Washington; when we put a tremendous concentration of dust and smog into the atmosphere, modifying the radiative balance; when we pave larger and larger portions of our country and change the albedo, or reflectivity, of the Earth; when we fly jet airplanes which on many occasions increase the cirrus coverage or trigger off the more prompt occurrence of cirrus clouds (in turn altering the radiative loss from the Earth out to space)—in each of these cases we are altering the atmosphere, and we are far from understanding the full implications of these events, some of which *may* have irreversible effects.[100]

The ever-present possibility of causing, through tampering with the natural forces in one place, undesirable, even catastrophic, weather alterations in another, compounds the dangers inherent in these activities: "To destroy a typhoon threatening Kyushu, for example, might deprive a drought-ridden corner of India of needed rain or even parch Eastern Europe."[101] It requires no great imagination to realize that any major deliberate weather modification could have

[99] According to Herman Kahn and Myron S. Wiener in *The Year 2000* (New York 1967), 53, some control of weather and/or climate is "very likely" in the last third of the 20th century.

[100] Roberts (fn. 98), 43.

[101] "Forecast: A Weatherman in the Sky," *Reader's Digest*, LXXXIX (October 1966), 123 at 124.

serious transnational consequences, on occasion not unlike the effects of nuclear war. For that reason no country can afford to be indifferent to extensive weather control activities, no matter where or by whom they are undertaken.[102]

The above survey illustrates in some measure the range and magnitude of the risks that may face mankind as a result of future applications of space and related technologies. The growing concern of the world community relating to these risks was first expressed in the U.N. Declaration of Legal Principles, and, more recently, in the Space Treaty. In sum, the Treaty, like the Declaration, recognizes that participants in space exploration might undertake experiments with potentially detrimental effects on other states; it places an obligation upon the contracting parties to conduct their experiments in outer space so as to avoid its "harmful contamination and also adverse changes in the environment of the Earth resulting from the introduction of extraterrestrial matter"; and it provides, in general terms, for international consultation before any potentially harmful activity is undertaken.[103] Having thus established the principle of international consultation, the Treaty regrettably neither prescribes the procedure for such consultation nor designates the agency to which states may turn for an authoritative evaluation of proposed experiments. On the all-important question of the legal consequences of disagreement in the assessment of an experiment, the Treaty is similarly silent. But what may well be its main shortcoming, is that the Treaty allows each state to decide unilaterally which of its planned activities or experiments might cause deprivations to other states.[104] This, combined with the absence of a competent international control authority, could in practice render ineffectual the principle of consultation. One must therefore conclude that the provisions of the Space Treaty relating to control over potentially hazardous space activities are still too general and rudimentary to offer adequate protection to the world community.

Yet, to any one concerned with the maintenance of international public order, not to mention the well-being of the human race, the urgency of devising appropriate machinery and procedures for controlling ultrahazardous space schemes *before* they are undertaken is

---

[102] See Rita F. and Howard J. Taubenfeld, "The International Implications of Weather Modification," *Bulletin of the Atomic Scientists*, xxv (January 1969), 43; C. Wilfred Jenks, "Liability for Ultra-Hazardous Activities in International Law," *Recueil des Cours*, cxvii (1966-I), 105, 160ff.

[103] Space Treaty, Article IX.

[104] For a critical appraisal of the parallel provisions in the Declaration of Legal Principles, see Lachs (fn. 23), 73.

obvious.[105] A series of recent disasters—e.g., the vast pollution caused by the *Torrey Canyon* shipwreck, the widespread damage to marine life and to the beaches of Santa Barbara, California, by oil leaking from an off-shore well, and the poisoning by an insecticide of all species of fish throughout 200 miles of the river Rhine—have dramatically demonstrated the gravity of threats to the ecology of our planet and, at the same time, exposed the inadequacy of our legal institutions to cope with these rather conventional threats.[106] The world community cannot be expected to face the possibility of major disasters caused by the reckless applications of space technology armed only with a grossly imperfect Space Treaty, the *Trail Smelter Case*[107] analogies, and the elusive "general principles of international law."

Admittedly, the regulation of these complex issues while the fund of relevant technical criteria remains modest and the military implications of space activities continue high may be difficult, but that does not mean that preventive measures should not and cannot be undertaken without delay.[108] The time is long overdue for institutions which will reassert man's supremacy over science and technology and make certain that science and technology will serve and not govern life and human values. The alternative may be a repetition, probably on a much larger scale, of the tragic consequences of prolonged neglect in controlling air and water pollution. The most immediate need is for the establishment of an impartial and truly representative international organ with global responsibilities, preferably linked to the United Nations, to which all experiments and programs potentially harmful to the earth-space environment would have to be reported in advance and whose determination in each case would be final. "Without such an impartial body," as one commentator cogently notes, "the scientific-technological connotation inherent in the term 'harmful,

---

[105] See, e.g., Resolution of the Institut de Droit International on "The Legal Regime of Outer Space" (pars. 11 and 12) adopted in 1963. *Annuaire de l'Institut de Droit International*, L (1963-II), 369. See also, Jenks (fn. 9), 314, and especially, the "Draft Rules Concerning Changes in the Environment of the Earth," prepared by the David Davies Memorial Institute of International Studies, reproduced in same, at 430.

[106] Some cogent thoughts on the capability of contemporary international law to meet the new situations created by the growing pressures of galloping science and technology can be found in Schachter (fn. 3), 423.

[107] Trail Smelter Arbitral Tribunal: Decision [United States v. Canada], March 11, 1941. Text in *American Journal of International Law*, XXXV (October 1941), 684.

[108] The David Davies Institute's "Draft Rules" (fn. 105) provide a superb basis for an intelligent discussion of these issues. Many solutions therein expressed are clearly in the common interest and in accord with the spirit of the Space Treaty. For some valuable thoughts on the potential role of law in safeguarding the integrity of the natural environment against the more traditional hazards, see the Institute's *Principles Governing Certain Changes in the Environment of Man* (1968).

or potentially harmful effects,' would give way to the play of power politics hardly different from that embodied in the presently used terminology, i.e. 'the peaceful uses of outer space.' "[109] The mere existence of such a control agency, even if initially granted more modest authority, would tend to have a restraining effect upon nations planning risky experiments.

COSPAR's Consultative Group on Potentially Harmful Effects of Space Experiments, which already acts in a quasi-official capacity on behalf of the world community,[110] could initially be given this assignment, at least until a better solution is found. But to become fully effective, the Group would have to be formally designated as the authoritative international control organ and reconstructed in a way that would preclude special interests from dominating its decision-making processes.

IV. The Pattern of International Cooperation

During the past decade much has been said and written on the subject of international cooperation in the conquest of outer space and about the "great prospects opening up before mankind" as a result of advances in space science and technology. The highest officials of many nation-states, particularly of space powers, and of international organizations have often spoken of the potentialities and the desirability of joint action. The U.N. General Assembly resolutions abound

[109] F. B. Schick, "A Subjective Approach to the Work of the United Nations Committee on the Peaceful Uses of Outer Space," *Diritto Aereo*, V (1966), 204-212.

[110] The Group, consisting of seven experts, was established in 1962 and through COSPAR it has since closely collaborated with the U.N. Committee on the Peaceful Uses of Outer Space. In its report of November 13, 1964, the Committee recognized the scientific competence of the Group and urged that all member states "proposing to carry out experiments in space should give full consideration to the problem of possible interference with other peaceful uses of outer space, as well as of possible harmful changes in the natural environment caused by space activities and, where Member States consider it appropriate, should seek a scientific analysis of the qualitative and quantitative aspects of those experiments from the COSPAR Consultative Group of Potentially Harmful Effects of Space Experiments, and should give due consideration to the results of this analysis." U.N. Doc. A/5785, Annex II, Recommendation No. 33, November 13, 1964.

For the text of COSPAR's 1964 report and resolutions concerning the potentially harmful effects of space experiments, see Jenks (fn. 9), 402. In 1968 the Group published a revised version of its "Sterilization Techniques for Instruments and Materials Applied to Space Research." M. Roy, "Benefits of Membership in COSPAR," *COSPAR Information Bulletin*, No. 48 (February 1969), 5.

A study of measures for preventing adverse effects of space experiments upon terrestrial environment is also conducted by the World Meteorological Organization. The World Health Organization and the International Atomic Energy Agency are also expected by the United Nations to participate in the investigation of these problems. Details in *International Cooperation* (fn. 13), 301 (WMO), 322 (IAEA).

in references to the surpassing importance of outer-space cooperation "for the betterment of mankind and for the benefit of States regardless of their degree of scientific and economic development."[111] In addition to the World Weather Watch, still in its inception, several multilateral agreements and a host of bilateral arrangements are commonly invoked as evidence that opportunities for transnational collaboration in space activities have not been neglected. Among these agreements, those widely regarded as the most important are: the Washington agreements of 1964 establishing Intelsat; the Geneva ITU agreement of 1963 allocating radio frequencies for various space uses; the ELDO and ESRO conventions of 1962 setting up two regional organizations for a joint exploration of outer space; and the United States-U.S.S.R. agreement which was originally concluded in 1962. In a further favorite illustration of the scope of international space cooperation, we are often reminded that the United States alone has dozens of bilateral agreements with countries as dissimilar from each other as the United Kingdom and Malagasy Republic.[112] To this seemingly vast network of joint activities, it is common to add the cooperative efforts conducted within the United Nations and its specialized agencies more intimately concerned with outer space problems, such as the World Meteorological Organization, ITU, and UNESCO, and within several nongovernmental organizations, notably COSPAR.

However, when this impressive formal evidence of international cooperation is more closely analyzed, the image of an apparently massive joint assault on outer space begins to fade rapidly, revealing a somewhat different reality. Despite the fact that advances in space science and technology have created new opportunities for the enhancement of a meaningful international cooperation and still further increased the interdependence of peoples everywhere, these opportunities remain largely neglected and the tangible benefits of space exploration are—more than a decade after Sputnik—still confined to only the most advanced and affluent countries. As U Thant has pointed out: "The space age is increasing the gap between the developed and

---

[111] Declaration of Legal Principles, U.N. G.A. Res. 1962 (XVIII) of December 13, 1963. See also, e.g., Space Treaty of 1967; U.N. G.A. Res. 1472 (XIV), of December 12, 1959; and U.N. G.A. Res. 1721 (XVI) of December 20, 1961.

[112] Texts of these agreements are reprinted in U.S., Congress, Senate, Committee on Aeronautical and Space Sciences, *United States International Space Programs*, 89th Cong., 1st Sess., 1965 [hereafter cited as *U.S. Space Programs*]. See also Arthur J. Goldberg, "International Cooperation in Outer Space," *Department of State Bulletin*, LIV (January 31, 1966), 163. More recent data on U.S. transnational space cooperation is in U.S., Congress, Senate, Committee on Aeronautical and Space Sciences, *Hearings on S. 2918*, 90th Cong., 2d Sess., 1968, Pt. 1, 55-60.

developing areas at an alarming rate."[113] The great expectations aroused with the advent of space technology in the less-developed nations have been only modestly fulfilled. Furthermore, even at this time, the agenda of the U.N. Outer Space Committee contains no items relating to the preparation of agreements envisaging major international space programs for the principal benefit of these nations. A review of relevant developments to date tends to confirm this appraisal.[114]

The two widely hailed multilateral agreements—the ITU Radio Regulations of 1963 and the Intelsat agreements—both relate to satellite communications, a type of enterprise which few citizens of the underdeveloped countries could afford to use in the immediate future without massive external assistance, and which, therefore, will probably for some time to come benefit primarily members of the affluent societies. That the needs of these privileged groups of users were foremost in the minds of those responsible for the inauguration of the first satellite communications system is evident both from the structure of Intelsat and the explanations offered in justification of the unequal allocation of managerial authority under the Washington agreements.[115]

The proposed Soviet global communications satellite system—Intersputnik—which was supposed to correct the undemocratic features of Intelsat and thus appeal to the developing countries, exists at this time only on paper.[116]

Cooperation along regional lines, apart from being painfully slow

[113] U Thant in a note addressed to the 1968 Vienna Conference on the Exploration and Peaceful Uses of Outer Space. U.N. Doc. A/AC.105/L.44, September 20, 1968, 1.

[114] For a more optimistic, official, survey, see U.N. Doc. A/AC.105/L.40, May 31, 1968.

[115] The 1964 Washington agreements grant to the Comsat Corporation at least 50.6 out of 100 votes on the Intelsat's governing board. Countries with a quota smaller than 1.5 percent, and the majority of the participants in the Consortium belong to this group, are not eligible for the governing board, unless two or more such countries, whose combined quotas amount to no less than 1.5 percent, elect a joint representative. For the U.S. position on the eve of the Conference on Definitive Arrangements for the Intelsat Consortium which convened in Washington on February 24, 1969, see *Department of State Bulletin*, LX (March 17, 1969), 224. After two plenipotentiary conferences, the second concluded in March 1970, members of Intelsat were still unable to agree on the text of the permanent treaty.

[116] For text of the "Draft Agreement on the Establishment of an International Communications System Using Artificial Earth Satellites," placed before the United Nations by the Soviet Union and seven other Communist countries (Bulgaria, Cuba, Czechoslovakia, Hungary, Mongolia, Poland, and Roumania), see U.N. Doc. A/AC.105/46, August 9, 1968.

in expanding, has yet to embrace the areas that need it most. The two major regional organizations for space exploration—ELDO and ESRO—consist of a handful of the most economically and technologically advanced states in the world.[117] The main concern of these organizations is and will probably remain for some time the development of space science and technology within the West European community, and for that reason the underdeveloped countries cannot expect in the near future much aid from this source. The prospects for these countries are not made any brighter by the current trend which obviously favors space cooperation among equals.

Examination of bilateral agreements on space cooperation concluded by NASA reveals that their principal beneficiaries are again the advanced nations. The usefulness of these agreements to the United States' space effort is obvious; many such agreements provide for the establishment, maintenance, and operation of NASA's tracking, command, and data acquisition facilities on the territory of the other contracting party, and for assistance in the testing of experimental satellites launched by NASA. Without the agreements the U.S. would experience considerable difficulties in the conduct of its space activities.[118] However, the technologically advanced partners of the

[117] For the text of the conventions establishing ELDO (European Space Vehicle Launcher Development Organization) and ESRO (European Space Research Organization) and a list of the contracting parties, see *International Cooperation* (fn. 13), 509 (ESRO), 522 (ELDO). Europe has another intergovernmental organization in the European Conference on Satellite Communications, established in 1963. The purpose of this organization is to coordinate European views on the Intelsat arrangements and to stimulate European programs of satellite research and development. U.N. Doc. A/AC.105/L.40, May 31, 1968.

Late in 1960, on the initiative of Argentina, the Inter-American Committee for Space Research was founded in Buenos Aires. The objective of this nongovernmental body is to "promote space research in the Latin American countries and assist in the creation of national bodies to encourage and co-ordinate space-related activities in the Latin American countries." Few of these countries have shown much interest in this Committee whose sole activity has been to hold occasional meetings of experts. See U.N. Doc. cited above, 99-101.

[118] See, e.g., U.S. agreements with Australia, Brazil, Canada, France, Germany, Italy, Japan, the Scandinavian countries, and Great Britain, in *U.S. Space Programs* (fn. 112). For example, the flight of Apollo 10 spacecraft, whose lunar module came within 9 miles of the moon's surface in May 1969, was tracked by a network of 17 ground stations. In addition to tracking stations on U.S. territory, stations in Bermuda, the Canary Islands, Australia, Spain, and Mexico were involved. *NASA News Release* No. 69-68 (May 7, 1969), 86.

The importance of appropriately deployed tracking facilities for major space activities was demonstrated by the Soviet effort to have the Space Treaty include a provision which would guarantee equal tracking facilities to all contracting parties under equal terms. The purpose of the Soviet proposal was obviously to obtain the tracking facilities of the vast network established by the U.S. through bilateral agreements with more than 20 countries. The version adopted in the

United States also receive significant benefits through bilateral exchanges. It is for countries such as the United Kingdom, Canada, Italy, France, Australia, and West Germany that the United States has provided the facilities necessary to enable them to place into orbit their national satellites; the next nation to benefit in the same manner will be Japan (since February 11, 1970, a space power in its own right). The nations of Western Europe have similarly profited through the launching by the United States of three ESRO-built satellites.[119]

In contrast, the benefits accruing to the bilateral partners of the United States who have only their territory to offer in exchange are minimal. In a typical agreement, the United States has agreed to build and operate a space vehicle tracking and communications station in Madagascar, whereas the government of the Malagasy Republic has undertaken to ensure that "land areas and rights-of-way required for the station shall be leased" to the United States.[120] The latter also undertakes, among other things, to pay the cost relating to the construction and operation of the facility, to employ local subcontractors, if available, and local labor, and to make "maximum use of materials and supplies available locally."[121] The agreement further provides that "qualified local personnel shall be utilized in connection with the operation and maintenance of the station to the maximum extent feasible,"[122] and that scientific data obtained by the station shall be shared with the Malagasy authorities as well as with the world scientific community.[123] Concluded in 1963, this agreement gave the United States the right to terminate it at any time within four years,

---

Treaty (Article X) merely states that requests for opportunities to observe the flight of spacecraft "shall be considered" on a basis of equality. The specific arrangements for such undertakings are to be determined by agreement between the countries concerned.

[119] The basic agreement between ESRO and the U.S., providing for cooperative launching of ESRO satellites, is reproduced in *U.S. Space Programs* (fn. 112), 315. On November 28, 1966, an additional agreement was concluded between the same parties providing for the establishment of an ESRO telemetry and telecommand station near Fairbanks, Alaska. For text of this agreement see *Department of State Bulletin*, LV (December 26, 1966), 979.

Commenting upon the U.S. international cooperative programs, James E. Webb, then the NASA Administrator, said that the "expenditures which cooperating countries are undertaking in these joint activities exceed our own [i.e., U.S.] costs allocated to them by something like two to one." *National Space Goals* (fn. 36), 12.

[120] Agreement between the United States and the Malagasy Republic effected by exchange of notes and signed at Tananarive October 7, 1963, Par. (2)A. *U.S. Space Programs* (fn. 112), 95.

[121] U.S.-Malagasy Agreement, Pars. (1) and (5).

[122] Same, Par. (7).

[123] Same, Par. (9)C.

"after appropriate advance notice," by closing the station.[124] In a similar agreement with Ecuador, originally concluded in 1960 and renewed in 1965,[125] the United States has undertaken the additional obligation of training a "limited number of qualified Ecuadorean personnel" in the operation of the tracking station, with no charge to the government of Ecuador.[126]

The record in space cooperation of the Soviet Union is incomparably poorer and directly contradicts its professed internationalistic ideology. The agreements concluded by the Soviets with other countries are few in number and limited in scope.[127] For example, among the almost five hundred satellites launched between 1957 and 1970 by the U.S.S.R., there is not a single one which was placed in orbit as a result of a cooperative effort. Ironically, while the Soviet Union does not seem to be particularly eager to enter into major space collaboration even with its Warsaw Pact allies,[128] much less with the underde-

[124] Same, Par. (11). In March 1967, the personnel of the Tananarive (Malagasy) station consisted of 89 U.S. nationals and 76 foreigners. U.S., Congress, Senate, Committee on Aeronautical and Space Sciences, *Hearings on S. 1296*, 90th Cong., 1st Sess., 1967, Pt. 2, 945. How many of the Malagasy citizens were assigned to menial chores in and around the station and how many to technical services, the available statistics do not reveal. However, the fact that after several years of operation the majority of the station's personnel were U.S. nationals suggests that not many locally recruited employees had been trained as replacements.

In view of the exceedingly generous terms given the space power in such bilateral agreements, one might expect that upon fulfilling its purpose, the tracking station would be transferred intact to the host country for its own use. The procedure attending the closing of the Kano station in Nigeria, following completion of the Gemini program, shows that such is not the case. NASA's Associate Administrator for Tracking and Data Acquisition described the procedure in these words: "We brought out all the portable equipment at Kano and shipped it back to the United States. The large antenna towers were not worth taking down. . . . It was not an economical proposition. The building itself, was a sheet metal structure. Once again, it was not an economical proposition to dismantle this and bring it back to this country. . . . All our electronic equipment was returned to the United States." Same, 943.

[125] Agreement Relating to a Cooperative Program in Ecuador for the Observation and Tracking of Satellites and Space Vehicles, signed at Quito on February 24, 1960, and Extension of the Agreement signed at Quito on May 10, 1965. Texts in *U.S. Space Programs* (fn. 112), 81.

[126] U.S.-Ecuador Agreement, Article IV; Extension of the Agreement, Article IV.

[127] For an account by a Russian author, see V. S. Vereshchetin, "Legal Forms of International Cooperation of the USSR in the Peaceful Utilization of Outer Space," *Sovetskoe Gosudarstvo i Pravo* (No. 1, 1967), 69. See also U.S., Congress, Senate, Committee on Aeronautical and Space Sciences, *Soviet Space Programs, 1962-65: Goals and Purposes, Achievements, Plans and International Implications*, 89th Cong., 2d Sess., 1966, 425ff [hereafter cited as *Soviet Space Programs*].

[128] The beginning of the Soviet Union's attempts toward some form of institutionalized cooperation with other Communist nations can be traced to an inter-bloc conference held in Moscow in November 1965. At the conference—attended by Bulgaria, Cuba, Czechoslovakia, East Germany, Hungary, Mongolia, Poland, and Roumania, in addition to the U.S.S.R.—it was agreed that the Soviets will

veloped countries[129] whose cause it so vigorously champions in the world's forums, in 1966 it concluded an agreement to undertake an ambitious program with France—a member of NATO and a highly developed nation.[130] Even the Intersputnik proposal, announced during the 1968 United Nations Space Conference, presumably for maximum publicity impact, could be construed as a propaganda maneuver rather than a genuine plan for international cooperation. The record of the third space power—France—is similar. Its most comprehensive bilateral space agreements are with the United States and the Soviet Union, and with the Federal Republic of Germany.[131]

The prime example of missed opportunities for maximizing the potential benefits of new technology through cooperative arrange-

---

provide the facilities for the launching of artificial satellites built by one or several of their allies. Same, 482, n. 156a. As of April 1970, no such launchings have taken place. On October 14 and December 25, 1969, the U.S.S.R. launched two satellites— "Intercosmos 1" and "Intercosmos 2"—which carried aboard scientific instruments built by several of its Warsaw Pact allies. This exception notwithstanding, Soviet cooperation with the bloc countries appears to be limited to exchanges of scientific data and optical tracking of Soviet spacecraft.

On December 28, 1966, *Pravda* reported that an agreement had been reached between the Soviet Union and Cuba on construction in Cuba of a communications station linked to Moscow through satellites. According to *Pravda*, the "construction and operation of this station will be carried out jointly by Soviet and Cuban specialists on the basis of the accord reached at the conference of representatives of the socialist countries in Moscow in the exploration and utilization of outer space." *Current Digest of the Soviet Press*, XVIII (January 18, 1967), 28. A similar agreement has since been concluded with Mongolia.

[129] The Soviet attitude toward space cooperation with the underdeveloped countries is illustrated by the magnitude of the contribution it made to the Thumba International Equatorial Rocket Launching Station in India. To this U.N. sponsored project, the U.S.S.R. has contributed one helicopter, one computer, and one "shake table." See U.N. Doc. A/AC.105/L.30, Annex I, September 1, 1966, 8.

[130] The agreement with France, signed at Moscow on June 30, 1966, is by far the most extensive cooperative program undertaken to date by the Soviet Union. It covers cooperation in space meteorology and telecommunications, exchange of scientists and information, and the launching of a French satellite from Soviet facilities. Text in *International Legal Materials*, VI (Washington 1967), 303.

[131] It seems that the principal cooperative project for France in the near future will be the construction with West Germany of an operational communications satellite designated "Symphonie." The project is based on a special treaty concluded between the two participating countries on June 6, 1967. The text of the treaty is reprinted in *Revue Française de Droit Aérien*, XXII (October-December 1968), 446. The Symphonie satellite is designed to cover Europe, large parts of Africa and South America, and the east coast of Canada and the United States. *Air and Cosmos*, VI (November 2, 1968), 15.

On March 10, 1970, as part of the Franco-German space collaboration, a West German satellite was successfully orbited aboard a French rocket launched from France's equatorial launch site in Guiana. *New York Times*, March 11, 1970, p. 6, col. 8.

ments is provided by the history of Soviet-American space relations.[132] Before the official announcement of the first United States-U.S.S.R. space agreement but after it became known that the negotiations were being held, hopes were entertained throughout the world that a new phase in the conquest of space was about to begin. However, upon the publication of the text of the agreement[133] it became obvious that even if fully carried out, the undertakings of the two space powers would only modestly contribute to the fund of human knowledge and to the more important objectives of international cooperation. Compared with the then existing practical possibilities of cooperation, the scope of the agreement was trivial. It provided for Soviet optical observation of the U.S. Echo II passive communication satellite; joint mapping of the geomagnetic field; and a regular exchange of meteorological data through the establishment of the Washington-Moscow communications link. Subsequent additional agreements did little to alter substantially the limited scope of the original undertaking.[134]

The unexpectedly rapid development of space science and technology, coupled with the apparent determination of both superpowers to embark upon the enormously expensive venture of landing men on the moon before 1970, presented especially favorable conditions for a major joint enterprise. The benefits that could thereby accrue to each participant and to the rest of the world community did not go unnoticed by their respective leaders. Thus in a letter of March 20, 1962, the Soviet Premier wrote to President Kennedy:

> ... I note with satisfaction that my communication to you of February 21 containing the proposal that our two countries unite their efforts for the conquest of space has met with the necessary understanding on the part of the Government of the United States.
>
> In advancing this proposal, we proceeded from the fact that *all peoples and all mankind are interested in achieving the objective of exploration and peaceful use of outer space,* and that the enormous scale of this task, as well as the *enormous difficulties which must be overcome, urgently demand broad unification of the scientific, technical, and material capabilities and resources of nations.*

[132] For an account, see *Soviet Space Programs* (fn. 127), 430ff.

[133] The texts of the original Dryden-Blagonravov Memorandum of Understanding, agreed upon on June 8, 1962, and of subsequent additional arrangements are reproduced in *U.S. Space Programs* (fn. 112), 409ff.

[134] The sum total of Soviet-U.S. cooperation as of March 1969, amounted to the following: exchange of information at meetings of scientists and engineers; trading of space-collected weather pictures; some coordination of efforts on geomagnetism; and attempts to write jointly a textbook on space biology. *Hearings on S. 1941* (fn. 89), 90.

The greater the number of countries making their contribution to this truly complicated endeavor, which involves great expense, the more swiftly will the conquest of space in the interests of all humanity proceed. And this means that *equal opportunities should be made available for all countries* to participate in international cooperation in this field. It is precisely this kind of international cooperation that the Soviet Union unswervingly advocates, true to its policy of developing and strengthening friendship between peoples.[135] (Emphasis added.)

However, at the end of his letter, almost as an afterthought, the Premier made the scope of such cooperation conditional upon the solution of the disarmament problem. "Considerably broader prospects for cooperation and uniting our scientific-technological achievements," he observed, "up to and including joint construction of spacecraft for reaching other planets—the moon, Venus, Mars—will arise when agreement on disarmament has been achieved."[136] The first Soviet-American space agreement, concluded a few months later, failed to incorporate any major joint programs.

In his last appearance before the United Nations, President Kennedy, in reference to areas where the United States and the Soviet Union could profitably cooperate, specifically suggested joint moon expeditions:

> Space offers no problem of sovereignty; by resolution of this Assembly, the members of the United Nations have forsworn any claim to territorial rights in outer space or on celestial bodies and declared that international law and the United Nations Charter will apply. Why, therefore, should man's first flight up to the moon be a matter of national competition? Why should the United States and the Soviet Union, in preparing for such expeditions, become involved in immense duplications of research, construction, and expenditure? Surely we should explore whether the scientists and astronauts of our two countries—indeed, of all the world—cannot work together in the conquest of space, sending some day in this decade to the moon not the representatives of a single nation but the representative of all of our countries.[137]

As is well known, the President's suggestions failed to materialize. What is worse, no serious attempt has been made or is now contem-

135 U.S., Congress, Senate, Committee on Aeronautical and Space Sciences, *Documents on International Aspects of the Exploration and Use of Outer Space, 1954-62*, 88th Cong., 1st Sess., 1963, S. Doc. No. 18, 248-51.

136 Same, 251.

137 U.S. Arms Control and Disarmament Agency, *Documents on Disarmament 1963* (Washington 1964), 528-29.

plated by either side to explore the possibilities of even a partial implementation of these rational proposals; competition rather than
cooperation characterizes U.S.-Soviet relations.

It is often asserted, and apparently with good reason, that the most
productive exchanges on matters relating to space exploration have
taken place through the United Nations specialized agencies and
through nonpolitical scientific organizations. While this may be true,
it is only fair to state that the restricted financial and manpower
resources of organizations such as the World Meteorological Organization or UNESCO severely limit their usefulness, especially to the
developing countries. As far as the nongovernmental organizations are
concerned, notably the International Council of Scientific Unions,
its member unions, and COSPAR, their limitations are still greater.
The essential condition for a meaningful participation in these organizations is a nucleus of highly skilled scientists within a member country, and that commodity is exceedingly scarce in many parts of the
world. Furthermore, the most directly relevant and the most active
among these nongovernmental entities—COSPAR—is "primarily a
means of communication, a coordinating body, and a non-partisan
forum in which scientific methods, problems, and results can be discussed."[138] So far the principal beneficiaries of these activities have
been the advanced nations which, not surprisingly, also account for
the majority of the membership.[139] Not one among all these governmental and private organizations is at the moment either equipped
or authorized to engage in any major outer-space undertakings.[140]

Some of the more important achievements and problems in the
legal regulation of space activities were outlined at the beginning of
this essay. The achievements must, of course, be attributed to the
readiness on the part of all states to cooperate in building a public
order in space. At this point, however, it is necessary to call attention
to a peculiar pattern of decision-making in outer space matters which

[138] Harold L. Goodwin, *Space: Frontier Unlimited* (Princeton 1962), 101. For
a fuller description of COSPAR's organizational structure and functions, see
International Cooperation (fn. 13), 378-400; 493-96.

[139] The present membership of ICSU stands at 59 nations and of COSPAR at
36. U.N. Doc. A/AC.105/L.40, May 31, 1968, 73 and 82-83.

[140] In the twelve years since Sputnik, the only tangible results of U.N. assistance
to the developing countries in matters relating to space science and technology
are: the sponsorship (granted in December 1965) of the Thumba Equatorial
Launching Station (TERLS) in India; the establishment by ITU of a center for
research and training in space communications at Ahmedabad (India); training
seminars conducted by WMO; preparation by UNESCO of a plan for the introduction in India of nationwide television for education. See, e.g., U.N. Doc. A/AC.
105/L.40, May 31, 1968, 9, 18, 27, 30.

has emerged in recent years, a pattern whose prolonged continuation cannot but negatively affect the future of space law and of international legal order as well. Even a superficial observer of the recent past must have noted that two nation-states, together controlling perhaps 90 percent of the world's nuclear and space power, have often been able to determine not only the substance of legal decisions affecting outer space but also the time when such decisions will be taken. In the early days of space exploration it seemed that the impact on the decision-making process of at least the middle-sized powers, if not of the minor ones, would be substantial though not necessarily decisive. Subsequent events, however, made it increasingly clear that neither the middle powers nor the new states possessed sufficient influence to effectively participate in the process.

In a semiformal manner, this situation was consecrated in 1962 by an agreement among the members of the U.N. Space Committee to dispense with voting and to reach all decisions on matters of substance unanimously.[141] While in theory this arrangement confers upon each of the 28 members of the Committee a veto power, in practice such power is accorded only to the United States and the Soviet Union. An attempt by a smaller country to have its proposals adopted will almost certainly be doomed to failure unless both superpowers find them acceptable. By and large, the role of the 26 members of the U.N. Space Committee has been reduced to efforts to reconcile differences between the United States and the Soviet Union. Before any proposal is formally put on the agenda of the Legal Subcommittee (or of its parent Committee), it appears that the uppermost consideration of the would-be proponent, and of most other members in the group, is not so much the urgency or the soundness of the proposal itself but whether it will be acceptable to at least one superpower, if not to both. The whole process of codification is largely geared to the desires of the Soviet Union and the United States. A few examples will illustrate the point.

The reader may recall that in the early years of the space age the question of fixing the boundaries between national airspace and free outer space was widely believed to be a problem in urgent need of international solution.[142] From the outset, however, the governments of the United States and of the Soviet Union made it known that they considered the raising of the issue premature. As a result, despite the efforts of some states to have the problem examined in

[141] U.N. Doc. A/AC.105/P.V.2, March 19, 1962, 5.
[142] A review of various proposals is provided in McDougal, Lasswell, and Vlasic (fn. 9), 323-59.

the U.N. Space Committee, the subject was given low priority.[143] The question of boundaries was finally placed on the agenda of the Legal Subcommittee in 1967, mainly on the insistence of France and several other countries. Even then, however, through the efforts of the United States and the Soviet Union the problem was sent for "technical" advice to the sister Scientific and Technical Subcommittee, which to this day has been unable (or unwilling) to provide the requested information. The genesis of the Space Treaty is another example. Since 1962 the Legal Subcommittee has been engaged in preparing a draft convention on liability for damage caused by space activities and a draft convention on assistance to astronauts in distress. By the end of 1965, the opinion had crystalized that the area of agreement was broad enough to permit the completion of the task, provided the Subcommittee would concentrate its future efforts on these two items. Accordingly, General Assembly Resolution 2130(XX) adopted on December 21, 1965, "urged" the Space Committee "to continue with determination" the preparation of these agreements. It was assumed that the Subcommittee would refrain from dealing with any other topic until these priority items were ready for submission to the General Assembly. However, when in May 1966, first the United States and then the Soviet Union suddenly decided they wanted a treaty on matters already covered by the Declaration of Legal Principles and by General Assembly Resolution 1884(XVIII), and requested a special session of the Legal Subcommittee for that purpose,[144] the commitment undertaken only six months earlier was readily forgotten and members of the Subcommittee soon embarked upon drafting a document which they knew would add little of substance to the policies enunciated with universal approval in 1963.[145] The history of the Treaty on Rescue and Return of Astronauts and Space Objects provides another example, in more than one way. In the first place, with so many other urgent problems unsolved, it is legitimate to question the high priority given this issue, not merely because it affects only two nations but also because the 1963 Declaration of Legal Principles had already provided astronauts with adequate protection. Secondly, by the end of 1967, following numerous unproductive meetings of the

[143] The boundary issue was for the first time acknowledged by the General Assembly in Resolution 2222 (XXI), of December 19, 1966. The Resolution requested the Committee on the Peaceful Uses of Outer Space, inter alia, to "begin . . . the study of questions relative to the definition of outer space . . ."

[144] See U.N. Doc. A/6341, May 31, 1966, for Soviet request, and U.N. Doc. A/AC. 105/32, June 17, 1966, for U.S. request.

[145] The Legal Subcommittee acted with unprecedented speed. The Soviet Union and the United States submitted their draft treaties on June 16, 1966, and the Subcommittee held its first working session in Geneva on July 12, 1966. U.N. Doc. A/AC.105/C.2/SR.57, July 18, 1966.

Legal Subcommittee, the prospects of reaching agreement during the twenty-second session of the General Assembly looked dim. Then, five days short of the adjournment of the General Assembly, the Subcommittee was suddenly convened in a special session at the request of the U.S. and U.S.S.R. and presented with the complete text of the treaty that had been bilaterally agreed by the two nations. With minor revisions, this text was unanimously approved by the General Assembly on December 19, 1967.[146]

The practice of the International Civil Aviation Organization offers comparable illustration of continuing deference to the desires of the superpowers. Although the necessity for studying the potential effects of space activities upon air navigation was brought to the attention of ICAO as early as 1956,[147] this organization formally discovered that "many of these activities affect matters falling within" its competence only in 1965.[148] The principal cause of ICAO's reluctance to concern itself with the problem is widely attributed to the influence of one of its powerful member states.[149]

The phenomenon described above and its potential implications for the future of space law and world public order generally, has been accorded far too little attention. Presumably, since consensus in the contemporary arena of politics is a scarce commodity, when achieved

[146] See Dembling and Arons (fn. 32), 630, esp. 638-41.

[147] During the 10th session of the ICAO Assembly, held in 1956 in Caracas, the report of the Legal Commission drew the attention of the Assembly to the anticipated space launchings and expressed the view that the Organization should concern itself with the problems of space flight. No action, however, was taken on this report. ICAO's "extremely cautious approach to the entire question of outer space activities," is discussed in *International Cooperation* (fn. 13), 340ff.

[148] At its 15th session held in 1965, the ICAO Assembly finally committed the Organization to a program of study "of those technical aspects of space activities that affect international air navigation. . . ." However, among the subjects to be studied, priority was given to meteorology and communications; legal problems are not even mentioned. U.N. Doc. A./AC.105/C.1/L.9, April 4, 1966, 34. See also "The Impact of Space Developments on Civil Aviation," *ICAO Bulletin*, XXIII (August 1968), 7.

[149] *International Cooperation* (fn. 13), 341-42. A more recent example of the virtual monopoly on decision-making held by the space powers was provided by the postponement of the U.N. Conference on the Exploration and Peaceful Uses of Outer Space, on request of the Soviet Union. Ironically, it was primarily on the urging of the U.S.S.R. that the U.N. "unanimously" decided to convene this conference in September 1967 in Vienna. U.N. G.A. Res. 2221 (XXI) of December 19, 1966. The date of the Conference was to coincide with the celebration of the tenth anniversary of the launching of Sputnik I. See statement by A. Blagonravov in U.N. Doc. A/AC.105/WG.I/SR.1-5, March 14, 1966, 10. Without giving any convincing reasons, the Soviets requested in early February 1967 that the Conference be indefinitely postponed and the Committee on the Peaceful Uses of Outer Space, on February 13, 1967, "unanimously" obliged. The Conference was eventually held in August of 1968. A summary of its proceeding is in U.N. Doc. A/AC.105/L.44, September 20, 1968.

it seems to generate euphoria which all but precludes a balanced appraisal of its overall effects. The point argued here, it must be emphasized, should not be mistaken for a plea to deny a special role in the world decision-making process to the superpowers, or as opposition to the principle of unanimity. The burden of responsibility which great powers carry in the world community should appropriately be reflected in the voice accorded them in the legal process. But that is not the same as conceding that these powers should hold a virtual monopoly on decision-making, the outcomes of which, after all, affect other nations as well. While enforced unanimity may on occasion accelerate agreement on some issues and thus contribute to the short-term interest in the evolution of a particular branch of international law, it would be unwise to dismiss too lightly its potential long-term consequences upon the elite of the new nation-states and upon the quality of participation of these states in the world lawmaking process.

Many of the so-called new states feel, as do the Communist states, that they cannot be automatically bound by traditional international law since they did not directly participate in its evolution.[150] Upon achieving independence, they have been admitted to the world's arenas of authority where formally they enjoy a status of equality with the older powers. Yet, to be formally an equal member of a decision-making body and in fact have no effective influence on its decision-making would seem to be bound to cause frustration leading eventually to alienation. If the present trend is permitted to continue, it should not come as a surprise when the current passive acceptance of their *de facto* inferior status at some point turns into obstructionism or withdrawal.[151] Obstructionism could express itself in many different ways. For example, nations so alienated could seriously interfere with future space activities by claiming sovereignty or "jurisdiction and control" to an altitude above the low orbits of spacecraft (i.e., 90 to 100 miles), and/or by refusing to grant transit rights through their airspace to foreign spacecraft, except for an exorbitant price.

150 "[C]onsiderable pessimism is expressed in some quarters," observes an eminent authority, "as to the prospects of codification under present conditions, when the Communist bloc challenge customary rules which do not suit them and and the new States of Africa and Asia are inclined to question customary law developed from the practice of European states." James L. Brierly, *The Law of Nations*, 6th edn. by Sir Humphrey Waldock (New York 1963), 85. An appraisal of the participation of the emerging nations in the development of international law can be found in Richard A. Falk, "The New States and International Legal Order," *Recueil des Cours*, CXVIII (1966-II), 1.

151 The temporary withdrawal of Indonesia from the United Nations and the continuing abuse of the world organization by the People's Republic of China may not be in this context entirely irrelevant phenomena.

The great powers could probably afford to pursue most of their space goals by ignoring such artificial obstacles, but the inevitable result of this practice would be a still further deterioration of relations among states, leading to a major breakdown of international legal order.

It requires no great wisdom to realize that this situation is directly related to the growing "capability gap" between a few technologically and economically advanced countries and the rest of the family of nations. Tremendous advances in science and technology achieved in recent decades have contributed little "to brighten the prospects of those who occupy the two-thirds of the world where poverty, disease, ignorance and lack of opportunity are the most conspicuous facts of daily life."[152] Science, in the apt words of one concerned observer, "in reaching for the planets and in probing into the genetic code, has somehow lost contact with the needs and aspirations of common humanity."[153] For the majority of the peoples of the world the promise of a new era of greater abundance and equality as a result of the advent of space exploration may remain no more than a promise unless corrective policies are devised and implemented without delay.[154]

The consequences of sharing the benefits of space technology with the underdeveloped countries can be reasonably expected to spread far beyond the problem of building a legal order in outer space. As the once monolithic power blocs continue to disintegrate, very different alignments are emerging in their place. The postwar division of the world into "free" and "Communist" states has lost much of its meaning; it is increasingly obvious that the distinctions between "haves" and "have-nots," or "rich" and "poor," will in the future far more deeply affect world public order than any conventional ideological distinctions. These developments strongly suggest that the preservation of our planet as a livable place will to an important degree depend upon success in securing the full participation of the new communities in the benefits which modern science and technology

152 Secretary-General U Thant, in his introduction to the annual report on the work of the United Nations, submitted on September 18, 1966. *New York Times*, September 19, 1966, p. 18, col. 5.

153 Schachter (fn. 3), 423, 429.

154 How to underestimate the expectations of the peoples of the world in regard to space activities may be illustrated in the following example. Speaking in the United Nations on the necessity of developing a transnational "sense of participation" in the space adventure, Ambassador Goldberg in all seriousness suggested that the "live radio and television reporting of our [U.S.] manned flight projects allows . . . this sense of identification." Goldberg (fn. 112), 163, 165. It is just as possible that the watching of the American space launchings enhances among the impoverished masses of the world a sense of nonparticipation and nonidentification.

have made possible. Traditional forms of "aid," such as loans, ship-ments of food, and technical assistance, while valuable, have demon-strably failed to alter the plight of the recipient communities.[155] The main weakness inherent in this modality of assistance, however, is not so much that it often comes too late and provides too little but that it is unable to create in the recipient the feeling of creative participa-tion. This can only be achieved if the peoples of the developing coun-tries are afforded the opportunity to take a direct part in activities which are materially beneficial to them and which generate self-respect, self-reliance, and a sense of belonging as an equal to the community of men. Meaningful space programs, undertaken by and for the benefit of the entire world community would seem, in contrast to the present forms of aid, ideal for the achievement of this over-riding objective.

Artificial satellites are already in use for many beneficial purposes such as weather forecasting and cloud survey, for global transmission of voices and data, for transcontinental television broadcasting, for mapping and navigation, and for scientific investigation of the earth environment and of the solar system. This is an impressive record considering that it was achieved largely through the unilateral efforts of a handful of countries and with only a modest degree of inter-national cooperation. Through joint ventures all these uses could be greatly expanded in the near future and new uses developed with ultimate benefits to all mankind. The more immediate priority should, however, be given to those projects which offer the best hope of bridg-ing the gap between the industrial and undeveloped societies in the shortest possible time.[156] The ensuing summary is illustrative of projects which promise to yield maximum beneficial impact upon the needy peoples of the world in the relatively near future.

The application of communications satellites for dissemination of essential knowledge and skills which the underprivileged nations could immediately put to practical use is perhaps the most important service that space technology can offer to man. While achievements such as the discovery of the Van Allen radiation belts, the acquisi-tion of new data relating to the shape of the earth, or the photographs

155 For a valuable analysis of U.S. foreign aid programs, see U.S., Congress, Senate, Committee on Foreign Relations, *Some Important Issues in Foreign Aid*, 89th Cong., 2d Sess., 1966, Com. Print.

156 The principal declared objective of the 1968 U.N. World Conference on the Exploration and Peaceful Uses of Outer Space was "to examine the practical bene-fits of space programmes on the basis of scientific and technical achievements, and the opportunities available to non-space powers for international cooperation in space activities, with special reference to the needs of developing countries." U.N. G.A. Res. 2221 (XXI) of December 19, 1966; U.N. G.A. Res. 2261 (XXII) of Novem-ber 7, 1967.

of the lunar surface are doubtless valuable additions to the common fund of knowledge, they can hardly be expected to affect the living standards of the underprivileged segment of mankind in the near future. By contrast, the establishment of a worldwide network of television satellites which would regularly carry first-rate educational programs, for example, in agriculture, engineering, sanitation, and medicine, to those parts of the globe where such educational facilities are nonexistent or inadequate, could not only greatly enhance the reservoir of skilled manpower available locally but also bring about immediate improvements in the living standards. The potentialities of direct television broadcasting via satellite seem particularly promising for the attainment of these goals;[157] at the same time, if used for the promotion of unilateral interests, this great technological innovation could easily aggravate an already tension-ridden international atmosphere.

One of the first practical applications of space technology has been in the field of meteorology. Meteorological satellites have already demonstrated their capability to identify and track various weather phenomena such as hurricanes, typhoons, cyclones, and sandstorms. Since atmospheric disturbances can propagate around the world in as little as three or four days, it is indispensable for the achievement of an accurate weather forecast to monitor the atmospheric conditions over the entire globe. Artificial satellites provide an unequal means for accomplishing this task. An effective worldwide weather forecasting service still lies in the future, and the available information now often reaches the potential user too late to be effective. The World Weather

[157] Direct broadcast satellites "can provide services and access to areas of the world which might not otherwise receive attention for generations, and they can provide for mass education in a time when conventional educational techniques are not able to fulfill the need." Jaffe (fn. 45), 167. A series of valuable studies on the use of space communications as a medium for spreading education and cultural exchanges appear in UNESCO, *Communication in the Space Age* (Paris 1968). Though a major technological breakthrough, direct broadcast of TV via space is within reach; according to some experts, it could be technically feasible by 1970 to provide TV education in this way to all schools within a country as large as India or Brazil. United Nations, Office of Public Information, *Space Science and Technology: Benefits to Developing Countries* (1968), 30.

Under the terms of a Memorandum of Understanding signed in Washington on September 18, 1969, the United States and India will cooperate in an experiment using satellite technology to bring instructional TV programs to some 5,000 Indian villages. The experiment will be a landmark in that it is designed to provide for the first time direct broadcasting of television programs from a satellite into small village receivers without the need for relay stations on the ground. The satellite is scheduled for launch in synchronous equatorial orbit by 1972. The programming, for which India assumes the sole responsibility, will be directed toward family planning, improvement of agricultural practices, and advancement of national integration. Text in *International Legal Materials*, VIII (No. 6, November 1969), 1281.

Watch[158] has barely begun. Obviously, through a more intense effort, the day could be brought much closer when a perfected system of meteorological satellites will be in operation, providing an accurate and timely forecast of weather conditions in any and all parts of the globe. The beneficial impact of a reliable weather forecasting system would, in the opinion of experts, be enormous. According to one estimate, "the ability to forecast weather accurately only three days in advance would be worth about $60 billion a year to the peoples of the world, not to mention the savings in human lives and the human misery which might be avoided."[159] An operational global system of weather prediction would be of inestimable value to predominantly agricultural societies, as are most of the developing countries.

Recent studies indicate that artificial satellites could also be profitably employed for the detection, protection, and continuous survey of earth mineral and other resources. A catalogue prepared by NASA reveals that earth resources satellites could provide useful information relating to: soil classification; land use capability; land use changes; natural vegetation; range surveys; crop identification; crop disease and insect invasion detection; flood control surveys; watershed and hydrologic studies; recreation site evaluation; wildlife habitat studies; forest species identification; forest fire detection; forest disease and insect invasion detection; soil conservation programs; irrigation development; agricultural development projects; and crop acreage control programs.[160] Moreover, according to the same source, a "capability to efficiently map monsoon regions during the critical period [initial rainfall preceding the monsoon season] would significantly enhance yield prediction capabilities in those portions of the world."[161] Be-

158 In response to the U.N. General Assembly Resolution 1721 (XVI) of December 20, 1961, which called upon the World Meteorological Organization to take measures for the improvement of weather forecasting capabilities, the WMO prepared a new global weather plan—the World Weather Watch—which was unanimously approved by the organization in April of 1967. The World Weather Watch is conceived as a worldwide meteorological network composed of the coordinated national facilities and services provided by international organizations. The key tools in this network are meteorological satellites. U.N. Doc. A/AC. 105/L.40, May 31, 1968, 21.

159 Glenn T. Seaborg, "Man Must First Choose Goals," *Technology Week*, xx (January 23, 1967), 32, 34. See also United Nations (fn. 157), 10-14; NASA, *A Survey of Space Applications* (fn. 98), 87-116.

160 Same, 39. The great economic potential of the "earth resources satellites" and their superiority over even the most advanced aerial survey techniques is ably explored in G.K.C. Pardoe, "Earth Resource Satellite Systems," *The Aeronautical Journal of the Royal Aeronautical Society*, LXXIII (April 1969), 297-306.

161 Same, 40. During a meeting held in May 1969, the Scientific and Technical Subcommittee of the U.N. Space Committee agreed, on the initiative of India and several other smaller nations, to recommend to its parent Committee investigation

cause of the chronic food shortage affecting a large segment of the human race and because of the rapid depletion of the earth's mineral and other resources, programs designed to apply space technology for the alleviation of these shortages obviously merit utmost priority. But to be meaningful, such worldwide resources management requires, in the words of Dr. von Braun,[162] "support on a world-wide basis. All nations that wish to benefit from its enormous potential must participate in its operation."

In addition, there are still other possibilities for joint action that should be explored with a view to bringing the benefits of space science and technology to all countries soon. For example, international space centers, such as the Thumba International Range in India, though with much greater capabilities and scope, could be established in various locations around the globe. Internationally owned, managed, manned, and financed, they would assure the widest dissemination of space science and technology and at the same time help develop among the participants a sense of self-respect as well as of transnational loyalty.

Although the United States and the Soviet Union decided to go their separate ways in landing men on the moon, measures should nevertheless be taken to begin thinking of arrangements for future joint exploration of the earth's natural satellite and of other celestial bodies. Why not begin planning an international scientific laboratory in earth orbit and another for the exploration of the moon and the planets? There are few enterprises that could do more for the cause of international understanding and for peace in outer space than having scientists from different countries work together in the greatest adventure ever undertaken by man. Apart from achieving these ends, nothing would better guarantee compliance with the Space Treaty than a truly international exploration of near-earth space and of the moon. Joint activities would also eliminate, or at least reduce, the danger of controversy about the allocation of resources found on celestial bodies. While in its early phases such a program might increase the cost of the venture for the space powers and decrease somewhat the efficiency of the operation, joint exploration of outer space including celestial bodies is eventually bound to result in a more equitable spread of the expenditures, thus enabling an ever-increasing

---

of earth-resources satellites capable of gathering information on crops, minerals, and the resources of the oceans. The U.S. and the Soviet Union failed to exhibit much enthusiasm for the recommendation. *Aviation Week and Space Technology,* XC (May 26, 1969), 57.

[162] Wernher von Braun, "Space Technology and Progress," *Technology Week,* XX (January 23, 1967), 36, 38.

number of states to allocate their resources to other projects. The experience gained in a pioneer moon program could later be utilized for the exploration of the planets and also for major international programs on the earth.

The possibilities for launching an internationally manned orbiting station—comparable to those now unilaterally planned by the Soviet Union and the United States—are particularly worth examining. Internationally constructed, owned, and manned, such a station could serve a number of useful objectives: as an experimental classroom where the representatives of different nationalities could learn to live and work together in amity; as a base for scientific experiments and the study of the universe; and as an instrument of international inspection for monitoring national activities in order to assure compliance with the Space Treaty and with possible future agreements on disarmament. The cause of public order in outer space would certainly be better served by assigning inspection duties to an international body than by continuing indefinitely with the practice of unilateral verification.

Since even the most comprehensive global assault on space could never satisfy all the needs and expectations of every country, nations will have to continue resorting to regional and bilateral arrangements. Many countries, both underdeveloped and developed, may find regional programs in addition to, or instead of, separate national projects particularly advantageous. By drawing upon the resources of several states, such programs would appear to offer to all the participants the best prospect for maximizing their particular interests in space exploration within the shortest possible time and at a minimum cost. The availability of multilateral space programs would not preclude the more advanced countries from continuing cooperation on a bilateral basis, especially with those nations with whom they have a unique community of interest—economic, scientific, technological, political, or otherwise. However, neither bilateral nor regional programs should be permitted to interfere with worldwide projects undertaken for the benefit of all mankind.

Two conditions must be fulfilled before most of the programs outlined above, and particularly the major ones, can be implemented. First, the two great powers must agree to substitute international cooperation for their present wasteful competition. As long as these two countries continue to control the major portion of the world's space technology and use it primarily for unilateral gain, no amount of enthusiasm on the part of other nations for global programs will suffice to transform them from idealistic dreams into reality.

The other condition for the implementation of major cooperative programs is the availability of appropriate organizational structures. Indeed, it has often been emphasized that the more serious limitations upon faster expansion of modern technology are to be found in the absence of institutions which would adequately reflect the common interest. The magnitude of the projects considered indispensable if all the peoples of the world are soon to obtain tangible benefits from the conquest of space is so great that no existing arrangements or agencies—intergovernmental or private—seem equal to the task. In view of this, it seems necessary to begin planning for an international space agency, with universal membership and attuned to the requirements of the nuclear-space age. To achieve its overriding goal—securing the active participation of all peoples in the exploration and exploitation of outer space under conditions of equality—such an agency should be an action agency; it should not be an organization engaged merely in the collection, exchange, and dissemination of information (such as the United Nations and its specialized agencies concerned with space activities). In brief, what is needed is an organization that would perform for the world community substantially the same role that NASA now performs for the United States [163]

Experience to date demonstrates convincingly that only through the large-scale internationalization of a major portion of nonmilitary space activities can the noble ideals of the Space Treaty be fulfilled. It is, perhaps, worth saying in conclusion that regardless of the magnitude of the resources allocated to the task of bringing the benefits of space exploration to the developing countries and irrespective of the existence of appropriate machinery for the purpose, space programs alone will never be able to alter substantially the disparities now dividing the community of man. This goal can be achieved only through massive and well-coordinated action that embraces many additional forms of assistance and cooperation. The space programs suggested above are conceived as being no more than a segment, though an important one, of the much wider international effort to provide in the foreseeable future by means of modern science and technology a better and fuller life for all. When a decade or two from now an analysis of our period is undertaken, the relevance of contemporary international law and institutions will probably be judged by the quality of the responses they have provided for the solution of these basic problems.

[163] A comprehensive examination of the various potential forms of transnational association and a review of contemporary and past experience relating to international organizations is provided in McDougal, Lasswell, and Vlasic (fn. 9), Chap. 8.

Index

BOOKS WRITTEN
UNDER THE AUSPICES OF THE
CENTER OF INTERNATIONAL STUDIES
PRINCETON UNIVERSITY

Gabriel A. Almond, *The Appeals of Communism* (Princeton University Press 1954)

William W. Kaufmann, ed., *Military Policy and National Security* (Princeton University Press 1956)

Klaus Knorr, *The War Potential of Nations* (Princeton University Press 1956)

Lucian W. Pye, *Guerrilla Communism in Malaya* (Princeton University Press 1956)

Charles De Visscher, *Theory and Reality in Public International Law*, trans. by P. E. Corbett (Princeton University Press 1957; rev. ed. 1968)

Bernard C. Cohen, *The Political Process and Foreign Policy: The Making of the Japanese Peace Settlement* (Princeton University Press 1959)

Myron Weiner, *Party Politics in India: The Development of a Multi-Party System* (Princeton University Press 1957)

Percy E. Corbett, *Law in Diplomacy* (Princeton University Press 1959)

Rolf Sannwald and Jacques Stohler, *Economic Integration: Theoretical Assumptions and Consequences of European Unification*, trans. by Herman Karreman (Princeton University Press 1959)

Klaus Knorr, ed., *NATO and American Security* (Princeton University Press 1959)

Gabriel A. Almond and James S. Coleman, eds., *The Politics of the Developing Areas* (Princeton University Press 1960)

Herman Kahn, *On Thermonuclear War* (Princeton University Press 1960)

Sidney Verba, *Small Groups and Political Behavior: A Study of Leadership* (Princeton University Press 1961)

Robert J. C. Butow, *Tojo and the Coming of the War* (Princeton University Press 1961)

Glenn H. Snyder, *Deterrence and Defense: Toward a Theory of National Security* (Princeton University Press 1961)

Klaus Knorr and Sidney Verba, eds., *The International System: Theoretical Essays* (Princeton University Press 1961)

Peter Paret and John W. Shy, *Guerrillas in the 1960's* (Praeger 1962)

George Modelski, *A Theory of Foreign Policy* (Praeger 1962)

Klaus Knorr and Thornton Read, eds., *Limited Strategic War* (Praeger 1963)

Frederick S. Dunn, *Peace-Making and the Settlement with Japan* (Princeton University Press 1963)

Arthur L. Burns and Nina Heathcote, *Peace-Keeping by United Nations Forces* (Praeger 1963)

Richard A. Falk, *Law, Morality, and War in the Contemporary World* (Praeger, 1963)

James N. Rosenau, *National Leadership and Foreign Policy: A Case Study in the Mobilization of Public Support* (Princeton University Press 1963)

Gabriel A. Almond and Sidney Verba, *The Civic Culture: Political Attitudes and Democracy in Five Nations* (Princeton University Press 1963)

Bernard C. Cohen, *The Press and Foreign Policy* (Princeton University Press 1963)

Richard L. Sklar, *Nigerian Political Parties: Power in an Emergent African Nation* (Princeton University Press 1963)

Peter Paret, *French Revolutionary Warfare from Indochina to Algeria: The Analysis of a Political and Military Doctrine* (Praeger 1964)

Harry Eckstein, ed., *Internal War: Problems and Approaches* (Free Press 1964)

Cyril E. Black and Thomas P. Thornton, eds., *Communism and Revolution: The Strategic Uses of Political Violence* (Princeton University Press 1964)

Miriam Camps, *Britain and the European Community 1955-1963* (Princeton University Press 1964)

Thomas P. Thornton, ed., *The Third World in Soviet Perspective: Studies by Soviet Writers on the Developing Areas* (Princeton University Press 1964)

James N. Rosenau, ed., *International Aspects of Civil Strife* (Princeton University Press 1964)

Sidney I. Ploss, *Conflict and Decision-Making in Soviet Russia: A Case Study of Agricultural Policy, 1953-1963* (Princeton University Press 1965)

Richard A. Falk and Richard J. Barnet, eds., *Security in Disarmament* (Princeton University Press 1965)

Karl von Vorys, *Political Development in Pakistan* (Princeton University Press 1965)

Harold and Margaret Sprout, *The Ecological Perspective on Human Affairs, With Special Reference to International Politics* (Princeton University Press 1965)

Klaus Knorr, *On the Uses of Military Power in the Nuclear Age* (Princeton University Press 1966)

Harry Eckstein, *Division and Cohesion in Democracy: A Study of Norway* (Princeton University Press 1966)

Cyril E. Black, *The Dynamics of Modernization: A Study in Comparative History* (Harper and Row 1966)

Peter Kunstadter, ed., *Southeast Asian Tribes, Minorities, and Nations* (Princeton University Press 1967)

E. Victor Wolfenstein, *The Revolutionary Personality: Lenin, Trotsky, Gandhi* (Princeton University Press 1967)

Leon Gordenker, *The UN Secretary-General and the Maintenance of Peace* (Columbia University Press 1967)

Oran R. Young, *The Intermediaries: Third Parties in International Crises* (Princeton University Press 1967)

James N. Rosenau, ed., *Domestic Sources of Foreign Policy* (Free Press 1967)

Richard F. Hamilton, *Affluence and the French Worker in the Fourth Republic* (Princeton University Press 1967)

Linda B. Miller, *World Order and Local Disorder: The United Nations and Internal Conflicts* (Princeton University Press 1967)

Wolfram F. Hanrieder, *West German Foreign Policy, 1949-1963: International Pressures and Domestic Response* (Stanford University Press 1967)

Richard H. Ullman, *Britain and the Russian Civil War: November 1918-February 1920* (Princeton University Press 1968)

Robert Gilpin, *France in the Age of the Scientific State* (Princeton University Press 1968)

William B. Bader, *The United States and the Spread of Nuclear Weapons* (Pegasus 1968)

Richard A. Falk, *Legal Order in a Violent World* (Princeton University Press 1968)

Cyril E. Black, Richard A. Falk, Klaus Knorr, and Oran R. Young, *Neutralization and World Politics* (Princeton University Press 1968)

Oran R. Young, *The Politics of Force: Bargaining During International Crises* (Princeton University Press 1969)

Klaus Knorr and James N. Rosenau, eds., *Contending Approaches to International Politics* (Princeton University Press 1969)

James N. Rosenau, ed., *Linkage Politics: Essays on the Convergence of National and International Systems* (Free Press 1969)

John T. McAlister, Jr., *Viet Nam: The Origins of Revolution* (Knopf 1969)

Jean Edward Smith, *Germany Beyond the Wall: People, Politics and Prosperity* (Little, Brown 1969)

James Barros, *Betrayal from Within: Joseph Avenol Secretary-General of the League of Nations, 1933-1940* (Yale University Press 1969)

Charles Hermann, *Crises in Foreign Policy: A Simulation Analysis* (Bobbs-Merrill 1969)

Robert C. Tucker, *The Marxian Revolutionary Idea: Essays on Marxist Thought and Its Impact on Radical Movements* (W. W. Norton 1969)

Harvey Waterman, *Political Change in Contemporary France: The Politics of an Industrial Democracy* (Charles E. Merrill 1969)

Cyril E. Black and Richard A. Falk, eds., *Future of the International Legal Order*, Vol. I, *Trends and Patterns* (Princeton University Press 1969)

Ted R. Gurr, *Why Men Rebel* (Princeton University Press 1969)

C. S. Whitaker, Jr., *The Politics of Tradition: Continuity and Change in Northern Nigeria, 1946-1966* (Princeton University Press 1970)

Richard A. Falk, *The Status of Law in International Society* (Princeton University Press 1970)

Henry Bienen, *Tanzania: Party Transformation and Economic Development* (Princeton University Press 1967, rev. edn., 1970)

Klaus Knorr, *Military Power and Potential* (D. C. Heath 1970)